FAT

FAT

A CULTURAL HISTORY
OF THE STUFF OF LIFE

Christopher E. Forth

REAKTION BOOKS

For Sarah Trulove, a long answer to a good question!

Published by Reaktion Books Ltd
Unit 32, Waterside
44–48 Wharf Road
London N1 7UX, UK

www.reaktionbooks.co.uk

First published 2019
Copyright © Christopher E. Forth 2019

Printed and bound in Great Britain by TJ International, Padstow, Cornwall

A catalogue record for this book is available from the British Library

ISBN 978 1 78914 062 0

CONTENTS

INTRODUCTION:
Life in the Wrong Place

Fat. The word conjures a range of images and evokes a multitude of feelings. Some of the these are positive. A fat body can appear beautiful and desirable. It may take up space in ways that are empowering and intimidating; it may also suggest an ability to enjoy abundance that other people cannot. Soft fat may feel comforting, sensual even, in ways that bony slenderness rarely does. At its best, fat may suggest the swollen fullness of life itself. In our current world, however, these positive impressions are often eclipsed by more negative ones. In medicine and the media, as well as in much scholarly and activist writing on the subject, the word 'fat' is usually considered in terms of its accumulation in the body in the form of 'obesity', which may be criticized on aesthetic and/or medical grounds and which is often the target of discrimination. Among those seeking to understand how large bodies have been stigmatized in recent years, a common-sense equation of fat with corpulence or fatness[1] has invited analyses that demonstrate how ideals about health, diet and beauty shift over time and across cultural boundaries while affecting various groups in different ways. The results of these studies offer many important insights. Corpulent men may be stigmatized as weak and effeminate, but fat women suffer greater discrimination and stigma in employment opportunities, salaries, medical care, romantic relationships and popular media. Fat, as well as the stigma attached to it, is also distributed along socioeconomic lines that disadvantage marginalized groups in terms of race, ethnicity and class. Body ideals and levels of dissatisfaction vary between Western and non-Western cultures, as well as between urban and rural contexts. Indeed, levels of body dissatisfaction among women in non-Western regions have been shown to increase with rates of exposure to Western media.[2] Regardless of where one stands on the issue, these facts seem to be more or less straightforward.

There is also no shortage of explanations for why these developments unfolded as they did. Here, too, scholarship on the subject reflects some broadly shared assumptions. When it comes to thinking about fat appreciation, a geographic division between the West and 'the Rest' is not only taken for granted, but is subdivided by a temporal one within Western culture. Several scholars demonstrate a distinction between a pre-modern acceptance of fat as a sign of health, fertility and beauty, and a modern rejection of what is often now labelled 'obesity' as unhealthy, disgusting and connected to the poor.[3] So self-evident does the modernity of anti-fat attitudes seem that one scholar has even dubbed the entire pre-modern world a 'time before fat'.[4] Many scholars implicitly reinforce this impression by contending that our current anti-fat stereotyping is a distinctly modern phenomenon that has developed in fits and starts since the 1500s to become much more pronounced since the 1920s. Even if they overstate the extent to which fat bodies were appreciated in previous periods, most persuasively show that fat aversion became particularly intense towards the end of the twentieth century. Weaving in and out of all these findings is the notion that concepts of health and beauty are culturally constructed, which is why media and medical warnings about the aesthetic and health risks of 'obesity' are often countered with reminders that what may appear to modern Western eyes as a source of disgust may in fact be viewed elsewhere or at other times as evidence of health, power and beauty. Building upon these assumptions, many scholars implicitly subscribe to some version of the idea that the history of so-called obesity is the story of 'how what was good became ugly and then bad'.[5]

From this perspective, fat is an instance of what anthropologist Mary Douglas described as 'matter out of place' in an ordered cultural system of ideas and images about health and beauty.[6] Conceived in terms of 'bodies out of bounds', to cite the title of an early fat studies anthology,[7] perceptions of fat are posited as *effects* of culture. While there is much truth in such claims, a kind of 'knee-jerk constructivism' is at work among many who, as they engage critically with reigning ideas about body size, often minimize or disregard how continuities interact with change over time. Moreover, in their reasonable concern with how culture shapes perceptions of bodies, they often do not consider how the material qualities of fat may also shape cultural ideas.[8] Just as what we already know about fat is refracted through the conceptual 'frames' we use to understand it,[9] many apparent certainties become less self-evident when we adopt a broader timescale and pose different questions about what we mean when we speak about fat. For instance, the much-discussed predominance of vision in the modern era has no doubt played an important role in the new aesthetic norms that circulated more widely and insistently from the sixteenth century onwards. But positing overly sharp or reductive distinctions in how people of different periods and cultures viewed the body is to overlook the multiple and sometimes contradictory ways in which bodies may be conceived and experienced at any given time.[10] Moreover, to assume that modern perceptions of bodies have become predominantly visual does not account for how the senses interrelate in perceptions of the world, nor does it consider the persistent role of non-visual senses in the assessment of bodies.[11] Emphasizing the *visual* without also considering the *visceral* is to reduce the richness of 'fat' to only a few of its dimensions. It is to disregard the possibility that other factors may be in play in our current obsession with slender fitness.[12]

More slippery than many assume, fat exceeds the frames used to contain it conceptually. One doesn't need to look far to see the complex visceral responses that fat can elicit in the twenty-first century. Consider, for instance, how many of these are condensed in one vivid scene from Joyce Carol Oates's novel *Middle Age: A Romance* (2001). Here the protagonist Roger encounters a seedy lawyer named Reginald 'Boomer' Spires, a 135-kilo/300-lb man whose 'obese, doughy-oily' flesh was ensconced in a shabby office, his body and surroundings proof of his fallen professional and corporeal status. At first glance this seems like a classic case of fatness symbolizing downward mobility.[13] Yet the specific terms of this fall from grace reveal issues not so easily reduced to socio-economic status. Roger's immediate reaction is one of disgust. Never had he encountered 'so repugnant a specimen of humanity. Boomer's body seemed to consist of layers of fat, oozing oily-fat . . . bloated as a drowned corpse.' The perceived threat of contamination further darkens this encounter as Roger fights the impulse to refuse to shake the fat man's 'moist and clammy' hand, wondering 'could a handshake be infectious?' Hinting at the proverbial notion that 'you are what you eat,' Boomer's flesh is itself 'doughy-oily' as if it has taken on the qualities of the edible fats and carbohydrates often said to promote fatness (and which, we are meant to assume, he has regularly ingested). The sight of his flesh invited tactile anticipations without requiring actual contact, just as it had at some point inspired a cartoonish nickname meant to conjure up the 'booming' sound that very large bodies are hyperbolically imagined to make when walking. Rather than simply making a displeasing appearance, Boomer's fat evokes for Roger the swollen-ness of death and decay ('a drowned corpse') and something barely human (a 'repugnant' specimen). Despite such strong reactions, though, Roger cannot accept the absolute otherness of the unfortun-ate lawyer. The fat, the failure, the intimations of mortality: no one is immune to such things, he tells himself. '*It could happen to you, pal. Never too late.*'[14] In his response to Boomer's body, Roger experienced what Stephanie Lawler calls the troubling 'recognition of (and horror at) sameness' that disgust-eliciting encounters may provoke.[15]

This fictional encounter encapsulates some of the revulsion that is widely reported in perceptions of fat today. 'If one were forced to come up with a six-word explanation for the otherwise inexpli-cable ferocity of America's war on fat,' Paul Campos writes in *The Obesity Myth*, 'it would be this: Americans think being fat is disgust-ing. It really is, on the most important cultural and political levels, as simple as that.' There is ample evidence to confirm this observa-tion. Not only is disgust at fatness widely registered in the media and popular culture, but numerous studies in a variety of countries reveal considerable anti-fat bias among healthcare professionals, who cite a patient's ugliness as well as lack of willpower and non-compliance with medical advice as the main reasons for the distaste and contempt they often fail to conceal.[16] Although the scientific jargon used to measure body mass and height presents the need to slim down as a simple but urgent matter of health and self-control, our prejudices against fat reflect a powerful emotion that is anything but detached or disinterested. And, despite Campos's focus on the United States, American attitudes towards fat are a local, if often exaggerated, version of a wider phenomenon. Given how anti-fat stereotyping proliferates in public contexts where it is generally unac-ceptable to express racist, misogynist and homophobic sentiments, Campos goes on to argue that disgust about fat is elicited 'by the sight of people who weigh anything from a lot to a little more than our current absurdly restrictive cultural ideal'.[17]

Campos is right about the similarities between anti-fat attitudes and other forms of prejudice.[18] But those who study disgust concur that sight is not paramount in this complex emotion. Summing up the findings of anthropologists and psychologists, the philosopher Martha Nussbaum points to the central role of touch in the generation of disgust. This is because 'the key idea is that of crossing a boundary from the world into the self.' As such,

> disgust would thus be closely connected to all three of the senses that the philosophical tradition regards as 'tactile' senses rather than mediated or distance senses: i.e., touch, smell, and taste, rather than sight or hearing.[19]

From this perspective, disgust is a response to the actual or anticipated contact with something material. Psychologists and philosophers studying disgust also tend to agree that, at its heart, this emotion is mobilized by unpleasant, perhaps intolerable, reminders of animality (or creatureliness) and mortality. Cohering most strongly around the activities of eating, sex and defecation, as well as our 'fragile body envelopes that, when breached, reveal blood and soft viscera',[20] the cognitive structure of disgust relies on a form of 'magical thinking' that denies the realities of impermanence and decay as necessary parts of organic life:

> Disgust . . . wards off both animality in general and the mortality that is so prominent in our loathing of our animality . . . The products that are disgusting are those that we connect with our vulnerability to decay and to becoming waste products ourselves.[21]

The structure of disgust is inherently idealist, almost utopian. Colin McGinn even calls it a 'philosophical emotion' in which 'we take the measure of the disjunction between how the world actually works and how we would like it to be.'[22]

Despite this talk of death and decay, at the heart of disgust is not a reaction to mortality in which the person faces eventual non-existence. This is because 'life' – that is, organic life – entails generative vital processes that precede and do not cease with the death of the person. The hard and dry bones of a skeleton may remind us of death and thus generate fear, but it is the rank and gooey softness of a rotting corpse that is more likely to elicit revulsion. A vexed response to organic life has been noted by many who have studied disgust. What is most horrifying about death, according to Georges Bataille, is not the 'bitter annihilation of being' that it brings, but the repugnance, this 'shipwreck of the nauseous', that comes with the awareness that 'I will rejoin abject nature and the purulence of anonymous, infinite life, which stretches forth like the night, which is death.'[23] Life and death thus exist on a continuum that is often at cross-purposes with human plans. It may be that what elicits disgusts is, from a humanist perspective, the 'wrong' kind of life, the kind that disregards our projects and dares to leaves 'us' behind.[24] Historian William Miller concurs:

> What disgusts, startlingly, is the capacity for life, and not just because life implies its correlative death and decay: for it is decay that seems to engender life. Images of decay imperceptibly slide into images of fertility and out again. Death thus horrifies and disgusts not just because it smells revoltingly bad, but because it is not an end to the process of living but part of a cycle of eternal recurrence.[25]

If disgust is a response to the often-unpleasant facts of organic life and human embodiment, then perhaps disgust at fat is elicited by a similar set of concerns. The grounds for making such a suggestion become firmer when we consider how often fat itself has been historically associated with vitality, fertility and creatureliness, even to the point of being described as the very 'stuff of life'.[26] In this sense, disgust at fat materializes ambivalence about the fact that humans are embodied as well as misgivings about the wider material world to which those bodies belong. As Miller puts it:

> ultimately the basis for all disgust is us – that we live and die and that the process is a messy one emitting substances and odors that make us doubt ourselves and fear our neighbors.[27]

Often approached as a response to 'matter out of place', then, disgust at fat may also be a reaction to 'life in the wrong place' – the latter a description used by Aurel Kolnai to describe bodies whose 'excessive vitality' has caused them to grow beyond what a given culture deems appropriate.[28]

✳

Broaching 'big' questions such as these may seem like an odd way to begin a work of history, but it is important for explaining the multifaceted and interdisciplinary approach that this book adopts. As a study of the formation of stereotypes, *Fat: A Cultural History of the Stuff of Life* contends that a contemplation of disgust is useful for thinking about the ways in which fat bodies have been apprehended over time. This is true, first, because studying disgust shows that there is nothing necessary or inevitable about the strong emotions that fat elicits today. Maintaining that 'core disgust' is an evolutionary adaptation serving to protect humans from the ingestion of potentially dangerous substances, some social psychologists suggest that disgust about fat occurs in a second-order, and therefore historically specific, cultural sphere where 'the focus of threat has spread from the mouth to the body in general'.[29] So, rather than being simply a 'normal' or 'natural' response to bodily variation, disgust about fat bodies has a history that can be explored and interpreted.

A second useful way of considering disgust is as an emotion that is not primarily related to visual impressions and so prompts us to think about fat in terms of touch, taste and smell as well as sight.[30] This expands the ways in which we can approach the stereotypes that have been attributed to fat people. Third, by drawing attention to the contact senses, disgust invites us to probe around in the very materiality of fat to assess what it is about fatty and fattening substances that may (but need not) provoke such an emotion under specific historical conditions. This allows us to examine fat as a noun as well as an adjective, to grasp it as something physical as well as visual.

Disgust is useful for thinking about fat in other ways as well. As the encounter above between Roger and Boomer suggests, disgust involves a recoil from bodies, as well as bodily processes and substances, that may remind us of those aspects of our own embodiment we might prefer to forget. Accompanying a simultaneous 'recognition of (and horror at) sameness', disgust reminds us how central the bodies of others are to our own culturally ingrained ideals of autonomy, ability and self-mastery. Acknowledging this 'intercorporeality'[31] is important for understanding the expansive ways in which fat stereotypes have been manifested, drawing together forms of difference like gender, race and class, but also age and disability. Much like food – but also *as* food – fat 'reminds us of others'.[32] Finally, insofar as disgust points to a tension between what we are and what we may prefer to be, it reveals misgivings about the paradoxes of embodiment. Disgust at fat throws into relief a deep-seated Western ambivalence about embodied life: despite its many rewards and pleasures, being a body means to be disappointingly and even terrifyingly connected to the transience of organic existence. In addition to reminding us of others, fat reminds us of the non-human materials and processes that comprise us. Alluding to the depth and pervasiveness of this recoil from organic life, one scholar contends that today the fat body is made to 'bear the full horror of embodiment'.[33] This suggests that, to varying degrees and at different moments, Western culture promotes fantasies about bodies capable of overcoming the limitations of embodiment – bodies that are alive yet, paradoxically, unaffected by 'life'. If there is something seemingly utopian or even transcendent in this wish for a body that is not a body, or at least a body purified of its messy and disappointing corporeality, this wish is hardly novel. It may not even be distinctly Western.[34] As Michel Foucault speculates:

> It may very well be that the first utopia, the one most deeply rooted in the hearts of men, is precisely the utopia of an incorporeal body.[35]

Beginning from these premises, this book offers a series of historical reflections on fat in the West, with particular attention to the ways in which negative stereotypes about fat people have unfolded over time. Agreeing that the modern era inaugurated a distrust of fat that has grown more intense since the early twentieth century, the book tries to understand this development by situating it within a longer time frame than other studies. By beginning its analyses with antiquity rather than the emergence of modernity, *Fat* demonstrates that people in pre-modern eras viewed corpulence with ambivalence rather than appreciation, generating many of the potent ideas and images that have provided crucial building blocks for contemporary stereotypes.[36] Rather than explaining how something 'good became ugly and then bad', in other words, the following pages show

how this something elicited an ambiguity that mutated over time to become commonplace and, for many, intolerable. Eschewing the impossible task of providing a comprehensive account of such a broad time span, this book necessarily adopts a selective and thematic approach to its topic.

Fat is also unique in terms of how it approaches its subject. Whereas others have approached the history of fat in terms of beauty, appearance and visual culture, or by charting the development of diets, dieting and exercise over time, this book complements their important work by showing that fat prejudices have some of their sources beyond the boundaries of the human body.[37] As a way of understanding the recurring ambivalence that pertains to corpulence in the West, here fat is also treated as a material substance located within bodies as well as in the wider environment. This prompts a conceptualization of fat in relation to vital processes of swelling or 'fattening' that involve agricultural experiences with fertility and decay. It also invites a consideration of how the materiality of fat plays a role in motivating cultural ideas about corpulence. More pointedly, fattening evokes perceptions of non-human animality, particularly that of domesticated creatures thought to occupy a 'lower' status in animal hierarchies. These three recurring themes – materiality, vitality and animality – expand the ways in which fat can be understood: as a material substance called fat, as the bodily situation of fatness, and as an effect of processes of fattening. They also provide ways of approaching how discussions of fat have, historically, been saturated with references to gender, race and status. Examining these themes over time highlights deeply rooted and recurring Western tendencies to associate the soft, flabby, bloated and viscous with the feminine and the feminizing, but also with the backward, primitive or uncivilized.[38] These themes circulate and intertwine through the history of Western perspectives on fat bodies, providing the basis for a number of negative images that crystallized in the last century.[39]

By examining the manner in which engagements with fat have historically moved back and forth between the material and social worlds, as well as across the human and agricultural realms, this book explores the mechanisms by which fat may offer 'a series of potentialities for signs' that resonate in various ways through to the present.[40] These signs produce 'sticky' layers of accrued meaning in which the residual remains latent in the new, constituting a cache of past ideas and images that remain ready-to-hand.[41] Drawing on just such a reservoir, our modes of perceiving and imagining fat have roots and implications deeper and subtler than the health and beauty concerns that preoccupy many scholars working in this area. Not only were most of these perceptions and images formed long before the modern era, but they often reflect engagements with the material qualities of fat that play an active role in the production of meaning.[42] The ways in which we imagine fat are thus at once tangible and intangible, physical as well as discursive, literal as well as figurative. In the cultural history of such imaginings, one encounters ambivalent responses to movements and transitions, growth and decay, fertility and sterility, swelling and shrinking, surplus and deficit, boundaries crossed and substances transmuted. One also engages with ideas and concerns about devouring and incorporation, mastery and subordination. Populated with animals and plants as well as people, there be 'monsters' here, too. Irreducible to any single set of concerns, stereotypes about fat emerge at the interstices of multiple fields of discourse and spheres of experience.

Fat is thus not simply 'good to think [with]', as Claude Lévi-Strauss famously said of animals.[43] Fat is *great* to think with, and it's been that way ever since Western peoples began reflecting upon their bodies and their worlds. Probing the history of how fat has been perceived and imagined may provide richer insights into the stuff our stereotypes are made of.

ONE

THE STUFF OF LIFE
Thinking and Doing with Fat

There are many reasons to consider fat as the 'stuff of life'. In its broadest sense, fat refers to a class of acids known as lipids: fatty molecules that are among those most crucial for organic life to exist. Indeed, being 'as fundamental to life as proteins and genes',[1] the presence of lipids may indicate all manner of life, terrestrial as well as extraterrestrial.[2] Here on Earth, the pivotal role of lipids in human development has received considerable attention in recent years. After a long period of emphasizing the centrality of proteins in prehistoric diets, a growing number of palaeoanthropologists underscore the importance for early hominins of fats derived from the bone marrow and brains of large game. Recent scholarship on the nutritional ceiling to growth posed by proteins and plants has focused greater attention on the importance of fats to early humans who 'managed, and in fact evolved, to obtain a substantial amount of the densest form of nutritional energy available in nature – fat – to the point that it became an obligatory food source'.[3] While meat-eating and game-hunting are still considered especially important for human evolution, 'animal-derived fat obtained mostly from marrow and brain is now seen as an essential part of the picture.'[4] To take one example, the Upper Palaeolithic bone assemblage discovered in the Las Caldas Cave in northern Spain provides evidence of concerted strategies to extract the marrow and fat from animal bones. This suggests that 'the extraction and exploitation of fat was part of the subsistence strategy of these human groups.'[5] Lipids, particularly omega-3 fatty acids, may even account for the expansion of brain volume that led to the emergence of modern humans (*Homo sapiens*). It is believed that this occurred after the migration of early humans to lakeshore and seaside locales in Africa, where they would have encountered animals rich in the fatty acids needed for brain growth. It may thus be no coincidence that this occurred around the same time that early peoples displayed new advances in intellectual and cultural development.[6]

Aside from nutritional benefits, the sensual pleasure of tasting fat has surely played a role in the attractions it held for early humans. Dietary lipids endow foods with particular tactile qualities, notably viscosity and lubricity, which contribute to their distinctive and appealing qualities. Mouth-feel, taste and a sensation of satiety count among the most appreciated gustatory experiences associated with the ingestion of dietary fats, and in recent years the pleasurable qualities of lipids have come to be viewed as especially important in understanding weight gain. Research even suggests that an ability to detect fattiness must be added to the other qualities we usually attribute to taste, alongside the sweet, sour, bitter and so on. The ability to provide this luscious sensual experience, preferably without recourse to potentially unhealthy additives, is the aim of many food manufacturers.[7] There is now 'definite evidence' for the existence of a sixth 'basic or primary taste quality for selected fatty acids (fat taste)', which has been dubbed 'oleogustus'.[8]

Lipids also play an active role in the body after they are ingested, potentially affecting moods, tastes and even volition. As scientists working in lipidomics contend, 'preferences for fat may be independent of the conscious ability to detect or assess the fat content of solid foods.'[9] Certain fatty acids have the potential to alter moods and attention levels, rendering prisoners less violent, schoolchildren more attentive and bipolar persons less subject to dramatic emotional shifts. The seemingly agentic potential of fats has encouraged philosopher Jane Bennett to remind us that the act of eating is not simply to adopt the role of a subject who actively consumes passive food, but 'to enter into an assemblage in which the I is not necessarily the most decisive operator'.[10] But we need not descend to the microscopic level to see how fats can challenge volition. Fatty foods, along with those that are sweet or salty, stimulate the pleasure centres of the brain, and may thus elicit more or less primordial responses.[11] Several studies have shown how non-human animals often display a seemingly insatiable appetite for fats, which they would eat excessively if given an endless supply.[12] In simple gustatory terms, then, greasy and sweet things 'have the capacity to make us eat more of them than we wish; they are will-weakening or will-deviating'.[13]

Despite ample evidence that animal fat has functioned as a symbol of health in many traditional societies, it is unclear whether, among early humans, a preference for dietary fats implied a corresponding appreciation of very fat bodies.[14] Consider the often-rotund figurines of women unearthed in many parts of the world. For decades, the belief that prehistoric corpulence was an unproblematic, if not intrinsically positive, symbol of female fertility generated a number of assumptions about the status, even reverence, accorded to fatness among early peoples. By exaggerating certain features of the female anatomy, these figurines seemed to emphasize a great respect for agricultural fertility in general and female fecundity in particular.[15] This view is widely disputed by archaeologists today. Some ask why female figures should necessarily be read as referring primarily to 'woman' in general or as reflections of social divisions based mainly on sexual difference.[16] Others speculate that the figurines may convey something else entirely, such as the impressions of what a female sculptor, deprived of the third-person perspective on the body that we take for granted, might see when looking down at her breasts, belly and feet.[17] Aside from the fact that 'there is no scientific support for the assumption that Neolithic and Copper Age religion was centered on cults of agricultural fertility',[18] archaeologist Douglass Bailey proposes that concepts of fertility may be more complex than we imagine. Just as sexual engagements can entail a 'physically, mentally, emotionally and sensually charged series of events', it is evident that a similar 'emotional atmosphere' surrounds the experiences of pregnancy and birth:

> pain, danger, worry, threat to life (maternal and infant), blood, viscera, but also the rudiments of generating life, and the pleasure this can entail; engaging the dangerous and moving through and beyond it.

In this treatment of fertility, Bailey invites us to remain open to the complexities that lived experience would have no doubt offered in the distant past: 'Opposites, contradictions and challenges are all at work here.'[19]

The long-standing belief that prehistoric corpulence was a symbol of female fertility is widely disputed by archaeologists today. The so-called Venus of Willendorf is perhaps the most famous of the often-rotund figurines of women unearthed in many parts of the world.

This chapter and the next take as their point of departure this suggestion that concepts of fertility involve experiences, processes and relationships that may be challenging as well as comforting; painful as well as pleasurable. They explore the ways in which ambivalence about the processes and substances associated with organic life has played a role in structuring Western cultural responses to fat. This chapter invokes recent scholarly work to show that a material symbol like fat is not completely arbitrary in relation to the concepts it signifies.[20] Rather, fat also refers to 'a physicality which resists and enables' and which plays an active role in the construction of meaning.[21] In symbolic terms, a corpulent body may act like a 'cultural trickster' that shifts between life and death[22] – even when the corpulence in question is attributed to some substance other than adipose tissue. But as a sticky and ambiguous substance, fat is itself literally liminal and connective, capable of sticking to bodies while shifting between solid and liquid states.[23] So this first chapter tracks the protean ways in which this physically and conceptually slippery substance has been perceived and employed. It considers how the unctuousness and soft moistness of fat have motivated a range of stereotypes about people who are corpulent, and have embedded fatness in masculine–feminine gender distinctions. Chapter Two expands this discussion to probe the ambiguity of organic life further while exploring the vexed relationship between fattening and images of animality and foolishness. Both chapters are driven by this book's central contention that understanding 'fat' requires us to think beyond our usual preoccupations with body size and shape, and framing in relation to (human) bodies alone.

Unctuousness

The science of lipidomics acknowledges no chemical distinction between fats and oils. Since in many respects what we call 'fats are just frozen oils', then, for the current discussion we will refer to fat in its solid as well as liquid forms.[24] If a range of dissimilar things may be described as 'fat', it is often because they share a certain greasy or unctuous quality. It is this unctuousness that facilitates analogies among various fat or fatty things across the registers of animal, vegetal and human. In addition to the greasy sensation it affords, the oiliness of fats has also implied the related qualities of inflammability and luminosity. The stone lamps used in Palaeolithic times employed animal fats as fuel, thereby allowing humans to remain active at night and facilitating cave painting, tool-making and other cultural advances.[25] Along with the expansion of brain volume that led to the emergence of *Homo sapiens*, fats played a critical role in human cultural and technological development. This burning of fat for illumination also revealed that, through combustion, fats can seemingly dematerialize into smoke and light.[26] In a process strikingly similar to alchemy, fat may be transformed from a state of 'gross' or 'dull' materiality – which, as we will see, is how it has often been described – into something subtle and even transcendent. If fat seemed to *symbolize* light and life to many early cultures, it was because such qualities were frequently considered intrinsic to the oily substance itself. Fat seemed to 'contain' rather than merely represent such powers.[27]

Despite this apparent capacity to contain life and light, fat was also an inherently ambiguous substance. In addition to their shared status as lipids, fat and oil may be viewed as cognates that refer to one another. Indeed, each is capable of *becoming* the other through a change in temperature. Fat's capacity to shift between solid and liquid states, as well as its apparent ability to dematerialize into the air, confirms its place in 'a group of ambivalent substances' that includes oil, tar, wax, tallow, grease, pitch and, arguably, honey.[28] Yet regardless of what form it takes, fat remains an intriguingly problematic substance, partly because it doesn't seem to follow the 'rules' we expect solids and liquids to observe. It isn't a very convincing solid when congealed. Neither easily grasped nor managed, fat jiggles and slides about, seemingly ready to collapse into a liquid state at any moment. But even melting does not restore fat to its 'true' state, for oil doesn't quite fit into the category of most liquids either. In addition to being somewhat viscous, oils evaporate at much higher temperatures than water, thus retaining their liquidity for longer periods. This durability may be why many ancient cultures associated fats and oils with strength, fertility and even life itself. For instance, Aristotle drew a distinction between aqueous moisture that easily evaporates and the unctuous sort that is separated from matter only with difficulty. For him, unctuous moisture was present in all matter, organic and inorganic. It was responsible for lending objects and substances their specific shape or consistency as well as whatever flammable capacities they might have.[29] Proposing that 'fat things are not liable to decay' and that 'a fat substance is incorruptible',[30] Aristotle perceived in fat the very stuff of materiality itself. Fat held the world together.

Yet fat's stickiness, whether as liquid or solid, may also be a source of frustration and even alarm. It is unclear how widespread a problem this has been, though a recent history of cleanliness and purity provocatively posits 'a deep psychology of slime, dirt, and stickiness that all hominids apparently share, in different degrees'.[31] Rather than passively yielding to a masterful human touch, fatty things seem to touch us back, adhering to surfaces and attaching themselves to our bodies. This is not only a matter of touch, for we often employ tactile metaphors to describe unpleasant sights.[32] Even our responses to the 'oleaginous' slip across the senses with surprising ease, from the greasy tactile sensation of oiliness to the odour that attests to the word's Latin root (*olere*, to 'give off' smell). The fact that oily things can absorb odours, flavours and colours from their surroundings – and that they are readily absorbed by the skin – makes them penetrative and boundary-crossing substances as well, capable of altering themselves as well as objects and living beings in various ways. As beneficial and revered as it can be, fat remains mutable and ambiguous, capable of switching between solid and liquid as well as between matter and 'spirit'. This may be one reason why certain early cultures viewed fats and oils as magical. Some even believed they could divine the future by watching how oil interacted with water through the practices of lecanomancy. Through the divination technique known as 'scrying', the future could be glimpsed by gazing for long periods at the lustre produced by oil rubbed on a smooth surface.[33]

From these general observations, we can examine specific historical understandings of fats in more detail. The ancient Hebrews usually used the word *šemen* to refer to oil, almost always that pressed from the olive, and the root of this word (*šmn*) 'refers to some underspecified concept of a "greasy, fatty, oily substance"'.[34] A dietary staple, this liquid fat was considered a blessing from God. As such it served as a metaphor for life, fertility and purity. Oil's capacity for luminosity could make the face, skin and hair shine, while its penetrative tendencies were thought capable of transforming the status of an object or person. The capacity of penetrative substances to elevate or contaminate the body partly explains the ambiguity with which oils could be perceived. Bodies penetrated by oils could either have their status elevated or diminished in some way.[35] Thus while the oil used to anoint high priests or kings in Israel partly facilitated their change in status, in other contexts the penetrative potential of oils

Probably fuelled with animal fat, this red sandstone lamp helped early humans to decorate the walls of the caves of Lascaux.

could make them seem contaminating and therefore dangerous. Drawing upon the purity codes found in Leviticus (11:33–8), the radical Jewish sect known as the Essenes viewed oil and other fluids as transmitters of pollution if they came into contact with 'impure' things. Fearful of contamination, Essenes kept their skin dry and avoided oil altogether.[36]

The ambiguous power of olive oil extended to more solid forms of fat. In Hebrew sacrificial rites, where substances symbolizing life were circulated between the divine and human realms, the 'best' part of the animal was reserved for Yahweh just as Yahweh had given humans the fat from animal and vegetal sources.[37] Hence the injunction 'all fat is the Lord's' (Leviticus 3:16), which referred mainly to the fatty layer of suet (*ḥēlebh*) that surrounds animal kidneys.[38] Considered the seat of life, partly due to their long-standing association with the genitals, and therefore with reproduction and sexual desire, the kidneys were also connected with such emotions as joy and agony.[39] It thus made some sense to assume that the fat in which they were encased possessed some of this potency. Yet since this suet was also considered especially tasty, and thus capable of propelling people to excess, it was forbidden to the Hebrews themselves: 'It shall be a perpetual statute throughout your generations, in all your settlements: you must not eat any fat or any blood' (Leviticus 3:17). Closely linked to blood, the vital fluid par excellence, in rare cases even human fat could be offered up as a form of sacrifice to the Lord. The Babylonian Talmud tells of a certain Rabbi Sheshet who believed he could, through the act of fasting, offer his own body fat as a proxy for the more traditional animal sacrifice:

> Now I have sat in a fast, and so my fat and blood have become less. May it be pleasing before you that my fat and blood that have become less be received as if I had offered them up before you on the altar and so be reconciled with me.[40]

Distinctive in many ways, the fatty offerings that the Hebrews made to Yahweh bore some resemblance to the sacrifices made by the Greeks. In Hesiod's *Theogony*, which recounts the mythical origin of such practices, Zeus was outraged when Prometheus tricked the gods into accepting the inedible parts of an ox concealed beneath a layer of white, glistening fat.[41] The sacrificial fat referred to here and in many Greek texts is the *omentum* (*epipolaion* or *epiploon*), a membrane of suet or lard (depending on the animal) that covers the stomach and intestines.[42] By being offered this fatty substance, the gods were 'being given the stuff of life'.[43]

Like the Hebrews, the Greeks too believed that the stuff of life was a pleasurable substance that could drive one to excess. It was the irresistible aroma of cooking fat that had compelled Zeus to fall for Prometheus' ruse, thus reflecting a rather earthly appreciation for the smell and taste of fat that was often cited in Greek comedies.[44] But it was not only the gods who were fond of the odour of fat. The word *knisae* refers to the steam and aroma of fat rising from roasted meat, and a greedy man who could not control his appetite for greasy things was sometimes described as a 'fat-licker' (*knisoloichos*), whether at the table or in everyday life. For this reason, a sycophantic social parasite who lingered around kitchens hoping for a handout could be ridiculed as a 'fat-flatterer' (*knisokolax*).[45] Such appreciation for fat was a variation on a more common antique theme. The Romans prized fat so much that they typically boiled rather than roasted their meat in order to preserve the fatty juices, an economizing practice that would persist among the European peasantry through the Middle Ages.[46] It is perhaps unsurprising that such greasy pleasures would attract the moralizing censure of Stoics as well as early Christian ascetics. Nor is it puzzling to discover that the Jewish philosopher Philo of Alexandria would enlist Hellenistic medicine to interpret the Hebrew taboo on fat as God's way of promoting health and morality.[47]

A matter of taste, fat also pertains to place.[48] Indeed, fat was not simply a vital substance observed in human and animal bodies. Being derived from vegetal sources as well, fat was bound up with the material environment. This becomes evident when we consider the important role that geographical and agricultural knowledge has played in shaping our concepts of fatness and thinness. For much of Western history, soil has been described as being 'fat' or 'thin', as well as loose or dense and wet or dry, and often as some combination of these qualities.[49] Fat soil had a distinctive texture and consistency that experienced farmers recognized. Aristotle's successor at the Lyceum, Theophrastus of Eresus, was just one among many Greeks who drew distinctions between 'fat' and 'lean' soil, applying a taxonomy that was shared by the Romans and which would persist in the Western imagination well into the nineteenth century.[50] According to the Roman writer Varro, the first thing a farmer must determine is whether a given soil is 'thin or fat or moderate' (*macra an pinguis an mediocris*) because that will indicate which sort of farming one can do.[51]

Since fat soil had a distinctive texture and consistency that experienced farmers recognized, touch was one of the most reliable methods of judging it. Virgil maintained that one could always tell which soil was fat (*pinguis*) because 'never does it crumble when worked in the hands, but like pitch grows sticky in the fingers when held.'[52] Since the tactile attributes of such soil called to mind the viscous and pliable qualities of oil or grease, describing a field as 'fat' was no simple metaphor. Rather there was something palpably unctuous about fertile soil that the agricultural writer Columella summed up by calling it 'fat' (*pinguis*) and 'glutinous' (*glutinoso*). Fat soil even possessed a kind of swelling tendency that could be discerned with a simple test. After removing a handful of soil to check for unctuousness, one had to pay close attention to what happened when the sample was reinserted into the hole one had made:

> if there is an excess as by some sort of leavening, it will be a sure sign that the soil is fat; if it is insufficient, that it is poor; if it makes an even fill, that it is ordinary.[53]

The abundance or 'increase' made possible by such soil did not refer solely to agricultural yield, but to the swelling potentiality of the substance itself.

The viscous and oily qualities that farmers understood as signs of fertility were not figments of the pre-modern imagination. Recent biogeochemical analyses of medieval soil composition reveal the biomarkers of fatty acids or lipids contained in the manure used to fertilize arable land.[54] Nor were such perceptions restricted to Greek and Roman culture. Similar observations about the oleaginous qualities of soil were registered among the Hebrews, for whom abundant crops and livestock were examples of the 'fat' (*ḥēlebh*) of the land (see Genesis 45:18). In Hebrew culture fat was used metaphorically to refer to the 'best' part of something, especially the choicest fruits of the harvest as well as the fertile land that produced them.[55] The fat cattle and ears of corn of which Pharaoh famously dreamt in

Genesis 41 were repeatedly cited in the West as a way of illustrating this connection between fat and abundance. As the Greeks and Romans also recognized, this metaphor was connected to the physical properties of fertile soil. It has even been argued that the oft-repeated biblical reference to a 'land flowing with milk (*ḥlb*) and honey' (Exodus 33:3) is probably a mistake. Rather, it should have been more correctly rendered a 'land flowing with fat (*ḥēlebh*) and honey'.[56] If we are to believe Isaiah (34:6–7), insufficiently fertile soil could even be enriched through the introduction of animal fat. In one of his righteous fits of violence, an enraged Yahweh declares his sword to be 'gorged with fat' and dripping with blood from the slaughter of countless animals, so that when the gore drops on the ground the 'soil [shall be] made rich with fat'. The fat that so abundantly and poetically gushed from the soil infused everything with its richness, from crops and animals to those humans fortunate enough to revel in its flow. One of the Dead Sea Scrolls even foretold a time when bodies would luxuriantly swell in tandem with the land: 'all who shall possess the land will enjoy and grow fat with everything enjoyable to the flesh.'[57] Unctuous richness thus provided tangible ways of thinking about increase, both in terms of agricultural yield and the growth of the body. As subsequent chapters will explore in more detail, what would come to be known as the 'fat of the land' affected how corpulence could be understood.

Doing Things with Fat

Among early peoples, fats derived from plant and animal sources were used for a variety of artistic, culinary and ritual purposes. We know this thanks to the work of scholars engaged in ancient lipid research, 'arguably, the most productive and informative area of biomolecular archaeology'.[58] Whether in solid or liquid forms, among early humans fats were employed as illuminants, sealants, lubricants, polishes, binders and varnishes, as bases for perfumes, and in medicinal and cosmetic ointments.[59] The medicinal and magical uses of fats are particularly interesting when discussing the stuff of life.

Mesopotamian and Egyptian pharmacopoeias made frequent use of fats and oils procured from plants and animals,[60] as did most peoples across the Hellenized world. In his first-century pharmacopoeia, *De materia medica*, which influenced European medicine for the next 1,500 years, Dioscorides recounted numerous applications for animal fats as well as the most effective methods of preparing, scenting and administering them. Melted fox fat could stop an earache, but so could goose fat if mixed with earthworms. He-goat fat was excellent for gout, but only when mixed with saffron and the dung of a she-goat. Bear's fat could cure baldness.[61] Such information reflected a widespread practice. The physician Soranus of Ephesus recommended goose fat and chicken fat for uterine problems,[62] and Pliny the Elder described numerous other medicinal uses for animal fats. Hog's lard, or what was called 'axle-grease' (*axungia*), was especially valuable:

> The men of old used lard in particular for greasing the axles of their vehicles, that the wheels might revolve more easily, and in this way it received its name.

Used in everyday life for the practical functions of 'softening, warming, dispersing, and cleansing', in earlier times *axungia* had religious applications as well. In Pliny's own day it was 'still the usage for the newly-wedded bride, when entering her husband's house, to touch the door-posts with it'. *Axungia* could be made from the fat of other creatures too, with its potency related to the intrinsic vitality of the animal that provided it. Thus, given that sexual reproduction expended considerable vital energy, the best fat was procured from 'a sow that has not littered', though *axungia* procured from the highly esteemed wild boar was 'much more excellent'.[63] The location of the fat in the body was also a consideration. The Greeks and Romans agreed with numerous other cultures that kidney fat was especially potent: 'All suet from the kidneys is highly valued.'[64] Other fats performed similar rejuvenating functions. Butter too was sufficiently fatty to be used in ointments, even if its culinary use was frowned upon by Greeks and Romans. Olive oil, for them, was a marker of civilization. Only the barbarians of the north consumed butter.[65]

As we have seen above, fat could be used to symbolize light and life because such qualities were thought to be intrinsic to – and thus *contained within* – the substance itself. We have also seen how oil could be used for the purposes of divination. It is therefore not surprising to note that the powers that seemed inherent to fat could be harnessed to perform protective and magical functions as well. What is called the logic of 'sympathetic magic' was often enlisted to explain how a substance might contain the powers of its animal source.[66] The fat of a brave lion thus 'protects against those who plot harm'. When smeared on the skin, elephant and deer fat can 'put snakes to flight'.[67] Similarly, wolf fat was said to possess very strong protective properties.[68] In other instances, the relationship to the animal is less clear. Pliny maintained that lion fat mixed with rose oil could keep the complexion fair, but cast doubt on what 'the lying Magi' said about those who rub it between their eyes to curry favour with kings.[69] The magical papyri from Hellenistic Egypt proposed even more mysterious uses for animal fats, including love potions, invisibility spells and the Powerful Spell of the Bear, 'which accomplishes anything'.[70] Numerous other magical texts describe how burnt offerings were pleasing to the gods, especially due to the agreeable aroma of the smoke produced by the fat of animals or even slain human enemies.[71] Beliefs that fat contained and conveyed the vital essence of a living being would persist through the Middle Ages. A text falsely attributed to the philosopher Albertus Magnus even included instructions for making a candle that would make men appear 'in the shape of that beast whose fat thou didst take'.[72]

Given that some fats seemed to contain the vitality and qualities of their plant and animal sources, it stood to reason that, by penetrating the skin, they could impart some of those vital powers to the human body. The Greeks believed that oil gave athletes greater strength, and appreciated how it tanned and softened the skin, causing it to shine with a luminosity that made the body seem divine.[73] The origins of this practice are uncertain. One theory is that the almost magical power the Greeks attributed to oil may be a residue of earlier uses of animal fats and other substances rubbed on the body by hunters to prevent their prey from smelling them, a practice evident in many ancient and traditional peoples. Such practices became ritualized once their original purpose was forgotten:

> As hunting gave way to agriculture, some ten millennia ago, the original purpose of the oil was lost sight of. But, since it had for so long brought success to the hunter, it was felt to possess the ability to improve the hunter's skill, to make him stronger and faster.[74]

Whatever the origin of athletic oiling, there was an implied connection between the oil that one applied externally and the fat and sweat of the body itself. Following exercise, athletes would typically scrape the dirt, sweat and oil off their bodies using a curved metal tool called a strigil. The healthy functioning of the body required one to replenish oil that was secreted and washed away from the skin. To scrape the excess oil and sweat from the skin without reapplying oil was to rob the body of something essential. This is why the Greek diviner Artemidorus considered it bad luck to have a dream about a strigil that did not also feature an accompanying oil flask. Such a device, he maintained, would 'scrape off one's sweat and add nothing to the body'.[75] This belief in oil's capacity to revive flagging vitality was based on personal experience. Non-athletes also reported feelings of rejuvenation when oil and water were rubbed on their bodies after a period of fatigue.[76] Even the mixture of sweat, oil and dirt that athletes scraped from their bodies had medicinal value. In fact, it was collected and sold at a very high price. Alongside the wide range of fats and oils that formed part of the ancient pharmacopoeia, this greasy gunk would be made into ointments to treat sprains, muscle pain and inflammation of the joints, vulva and anus. But it was not only athletes' sweat and oil that healed. The layer of 'filth' that collected on the walls of baths

The healthy functioning of the body required one to replenish oil that was secreted and washed away from the skin. Greek athletes would typically scrape the dirt, sweat and oil off their bodies using a curved metal tool called a strigil. Athlete holding a strigil. Side A from an Attic red-figure skyphos, 475–450 BCE.

and gymnasia, as well as on the surface of statues, was also sold as a medicine.[77] This tacit link between oil and sweat may support the notion that the main function of anointing the body with oil after a bath was 'to feed, to introduce into the body through the pores, the stuff of life and strength, which appears to come out through the pores in the form of sweat'.[78] Such belief in the rejuvenating and strengthening power of oil persisted through the Middle Ages and beyond.[79]

As the next chapter will explore in greater depth, the ambiguity of fat persists throughout its various uses. In its refined state, oil may motivate impressions of purity, even spirituality – consider our modern fascination with essential oils or extra virgin olive oil. Yet when encountered as sticky grease, oil is also capable of eliciting disgust, a culturally inflected emotion that the Romans called *fastidium*. The poet Horace reported 'the great feelings of *fastidium* [that are stirred up] in the stomach, if the slaveboy has pawed the winecup with greasy hands while stealing a sip'.[80] Emperor Marcus Aurelius had a similar reaction to the thought of immersing himself in the less-than-pristine waters of a public bath: 'What is bathing when you think about it – oil, sweat, greasy water, everything loathsome.'[81] Even Dioscorides, we have seen, who endorsed the medicinal value of the greasy scrapings from the walls of baths, did not hesitate to call this mucky matter 'filth'.[82] The less commendable qualities of fat also made it available for the purposes of invective. The Romans, who were less fond of athletes than the Greeks, often described them as sweaty, stupid, oily, greedy, frivolous and fat, unflattering adjectives evoking qualities they associated with the sticky, clinging and bulging.[83]

Not even olive oil was free of ambiguity. Despite having adopted the Greek custom of rubbing themselves with oil, the Romans retained a certain distrust of a practice they associated with luxury and effeminacy.[84] Even some Greeks registered ambivalence about olive oil. Plutarch tells the story of the luxury-hating Theban general Epaminondas, who, after being presented with an account of the meal expenses that he and his fellow officers had recently incurred, 'showed indignation only at the great amount of olive oil'. It wasn't the financial expense that bothered him, but the fact 'that he had taken into his body so much oil'.[85] Interestingly, Epaminondas' distrust of oil was echoed in his contempt for fat men, whom he believed were woefully unfit for the rigours of war.[86] As the following section explains, what made fat substances and corpulent soldiers problematic for Epaminondas was their shared connection with 'softness'.

Softness and Moisture

As a vital substance closely connected to organic processes of growth and decay, fat is implicated in life as well as death, increase as well as excess, growth as well as decline. We can understand this in more detail by considering the effects that fatty substances have in the body itself. When contained within the bodily envelope, greasy and sticky fat enhances the 'softness' of soft tissues, fills in potentially unsightly concavities and blunts the hard edges of bones. This erasure of the most telling signs of the skeleton, which many cultures see as an unpleasant reminder of mortality, may be one reason why varying degrees of plumpness have functioned in many cultures as evidence of health, youth and vitality. But the very soft and yielding qualities that offered reassuring signs of healthy life could also be viewed as problematic. As we will see, in Graeco-Roman antiquity the yielding capacity of fat did not remain a simple tactile impression, but was related to gendered concepts of softness that, depending on the circumstance, could be viewed as the cause or effect of corpulence. While at times this softness pertained to qualities attached to females, who were typically seen as being colder, fatter and moister than males, it also denoted organic decay as well as moral corruption.[87] A slippage between the 'feminine' and the 'rotten' is an enduring feature of the softness that fat, and flesh in general, have manifested in Western culture.[88] What gets highlighted as being alarmingly soft changes over time; yet despite its changing content, 'softness' as a cultural category seems to resist profound transformation.[89]

Softness and moisture have been connected to images of the feminine since antiquity. Some of the reasons for this were medical. 'Plethora', or a superabundance of blood, was central to how the Hippocratic authors viewed female bodies, with an emphasis on wetness as dominating the female temperament. Moisture was feminized in a gendered typology of bodily fluids and textures that generated concern when one predominated over the others.[90] Female flesh was seen as especially absorbent and porous. Like wool, it was thought to soak up excess blood produced in a woman's stomach (which is what food had been converted into through digestion). Whereas in men it was only the glands that were described as spongy and porous (and the main avenue through which males absorb excess moisture), the whole of the female body was just as porous as the glands. What made a woman lesser than a man in this scenario, and what was cited as a rationale for her exclusion from the life of the polis, were the implicit value judgements that deemed the loose and spongy as inferior to the firm and compact.[91] Classical sources are unclear on the precise nature of the moisture said to predominate in female bodies. Recall Aristotle's proposal that unctuous moisture is present in all matter. Did this mean that the moisture said to predominate in women's bodies was therefore especially *unctuous*? The Roman writer Macrobius suggested as much when he commented on the uniquely oily qualities of female flesh:

> The fact that a woman's corpse helped men's corpses to burn was a function not of its warmth but of its rich [or fat] and oily flesh [*pinguis carnis et oleo*], a condition male corpses lacked because of their innate warmth.[92]

Whatever we make of Macrobius' unusual claim, physicians counted moisture and fat among the most conspicuous signs of the female body. If male bodies were considered to be naturally drier and thinner, it was because their innate heat and greater activity tended to 'melt' away much of their fat. Since fat, like semen, was viewed as concocted blood, a preponderance of fat represented a deficiency of blood capable of disturbing the normal functioning of the body. Women were said to be especially moist, partly because their 'feminine' sedentary lifestyle gave rise to fevers and poor health generally. Unable to make use of all the food they consumed, women tended to be fleshier than men, and only menstruation and pregnancy would properly evacuate their excess. Soranus, whose gynaecological ideas would hold considerable sway into the early medieval era, observed numerous factors that affected menstrual flow, such as season, constitution, age, physique and lifestyle. Among the very fat, he explained, menstrual flow is light, 'perhaps because the material is spent on their good nutritional state . . . for what nature does not use up for abundant nourishment, she adds to the excretion'. This economy of fluids is similarly affected by 'habits and modes of life', with more active women also experiencing lighter flow. This is how women easily become 'fat and ill-proportioned'.[93] Writers of late antiquity would build upon these ideas, arguing that, among fat women, menopause could occur as early as age 35 (as opposed to around forty to fifty, which was thought typical of most women).[94]

Lifestyle, then, played an important role in structuring the ways in which one's 'natural' constitution would manifest itself. This applied to males as well. Although viewed as naturally drier than females, some males had more humid constitutions than others. While they might regain some equilibrium through exercise and other measures, such males could also become overly corpulent if their lives were sedentary or, upon attaining old age, ceased to be as active as they once had been.[95] The masculinity of such soft and fat males could be called into question, mainly because the gendered typology of fluids and textures could be invoked to support the supposed moral inferiority of all 'feminine' traits. Adamantios made this clear in his fourth-century CE gloss of reigning physiognomic wisdom:

> Masculine parts are better than female. Since for the most part what is masculine is noble, without deceit, just, spirited, competitive and simple. What is female, on the other hand, is ignoble, bitter, deceitful, light-minded, unjust, contentious, and impudently cowardly.[96]

There was a wider geographical dimension to all of this. Some of the softness and moisture associated with 'feminine' qualities was explained with reference to different physical environments where climate and terrain were said to mould bodies and character in definite ways. The Hippocratic authors maintained that people residing in 'fat' and moist lands were more likely to have similar features in their bodies and characters. This cluster of tactile qualities was freighted with moral significance. 'For where the land is rich, soft, and well-watered . . . there the inhabitants are fleshy, ill-articulated, moist, lazy, and generally cowardly in character.'[97] This more or less geomorphic perspective facilitated a mesh of mutually supporting qualities within which fatness was entangled with physical and cognitive traits. In addition to being prone to 'slackness' and 'sleepiness', such people would lack the 'hard' and 'taut' articulation of joints that distinguished men from women, warriors from farmers, and Greeks from 'Asiatics'.[98] Instead they would manifest an overall laxness in their lifestyles and characters that aligned them with slack effeminacy and corruption. This was the kind of 'softness' implicit in the Greek word for luxury (*tryphē*), which has origins in the idea of receptiveness that is at odds with the 'hard' virile ideal publicly celebrated in Hellenistic culture.[99] This is why Herodotus could declare categorically that 'Soft lands breed soft men; wondrous fruits of the earth and valiant warriors grow not from the same soil.'[100]

The tactile properties of fat thus played an important role in constructing the moral category of softness as well as the gendered distinctions that it enabled. In fact, it was not uncommon to contrast the softness of fat with the relative hardness of muscle. As the next chapter explains, the Greek fascination with muscularity that developed from the Homeric period onwards reinforced this cultural validation of the hard and taut, establishing a connection between muscles and willpower that has arguably shaped our Western sense of the self ever since.[101] As a substance whose properties include the soft and greasy, fat has functioned since antiquity as the moral and physical 'other' of muscle and sinew, whether this tension has been manifested literally in the validation of hard and taut bodies over soft ones, or figuratively through references to a softness of character and a lack of willpower. Either way, it seems that the cultural stock of fat declines whenever muscularity and willpower are privileged.

＊

From this overview, fat's connection with organic life should be fairly obvious. Not only are fatty molecules essential for life, but many of the material substances and processes associated with organic existence are considered to be 'fat' to one degree or other: thick, greasy and viscous in texture and consistency. In addition to containing vitality, such substances were also thought capable of causing and materializing the *swelling* that is widely viewed as evidence of growth, increase and ripening – 'different manifestations of the fullness of life'.[102] In fact, when we consider the myriad ways in which fatness is observed in the processes and products of the natural world, one marvels at the extent to which softness, thickness, unctuousness and viscosity are cross-culturally viewed as qualities representative of – if not intrinsic to – organic life in all of its richness. It is, as Steven Connor puts it, as if 'at the essence of a living being is not something solid, but a powerful, viscous semi-liquid – in fact, an oil'.[103] This is why in Christianity, but surely in other religions as well, oil has been viewed as 'the fatty substance of life itself, the unctuous flow with which life persists, the viscosity of its slow growth, the syrup hidden at its core, its secret exuberance'.[104] If it is an exaggeration to say that fat *is* life, there is ample evidence to propose that, in its vital materiality, *life is fat*.

At the same time, this chapter has also gestured toward the ambiguities that fats and oils may materialize, and these need to be examined in greater detail. As is the case with other substances, the sensuous qualities of fat do not exist separately from culturally shaped perceptions and discourses that make sense of them. Rather than determine culture in any direct way, these qualities offer 'a series of potentialities for signs'[105] that may be 'bundled' together and mobilized within systems of value that privilege certain qualities over others.[106] As the next chapter explains, the stuff of life has rarely been viewed as an unmitigated good.

TWO

FERTILE AMBIGUITIES
The Agricultural Imagination

As the 'stuff of life', fat is imbued with vitality. Yet vitality involves processes of birth, growth, illness and death that 'pose existential challenges which all societies must interpret and react to physically in some way'.[1] This is especially evident when we add the phenomenon of *fattening* to our discussion of fat and fatness. Whether involving plants or animals, agricultural fattening is a process that includes ripeness, fullness and abundance, all of which may be viewed as beneficial and welcome. Swollen fullness, however, is also a moment on a continuum that moves through death and decomposition to create the conditions for new life, even if this life is not human, is not 'my' life. Whether or not we accept anthropologist Maurice Bloch's claim that 'the vast majority of societies represent human life as occurring within a permanent framework which transcends the natural transformative process of birth, growth, reproduction, ageing and death',[2] a case can certainly be made for the Western world's fraught relationship with organic process, materiality and animality. Engagements with these phenomena form part of an antique yet durable agricultural imagination that, by evoking models inherited from farming and animal husbandry, apprehends fat and fatness in terms of swelling or fattening.

Looking to the ancient world as a way of making sense of our current issues concerning corpulence may seem counterintuitive to those who assume that misgivings about fat are a distinctly 'modern' development. Yet this is not the first book to make note of certain continuities between ancient and modern ideas. Writing of 'the historical tenacity of cultural disdain for the fat body', Susan E. Hill shows how our current symbolic links between fatness and death, irrationality, femininity, animality and dirt have important antecedents in the classical and biblical sources of Western culture.[3] Whereas the previous chapter surveyed some of the complexity with which fat as a substance has been understood in the ancient world, this chapter examines the ambiguities of the fatty as well as the fattening. It complements Hill's analyses of ancient gluttony and fatness by examining fat's broader connection to the concept of 'life' as a process. At times, this involves a consideration of substances that may fatten without necessarily being fat. It will show that, in the agricultural imagination, fat may be seen as a borderline concept located on the cusp of ripeness and rottenness, fertility and barrenness. It will also examine the deep sources of animal invective applied to fat people that continues to speak to one's status in social and cultural hierarchies. We will see how, whether referring literally to soil or figuratively to the human body, the agricultural imagination generated powerful and enduring root metaphors that have become so deeply buried in Western culture that their origins in dirt, vegetation and animal husbandry have been largely forgotten. To think fat, then, one must be prepared for frequent and often surprising intersections between plants and animals which provided important models for thinking about the moderate and the excessive, the ripe and the rotten, the dominant and the subordinate, and the consumer and the consumed.

Matters of Life and Death

The ambiguity of fat relates, at least in part, to its connection to processes of fertility, growth, death, decomposition and regeneration. Ambivalence about such phenomena is not a novel feature of modernity. Historian Caroline Walker Bynum offers a detailed tracking of the denial of organic process among Christian theologians from the third century through to the fourteenth. As they imagined the resurrection of bodies at the end of time, these authors repeatedly rejected the apostle Paul's claim that the dead body is like a seed that rots in the ground. They preferred instead to imagine the corpse using non-organic metaphors of a broken vessel or crystal capable of being reconstructed rather than having to undergo putrefaction. Bynum observes that death was a problem for these men, 'not because it was an event that ended consciousness, but because it was part of oozing, disgusting, uncontrollable biological process'.[4] The recurrent association of female bodies with the organic process that so disturbed most male (and even some female) theologians reinforces impressions that certain exalted forms of masculinity are imagined as being 'beyond process' and therefore transcendent in utterly phantasmatic ways. In the Western world, being subject to organic processes may in fact be more of an affront to human dignity than death itself. In his cultural history of perceptions of death, Jonathan Dollimore proposes that 'the process of change and decline *in time* is more disturbing than the idea of not being at all.'[5] By considering the longevity of such vexed responses to human corruptibility, Bynum and Dollimore gesture towards perceptions that bridge conventional divisions between ancient, medieval and modern. If fat is intrinsically ambiguous, it is partly due to its close connection to processes that may evoke positive as well as negative feelings.

The examples offered so far have been drawn from European culture, so perhaps such concerns should be treated as distinctly, or at least primarily, Western. There is, after all, ample evidence – too much to survey here – demonstrating how fat and fatness have functioned as evidence of privilege, fertility, power and beauty in many non-Western societies.[6] Archaeological research provides some of the earliest clues. To take one example, the search for fat was paramount for the native hunting peoples of northeastern America, influencing 'almost all aspects of their lives, including the spiritual world'. Specific animals were hunted and revered for the fat content of their flesh and bones, and techniques were developed to extract as much fat as possible from the meat during cooking. Various Native American myths even associated fat with survival and immortality.[7] Related disciplines, notably anthropology, provide numerous cases of societies in which human body fat is especially valued. It is widely known that many cultures in Africa force-feed girls in order to fatten them for marriage. While not all of these societies draw direct associations between fatness and fertility, in some cases the practice of fattening is explicitly likened to a process of 'ripening' based on agricultural analogies.[8]

Beyond certain societies in Africa, other cultures manifest quite expansive understandings of fat. In several Australian Aboriginal traditions, fat is a substance located within the land as well as in plants, animals and humans. Linked to sweat, semen and milk as cognate fluids that that are similarly imbued with vitality, animal fats are seen as providing health and energy. Some fats have been considered too powerful for certain kinds of people to bear. Historically speaking, human fat has been considered especially potent. In addition to signifying health and vitality, human fat, especially the kind attached to the kidneys, was traditionally cut from the bodies of enemies in wartime. It was also believed that a person's kidney fat could be actually or magically removed by enemy sorcerers.[9] A world away, in the Andean culture of South America, fat (like blood) is a particular manifestation of *chuyma* or 'heart' and associated with the qualities of spirit or 'soul' and courage. Here, as in Australia, loss of body fat is a sign of sickness. Serious illnesses may even be attributed to the mysterious operations of a *kharisiri* or *pishtaco*, a bogeyman said to steal kidney fat whose origins are traceable to the Spanish conquest.[10] Whether diminished through ill-health or spirited away through sorcery, diminished body fat signifies the loss or removal of that which promotes health and vitality.

Despite its importance, fat is not the only vital substance in the body. Similar powers, and even similar qualities, may be noted in milk and semen. In addition to being described as thick and rich, milk and semen have often been viewed as sharing a substantial relationship with fat as well as with the swelling of bodies through feeding and pregnancy, respectively. Calling to mind 'ideas about process, change, vitality, and decay', vital bodily substances like semen, milk, blood and fat are not simply 'felt to be dirty – they are powerful'.[11] In many cultures, then, fat belongs to a group of bodily substances that are 'ambiguous in the most fundamental way' partly because, by coming out of the body, they call into question the precise boundaries of the self.[12] A few examples of this ambiguity should suffice. In Papua New Guinea, as well as in Borneo and the Andes, pig fat is explicitly likened to semen and, as such, associated with male sexuality in ways that may provoke anxiety as well as disgust.[13] In the former case, it is not necessarily fatty tissue that is thought to make one 'fat'. Rather, what seems to fatten a body may also be certain contact with female bodies – often seen as potentially polluting – and substances that predominate in boys but are considered inappropriate in adult males. In the male initiation rites of the Bimin-Kuskusmin people of Papua New Guinea, fatness is associated with the 'filth, putrefaction and moral degeneracy of female substance and behavior'. This is especially so when it appears in the bodies of young male initiates that have been 'defiled' by the fattening 'effects of female foods and female substances . . . the elders loudly observe that the novices are polluted, weak, and ugly – as is apparent by their round, fat stomachs'.[14] Inflected by gender ideals, swollen fatness may be acceptable in female bodies while seeming more problematic in those of adult males.

In certain cultures, then, fatness may symbolize the storing up of substances imbued with vital energy. Such swelling may be viewed in different ways. The corpulent monarch of the remote Mankon king-dom in western Cameroon is 'the archetype of male fertility' because his body is swollen with the ancestral substances that he dispenses to the community in the form of semen, saliva, breath and other mate-rials.[15] Failure to dispense these vital substances would be viewed as a menace to the community. In other cultures one can indeed find examples of negative reactions to a body's perceived hoarding of com-munal powers. The Etoro people of the Strickland-Bosavi region of Papua New Guinea have been known to kill plump 'witch-children' at birth precisely because, by being considered too fat, they appear to have accumulated in their bodies the life force that should in principle circulate throughout the community.[16] In other cultures, bodies bearing the signs of swollen fertility are plotted along the tra-jectory of organic processes. Utilizing analogies directly drawn from agricultural knowledge, in rural Jamaica fat bodies are appreciated as evidence of health and beauty. Yet this appreciation wanes when bodies that were once robustly plump begin to seem 'spongy, soft, hanging slack, and denoting declining fitness as if a person was an overripe fruit, beginning to break down and rot'.[17] This reveals how, in certain contexts, fatness can mark a moment on a continuum in which vitality and fertility may easily slip into death and decay. Insofar as fatty substances may evoke images of growth and life as well as corruption and sexuality, they are capable of eliciting a range of responses, positive as well as negative.

The Jamaican case reveals how fat can seem to *represent* growth and increase while remaining a *material instance* of that increase. This case also identifies situations where increase that extends beyond ripeness may seem to transform itself into waste and decay. Similar themes circulated in European agricultural thinking. We have already seen how the Greeks and Romans related the fattening of humans to the 'fattening' of farmland. Whereas some degree of fatness was beneficial, there were limits that the wise farmer needed to recognize. Despite heaping praise on fat soil, Columella warned that extremes in soil types could lead to problems. While very lean soil tends to become barren, 'the fattest and most fertile soil suffers from rankness of growth.' To make his point, Columella had recourse to common-sense wisdom about human bodies:

> There is need ... of much intermixture among these so different extremes, as is requisite also in our own bodies, whose well-being depends on a fixed and, so to speak, balanced proportion of the hot and the cold, the moist and the dry, the compact and the loose.[18]

By drawing such distinctions, especially the one separating 'hot' from 'cold' soil qualities, Columella revealed his reliance on the humoral model of the body that, based on Hippocratic precedents, would structure European medical thinking through to the seventeenth century.[19]

If acceptable fatness was capable of resulting in decay rather than fertility, there was also something potentially repulsive about the substances that helped to make a particular soil 'fat'. Soil was typically fattened with rotten organic matter as well as faeces, substances that are often viewed as ambiguous even if they yield beneficial results. Greasy excrement, which 'the Greeks, early and late, unequivocally regarded ... as dirty or disgusting, indeed as polluting',[20] was an unavoidable ingredient in the fattening of 'thin' soil. Thus Columella described 'the very best soil' as being fat (*pinguis*) because of its greasiness, as well as 'rotten' (*putris*) due to the dead and decaying matter it contained.[21] Fertile soil thus gives life precisely *because* it is composed of greasy and decaying substances, thus achieving that state of 'fecund putrescence' that is the middle stage of the organic process of death and rebirth.[22]

Just as agricultural authors borrowed insights from physicians, the Hippocratics derived a great deal of their knowledge of human nutrition by observing what took place in plants.[23] Even if the substances and processes being described were not exactly the same, then, it still made sense to identify homologies between the fat of animals and that of soil and plants. Associations between crops and people had been the stock-in-trade of educational theory since fifth-century Athens. When extended to bodies, these analogies formed the basis for a set of tropes that would proliferate in the West well into the modern era.[24] If fatness oftentimes seemed to imply abundance, for instance, it could also denote surplus and superfluity. Etymologically speaking, the Latin word *prosperus* suggested a kind of 'thriving' that was closely associated with concepts like fullness, fatness, increase, satiety and ripening.[25] Yet if prosperity implied abundance and growth grounded in observations about plants and animals, agricultural knowledge maintained that growth beyond acceptable bounds could be problematic. Hence the *luxuria* or 'rankness of growth' that was for the ancients a consequence of overly fat soil referred to organic increase that must be cleared away lest the land become unproductive.

Moralists also harvested some of their key ideas from agricultural models. In addition to denoting overgrowth, *luxuria* was also the term that Romans used to describe a chief cause of personal and social 'corruption', a concept also grounded in agricultural experience. As defined by the *Oxford English Dictionary*, 'corruption' denotes physical decomposition along with the loathsome putrefaction that accompanies it, which seems implicit in related definitions describing 'the perversion of anything from an original state of purity', be it something organic or moral. That decay implies a pre-existing state of purity or integrity is revealed by the fact that *corruptio* is also a biblical term denoting mortality in the face of God's eternity and therefore human distance from divinity. More explicitly than the concept of luxury, corruption points to the decomposition of a body as well as the emotional responses this process may elicit.[26] The qualities that helped to explain agricultural abundance were thus capable of giving rise to negative consequences: overgrowth, rottenness and barrenness instead of moderation and fertility. As a product of the agricultural imagination, fatness may evoke impressions of fertility as well as sterility and corruption. These ideas pertained to animals as well.

Fertility, Fattening, Animality

If vegetation was not the only model for thinking about reproduction,[27] non-human animals were also a regular point of reference for ancient ideas about generation. Here, too, fatness and fertility were not always synonymous. In some cases, they were clearly in a state of tension. Traditional beliefs linking fertility to the lunar cycle played a role in determining the best time to fatten certain animals. It was most prudent to fatten birds and other animals as the moon waxed – that is, as the moon itself seemed to grow and 'ripen' to fullness. It thus stood to reason that castration was best carried out as the waning moon seemed to decay or fade away.[28] Yet the removal of an animal's sexual capacity was also believed to promote fattening. Ancient beliefs held that one could fatten sows and camels by cutting out their wombs.[29] Roosters, it was said, grew fat after castration.[30] The reverse was also true: fattening diminished fertility. 'He-goats are made sterile by over-fattening,' noted Pliny.[31] The same thing was observed among deer:

> The males when at last freed from lustful desire greedily seek pasture; when they feel they are too fat, they look for lairs to hide in, showing that they are conscious of inconvenient weight.[32]

Ancient medicine tried to account for this unstable relationship between fatness and fertility with reference to other vital bodily substances. The connection between blood and fat was important: fat was viewed as having been concocted from blood and from the nutriments that helped to create blood. This is why Pliny could state that 'Fat animals have a smaller supply of blood, because it is used up in the fat.'[33] Yet insofar as the 'normal' itinerary of blood is to be turned into sperm in the male and milk in the female, the presence of large amounts of fat in the body could indicate qualities at odds with fertility. Here, too, certain animals shed light on this relationship. Pigs that are 'too fat ... experience lack of milk'.[34] As a 'residue' of other vital bodily substances, fat enjoyed a double status as both a vehicle of vitality and a form of surplus that could be viewed as 'excremental' in that it is secreted from the body. As opposed to certain African cultures, where fatness may be deliberately cultivated as a means of storing up the forces of life and reproduction, Western societies have typically held that the production of fat and the production of sperm are in a state of tension. For us, 'fat is considered as a deviation of that which should be devoted to sexual activity.'[35] While this is really only true when fat is thought to be excessive, this statement aptly accounts for some of the ongoing claims that very corpulent people are less fertile than others, either through sterility or impotence. Insofar as this diversion of blood from its fertile aim results in infertility, in the case of fat men excess nutriment becomes the symbolic equivalent of castration.[36] Swollen fatness may denote fertility and ripeness as well as death and decay, such as in the swollenness of a corpse.

Classical sources elaborated on the sometimes inverted relationship between fatness and fertility. Aristotle noted that in fat animals 'what needed to go from the blood into semen and seed is converted into soft and hard fat.'[37] His description of how fatness diminished male fertility drew upon plant as well as animal registers. Men who gain weight are much like grapevines that 'go goaty' in that they 'behave just like he-goats, which when they get fat indulge less in copulation, and incidentally this explains why goats are made to slim before the breeding season'.[38] In addition to corroborating this idea, Pliny evoked the spectre of physical decline: 'All fat animals are more liable to barrenness, in the case of both males and females; also excessively fat ones get old more quickly.'[39] Sustaining an association between plant and animal anatomies, Pliny contended that both suffer from

> hunger and from indigestion, maladies due to the amount of moisture in them, and some even from obesity [*obesitate*], for instance all which produce resin owing to excessive fatness [*pinguitudine*] are converted into torch-wood, and when the roots also have begun to get fat, die like animals from excessive adipose deposit.[40]

Whereas fatness and fertility go together, it has been noted since antiquity that men and women who are exceptionally large may also be as infertile as those who are very thin.[41] Animals that grew fat thus succumbed to the same problems as overly fat fields.

If fattening is an ambiguous phenomenon, food and eating are similarly equivocal. Beyond the obvious benefits that make it essential for life, food is also organic and thus subject to adulteration and decay. 'Food is unclean, a highly unstable substance,' sociologist Deborah Lupton reminds us; and it is messy and dirty in its preparation, its disposal and its by-products; it inevitably decays, it has odour. Delicious food is only hours or days away from rotting matter, or excreta.[42]

Eating food thus involves the introduction of potentially harmful matter into the body and, in so doing, activates processes that humans share with non-human animals. The act of eating is ambiguous in other ways as well. It implies relationships with others that are also redolent of animality.[43] The *Oxford English Dictionary* shows that the verb 'to feed', which for a time meant the same thing as 'to grow fat', could refer to the grazing of animals as well as 'feeding on' someone else, or parasitically living at someone else's expense. The verb could thus place one in a position of agency (*to take food*; *to eat*) or subjection, as in the nineteenth-century phrase *to feed off*, meaning 'to fatten (an animal) for sale or slaughter'. Something similar occurs in other Indo-European languages, where the verb *to feed* means the same thing as 'to fatten', and fattening has a close relationship to the fattening of domestic animals. In her study of words relating to eating, Christine Hénault observes that

> Languages indeed have a semantic link between, on the one hand, the act of eating, and on the other hand, the situations where the individual is faced with certain events imposed upon him and that he has to undergo.[44]

The root of the term 'obesity' reflects some of this ambiguity. As the past participle of the Latin verb *obedere* (to eat away, eat into), the term *obesus* originally meant 'skinny, all skin and bone' but, for reasons that are unclear, developed over time to refer mainly to one 'who devours'.[45]

Processes of fattening and devouring revealed a power differential that played a role in the analogies the Greeks and Romans drew between human and non-human animals but also among animals themselves. To the extent that there is a 'hierarchy of sympathy' structuring the degree of ethical interest a given society affords the living things it consumes, the category of the 'animal' is often subdivided into those worthy of human respect and even symbolic emulation and those considered inherently ignoble and deserving of their lesser status.[46] Just as plants were made for animal consumption, it was said, non-human animals were made for human use.[47] A similar hierarchy based on predation was applied to animals themselves. Aristotle noted that animals 'differ from one another in regard to character'. Some are brave and ferocious. The lion, for example, is 'free and courageous and high-bred'.[48] Although dangerous 'wild' animals could be described in a variety of ways, these predators were rarely used for food and were thus viewed as somewhat higher in the hierarchy of non-human animals. This was not the case with 'prey' animals like cows, sheep, pigs, goats and poultry that were often fattened for human use.[49] The relatively low status of livestock in the animal hierarchy has hardened since the Neolithic era, by which time domesticated animals were viewed more as property than as sentient peers.[50] Although in antiquity prey animals were capable of being represented in complex ways, they were often associated with traits like meekness, slowness, docility and even stupidity. If fattened farm animals may have been looked upon as slaves and thus objects of disdain during Roman times,[51] by the Middle Ages creatures like sheep and lambs were considered cowardly and stupid, almost deserving the fact that they would be slaughtered and devoured by humans.[52]

These developments have implications for human cultures, not least because they have to do with status in hierarchical systems. Speaking in broad terms, historian Keith Thomas proposes that the domestication of animals 'became the archetypal pattern for other kinds of social subordination'.[53] The contempt that has often been heaped on prey animals may spring from the fact that domestication entails specific forms of disempowerment connected to their fattening. In addition to undergoing gradual bodily changes, with their brains becoming smaller relative to their bodies as their fat content increases,[54] domesticated animals may be subjected to restriction of movement as well as castration to ensure that their flesh remains palatable and their dispositions mild.[55] For the Roman agronomer Varro, barnyard fowl demonstrated how the fatness produced by fattening could function as a kind of prison or slavery: 'These are shut into a warm, narrow, darkened place, because movement on their part and light free them from the slavery of fat [*quod motusearum et lux pinguitudinis vindicta*].'[56] Domesticated male animals, as every farmer knew, tended to grow fatter once they had been castrated, with the result being that their flesh became more tender and palatable while their dispositions were said to grow softer.[57] The figure of the eunuch most vividly illustrated this association between emasculation and fattening. A fourth-century Latin physiognomy text recounts the telltale signs of such a man: 'forehead taut, cheeks soft, mouth relaxed, skinny neck, fat calves, thick feet like lumps of meat, a feminine voice, women's words, all limbs and joints without vigour, lax and loose.'[58]

Associations between fattening and livestock reveal what we might call a 'vertical tension' between the earthy downward tendencies of 'animal' behaviour and the upward or transcendent aspirations connected to 'human' existence.[59] In this way, the presumed 'low' status of non-human animality related also to assumptions of immanence and the almost principled rejection of transcendence displayed by the mass of humans. This vertical tension is at the origin of the Western philosophical tradition, which was itself inaugurated by pronounced misgivings about embodiment.[60] The kind of 'life most people lead', Plato explained, consisted of feasting and always seeking out the low and vulgar:

> They never look up at the true top, or go there . . . They are like cattle, their gaze constantly directed downwards. Eyes on the ground – or on the table – they fatten themselves at pasture, and rut.[61]

As it was lived by most people, then, 'life' was animalistic and fleeting, bereft of loftier aspirations. It was certainly not 'the good life' befitting human beings. Plato wondered what people would be like in a society that freely provided basic necessities and eliminated the need for vigorous effort to obtain them: 'is each of them to live out his life getting fattened up, like a cow?' In his view, such people had become fit for slaughter by stronger and harder types: 'it's appropriate that an idle, soft-spirited, and fattened animal usually is ravaged by one of those other animals who have been worn very hard with courage and labors'.[62]

The Stoics extended these ideas in their sharp criticisms of luxuries that threatened to reduce men to the level of the most ignoble of beasts. Seneca described how dissolute fat men who keep late hours and get no exercise are like birds being fattened for the slaughter. The key difference was that, unlike animals that have been captured and fattened by humans, such men are personally responsible for the fact that 'their idle bodies are overwhelmed with flesh.'[63] While fattening was not necessarily a result of gluttonous excess – and, conversely, at this time corpulence was not consistently equated with gluttony – the idea that a man could be ruled by his appetites seemed to reduce him to the level of a beast or a slave. This is how, in Athenaeus' *The Learned Banqueters*, Ulpian could amuse his fellows by likening luxurious eating to being 'foddered' like farm animals.[64]

To the degree that it may suggest the result of processes of fattening, then, fatness is capable of being viewed in contradictory ways. The same logic that compelled Graeco-Roman observers to link 'fat' lands to 'soft' characters, and to compare animal and human physiques and characters, offered a potent way of combining these qualities with reference to fat people. According to classical models of appetite, the act of consumption could easily drift from the moderate enjoyment of sensual pleasures to excesses reflecting a 'slavish' submission to one's desires. The corpulent could be depicted as physically and morally 'soft', unable to assume a 'firm' or 'hard' stance in relation to external stimuli or their own appetites. By seemingly living in 'a state of nonresistance with regard to the force of pleasures', they could appear to be 'in a position of weakness and submission'.[65] In addition, as we will see below, such people could be viewed as 'insensate', as if the fatty layer under their skin rendered them mentally or emotionally dull.

Situations in which one's control over the process of consumption might be called into question – as revealed in the case of 'fattened' animals – could imply very different traits. This is one reason why deliberately fattening oneself or one's children was viewed in Graeco-Roman antiquity as something that 'belonged to the sphere of the strange and exotic'.[66] The latter will become clearer when we consider how Asiatic peoples could be perceived during this period. If fattened bodies ever became objects of revulsion in the Hellenized world – and such strong responses were not as common among pagans as they would be among early Christians – it would have had more to do with the 'ideological disgust' elicited by violations of the rules governing social hierarchies than the kind of feeling elicited by grease or faeces.[67] Given that disgust often overlaps with related emotions, such ideological disgust might have easily been taken for contempt, disgust's 'closest neighbor'.[68] Fatness and fattening were thus enmeshed in status hierarchies where the human was privileged over the animal, the masculine over the feminine, the free over the slave, and the familiar over the exotic.

Albeit less pronounced, links between fatness and abject animality are evident in the Hebrew Bible as well. The Book of Judges (3:12–22) tells the story of what happened to King Eglon of Moab. King Eglon was 'a very fat man' empowered by Yahweh to dominate the Israelites for eighteen years because they had once again done 'what was evil in the sight of the LORD'. This period of servitude was ended by the deliverer Ehud, who rose up to assassinate the king. With a name that meant 'big [or young] calf', Eglon would suffer the fate of fattened sacrificial animals – the 'message from God' that Ehud delivered took the form of a double-edged sword plunged into the fat king's belly. So corpulent was Eglon that his fat (*ḥēlebh*) completely swallowed up Ehud's sword, hilt and all. Unable to 'draw the sword out of his belly', Ehud observed instead that 'the dirt came out'. In addition to signifying the corruption of the wealthy, Eglon's fatness has been interpreted by scholars as establishing a contrast between Israelite and Moabite, human and animal, masculine and feminine, dominant and subordinate, but also between intelligence and stupidity.[69] By noting the appearance of excrement ('dirt') that flowed from Eglon's ripped belly, the episode took the extra step of connecting great fatness with the filth and impurity that would surely elicit disgust as well.[70] Planted in the Hebrew Bible, the connection between fatness and excrement would be cultivated by early Christians, as the next chapter will show.

Historical experiences with crops and livestock provided the deepest sources of an enduring yet tacit cultural intuition in the West: that fattening may signify an abdication or restriction of agency resulting in subordination and even fleshy incarceration. To *grow fat* through good living could signify agency, status and enjoyment. It could even indicate a predatory role in which a person 'devoured' others in a manner commensurate with his or her power. Yet being an eater contains the possibility of someone else acting as a feeder. When this did not imply a kind of infantile position vis-à-vis a mother or caregiver, to *be fattened* by someone else, in the manner of a pig or goat, could suggest passivity and a resemblance to livestock destined for the chop. As a consequence of the methodical and even forced ingestion and incorporation of edible things, fattening also carried the troubling reminder that humans too are edible and may be 'devoured' by those who are more powerful than they. The disturbing fact of human edibility was driven home by stories of ancient and indigenous peoples who supposedly fattened captured prisoners for the express purpose of feasting on their flesh.[71] Fattening is a process whose troubling associations with subordination, animality, and even anthropophagy, have never been completely shrugged off. As the next section explains, it also has links to cognitive 'thickness' and foolishness.

Insensateness and Stupidity

Fat's association with 'lesser' animals extended to the cognitive domain as well. Here, too, connotations of animality were accentuated by the ambiguous materiality of fat. In addition to its connections to greasiness and softness, fat has been viewed since antiquity as a dull and insensate substance that could align corpulent individuals with unflattering forms of animality but also stupidity. Arguing that blood itself lacks perception, as does anything (like fat) concocted from blood, Aristotle speculated that 'if the entire body were to become fat, it would lack perception entirely.'[72] The Romans adopted a similar perspective with reference to animal examples. Explaining that 'greasy fat has no sensation [*adips cunctis sine sensu*], because it does not possess arteries or veins,' Pliny declared that most fat animals are more or less insensitive: 'it is recorded [by Varro] that because of this, pigs have been gnawed by mice while still alive.'[73] The third-century writer Aelian notes a similar perceptual barrier in the aquatic world. When a 'large fish becomes very fat it can no longer see or hear, the vast bulk of its flesh being an obstacle to sight and to hearing'.[74]

Such examples present fat and fatness as intruders in the animal body. In the case of humans, great masses of flesh were seen as supplemental to – and thus not really part of – the 'true' body, which was considered to be neither too thin nor too fat.[75] Pliny claimed that it was due to the insensateness of this surplus matter that 'the son of the consular Lucius Apronius had his fat removed by an operation and relieved his body of unmanageable weight.'[76] The contention that layers of fat were not really part of the human body is further illustrated in the oft-told tale of Dionysius of Heraclea, tyrant of a city-state in Asia Minor. Dionysius' 'addiction to luxury' and 'overeating every day' caused him to gain so much weight that he found it difficult to breathe and, out of shame, held audiences while seated behind a chest that concealed all but his face.[77] In Aelian's version of the story, Dionysius' physicians recommended inserting long needles into his ribs and stomach while he was in a deep sleep so that, by passing through his fat – since 'it was insensitive, and in a sense not part of him' – they could discover where his fat ended and his flesh began. The idea was that the slumbering king would be roused only when the needles hit something 'not transformed by the excess of fat'.[78] Dionysius' fat could be cut away because, strictly speaking, it was a form of surplus that was not bound up with his body in the same way as a limb or internal organ. But this did not save him from the nasty barbs of his countrymen. According to Athenaeus, some of them likened their ruler to 'a fat pig' who thought it was fine 'to be fat and lie on your back, with an enormous gut, barely able to speak or breathe in and out, eating and saying "I feel so good that I'm rotting"'.[79] A consequence of having been 'addicted to luxury', Dionysius of Heraclea's fatness conjured images of animality and decay as well as insensateness. As the next chapter explains, it also evoked the dangerously exotic foreignness of Asiatic cultures.

In the form of adipose tissue, fat served as an interface between the self and the world in ways that might affect mental and emotional experience. Perceived since antiquity as a surplus accretion upon the 'true' body, layers of fat have been regularly imagined as encasing the self, insulating it from the blows of the world while functioning as a kind of security blanket. The insensateness of fat was thus readily extended to the characters of individuals burdened with a form of dull materiality that constrained as well as yielded. If the softness of fat denoted a potentially troubling non-resistance to external stimuli, its insensate 'thickness' suggested a kind of insulation through which things pass only with difficulty. In the fourth-century BCE *Physiognomics*, erroneously attributed to Aristotle, insensitivity was closely bound up with bodies in which 'the distance from the navel to the chest is greater than the distance from the chest to the neck.' People with such physiques are

> gluttonous and insensitive; gluttonous because the receptacle into which they admit their food is large, and insensitive because the

senses have a more cramped space, corresponding to the size of the food receptacle, so that the senses are oppressed owing to the excess or defect of the food supply.[80]

In such persons, the capacity for delicate emotions and even perception itself is diminished through the constriction of those regions of the body in which the senses are located.[81]

Insensateness was also coupled by some classical thinkers with the qualities attributed to animals domesticated for human consumption and therefore deliberately fattened through restrictions on diet and movement. Thick and 'sluggish' bodily movement thus found parallels in the torpor and clumsiness of the mind, perhaps encouraging the notion that 'the body and soul of the same creature are always such that a given disposition must necessarily follow a given form.'[82] It may also be why Pliny claimed that animals with very large abdomens are 'less clever' than those with smaller ones.[83] This association of stupidity with non-human animals is preserved in the French word *bête*, which means 'animal' as well as 'foolish'. Ancient physiognomic analyses of gluttons were informed by analogies drawn with voracious non-human animals, especially pigs and crocodiles, whose especially thick hides also contributed to their stupidity. The pig was identified as most similar to the glutton in that both were less interested in their souls than in bodily pleasures.[84] Fat's capacity to provide insulation from external forces was literally true in the case of boxers and gladiators, whose extra fat was thought to function as a kind of padding.[85] And no one in Antiquity credited boxers and gladiators with being the cleverest of men.

For classical writers the insensateness of fat thus seemed to produce cognitive insensitivity as well as motoric sluggishness, both of which would form durable stereotypes that would circulate in the West for centuries. The Latin term *crassus*, meaning thick, dense and grossly stupid, allowed one to draw assumptions about character and intelligence based on bodily traits. Nor was this restricted to the classical period. The English *crass* and the French *gras* (fat) both have etymological roots in *crassus*.[86] While sometimes admiring fat bodies as evidence of wealth and status, the Romans were also likely to suggest that intelligence and corpulence were mutually exclusive. As a joking reference to the goddess of intellect, a popular means of denoting dim-wittedness was to say that such a person had a 'fat

Minerva' (*crassa* or *pingui Minerva*), thus suggesting a gap between corpulence and wisdom.[87] The physician Galen offered medical support to this popular association of fatness and foolishness by declaring that 'it is truest of all that a full stomach does not beget a fine mind'.[88] This statement would go on to be a proverb in Western culture. Although subsequent versions of this saying tended to insist upon fatness rather than fullness, it may be that Galen was referring to the experience of sluggishness and tiredness that can follow a big meal.[89] If so, over time this phenomenological experience of sluggishness resulting from fullness came to be applied to fat bodies in general.

If insensateness could slide from the literal to the figurative as well as between the animal and human, it was equally capable of being bundled together with the other qualities of fat. This is how

In a striking departure from the Greek physical ideal of beauty, health and morality, boxers were renowned for being misshapen and fat. On pottery they were often represented with pot-bellies and massive thighs. Nikosthenes, black-figured amphora showing a boxing contest.

all of those 'soft' and cowardly inhabitants of 'fat' lands described by Hippocrates could be relied upon to be 'thick-witted, and neither subtle nor sharp'.⁹⁰ The high living that may contribute to corpulence, and therefore to moral and physical 'softness', could just as easily bring insensateness or foolishness along with it. Railing against the ruinous luxury he saw all around him, the first-century poet Persius described a particularly villainous man as being 'numb with vice' because 'prime fat has overgrown his heart' (*fibris increvit opimum pingue*), as if the substance had worked its way into his very innards.⁹¹ The satirist Lucian described as '*pacheis*' (fat or stupid) all those gullible, rich people who had been fleeced during the second century by the mystical fraud, Alexander of Abonoteichus.⁹²

None of this was exclusive to the Hellenistic tradition. The Hebrews also registered concern about fat's desensitizing effects on the person. In biblical texts, words for fat (such as *ḥēlebh*) were undoubtedly positive when referring to bounteous land, but took on negative implications when observed in the human body. This was especially true for the wealthy, whose enjoyment of 'fat things' could lead to arrogance, selfishness or financial ruin.⁹³ Insensibility was a primary trait of wealthy people who showed no compassion for the needy: they have been rendered insensate and dull by their own prosperity and suffer the ill-effects of fat regardless of their actual corpulence: 'They close their hearts to pity [literally: they are enclosed in their own fat (*ḥēlebh*)]; / with their mouths they speak / arrogantly' (Psalms 17:10). In a number of biblical passages, fat is synonymous with being mentally slow or 'thick'. Here, too, it is manifested most often among the prosperous: 'Their hearts are fat [*taphash*: unreceptive or stupid] and gross [*ḥēlebh*]' (Psalms 119:70). Such people become obdurate, suffering from a 'hardening' of the heart, which also happened to be the seat of the 'mind'. Thus the hard-hearted person is literally 'fat-hearted', and so deprived of spiritual wisdom.⁹⁴ In Deuteronomy (32:15), Moses recites the words of God to the Israelites, explaining how, after being provided with the bounty of the land, Jacob became complacent and turned his back on God. 'Jacob ate his fill; / Jeshuran [that is, the people of Israel] grew fat [*šemen*], and kicked. You grew fat [*šemen*], bloated, and gorged!' Even if abundance and good living had caused these bodies to become grotesque to the eye, the Hebrew tradition was more concerned with the spiritual and cognitive effects of this fattening.

*

While it is true that the distant past evinced a more tolerant approach
to body size and shape, the cultural history of fat in the West does
not reveal eras of history when fat, fatness and fattening were valued
without qualification. Rather, fat referred to ambiguous substances
and processes that were capable of straddling cultural categories
of the fertile and the rotten, the beneficial and the dangerous, the
high and the low. In one form or another, then, fat is implicit in most
of the main categories of Western culture: pleasure and pain, vice
and virtue, illness and health, dirty and clean, moist and dry, animal
and human. The qualities associated with fat (softness, greasiness,
dullness) are among the structuring elements of many ancient cultures
and thus part of the conceptual frameworks through which they
viewed the world. It is soft, loose and flabby; capable of slipping
between solid and liquid states, it is disturbingly unstable and protean, qualities that rarely represent positively in Western culture. As
the next chapter demonstrates, many of these qualities were applied
to bodies in the Greek and Roman worlds, where fattening oneself
through luxurious living implied an abdication of self-mastery. While
the following chapters focus more closely on perceptions of corpulence, we will repeatedly see how the materiality of fat, as well as the
agricultural connotations of fattening, recur as ways of thinking
about fatness.

THREE

ANCIENT APPETITES
Luxury and the Geography
of Softness

When Socrates announced that he wanted to take up dancing, all his friends at the drinking party broke out with laughter. What was so funny about this declaration? Socrates wondered. Was it because dancing might be good for his health and well-being, or that it would exercise all of his muscles and render his proportions more balanced and beautiful? 'Or is *this* why you're laughing,' Socrates asked, indicating his round belly, 'because my stomach is larger than it should be and I want to reduce it to a more normal size?'[1] If these questions were largely rhetorical, this is not the first time Socrates' body was discussed in ancient texts. Widely depicted as pudgy and ugly, Socrates was sometimes likened to the ancient woodland god Silenus, often depicted in Greek statuary as fat, bald and drunk. It was even reported that Socrates had been examined by the physiognomist Zopyrus, who concluded that he was 'stupid and thick-witted' and 'addicted to women', though not because of his belly.[2] Said to pay no attention to the beauty or ugliness of other people, the ageing philosopher left no evidence that he was concerned about his own physical shortcomings. His friends agreed that these defects – and the Greeks *did* see them as defects – were compensated for by his excellent mind. It may also be that Socrates' status as a great thinker shielded him from the kinds of insults that another man's belly might invite.[3]

Albeit viewed as a deviation from aesthetic norms, the fact that excessive flesh was not a particularly vexing moral or medical issue in antiquity needs to be stressed from the outset. It was not the master pathology it would become by the late twentieth century. It is true that the Greeks expressed concern about the possible consequences of overconsumption and sedentary lifestyles. But, whereas developing a soft, fat body was one possible result of immoderation, they remained primarily concerned about the moral effects that 'luxury' could have on the person. In *The Republic*, Plato argues through the mouthpiece of Socrates that the 'feverish city' of his own day, described as 'swollen and inflamed', suffered in part from culinary refinements and a growing idleness that generated many diseases. Concerned here with bodies bloated through an accumulation of unhealthy 'gas and ooze, like a marsh',[4] Plato also frowned on fatness as tangible evidence of laziness, overconsumption and beastlike submission. Despite this imagery, though, neither the Greeks nor the Romans tended to link corpulent bodies to 'gas and ooze' or any other abject substance. For that we must wait for the arrival of Christianity. Whatever disgust they might have felt towards fatness was usually of the 'ideological' sort – somewhat closer to contempt – in which the fattened person seemed to 'descend' to the level of a slave, woman or animal. Not primarily an aesthetic concern, fat mattered to the Greeks and Romans partly because it was bound up with ideas about status.

Having mapped some of the ways in which fat, fatness and fattening were approached in antiquity, we can now look more carefully at Graeco-Roman perceptions of corpulent bodies. Beginning with a discussion of how classical bodily ideals were complicated by the moral and physical problems of luxury as well as allowances made for lifestyle and profession, this chapter probes the ways in which Greek and Roman ideas about 'softness' were partly constructed out of anxious encounters with Asiatic cultures that would form a counterpoint to Western bodily ideals and aspirations for centuries to come.

Luxury and Effeminacy

By pointing to his belly, Socrates was indicating far more than the place where food is digested. Neither the Greeks nor the Romans saw the belly as a simple anatomical referent, nor did they associate food and drink with nutrition alone. Since Homeric times, the Greek terms *gaster* and *nedus* referred to the stomach, loins, intestines, womb and genitals. This suggested that the belly was viewed broadly as the seat of hunger as well as the location of abdominal viscera and reproductive organs. Without designating a specific organ, *gaster* could denote either the idea of gluttony or a large belly.[5] The Romans

Socrates was often likened to the plump woodland god Silenus, shown here holding a *kantharos* or wine cup, 4th century BCE.

continued these associations, frequently linking women's bodies to sexuality and eating, often with rather racy language. For them, the womb was referred to as the 'belly' (*uenter*, *aluus*), and whereas the 'cunt' (*cunnus*) was often described as 'devouring' the 'cock' (*mentula*), either organ could be said to have been 'eaten' during an oral sex act.[6] In classical antiquity, then, the belly and what were euphemistically referred to as the regions 'below' were closely linked, illustrating at once the anatomical slipperiness between stomach and genitals and the intimate connection between eating and sexual desire. An unbridled appetite for food was widely believed to give rise to sexual desires as well.[7] Mentioned by pagan, Jewish and Christian moralists alike, the belly was the location of that 'intimate and unholy trinity' that eating, drinking and sensual indulgence represented in the ancient world.[8] Insofar as these 'appetites' were interlaced, the stimulation of one risked awakening the others too.

If the belly was home to sexual as well as alimentary appetites, doctors felt these were best satisfied in moderation. What the Hippocratic authors noted would go on to inform Roman medicine as well: 'Neither repletion, nor fasting, nor anything else is good when it is more than natural.'[9] This moderation should pertain also to the substances that comprised a person. These the Greeks viewed in terms of four bodily fluids, or 'humours', that were present in all people: blood, phlegm, yellow bile and black bile. The proportion of humours within a given person differed, with each individual having a particular humoral make-up or 'complexion' in which one humour predominated. A person whose complexion was marked by the predominance of phlegm would be naturally colder, moister and thicker, and therefore more prone to corpulence. Humoral complexion affected temperament as well, so that the phlegmatic person was said to tend towards being lazier, paler and colder than others.[10] The accumulation of substances capable of causing 'excess flesh' could also consist of surplus humours that should be evacuated for the sake of equilibrium. Beyond identifying a phlegmatic complexion, a common way of assessing fat bodies was with reference to 'plethora', or the accumulation of excessive blood. Another was to relate it to what was called 'dropsy' or 'hydropsy' (now called oedema), a pathological form of water retention in which individuals experience unquenchable thirst even though their tissues are in fact swollen with fluid. This tendency to view corpulence in fluid terms – as an effect of the unhealthy accumulation of noxious humours in the body – would persist for about two millennia. Some were still conflating dropsy with 'obesity' into the early nineteenth century.[11]

Being born with a tendency towards corpulence did not exempt a person from taking steps to restore the equilibrium that might result in a more moderate physique. Such a person would be counselled to lead a lifestyle designed to counteract such tendencies, which included eating foods that were not phlegm-producing and taking more exercise.[12] Failure to do this could have dire consequences: 'Those who are constitutionally very fat are more apt to die quickly than those who are thin.'[13] Attention to diet and exercise were recommended for the sake of health, but also for the sake of that fusion of beauty-and-goodness that the Greeks called *Kalokagathia*. Thought to be particularly evident in the bodies of aristocrats, *Kalokagathia* functioned as a marker of status as well as health, beauty and morality.[14] We have already seen this concept at work in ancient physiognomy, which maintained that a person's character could be read in the shape and appearance of the body. Great corpulence was seen as ugly and thus as a breach of this ideal of beauty-and-goodness. It may have been this violation of the logic of *Kalokagathia* that caused the admirers of Socrates to be disappointed that a beautiful soul like his was incarnated in such an unimpressive physique.

As a sign of ill-health that could lead to further problems, then, great fatness could appear as an aesthetic and moral failing. Writing during Roman times, Soranus of Ephesus considered 'excess flesh' (*polysarkia*) to be a disfiguring disorder. Having such 'an abnormal and excessive amount of flesh, which bulges out in full prominence', is not only 'unsightly' or 'disgraceful'. It also signifies serious health problems for the patient, including sweating, sluggishness, shortness of breath and the sensation of being 'suffocated by his own body'. Soranus likened such large bodies to domesticated animals confined to feeding stalls 'so that their bodies become large and bulky and puffed up'. In this way, he took issue with physicians who reassured their patients that great corpulence was a sign of health:

> there is only one kind of good habit of body, namely, that in which there is strength with a moderate amount of flesh; and that is a condition to preserve rather than alter.[15]

A moderate level of fleshiness was natural and evidence of good health. The influential physician Galen commended constitutions that sat 'midway between thin and corpulent'.[16] We have seen above that *polysarkia* counted among the diseases caused by excessive blood in the body. Ancient doctors reasoned that blood was created from the food one eats, so that overeating and not exercising threatened to create more blood than was required for healthy functioning. Not only did surplus blood generate numerous diseases, Galen thought, but it created sensations of heaviness, sluggishness and pain in both body and mind. Overeating could thus result in mental lethargy. While moderate fasting was considered a useful way of minimizing the bloating effects of plethora, a more effective measure was therapeutic bloodletting or phlebotomy.[17] Others corroborated Galen's basic points. In his compendium on medicine, Celsus also noted that the healthiest body was a moderate one:

> The square-built frame, neither thin nor fat, is the fittest; for tallness, as it is graceful in youth, shrinks in the fulness of age; a thin frame is weak, a fat one sluggish.[18]

Very fat people, moreover, suffer from certain health problems. They 'are throttled by acute diseases and difficult breathing; they die often suddenly, which rarely happens in a thinner person.' This is why a man who has 'become fatter and better looking and with a higher colour ... should regard with suspicion these gains of his'.[19] Without moralizing about those who ate to excess, Celsus recommended different health regimens so that individuals of various constitutions could alter their lifestyles to more closely approximate the mean:

> But above all things everyone should be acquainted with the nature of his own body, for some are spare, others obese [*obessi*]. .. So then a thin man ought to fatten himself up, a stout one to thin himself down.[20]

Classical writers also evinced a concern with well-articulated male bodies and frowned upon those whose joints and sinews were not readily visible. This preoccupation was more fully developed by the Romans, whose interest in anatomy propelled fantasies of muscularity to the centre of their culture. Shigehisa Kuriyama sees in the movement from Homer to Plato the gradual development of a notion of the human agent whose muscular activities express the volition of the soul:

> the rise of the preoccupation with muscles . . . is inextricably intertwined with the emergence of a particular conception of personhood ... Interest in the muscularity of the body was inseparable from a preoccupation with the agency of the self.[21]

Fatty tissue softened and rounded out the body in pleasing ways, but too much of it diminished the visible articulation of muscles and joints and could contribute to a 'feminine' look that frustrated ideals of virile hardness. Reflecting the concept of *Kalokagathia*, physiognomy maintained that excessively soft and flabby flesh could speak volumes about a person's character. The pseudo-Aristotelian *Physiognomics*, which would go on to influence Roman and medieval analyses of the body, linked personal character to bodily traits like movement, shape, colour, facial expression, skin texture and voice. From it we learn that signs of the brave man include 'strong and large' bones and sides of the body with a 'broad and flat belly'. Excess flesh, however, indicated foolishness and gluttony, but also femininity.[22] Appropriated by Greek sculptors as a way of representing how human excellence was manifested in the external traits of the male body, physiognomic wisdom about fat, muscularity and proportion was cast in bronze. Rather than representing an unattainable ideal, sculpture instead sought to capture the universal and general, thus a snapshot of 'Everyman' as he was perceived at the time.[23]

Like everything else in the world, though, Everyman was subject to change over time. By the fifth century BCE, that perfect fusion of body and mind that had been promoted since the earliest times had fallen out of favour among the Athenian elite. The athletic life was not especially conducive to the balance and equilibrium promoted by most physicians, and Plato discouraged devoting such attention to the body without a similar concern with the mind. Among athletes, we have seen it was boxers who were renowned for being especially misshapen and fat. When represented on pottery they frequently appeared with pot-bellies and massive thighs. The presence of the past, at least as it was nostalgically imagined, played a role in how fatness was understood. While perhaps uncommon in everyday life, excessive corpulence was cited as proof of how contemporary society had drifted from older ideals. In this way, it could be a target of ridicule in Greek comedies, where fat bodies were the stuff of political satire directed against the greedy and lazy.[24] Ever on the lookout for new material, the playwright Aristophanes regretted the moral and physical slackening that he observed in young people. When the character Aeschylus in *Frogs* complains that today 'nobody takes any exercise', the god Dionysus agrees:

> You couldn't be righter. I almost doubled up
> At the Panathenaea laughing when

A slow coach [*sic*] of a booby thumped along,
Stooped, white as a sheet, fat.
And when he got to the Gates by the potter's [*sic*] field
People whacked him on his belly and butt
And ribs and sides and all his miserable hide.[25]

The supposed decline from an even more ancient ideal received comment elsewhere too. An early fifth-century BCE vase depicts a fat male at the *palaestra*, perhaps embarrassed by his physique, arguing with a slender youth while more athletic types exercise with the javelin and discus.[26] Even if corpulence was not the most common bodily sign of softness, it remained available for scrutiny among critics of the present state of the body.

Establishing a pattern that would be repeated for the next two millennia, the Greeks described the present state of their bodies as inferior to those of earlier times. Luxury (*tryphē*) was most often cited as the cause of this decadence, and the problem was usually traced to the belly. Overly refined or excessive eating was seen as the clearest proof that 'modern' people had degenerated from hardier ancient times. Plato was especially worried about such things, and perceived moral as well as physical problems in the spread of fat and the atrophy of muscle tissue. Bakers, wine vendors and authors of cookbooks may 'fill up and fatten people's bodies, and be praised by them for it', but they also 'destroy their original flesh as well'.[27] Roman culture, which built upon and extended many Greek ideals and anxieties, also contended that luxury and vice were rife in the present. Dinner parties (*convivia*) were to Rome what drinking parties had been to classical Athens, and many observers commented on the greater (some said excessive) emphasis the Romans placed on food. Satirists frequently contrasted the virtues of a simple rustic life – which they, like most of their contemporaries, believed characterized the Roman past – and lampooned the refined and extravagant tastes of gourmands and gastronomes who lavished attention on money and food. The philosopher Epicurus' claim that 'the beginning and the root of all good is the pleasure of the stomach' was misunderstood by many as an endorsement of lavish banquets, even though the thinker explicitly prescribed virtue and moderation. This was not helped by rumours that Epicurus himself indulged in sensual escapades ranging from the table to the bedroom.[28] In popular culture, animals could be used

Red-figure cup by Pheidippos showing (on the outer rim) a sequence of athletes with contrasting body shapes, *c.* 500 BCE.

to describe the problem of gustatory excess. Before the scene was repeated in Aesop's story of the weasel in the granary – and acted out, centuries later, by Winnie-the-Pooh – a Roman fable told of a fox who, upon discovering a goatherd's supply of food hidden in a hollow tree, ate so much that he became too fat to squeeze out again.[29]

The Stoic philosophy that predominated during the late Republic and early Empire frowned upon such popular Epicureanism. To the Stoics, living for one's belly implied selfishness rather than civic virtue, suggesting that those who conducted themselves in such a way would be useless to the community in times of need. Unbridled appetites thus threatened to make one a bad citizen.[30] This was both a matter of moral fibre as well as physical capacity. In the face of the culinary excesses that received so much attention in the Graeco-Roman world, it was not uncommon to see Sparta celebrated for its famously strict approach to sensual pleasures. According to Plutarch, the greatest innovation of the Spartan statesman Lycurgus was the creation of common messes in which freemen dined together rather than in the seclusion of their homes. Reflecting upon the vices of his own day, Plutarch admired the fact that luxury could find no foothold in bodies that were prevented from

> reclining on costly couches at costly tables, delivering themselves into the hands of servants and cooks to be fattened in the dark, like voracious animals, and ruining not only their characters but

also their bodies by surrendering them to every desire and all sorts of surfeit, which call for long sleeps, hot baths, abundant rest, and, as it were, daily nursing and tending.[31]

Plutarch also seemed to admire the Theban general Epaminondas, who defeated the Spartans but shared their contempt for fat soldiers. Epaminondas even reportedly expelled one of these soldiers from the army, sarcastically claiming that 'three or four shields would scarcely serve to protect his belly, because of which he could not see a thing below it.'[32] As it seems unlikely that Epaminondas was speaking of legs and feet here, this visual eclipse of 'what lies below' the belly offered a withering comment on the virility of fat soldiers.

Epaminondas' admiration for Spartan hardness reveals a recurring motif among ancient moralists. What classicists sometimes call the 'Spartan mirage' has fascinated observers throughout Western history, not least for the intolerance the Spartans showed for corrupting softness.[33] It is partly for this reason that Sparta became 'the model for the utopianism of Plato and Aristotle' as well as that of many other moralists over the centuries.[34] The Spartans, or at least what was often said about this warrior people, played an important role in shaping classical ideas about luxury and fat. Tradition claimed that Spartans held beauty contests to celebrate the most appealing men and women in their society,[35] but, unlike the Athenians, actually penalized those who drifted too far from the ideal. Anecdotes about the Spartan treatment of fat men circulated widely. Athenaeus wrote that every ten days young men were required to present themselves naked before the magistrates who scrutinized their physiques for signs of slack effeminacy, which included having 'a large potbelly'. He then related the story of a certain magistrate, Naucleides, son of Polybiades, who was brought before the Assembly because he had become 'extremely corpulent and fat, as a result of his addiction to luxury'. After being subjected to public ridicule, Naucleides was threatened with banishment if he did not reform his life.[36] The enslaved population of Helots supposedly had it much worse. They could be killed if they became too fat and robust, and their masters punished for allowing it to happen.[37]

If Sparta provided one of the earliest models of a corporeal utopia, one that would be invoked in the West even to the present, it was not most people's idea of the perfect world. Notwithstanding bracing tales of Spartan austerity, in Roman life the social consequences of fat and flabby bodies were more complex. Despite the negative connotations of fleshiness and the implicit assumption that a fat person might also be morally lax, there is little evidence that the immoderate feasting of Roman patricians was ever condemned as a detestable immersion in *luxuria*. There is only one reported case of a censor explicitly dishonouring a cavalryman for being so overweight that he could not perform his duties on horseback. In addition to being an unusual thing for a censor to do, none of the Latin terms used to denote fleshiness seemed to invite political dishonour. *Pinguis* described a degree of corpulence that was viewed as evidence of prosperity and even health, while *obesus*, which referred to the very fat, was considered a health problem rather than a moral failing. The stronger term *crassus*, moreover, with its connotations of sluggishness and stupidity, was not necessarily pejorative when observed among elites. Renowned for his contempt for luxury and tendency to pick out the physical shortcomings of his opponents, even the sharp-tongued Cicero failed to exploit corpulence in his withering critiques of fellow statesmen. Rather he, like many Romans, seems to have accepted patrician fat as evidence of wealth and status. The relative immunity from politically damaging ridicule that most fat nobles enjoyed shows how Greek theory failed to instruct Roman practice.[38] Here, too, it may be that their status shielded patricians from the kind of stereotyping that would be applied to others.

There are other places where Hellenic ideas failed to sway Roman customs. Greek athletic ideals made few inroads in Rome, where doctors were more interested in adjusting health regimens to the needs of individuals according to sex, age, class and profession. Not only was athletic exertion considered unseemly for a gentleman, but most understood that the various demands that public service made upon elites left them with little time for regular exercise or even a proper amount of sleep.[39] Nevertheless, if a large belly could function as a sign of the good life – and this despite medical warnings about the health problems caused by excessive weight – it remained an ambiguous feature that was subject to ridicule depending upon the status of the person and how he comported himself publicly. The moralizing tone of orators about the pitfalls of luxury would have generated complicated responses among elites: 'Romans love to catalogue the manifold luxuries that Empire brought, even as they castigate themselves or others for wanting them.'[40] Research into aristocratic portraiture suggests that, from at least the late Republican era, corpulence was a personal feature that could be highlighted and even exaggerated in order to underscore the character of an individual. This 'respectable minority tradition' could even enhance the subject's flesh in order to signify energetic strength and power.[41] Laying the groundwork for a pattern that would persist through to the Middle Ages and to some extent beyond, a somewhat fat leader could enjoy public esteem so long as he continued to demonstrate energy and a capacity for work. If his corpulence prevented him from leading an active and assertive public life, his fat could easily morph into a symptom of effeminate softness.[42] Fatness was capable of signifying monumental power or corrupting softness.

How did women fit into ancient representational schemes? The answer is complicated, especially when we consider the wider Hellenized world. The ancient Egyptians, for instance, evinced a rather conflicted view of fat. If predynastic art from around 3000 BCE often featured fleshier women, this preference was eclipsed by an artistic idealization of slender youthfulness that lasted for over 2,000 years. Egyptian depictions of women often emphasized their sexuality and were apparently designed for a male gaze. Whereas 'women had to be youthful, shapely and free from the ravages and realities of childbirth', male bodies were also idealized with limbs that 'were shown well muscled, and biceps . . . indicated by a prominent bulge in the upper arm'.[43] Archaeological digs reveal how far from reality this fantasy of physical beauty could deviate. While pharaohs were typically represented in art with young and vigorous physiques, the mummies of several rulers (such as Amenhotep III and Ramses III) reveal large folds of skin suggesting they had been quite fat when they died. Indeed, the recently discovered body of the female pharaoh Hatshepsut has been described as having been 'hugely obese' in life.[44]

Despite what we might call an 'official' scorn for fat, other important Egyptians were represented in more 'realistic' terms in the art adorning their tombs, sometimes with rolls of flesh, prominent bellies and pendulous breasts. This apparent deviation from the pharaonic ideal may have corresponded with a canonical depiction of important Egyptian men who had been able to enjoy prosperity without exerting themselves physically. Yet despite this relaxation of physical expectations for elite males, as well as the actual fleshiness sometimes suggested by their remains, the wives of prominent men were still depicted in funerary art as tall, slender and beautiful.[45] This sketchy information may indicate that corpulence was considered unworthy of those believed to be divine (as the pharaohs were), but that it was a more or less acceptable way for powerful and wealthy males to appear.

If Greek and Roman women did not receive much artistic attention, they too could be judged according to appearance. Among the physical features considered pleasing in a Roman woman were firm breasts, shapely hips and a flat stomach.[46] If we believe the comic poet Terence, in the second century BCE women were encouraged to be very slender, and if one showed the slightest tendency towards plumpness she could be jokingly said to be in training to be a boxer.[47] Things had not changed much by the time of the Empire. A character in one of Martial's satirical epigrams was explicit on this point:

> Flaccus, I don't want a slender girlfriend whose arms would be encircled by my rings, who would shave me with her bare haunch and prick me with her knee, who has a saw projecting from her loins and a spearhead from her arse. But neither do I want a girl-friend weighing a thousand pounds. I am a flesh-fancier, not a fat-fancier [*carnarius sum, pinguiarius non sum*].[48]

As was often the case, beauty ideals were closely linked to conceptions of health and morality. Greek medical advice for females recommended dietary vigilance and exercise, as well as avoiding warm baths, so that they did not become too fat. Rufus of Ephesus urged mothers to monitor their daughters for signs of 'plethora' or weight gain. Pregnant women were particularly warned not to gain too much weight lest they become, as Soranus wrote, plethoric as well as 'fat and ill-proportioned'. Building upon the idea that sexual intercourse was a heat-generating activity capable of 'melting' fat, and that excess flesh to some extent resulted from the accumulation of humours, Soranus also said that frequent and vigorous coitus was an ideal method for women to maintain their figures. It was the lack of sex that could cause weight gain as well as menstrual problems.[49] As we have seen, then, cold, moist and less active female bodies were considered more likely to succumb to fleshiness and softness. Among males, the latter were often treated as signs of vice and effeminacy, disturbing phenomena whose apparent sources could be mapped across the Mediterranean basin.

The Geography of Softness

Classical perceptions of 'softness' were relational, and heavily reliant upon beliefs about how the Greeks and Romans measured up to other peoples in the Mediterranean and beyond. The Greeks were particularly sensitive to what their neighbours were up to. They perceived the unholy trinity of eating, drinking and sexuality everywhere around them, from the Sybarites and Sicilians of southern Italy, famous for their pastries and cookbooks, to the Syrians, Lydians and Persians of the east. Imagining themselves as an island of virtue amid a sea of moral and physical corruption, Greeks loved to tell tales about the 'effeminate' luxury of others in the region. They were particularly appalled by the 'decadent' Persian custom of lavishing upon their rulers the most delicious, refined and costly food and drinks from across their empire,[50] and often depicted the Persian army as plump, lazy and wallowing in luxury.[51]

Physical and moral softness were thus central features of how the Greeks perceived cultural difference. Much of this was explained with reference to environment. In *Airs, Waters, Places*, the Hippocratics contended that 'in general you will find assimilated to the nature of the land both the physique and the characteristics of the inhabitants'. It was with such environmental and climatic premises in mind that the Greeks judged the Scythians, that ancient nomadic people of Central Eurasia. Residing in a cold, moist and windy environment for much of the year, the Scythians did not experience dramatic seasonal variations that would require them to develop endurance.

> For neither bodily nor mental endurance is possible where the [seasonal] changes are not violent. For these causes their physiques are gross, fleshy, showing no joints, moist and flabby . . . because of their fat and the smoothness of their flesh their physiques are similar.[52]

The typical Scythian man fell far short of the Greek ideal. Not only did he lack the strength to throw a javelin or draw a bow properly, but the moist flabbiness of his body when combined with the effects of constant riding did much to diminish his sexual ardor. He was thus reduced to a life of impotence and what the Greeks would have considered women's work. Even if Scythian males could be coaxed into attempting coitus, the bodies of the women posed obstacles of their own: 'the mouth of the womb is closed by fat and does not admit the seed. They are personally fat and lazy, and their abdomen is cold and soft.'[53]

The Hippocratic explanation for why the Scythians differed from Greeks reflected ancient understandings of human variation. Culture and environment played more important roles than the innate and unchangeable qualities that would later be associated with the concept of 'race'. Their fleshy bodies offered evidence of the same *inarticulateness* so widely attributed to the ways in which 'barbarians' spoke. When the Greeks encountered other Asiatics, they often saw replications of the Scythians whose rounded and less differentiated physiques were evidence of their soft, flabby and cowardly character.[54]

If many ancient categorical distinctions were gendered, they were equally inflected by the powerful rhetoric of submission and servitude, either to another person or to one's own appetites. This was at the heart of Aristotle's understanding of 'natural' slaves, especially those who hailed mainly from non-Greek societies, as people whose desires did not submit to practical reason or deliberation. Formed in this way through the effects of climate, they were thus incapable of the virtue conducive to the good life of human flourishing.[55] Actual slaves were most often associated with raw physicality, manual labour and, above all, unbridled passions, which Aristotle described as that part of the person most in need of mastery. So pervasive was this alignment of slaves with sheer matter in the Hellenistic world that it was not uncommon to simply call a slave *soma* (that is, 'body').[56]

Kalokagathia, that noble fusion of beauty, health and morality, was often invoked to demonstrate just how coarse and vulgar the bodies of slaves were – or at least, how they were made to appear. Slave bodies were widely lampooned for their lack of beauty, and enslaved males were often portrayed as deformed, ugly and beardless with pro-truding backsides. The pot-belly was also a common trait associated with slaves. Even if we might view this feature as the result of mal-nutrition rather than high living, bloated bellies represented slaves' understandable (and to elites, laughable) obsession with food.⁵⁷ But it was also an aesthetic defect that provoked humour. In order to make guests laugh, or to flatter their sense of superiority, the slave dancers and other artists who performed at symposia often played upon (or, with the use of padding, deliberately exaggerated) their physical deviation from classical ideals.⁵⁸ Such bellies were obviously not 'fat' in the same way as those padded with adipose tissue or bloated with air or fluids, but they nonetheless indicate a deviation from aesthetic standards as well as an overarching focus on appetite. Aesop, the famous author of fables, is said to have been a slave. He was described by his ancient biographer as 'an absolute miscreant' on account of his bloated belly, misshapen head, snub nose and thin lips. Much like Socrates, Aesop was praised for the beauty and wisdom of his ideas

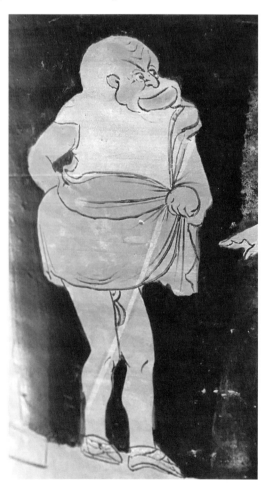

The pot-belly was commonly associated with slaves, who were often lampooned for their lack of beauty. Enslaved males were often portrayed as deformed, ugly and beardless with protruding backsides. Some were made to perform at symposia or, as in this case, the theatre. Slave wearing the short tunic, from a Sicilian red-figured calyx-krater, c. 350–340 BCE.

This woman, also possibly a slave actor, theatricalized corpulence as a deviation from Greek aesthetic ideals. Theatrical type: Fat woman. Terracotta from Cyrenaica, made in Attica(?), *c.* 350–320 BCE.

with full awareness of how much the fabulist's noble mind contrasted with his disappointing physique.[59]

Wishing to use physical difference as a way of setting themselves apart from other peoples, the Greeks observed a kind of 'inverted *Kalokagathia*' among foreigners, non-citizens and the socially marginal.[60] The Romans also drew attention to physical differences as a way of accounting for the surprising habits of their neighbours, whether across the Mediterranean or simply elsewhere on the Italian peninsula. When towards the end of the Republic the Romans looked upon their Etruscan neighbours to the north, they noted that their sarcophagi and ash urns often included statues of their occupants (and sometimes their spouses) reclining at a banquet, oftentimes with the flabby bellies of males proudly displayed.[61] Such spectacles of luxuriant softness prompted Catullus to ridicule the 'plump Umbrian and obese Etruscan',[62] even though many Romans themselves had similar plump figures carved on their own sarcophagi. The rather dismal opinion the Romans had about other cultures enhanced their own sense of virtue and self-mastery.

If physical differences pointed to the invisible traits of morality and character, this was especially the case when Romans reflected upon Asiatic peoples. Even something as seemingly straightforward as oratory could denote physical and moral differences across cultures. In theory, at least, orators were expected to possess physiques and verbal skills that lacked the excess and softness associated with Asiatic cultures. The Stoically inclined rhetorician Quintilian claimed that orators need

> firmness of the body, lest our voice be attenuated to the thinness of eunuchs and women and sick people; this is achieved by walking, applying body lotion, abstinence from sex, and the easy digestion of food – that is, frugality.[63]

The quality of one's voice thus sprang naturally from the condition of the body. When Romans debated different kinds of oratorical styles, especially those traceable to Athens rather than Asia, they typically conflated the latter with decadence, luxury and effeminacy. When Quintilian discussed Attic and Asiatic styles of speechmaking in his *Orator's Education*, his description of their differences evoked contrasting bodily states:

> The Attici, refined and discriminating, tolerated nothing empty or gushing; but the Asiatic race, somehow more swollen (*tumidor*) and boastful, was inflated with a more vainglory [*sic*] way of speaking.[64]

Asiatic rhetoric needed self-control and a crash diet if it was to approximate the sinewy virility of Roman oratory. In a sense, then, Quintilian's book functioned as a kind of verbal fitness manual.

If the rhetoric of Asiatics was supposedly 'inflated', their bodies were thought to be even more so. Or at least this is how stories of Asiatic monarchs made it seem. We have already encountered Dionysius of Heraclea, tyrant of a city-state in Asia Minor, whose habitual gluttony and luxury caused him to gain so much weight that he found it difficult to breathe, much less move. But stories were told of other fat tyrants. Athenaeus offered this garish portrait of Ptolemy VII of Egypt: 'His addiction to luxury led to him being physically disabled, as a result of his obesity and the size of his belly, which was too large to get one's arms around easily.'[65] To make matters worse, his tunic was diaphanous, so that all could gaze upon what was beneath, an extravagance that would have immediately registered as 'effeminate' in Rome. For these reasons, the Alexandrians referred to their king as 'Physcon' (pot-belly or bladder), which was a compliment in a dynasty for which lavish displays of wealth, abundance and excess were a carefully orchestrated strategy of political propaganda.[66]

Even more fascinating were those tyrants who had actually been incapacitated by fat. Like his predecessor, Ptolemy VII's son Alexander 'also surrendered to obesity', reputedly being so fat that he could not take a leisurely stroll 'unless he leaned on two people as he moved'. As was often the case in his lively writing, Athenaeus' words were carefully chosen. To become fat to the point of incapacitation sig-nified powerlessness in the face of one's appetites. Such subordination could only be called 'surrender', except here it was fatness itself that had conquered and disabled the king. Worse, perhaps, was the fate of the luxurious King Magas of Cyrene. Here was a ruler who was so 'enormously heavy near the end of his life' that he 'ultimately suffo-cated because of his obesity, since he never got any exercise and consumed large amounts of food'.[67] In addition to its insulating capacities, fat seemed to exercise a kind of agency of its own, 'suffo-cating' those who 'surrendered' because they lacked the capacity to overcome their 'addiction to luxury'. Designed to leave readers aghast at the extremes one might find among Asiatic peoples, such stories also functioned as cautionary tales for those who might suc-cumb to similar vices. In the case of elite bodies bloated by luxurious living, fatness was a reminder of how the ideals and practices of other peoples might end up softening Rome itself.

'A Belly without Ears'

Hellenistic culture might have scoffed at the perceived excesses of other cultures, but the problem of luxurious overindulgence was no foreign affair. This was especially so since many of the luxuries that worried moralists were a consequence of trade links with the rest of the Mediterranean. While a great deal of merriment was had at the expense of slaves, the fact that *anyone* could become a slave by being captured during wartime highlighted the fluidity between the states of freedom and bondage, as well as indeterminacy about what made someone a 'natural' slave.[68] Most Roman elites didn't concern themselves with such possibilities, and the more common scenario in which a freeman might become a slave was metaphorical. 'Show me a man who isn't a slave,' Seneca declared; 'one is a slave to sex, another to money, another to ambition; all are slaves to hope or fear.'[69] While manifesting concern for the souls of men who had enslaved themselves through lack of exercise, excessive eating and drinking and late nights,[70] Seneca perceived the external signs of this defective lifestyle in 'the belly growing to a paunch [*distentusque venter*] through an ill habit of taking more than it can hold'.[71]

Applying such images of dissolute swelling to the rapid expansion of Rome allowed moralists to combine the organic roots of *luxuria* as 'overgrowth' with the related notion of decomposition, not unlike the fat that Seneca saw 'creeping' all over the bodies of the profligate. As the majority of Romans lived at subsistence level, however, the decadent feasts recounted in satirical texts would have never been a possibility for most people.[72] If Rome really was wallowing in luxurious excess, as some complained, then the 'Rome' they had in mind referred at most to a tiny ruling elite whose lifestyles and consumer habits became the focus of public scrutiny. If Rome itself had become a 'belly without ears', as Cato had put it, then citizens were microcosms of this voracious body.

Satirists were at the ready when they noticed evidence of Asiatic indulgence in Rome itself. Animal metaphors were on hand to spice up their invective. Juvenal wrote of a fat lawyer who was one of those wealthy elites who 'consume entire fortunes at a single table . . . What a monstrous gullet, that serves itself whole boars, an animal created for parties!' he marvelled. Such gluttons would get their just desserts:

> The punishment is instant, though, when you take off your cloak and, completely bloated, carry an undigested peacock to the baths. The result: sudden death and intestate old age.[73]

The bitter satires of Persius, sharpened by the author's Stoic worldview, probed the innards of a corrupt elite whose degeneracy was marked by overloaded tables and bloated bellies. Commenting periodically on the prominent paunches of writers and elites, Persius conjured up the image of a pig's stomach (*aqualiculus*) to describe these pot-bellies, thus reinforcing the bestial qualities of Rome's gluttons.[74]

This is perhaps one reason why Romans sometimes fretted over the spread of foreign habits throughout the empire. The Roman virtue of *gravitas* (weightiness, seriousness) implied that a man was grounded in the realities and responsibilities of his world, but this moral ideal was only contingently related to physical weight and size. If a large and fleshy body could signify status and achievement, excess flesh could just as easily suggest a kind of moral *levitas* (lightness) that could cause one to behave irresponsibly. Lavish public feasts were hardly unknown among emperors and aristocrats, and rather than being viewed as necessarily immoral, their public nature qualified such extravagances as benefits to the city – benefits that signalled the ruler's willingness to associate with his subjects. The emperors Domitian, Augustus and Vespasian all hosted large banquets to celebrate and share their abundance, and such public luxury was generally viewed as a civic act of commendable largesse. Even the bloated and shamelessly self-indulgent Nero was not reproached when entertaining his fellow elites, but only when his feasting seemed to distract him from political duties. The latter was seen as a purely personal immersion in luxury that disregarded, and seemingly dismissed, the virtues of commensality and hierarchy that cemented the Roman elite.[75]

One could expect little mercy when luxury was purely personal. Searching for some kind of moral failing as an explanation for the fall of this or that statesman, late antique historians made ready use of the charge of gluttony to oversimplify otherwise complex social and political phenomena. Insofar as appetite signified the passions and was thought inconsistent with *gravitas*, accusing statesmen of gluttony was a powerful way of tarnishing their reputations.[76] According to Suetonius, the emperor Claudius was a notorious glutton much given to excesses of sexuality, cruelty and paranoia:

He was eager for food and drink at all times and in all places . . . He hardly ever left the dining-room until he was stuffed and soaked; then he went to sleep at once, lying on his back with his mouth open, and a feather was put down his throat to relieve his stomach.

Despite having to behold this image, which was hardly consistent with imperial *dignitas*, Suetonius' worried readers could breathe a collective sigh of relief. 'Immoderate in his passion for women', at least Claudius was 'wholly free from unnatural vice'.[77]

Claudius' successor, Nero, saw no problems in being represented as corpulent in official art. Rather, in the portraits he commissioned, Nero seems to have emphasized this trait, and his final portraits were even modelled on Ptolemaic styles in which fleshy faces were intended to convey royal abundance and beneficence.[78] The flesh that Nero relished was grist to the mill of critics eager to reduce deeds to physiques. Suetonius' head-to-toe sketch of the tyrant counts his fleshiness as evidence of an aberrant physiognomy:

> He was about the average height, his body marked with spots and malodorous, his hair light blond, his features regular rather than attractive, his eyes blue and somewhat weak, his neck over thick, his belly prominent [*cervice obesa, ventre proiecto*], and his legs very slender.[79]

The physiognomic texts of the day that probably informed Suetonius' portrait would have interpreted his thick neck as a sign of strength, temper and insensitivity, and his fat belly as evidence of licentiousness or deceitfulness, or of insensitivity, drunkenness, intemperance and debauchery.[80]

Those who succeeded Nero fared no better in the eyes of ancient historians. When the first-century CE emperor Aulus Vitellius failed to emerge victorious from a civil war launched by his rival Otho, Tacitus blamed his failure on moral turpitude connected to his penchant for good food. That Vitellius was also a rather fat man is evident in the statues and busts of him that survive. Considering the conventions of elite portraiture of the period, it may be possible to read these as proudly projecting imperial power.[81] Yet when the emperor fell from grace, his status shield slipped as well. What might have previously been viewed as a positive feature would become proof of weakness and vice. Tacitus claimed that Vitellius loved the company of Nero because he sensed in him a kindred spirit: he too was a 'slave to his stomach and had sold himself to luxury'.[82] Cassius Dio reported that 'He was insatiate in gorging himself, and was constantly vomiting up what he ate, being nourished by the mere passage of the food.' Typically eating three or four big meals a day, Suetonius observed, Vitellius had an appetite that was 'insatiable, coarse and constant; he could not hold it in check even when he was conducting sacrifice or travelling.'[83]

These moralizing historians made much of these matters when Vitellius met his unfortunate end. As the captured and bound emperor was being dragged along the Sacred Way towards the Forum, where he would be murdered, angry Romans rained abuse upon his bloated flesh:

> Some threw rubbish and sewerage at him, whilst others called him 'Firebug' and 'Fatty'; indeed some of the crowd even mocked him for his bodily defects, for he was extremely tall [*enormis*, which can also mean 'shapeless'], with a face flushed due to excessive drinking, and a protruding stomach.[84]

Recounting the same humiliating scene, Dio Cassius underscores the perceived connection between gluttony and fatness:

> Some buffeted him, some plucked at his beard; all mocked him, all insulted him, making comments especially upon his riotous living, since he had a protuberant belly.[85]

✳

What happened to Vitellius on the way to the Forum was not remotely funny, but the raucous crowd clearly enjoyed reducing its former leader to his most conspicuous physical trait. As Mark Bradley observes:

> excessive flesh in the Roman world tapped into a highly subjective and versatile set of traditions about the relationship between personal appearance and social, political and economic status. Fat mattered.[86]

If Socrates and Vitellius had anything in common, it is that they both had prominent bellies and were eventually killed by the will of the majority. Yet their respective bellies were perceived in different ways. Socrates' corpulence was hardly invisible. Rather, it invited comment and even some good-natured ribbing by his friends. Yet this deviation

When the Emperor
Vitellius fell from grace,
his once monumental
body became the target
of ridicule and contempt.
As the angry mob
dragged him off to
be killed, Dio Cassius
observed, 'all insulted
him, making
comments especially
upon his riotous
living, since he had
a protuberant belly'.
Vitellius, 69 CE.

from aesthetic and moral standards was forgivable since the 'beauty' of his mind conferred upon him a status that may have shielded him from potentially damaging stereotypes. No matter what the physiognomer Zopyrus read in the philosopher's body, Socrates could sport a prominent belly while continuing to be esteemed by his friends. Although this circle was not wide or powerful enough to prevent Socrates from being put to death as a menace to society, the philosopher's belly was never mentioned as evidence of his alleged crimes. If Emperor Vitellius had at some point benefited from a similar status shield, he had clearly lost it over time. For the Roman mob that killed him, Vitellius' fat belly was a vivid symbol of political failure wrought by luxury, corruption and weakness. Had he been a more successful leader, his towering physique might have radiated monumental power and unimpeachable character. As things stood, though, circumstances dictated how his fat would be perceived: if the act of fattening could suggest an animal fit only for the slaughter, that is exactly what happened to Vitellius.

In addition to sketching some of the ways in which fatness related to status, this chapter has shed light on other developments as well. For instance, there is a temporal dimension to note: the Greeks and Romans often described their present as marked by vices supposedly unknown in earlier, simpler times. Along with other perceived forms of physical and moral weakness, the bodies of the present invited comparisons to the fitter and more virtuous specimens that were said to populate the past. There is also a spatial or geographic dimension to consider: observing that natural environments could be literally 'obesogenic', Graeco-Roman culture sometimes traced the kind of luxury that fattened Vitellius to Asiatic sources. From this perspective, the unfortunate Vitellius might have resembled Dionysius of Heraclea, Ptolemy vii of Egypt, Magas of Cyrene and other fat Asiatic kings. When it occurred, Hellenistic contempt for corpulence reflected a culture that lamented 'corruption' at home as well as abroad. As the next chapter explains, early and medieval Christianity was able to build upon these ideas while placing even more emphasis on the feelings of disgust that fat could awaken. Unlike the Greeks and Romans, among Christians the viscosity and weight of fat could represent a disturbing clinging to the world that revealed the sinful soul's unreadiness for transcendence.

FOUR

CHRISTIAN CORPULENCE
The Belly and What
Lies Beneath

A ccording to an early Christian legend, Judas Iscariot spent his last days as a disgustingly bloated fat man. Although Matthew (27:3–8) says Judas hanged himself out of remorse at having betrayed Jesus for thirty pieces of silver, other Judas stories in circulation during the early days of the faith offered different accounts. In the book of Acts (1:18), for instance, Luke claims that Judas' belly burst apart in the field he purchased with his ill-gotten gains. A fate like this was not quite gruesome enough for Papias, Bishop of Hierapolis and a prominent Christian leader of the early second century. Expanding upon Luke's graphic image, Papias depicted the traitor as having become inexplicably yet monstrously 'swollen up' prior to his death, transforming his body into 'a terrible paragon of ungodliness' that was so massive it 'could not pass where a chariot could pass easily'. Papias even elaborated on the Hebrew motif of the spiritually numbed 'fat heart' by claiming that Judas' eyes were so swollen that 'he was not able at all to see the light.' Rather than restrict his comments to spiritual matters, Papias lingered over the disturbing physical consequences of Judas' fall. Not only was the disgraced apostle's body swollen beyond measure, but his penis 'appeared more disgusting and bigger than any other shameless thing', so disgusting, in fact, that when he relieved himself 'pus with worms' poured onto the ground. When Judas finally died, the nauseating stench of his corrupt body penetrated the earth itself, fouling it forever: 'up till the present day nobody can pass that place without stopping up his nose with his hands. So big was the efflux of his flesh that spread out also on the earth.'[1]

More corpse than corpulent, the bloated body of Judas had little to do with immoderate eating and drinking. Rather, his flesh displayed a corruption so extreme that it had become rank and rotten through and through. That Papias did not disclose the cause of Judas' swollen body is less important for our purposes than the probable significance of the swelling itself. Jesus had been dead for decades by the time Emperor Vitellius was killed in 69 CE, and the movement he inspired was evolving beyond a narrow sect of Judaism to become a more 'universal' faith around the Mediterranean. The abuses that Christian moralists and political thinkers observed in Roman society, and which they saw as being partly exemplified by luxuriantly fat bellies, were ideologically useful for their fledgling movement. Whether bloated through pride or excess, the grotesquely distended body became a powerful stock image that early Christians used to describe how the enemies of God met their deaths.[2]

We have seen how, in the late Republican era, nobles would sometimes have themselves officially represented as corpulent in order to promote positive personal traits, a practice that was adopted by several emperors of the period. This allowed admiring pagan biographers to celebrate the battlefield prowess of the Emperor Galerius (*c.* 260–311), whose large body was meant to suggest his monumental strength and power. As the case of Vitellius shows, such interpretations did not go uncontested. Refusing to forgive Galerius for causing the persecutions of 303–11, Christian writers instead saw his large body as evidence of fatness, illness and animality. Lucius Caecilius Lactantius, who would go on to advise the Christian emperor Constantine on religious matters, described Galerius as

a beast, with a natural barbarity, and wildness quite foreign to Roman blood ... His body matched his character: he was tall in stature, and the vast expanse of his flesh was spread and bloated to a horrifying size.[3]

Depending on one's perspective, the swollen flesh that was officially meant to symbolize power could also be read as a symptom of vice and corruption. It could also be a source of cruel ridicule, at least for some pagans. One of the tamer forms of entertainment ordered by the rather eccentric teenage emperor Elagabalus (r. 218–22) was to have eight fat men try to sit on a single couch. This would 'call forth general laughter' since not all would be able to fit.[4]

This chapter examines how early Christians turned the Roman critique of *luxuria* against the pagan establishment while using the same ideas to bend Hebrew writings to their own agenda.[5] Fully capable of being aligned with the sin of gluttony, in Christian hands corpulence could also denote an egotistical swelling of the self beyond what was considered proper for the maintenance of community. By spiritualizing the vertical tension introduced by Plato, who lamented the earthbound animality of those who seemed to live only to eat, Christians claimed that fatness exerted a downward tug on minds and even souls imagined to be capable of 'higher' and more transcendent things. Drawing upon the ideas of Philo of Alexandria, the contempt that early Christians sometimes heaped upon fat bodies referred as much to the sticky domains of organic life as it did to concerns about size and shape. Moreover, by obsessively indicating the location of the 'appetites' in the body – specifically in 'the belly and what lies beneath' – they connected excess body fat to the abdomen and the genitals as seats of desire and consumption, digestion and excretion. If Christians applied to fatness some of the 'ideological disgust' that Roman elites associated with slaves, servility, indiscipline, cowardice and 'softness',[6] they also exploited the intrinsically greasy and excremental aspects of fat in ways the Greeks and Roman rarely did. In this way, Christians connected corpulence to the grease and filth of the material world, establishing a set of ideas that would remain operative through to the Middle Ages.

Belly-slaves

As is often the case when considering early Christian texts, it is helpful to return to Hebrew sources. In common with the Egyptians, the Hebrews envisioned the belly as a 'casket' enclosing a person's thoughts and 'heart' – the latter included emotions like fear, joy, bitterness, greed and lust.[7] What one put into one's belly thus held considerable significance, and as the Hebrews engaged more closely with Hellenistic ideas over time, they refined how they reflected upon their long-standing dietary restrictions. Drawing upon Roman terms, those apostate Jews who disregarded such prohibitions could be called 'belly-slaves' in that they seemed to allow their appetites for illicit food to govern their judgement.[8] Such Hellenistic reflections were integral to how the Jewish philosopher Philo engaged with these texts in Alexandria during the early years of the first century. Philo viewed fat in a variety of ways. For one thing, he saw it as an oleaginous substance that preserved the vital organs, preventing them 'when dried, from very quickly dissolving and melting away. For one who has the moisture of fatness receives the moisture as most vital nourishment.'[9] Philo's medical approach to fat was useful, not least because he believed that health considerations played a role in Mosaic dietary codes. After all, fat was not only sacred, but tasty as well. It was the fattest and most delicious animals that were most likely to drive people to excess. By placing a taboo on fat, Philo contended, Yahweh was doing his chosen people a favour. Prohibiting them from eating the 'richest part' of the animal would allow them to become accustomed to

> self-restraint and foster the aspiration for the life of austerity which relinquishes what is easiest and lies ready to hand, but willingly endures anxiety and toils in order to acquire virtue.

In addition to this very Hellenistic ideal of moderation, Philo maintained that Yahweh also prohibited the eating of certain animals for health reasons, knowing that 'gluttony begets indigestion which is the source and origin of all distempers and infirmities.' Like a wise doctor, then, Yahweh prescribed a moderate regime that avoided both the stark austerity of the Spartans and the freewheeling excess of the Sybarites.[10]

Health issues were just the beginning of Philo's concerns. Despite his nod to classical medicine, Philo's interpretation of Hebrew texts was driven by a puritanical ethos that had much in common with the neo-Platonist idealism that informed early Christian theology. Commenting on the book of Genesis, Philo described Thobel, maker of bronze and iron tools, as a supplier of weapons who knew that armies and navies willingly face 'the greatest dangers for the sake of bodily pleasures'. To illustrate the folly of such rationales for war, Philo pointed out that 'the sister of Thobel was Noeman (Genesis 4:22), meaning "fatness".' Echoing Plato, who had argued in *The Republic* that the quest for luxury was the origin of warfare, Philo claimed that when those who 'make bodily comfort and the material things of which I have spoken their object, succeed in getting something which they crave after, the consequence is that they grow fat'.

The fat that Philo had in mind referred to bodies, and metaphorically to souls, that had become so bloated through excess that they resembled overripe fruit or decomposing corpses: 'These, suffering from the effects of fatness and enjoyment spreading increasingly, swell out and become distended till they burst.' Yet not all swelling was bad. As opposed to the fattened body that evoked organic corruption, Philo praised souls that had been 'fattened by wisdom', for they will 'acquire a firm and settled vigour' symbolized by the sacrificial fat ritually offered to God. Being unencumbered by the coarse materiality of the world, this spiritual 'fattening' was qualitatively superior to the swelling of 'the body and outward things'. The reason was that the latter, being material, are ephemeral and prone to decay.[11]

Implicit in agricultural concepts of fattening, the association of fatness with decay was emphasized by Philo in ways that were uncommon among most pagan writers of the period. Greek and Roman physicians acknowledged fat's soft, unctuous and insulating qualities, but they did not usually connect fat bodies with filth, much less putrefaction. With his emphasis on transcending the material world, Philo's notion of fat contained the idea of surplus organic life as well as the rotten, bloated and viscous qualities of a fallen world. Yet, for all of his apparent singularity, Philo was not alone in thinking about fat in terms of a vertical tension between the transcendence of the soul and the sticky immanence of materiality. Similar ideas were echoed in Porphyry's *On Abstinence from Killing Animals*, which was written during the last quarter of the third century and is the oldest existing account of Graeco-Roman philosophical asceticism. Fat was 'a philosophic issue' for Porphyry, as it was for Philo.[12]

Framed as an attempt to persuade a friend who had converted to Christianity to resume a pagan life and a vegetarian diet, *On Abstinence* recommended moderate eating and drinking as being beneficial for body and soul. Animal flesh was to be avoided because it causes one to become fat (*pachos*) while promoting physical strength that, while appropriate for wrestlers and labourers, does little to promote contemplation. Encumbered with excess flesh, the meat-eater may become stronger but also 'more inert and feebler about one's own concerns'.[13] Corpulence posed an obstacle to reason, so it was better to 'fatten' the soul through intellect than 'to fatten our flesh on meat'. There was something uncomfortably heavy, contaminating and even parasitical about fatty matter that placed it at odds with the ideally upward trajectory of the soul:

> when the body is fattened it starves the soul of the blessed life and enlarges the mortal part, distracting and obstructing the soul on its way to immortal life, and it stains the soul by incarnating it and dragging it down to that which is alien.[14]

As the soul was meant for higher and purer things, fat and fatness represented forms of spiritual disability and impurity that pulled one back to earth.

Philo and Porphyry were thus of a similar mind, and both had an influence on early Christianity. Fat's inherent tendency to cleave to the material world, either through viscosity or weight, was further complicated by Philo's contention that the belly was the seat and generator of sensual appetites. Sexual pleasure seemed to ebb and flow depending upon whether the belly was empty or full, a fact that made some sense given the anatomical proximity of reproductive and digestive organs. 'This is apparently the reason why Nature placed the organs of sexual lust where she did,' Philo speculated, for the genitals are 'roused to their special activities when fulness of food leads the way'.[15] As Philo insisted, and many Church Fathers would later agree, it is 'the belly and what is below it' that posed the gravest obstacles to moral life. Whether obsessed with food or sex, 'belly-centred' people betray their selfish preference for carnal pleasures over the needs of the community. Unable to govern their own appetites, such individuals have neither the inclination nor the capacity to govern others. Moreover, insofar as the belly could be worshipped and serviced almost like a divinity, the commitment to earthly pleasures symbolized by excessive eating also suggested a denial of God.

Philo's concept of the belly-centred person was more of a commentary on gluttony than on corpulence. As we have seen, the two were not consistently bound together in the Hellenistic world. While it was reasonable to assume that excessive eating could cause a person to become fat, one who pursued a modest and frugal lifestyle might be naturally stout without fearing moral judgement. Just as the belly itself had a spectrum of anatomical referents, being 'belly-centred' referred to the location of desires that were expressed in more than the immoderate love of food. This is how Athenaeus' learned

banqueters could ridicule a glutton, one ruled by his appetites, as a
'Worshipper of your own belly!'[16] So devoted was a certain Arches-
tratus to sensual pleasures, Athenaeus added, that he 'circumnavigated
the inhabited world for the sake of his belly and the portions of his
anatomy below the belly'.[17] Worshipping one's belly as a god was
no laughing matter for the religiously inclined. For writers like
Philo, the stomach and the genitals symbolized an 'animal-life
force' that had the capacity to divert humans from their more
properly divine trajectories.[18] By obsessing over the proximity of the
belly to the reproductive and excretory organs – and by underscor-
ing the troublingly viscous properties of fat as a substance – Philo
suggested that immoderate indulgence in the pleasures of the flesh
all came together in grease, filth and shit. By subjecting Hellenistic
ideas about the belly to 'a biblical filtering', Philo foregrounded the
rotting and excremental dimensions of food, fat and sex that were
less pronounced in pagan sources.[19]

Until the fifteenth century, mainstream Judaism developed more
or less unhindered by Philo's classical readings of scripture, a fact that
reflects the anti-Hellenizing bent of the early rabbinic movement
as well as Judaism's generally more positive view of the body. Philo's
ideas were nonetheless attractive to early Christian theologians who
shared his concerns about the linkages between food, drink and sexuality.[20] Paul of Tarsus registered similar concerns in his missionary
work and letters to early Christian communities. Recommending
neither fasting nor dietary restrictions as conducive to Christian
piety, Paul was adamant about the problem of the belly, whose worship he saw in terms similar to those that animated Philo and others.
Just as Hellenistic moralists criticized belly-slaves for indulging their
own appetites at the expense of the community, Paul saw in gluttons
a shirking of their responsibilities to the flock. They were bad citizens
of the Heavenly kingdom. In this way could Paul accuse the biblical figure Onan of belly-slavery. By spilling his seed on the ground
instead of impregnating his dead brother's widow, Onan too was a
pleasure-seeker who neglected his duties to family, city and God. One
could not therefore claim to follow Christ while also submitting to
personal desires, which was a form of slavery as well as idol-worship.[21]
While Paul warned against becoming overly attached to the belly
and the parts underneath, he was less concerned with appearance
than with desire itself. Paul likened the Christian struggle against

the passions to what an athlete might do, in this way reworking Hellenistic material into his account of the model Christian.

How did Jesus himself stack up against these concerns? According to the Gospels (Matthew 11:19; Luke 7:34), Jesus was accused by his enemies of being a glutton and a drunkard because he dined with publicans and other groups frowned upon by the religious establishment.[22] Yet these texts say virtually nothing about the Son of Man's physique. While the reason for this omission is uncertain, it may indicate a desire to represent Jesus as a freeman rather than as a slave: according to the literary conventions of the day, slave bodies were often described in detail to emphasize their grotesque and deformed qualities.[23] What we do know about Jesus' body is that it has almost never been depicted as fat in medieval or early modern art. The Word might indeed have become flesh, just not *too much* flesh. If the body of Christ went conspicuously unmarked in the Gospels, the same is not true of the sinners Jesus occasionally encountered. Although corpulence did not count among the afflictions Jesus is credited with healing, Luke (14:1–6) relates an episode where Jesus encounters a man suffering from the bloating effects of dropsy (oedema). Observing that dropsy occurs in a scene where Luke is commenting on the pitfalls of socio-economic success, one scholar persuasively reads this disease of artificial and excessive thirst as a well-known Hellenistic metaphor for limitless desire and thus 'addiction to luxury'.[24] Whether physically bloated with excess water or flesh, or metaphorically puffed up with pride, for early Christians the swollen self was capable of signifying many forms of excess that set one apart from the righteous.

Swollen Bottles and Resurrected Bodies

Hellenistic recommendations about moderation were widely known in the ancient world, but it was Clement of Alexandria who extended pagan medicine to the Christian context in the late second century CE. Registering his respect for the Spartan way of life, Clement emphasized the virtues of plain and simple food while warning against luxuries that might corrupt body and soul.[25] In this context fat and greasy things were particularly problematic. When improperly used, Clement warned, oil and oil-based products could destroy the virility of men and the morality of women. Concerns about oil were extended to the fatty flesh of certain animals:

The divine law, then, while keeping in mind all virtue, trains man especially to self-restraint, laying this as the foundation of the virtues; and disciplines us beforehand to the attainment of self-restraint by forbidding us to partake of such things as are by nature fat, as the breed of swine, which is full-fleshed. For such a use is assigned to epicures.[26]

Variation on such themes may be found throughout patristic literature. Even the moralizing theologian Jerome enlisted pagan medical authority to make a religious point. Conceding that 'gorging gives rise to disease' and awakens sexual desire, it was Jerome who translated into Latin Galen's claim that 'a full stomach does not beget a fine mind' (*pinguis venter non gignit sensum tenuem*).[27]

In a pattern that would repeat itself through the early Middle Ages, though, whatever claims medicine might have for regulating conduct and promoting healthy practices could be trumped by theological obsessions with sin and damnation that appeared to be concretized in the 'heaviness' of the flesh and matter generally. This is why Clement could claim that 'Fasting empties the soul of matter and makes it, with the body, clear and light for the reception of divine truth.'[28] Fat and food were seen as frustrating the upward trajectory of the soul, literally weighing it down with filthy and rotten substances. Images of heavy and swollen putrefaction were employed by others as well. 'But my pleasure is to have no pleasure,' declares the character 'Pneuma' in Gregory of Nazianzus' fourth-century dialogue *Comparatio vitarum*; and:

> not to have my body swollen with things filling it inside, sick with the infirmity of the wealthy, breathing from my throat the sickly, sweet odor of filth, constraining my mind with the weight of my fat.[29]

As with Philo and Porphyry, among early Christians the negative qualities of fat included a heavy and greasy clinging to corruptible worldly things that prevented the transcendence of the soul. Fat was a problem, as was all flesh, but more so because fat was literally *more flesh*.

Fat, gluttony and belly-slavery affected Christians differently depending on whether they were clerics or laypeople. Take the so-called

Desert Fathers, who formed remote monastic communities in Egypt beginning in the third century. For these world renouncers, chastity and bodily mortification were central to the Christian life. What *they* called 'gluttony' consisted of taking more than one's usual meagre ration at mealtimes or even requesting to have some vegetables with one's bread. Insofar as great corpulence was less of a possibility for these world renouncers (whose 'sinfulness' might result in what the outside world would have seen as healthy fleshiness), the connection between gluttony and fat seems to have been reserved for the laity.

This was quite evident to John Chrysostom, who preached in fourth-century Antioch before becoming Archbishop of Constantinople. Nicknamed 'golden-mouth' for the honey-like eloquence of his orations, what flowed from his pen wasn't always so sweet, especially when the subject of luxury came up. Motivated by the high levels of poverty he had encountered as a young priest, Chrysostom made charity the central theme of his mission. This meant breaking down the complacency and selfishness that tightened the purse strings of the wealthy. Chrysostom railed against the well-to-do whose luxuries closed them off from their less fortunate brothers and sisters. In so doing, he focused unusual attention on the body as a way of encouraging people to overcome barriers toward true community. As physical vulnerability was a universal shared by all people, 'John preached a brotherhood of bodies at risk.'[30] Some were more at risk than others, though, and Chrysostom evinced a general disgust with the desiring body as a container that was too often filled beyond its limits: 'for as a man who shall draw into a leaking vessel labors in vain, so also does the one who lives in luxury and self-indulgence draw into a leaking vessel.'[31] As Chrysostom declared elsewhere, 'The body is like a swollen bottle, running out every way.'[32]

Of all early Christian writers, Chrysostom was perhaps most obsessed with fat bellies and bloated limbs. They crop up frequently in his writings, usually as the sorry evidence of gluttony, and frequently in connection with filth and excrement. As opposed to the harsh austerities practised by world-renouncing ascetics, a lifestyle that as a young man Chrysostom had tried and failed to follow, the Church generally expected laypeople to pursue lives of moderation. The reasons Chrysostom gave for leading a temperate life combined spiritual, medical and aesthetic rationales. Targeting luxury as one of the central obstacles to charity, he had no problem employing the pagan wisdom of Galen to make a Christian point. 'Luxury and sobriety cannot exist together: they are destructive of one another. Even the Heathens say, "A heavy paunch bears not a subtle mind".'[33] His suggestions for moderation in food and drink were moralized versions of Graeco-Roman hygienic recommendations: 'Dost thou wish to nourish the body? Take away what is superfluous; give what is sufficient, and as much as can be digested. Do not load it, lest thou overwhelm it.'[34] As was the case with Philo, however, Chrysostom's association of fat and gluttony with excrement was more pronounced than one would have ordinarily found among pagans. In a homily on Paul's letter to the Corinthians, Chrysostom asked believers to think not of the luxurious themselves but of what was in store for them: 'here indeed filth and obesity, there the worm and fire'.[35]

Animality was another pagan metaphor that Chrysostom employed – and exaggerated – in his 'honey-like' homilies. Like other key authors of the patristic era, Chrysostom frowned upon the relative fluidity that pagans acknowledged between human and non-human animals, along with many of the pleasures and pastimes enjoyed by others in the Hellenized world. Early Christians thus railed against 'species ambiguity and established a principle of a qualitative difference between humans and animals'.[36] More than that, Christianity effected what might be called a 'purification operation' whereby humans become 'exterior and superior to nature' in ways that were less conceivable to the Greeks and Romans.[37] This purifying distinction between humans and animals would harden over time. By the twelfth century, Thomas Aquinas was declaring that the 'life of animals . . . is preserved not for themselves, but for man'.[38]

As one effect of this transformation, Chrysostom's vivid depictions of fat sinners are laden with the materiality and animality that the faithful were supposed to transcend. Those aspiring to purity were encouraged to read the physical evidence of sin on the bodies of others.[39] Spending one's wealth on self-indulgence rather than on the good of others could reduce a person to a quivering, stinky mess that Chrysostom seemed to enjoy describing: 'grossness of body, flatulence, pantings, fullness of belly, heaviness of head, softness of flesh, feverishness, [and] enervation'.[40] While many Church Fathers condemned the appetites that seemed to drive such excesses, Chrysostom lingered over the physical repulsiveness that such appetites could produce. He especially dwelled on the animalizing consequences that corpulence might bring about. Could there be a more 'disgusting spectacle', Chrysostom asked rhetorically, than 'a man cultivating obesity, dragging himself along like a seal?' Certainly not! his readers were expected to respond, but Chrysostom didn't want to be misunderstood. 'I speak not this of those who are naturally of this habit,' he hastened to add, 'but of those who by luxurious living have brought their bodies into such a condition, of those who are naturally of a spare habit.' The latter transform themselves into 'brute beasts' that feed the entire day 'because their only use is to be slaughtered'. A man who comports himself 'as if he were indeed a hog in fattening' becomes 'a spectacle of unseemliness, with nothing human about him, but with all the appearance of a beast with a human shape'. Like Philo and Porphyry before him, Chrysostom invoked the motif of spirit encumbered by an engulfing materiality, but he enhanced it with images of disabling animality: 'the miserable soul, just like the lame, is unable to rise, bearing about its bulk of flesh, like an elephant.'[41]

Despite appearances, there were nuances to Chrysostom's view of fatness. Being naturally corpulent was, it seems, not a problem in itself. Given Chrysostom's vitriolic invective – spiked as it was with references to hogs, seals and elephants – one wonders how he or any of his readers would have been able to tell whether any given person's corpulence resulted from gluttony or constitution, or whether they would have even bothered trying. Despite the transcendent aims of his ideas of the good Christian life, there is something inescapably 'worldly' about Chrysostom's relentless emphasis on appearance, suggesting that what some modern theorists refer to as 'the gaze' was already very much operative when it came to scrutinizing the bodies of believers. This may explain why Chrysostom reserved some of his nastiest barbs for women, whose potential fall from grace was something of an obsession for him. Some of his concerns about female corpulence were health-related: 'For why dost thou, O woman, continually enfeeble [thy body] with luxury and exhaust it? Why dost thou ruin thy strength with fat? This fat is flabbiness, not strength.'[42]

As always in the ancient world, though, health went hand-in-hand with beauty and morality: 'in truth luxury makes the beautiful woman not only sickly, but also foul to look upon.' Vision was but one of the senses that a sinful fat woman could offend:

she is continually sending forth unpleasant exhalations, and breathes fumes of stale wine, and is more florid than she ought to be, and spoils the symmetry that beseems a woman, and loses all her seemliness, and her body becomes flabby, her eyelids blood-shot and distended, and her bulk unduly great, and her flesh a useless load.

Insisting that his readers share his revulsion, Chrysostom asked them to imagine for themselves 'what a disgust it all produces'.[43] To make his point, Chrysostom offered a before-and-after comparison that is worth quoting in full:

For tell me, suppose one had a comely person, and passing all in beauty, and wealth were to go to him and promise to make it ugly, and instead of healthy, diseased, instead of cool, inflamed; and having filled every limb with dropsy, were to make the counte-nance bloated, and distend it all over; and were to swell out the feet, and make them heavier than logs, and to puff up the belly, and make it larger than any tun . . . well then, tell me, when wealth works these effects in the soul, how can it be honourable?[44]

If a faithful person failed to achieve in life the kind of body that Chrysostom thought was most appropriate, what would happen when the bodies of the righteous were raised from the dead in the hereafter? The Christian belief in bodily resurrection would have resonated with pagan Hellenistic peoples, who associated bodily immortality with the gods while fully expecting that they themselves would endure the afterlife as bodiless 'shades'.[45] Unfortunately, the Christian hereafter was not without certain size requirements. In a variation of the saying that a rich man would have a harder time getting into Heaven than a camel would through the eye of a needle (Mark 10:24–7), Tertullian claimed that

More easily through the 'strait gate' of salvation will slender flesh enter; more speedily will lighter flesh rise; longer in the sepulcher will drier flesh retain its firmness.[46]

Although it bore some relationship to Hellenistic body ideals, this emphasis on slenderness, lightness and dryness related less to aesthetic standards of size and shape than to anxieties about human flesh that were as bound to processes of dissolution and putrefaction as any other form of organic life. The ascetic life thus promised a body immune to the ravages of time and organic process.[47] This understandably raised questions about what the reanimated corpses of the righteous would look like in the New Jerusalem. Paul (1 Corinthians 15:38–54) was light on the details of what this 'spiritual body', so superior in glory, power and imperishability to its earthly version, would actually be like. Declaring that 'flesh and blood cannot inherit the kingdom of God,' Paul was certain that human flesh differed from animal flesh, and that God would give this or that person 'a body as he has chosen'. Later writers offered more specifics. In his early writings, Augustine of Hippo made no promises about what believers could expect after being resurrected, conceding only that it is not certain 'that the lean shall rise again in their former leanness, and the fat in their former fatness'. Even if God decided on a 'well-ordered inequality' of bodily shapes and sizes, Augustine assured readers that Heaven's inhabitants would be easy on the eyes: 'whatever shall be there shall be graceful and becoming: for if anything is not seemly, neither shall it be.'[48]

If statements like this suggest that Heavenly ideals respected Graeco-Roman aesthetic standards, they also reveal early Christianity's insistence that the resurrected body would be 'perfected' and 'complete' in ways that pagans never imagined in their own views of the afterlife.[49] Augustine had it all worked out by the time he wrote *The City of God* years later:

> let neither fat persons nor thin ones fear that their appearance at the resurrection will be other than *they would have wished it to be* here if they could [emphasis added].

Since 'all defects will be corrected' in God's kingdom, it stood to reason that 'the body will have that size which it either attained in the prime of its life or would have attained had it achieved the pattern implanted in it' as well as 'the beauty which arises from preserving the appropriate arrangement of all its parts'. Anticipating the aim, if not quite the actual procedure, of the modern liposuction technique of 'fat transfer' or 'fat grafting', Augustine thought it reasonable to assume that 'any part of the body's substance which, concentrated in one place, would give rise to a deformity by reason of excessive size will be redistributed throughout the whole.' This is how the overall stature of an individual would be only slightly enlarged at the resurrection. Any physical feature that 'would have been unsightly if concentrated in one place' would simply be moved elsewhere.[50] The perfected resurrection body would not simply be well proportioned and appealing – and, it seems, Hellenized – but it would also be immune to the disability and decay inherent to earthly embodiment. It is in this sense that one might say that today's cosmetic surgeons aspire to do God's work.

Corpulence in Medieval Christianity

Augustine thus seemed less concerned than other Church Fathers about whether or not one was corpulent during one's life. So long as a person had lived a righteous life, his or her resurrection body would assume its properly beautiful form. Yet the fourth century, during which Augustine wrote, marked a turning point in the history of Christianity. Not only was the faith legalized and orthodoxy formed, but the diminishing of its outsider status was accompanied by a re-valorization of the material world, including the body, as religiously important.[51] If fat can be said to have been important for late antique and medieval Christianity, it would have been mainly in the form of oil. Peter Cramer's explanation for the significance of holy oil in the eighth-century *Gelasian Sacramentary* underscores how theologians tapped into the material qualities of fat that had captured the attention of pagans and Jews. Noting how often anthropologists have observed the significance of oil 'across a huge variety of societies, with a multi-plicity which has its own exuberance', Cramer proposes that

> Everything is in the oil, the inner principle of the vital, which when smeared on the body – the chrism, a mixture of oil and balsam, would be smeared on the forehead of the baptized by the priest on the vigil of Easter, after the bath of baptism – makes manifest this inner principle, brings it to the surface, 'for all to see'.[52]

Oil was so important that the bodies of certain saints were believed to excrete forms of it after their death.[53] In the thirteenth century, Caesarius of Heisterbach noted the healing properties of the oil that flowed from the bodies of saints like Elizabeth of Thuringia as well as Demetrius, Catherin and Nicholas.[54] Even in cases where the precious substance exuded from the bodies of holy women was not oil – as in the case of the milk said to flow from Flemish mystics – the substance in question was still fatty and life-giving.[55]

In the form of holy oil, fat retained its ability to convey vitality and fertility, but we have also seen how, as a delectable foodstuff that was connected to sensuality, it took on other meanings as well. This was true when bodily fatness was loosely connected to the sin of gluttony. Indeed, it was also during the fourth century that the first list of major sins was compiled by the Church. Given the predominance of world-renunciation in early Christianity, gluttony topped the list. Viewed in social terms, the glutton took more than his or her share, and thus potentially deprived others of nourishment. As we have seen, gluttony usually had more to do with an uncontrollable appetite than with personal appearance. Individuals might be guilty of gluttony, and gluttony could easily be seen as manifested in corpulence, but they were not necessarily held morally responsible for their fat, which could also be seen in medical terms as an effect of individual humoral complexion and of lifestyles linked to professions that might require more or less physical work.[56] As the diatribes of Chrysostom suggest, though, it was tempting to draw inferences about one's spiritual worth from bodily clues alone.

Despite this fixation on gluttony, it was unusual in the Middle Ages to find communal fasting that bore much resemblance to the hardcore asceticism of Christianity's early days, even though some religious orders demanded greater austerities than others. Vegetable gardens, fruit trees, wheat, vineyards and livestock were common features of Pachomian monasteries of the fifth and sixth centuries, suggesting that the monks there enjoyed a diet more than ample for supporting health.[57] Some monasteries even became notorious centres of gluttony and laziness. This eventually earned monks a reputation for rounded bodies that generated proverbs like 'fat like a monk' to stand alongside sayings like 'fat as a pig'. The tone of such statements suggests degrees of corpulence beyond what would have been considered simple evidence of health.

Some monks took their feasting rather seriously. When in the tenth century the reform-minded Bishop Aethelwold became the head of the Winchester monastery and tried to enforce a more sober regimen, the monks most attached to eating and drinking tried to poison him.[58] Criticism of the luxurious living of fellow monks and calls for a return to austerity may have been a pattern when new monastic orders appeared on the scene. 'Does salvation rest rather in soft raiment and high living than in frugal fare and moderate clothing?' was the question the Cistercian Bernard of Clairvaux posed to the Cluniac order in the mid-twelfth century. His answer to his own question – 'The soul is not fattened out of frying pans!' – might have made Porphyry proud.[59] While we cannot speak to the state of monks' souls, archaeologists offer glimpses of the condition of their bodies. A recent excavation reinforces the view that a 'monastic way of life', featuring a diet high in saturated animal fats and alcoholic beverages coupled with a more or less sedentary lifestyle, predisposed monks to a bone condition that has been closely linked to corpulence, gout and diabetes.[60]

Closely connected to issues of morality and appetites, corpulence was also a matter of appearances in the Middle Ages. At least among spiritual leaders, physical beauty continued to be seen as evidence of goodness. Saints were not only thought to have certain spiritual advantages over others, but were said to possess seven gifts of the body as well: beauty, agility, strength, freedom of movement, health, voluptuousness and longevity. In the symbolic system that structured medieval iconography, flat stomachs were privileged over swollen ones, not least because the latter were often associated with sinfulness.[61] Medieval people may have been unclear about what the 'moderate' body looked like, but they surely knew great fatness when they saw it. Yet corpulence in itself was not enough to condemn a person as profligate. Rather, it had to be accompanied by morally questionable behaviour that allowed critics to propose that such misdeeds were in fact legible on the body.

Such a conclusion might have been counterintuitive to the most austere of medieval ascetics, who implored believers not to be seduced by the physical appearance of health and prosperity. Putrefaction was, after all, 'inherent to life' rather than something that unfolded after death, and its effects were said to be especially pronounced in bodies fattened on fine food and drink.[62] 'A well-fed body and delicate complexion', argued the Cistercian monk Hélinand de Froimont, 'are but a tunic of worms and fire. The body is vile, stinking and withered.'[63] To die with a hard and gaunt body meant never having to know 'the horror of sudden decay' awaiting those pampered by soft and indulgent living.[64] But such pronouncements were extreme, and distract us from the fact that, for all of their suspicion of sexuality and decay, medieval theology still considered the person to be a psychosomatic unity of which the body was an essential component.[65]

Appearances thus mattered, even if they were not paramount. Questions about the beauty of the resurrected body were not put to rest with Augustine, but cropped up periodically throughout the Middle Ages.[66] Pondering the same question centuries later, the angelic doctor of the Church, Thomas Aquinas, agreed that in the afterlife 'We may expect that to be resumed by preference, which was more perfect in the species and form of humanity.'[67] One might thus assume that Aquinas' resurrected body would differ from the one he sported on Earth. Although Aquinas was reputed to have been so fat that he could only sit comfortably at a table if a space had been cut away for his belly, no one doubted that he faithfully observed the required austerities of the Dominican order. While some might have made comments behind his back, there was no reason for Aquinas' girth to signify anything negative to fellow clerics.[68]

If, somewhat like Plato, Aquinas' spiritual and philosophical credentials shielded him from whatever stigma his fat body might otherwise have attracted, the reverse was true of clergy who had earned reputations for vice. In some cases, great fatness was described as monstrosity. The German chronicler Lampert of Hersfeld expressed dismay when Adalbero, a monk of the monastery of St Gallen, was offered the bishopric of Worms in 1065. In addition to being 'completely lame in one foot', Lampert reported, Adalbero was

> in all respects a sight to behold. For he was a man of great strength, of extreme gluttony and of such great fatness/thickness [*crassitudinis tantae*] that he struck beholders with horror rather than admiration.

To give readers a sense of the kind of spectacle that Adalbero made of himself, Lampert included partial quotations (italicized here) from Roman writers like Livy, Horace and Sulpicius Severus:

> *No hundred-handed giant* or any other monster of antiquity, if *it rose from the underworld*, would *turn the eye* and *gaze* of the astonished populace *upon himself to this degree.*

The populace would not be astonished for long. Five years later the fat bishop died, 'suffocated (so it is said) by his own fatness [*crassitudine*]'.[69]

Despite this perceived connection between fat monks and gluttony, great fleshiness was not a reliable sign of a voracious appetite. In medieval art, gluttons were often depicted as gaunt creatures whose bodies were seemingly incapable of ever achieving repletion. Theological concerns about the sin of gluttony were sometimes complemented by medical warnings about the dangers of overeating, but the connection between gluttony and fatness developed more slowly. The allegorical figure of Gluttony in William Langland's *Piers Plowman* (*c.* 1370–90) suffered from health complaints (indigestion, flatulence, vomiting), indicating the persistence of Galenic dietetic wisdom throughout the medieval era.[70] The Pardoner in Chaucer's *Canterbury Tales* (1387) also viewed gluttony as having implications extending beyond the strictly religious. It was also a practical problem in that it caused forgetfulness and loss of wit, as well as an unhealthy imbalance of the bodily humours:

> Oh, if a man knew how many maladies
> follow from excess and gluttony
> he would be more temperate
> in his diet when he sits at his table.[71]

Often the problem of fat was eclipsed by other physical ailments caused by overindulgence, so much so as to be nearly invisible. Elsewhere, the fat belly was treated as the most conspicuous sign of gluttony. In Dante's vision of Hell the third circle was reserved for gluttons, and featured the three-headed demon Cerberus who, with 'his belly large' [*'l ventre largo*], would have been recognized as bearing what many would have seen as one effect of that particular sin.[72]

Even if there was no consistent connection to gluttony, fatness was certainly available for moral comment under the right circumstances. Writing about the proper training of novices in monastic schools, in the early twelfth century, Hugh of St Victor encouraged teachers to search for the hidden defects of their students' characters in involuntary gestures and bodily features. In particular they were encouraged to be on the watch for fatness, which betokened lasciviousness if not gluttony per se, as well as 'loose' or quick physical movements that denoted, respectively, negligence and inconsistency.[73] A few decades later, a monk at the Abbey of Montecassino known for his strict fasting was reputed by lay people to be a 'glutton' precisely because he was fat.[74] A similar depiction of corpulence as a sign of corruption may be found in the *Garcineida*, a twelfth-century 'money-gospel' satirizing the wealth of the Church by depicting a world representing the inverse of the values preached in the Gospels.[75] By the early thirteenth century, the Dominican monk Jean de San Gimignano was trotting out some ancient truisms when he claimed that great fatness not only 'engenders the worst maladies' but 'impedes the activity of the soul' and is thus an 'obstacle to sense and intelligence'.[76]

Constructed out of ideas circulating in Hebrew and Hellenistic culture, fatness had become a problem of mind, body and spirit, while the substance that produced corpulence retained its links to excrement and filth. As one might expect, images of eating and defecating were common in a culture that continued to recognize a slippage between the belly as the site of reproduction as well as digestion and excretion. When they weren't likening diseases to weeds threatening to invade the 'garden' of the body, medieval doctors described illnesses as wild animals that could 'devour' a person. Death itself was imagined as a hungry animal that devours. According to Bartholomew of England, 'death [*mort*] is so called because it bites [*mord*] horribly.'[77]

If the righteous could at least look forward to redemption in the 'womb' of Paradise, for sinners there was more devouring to come. The Devil, it was said, was a 'twisting, many-shaped serpent-demon' who always '*goeth about seeking* men and women *whom he may devour*'.[78] In the feverish visions of some clerics, the journey to Hell was itself a process of being devoured and excreted. Hence the widespread use of scatological imagery to depict Satan and Hell. In his *Inferno* (*c.* 1410), Giovanni da Modena's gripping image of Satan devouring sinners and shitting them into Hell aptly conveys this long-standing view of digestion as a perversely inverted process of gestation and reproduction. The nastiness continued below, where gluttons who had fattened themselves like beasts would now be force-fed unclean animals and other foul victuals for all eternity. As late as the fifteenth century, the Flemish theologian Denis the Carthusian imagined Hell as a vast intestine swollen with all manner of grease and filth,

In the medieval imagination the path to Hell passed through Satan's devouring and excreting body. The centre-right section of Giovanni da Modena's fresco *Inferno* shows slender gluttons being force-fed for eternity. Their slenderness may suggest appetites that can never be sated. Giovanni da Modena, *Inferno*, *c.* 1410. Cappella Bolognini, Bologna, Italy.

especially rotting and stinking human fat. In this vile place, the bodies of sinners will be 'fat and despairing' as well as 'disgusting, liable to suffering, gross and slow, heavy, foul and smelly'. Shocked by their appearance, they will be 'astounded by the so great and so horrible shapelessness, ugliness, and obscurity of their own bodies'. In stark contrast to the bloated bodies of the damned, the righteous would enjoy Heaven as beautiful, slim, lithe and graceful beings, just as Augustine and Aquinas had promised.[79] The fatness of the sinful is vividly depicted in Taddeo di Bartolo's *The Last Judgment* (*c.* 1394), where the gluttonous and the greedy are all corpulent. Closely connected to the filth and decay of this world, fat was the stuff of organic life that good Christians hoped one day to overcome.

＊

Things are getting a bit messy now, so it's worth reviewing the developments encountered so far. The Greeks, Romans and Hebrews connected fat's agricultural and moral implications, laying the groundwork for enduring ambivalence about fertility, animality and consumption. While corpulence could be appreciated as evidence of wealth and power, on other occasions the Greeks and Romans were prone to perceiving the fat body as an object of ridicule, and at times astonishment. But it would be a stretch to argue that fatness was for them a simple disgust elicitor. The excremental implications of the act of fattening the soil, as well as the potential unpleasantness of greasiness, were not typically extended to descriptions of fat people. These potentialities of fat, in other words, were not fully actualized in Hellenistic or Hebrew views of corpulence. Often cited as evidence of poor health and something to be avoided, fatness was at worst capable of eliciting what has been called ideological disgust. The latter, we have seen, was triggered by the subversion of established hierarchies, and overlapped with the contempt expressed at men whose submission to feminizing appetites aligned them with women, slaves and Asiatic peoples. Regular references to livestock fattened for exploitation by the more powerful offered one way of demonstrating how fattening could align a person or group on the 'low' end of a hierarchy.

The diminished status and power sometimes associated with corpulence was enhanced by the ways in which Hellenistic and Hebrew culture made use of the materiality of fat. Among the former, the feminine 'softness' that luxury implied was literally embodied in the fatty tissue of the corpulent, as if their flesh materialized the weak and yielding character of those who lacked virile firmness. The fact that softness might also suggest putrefaction and corruption was not often foregrounded in Hellenistic and Hebrew descriptions of fat bodies. The insensateness of adipose tissue was also identified as providing a material insulation that diminished sensitivity as well as cognition and, for the Hebrews, spirituality. This is how the supposed foolishness or stupidity of fat people was explained with

Corpulence was an inconsistent sign of gluttony in early and medieval Christianity, but in Taddeo di Bartolo's vision of Hell it marks the gluttonous as well as the greedy. In this fresco detail, perpetually hungry gluttons are prevented from eating the food in front of them. Taddeo di Bartolo, *The Last Judgment*, c. 1394. Collegiata di San Gimignano, Tuscany, Italy.

reference to a physical barrier to perception as well as the dumb docility of livestock. Fatness could now be connected to the unhealthy, the ugly and the immoral; it might suggest a kind of 'feminine' weakness in the face of the appetites of the body; and it could evoke the character traits as well as the physiques of non-human creatures that occupied the lowest rungs of the animal hierarchy. It could also be used as a way of mapping those regions of the world where such

In this fresco detail, the punishment of the greedy includes being force-fed gold shat by a demon. Taddeo di Bartolo, *The Last Judgment*, *c.* 1394. Collegiata di San Gimignano, Tuscany, Italy.

abject traits were said to predominate. For some, visions of the iron utopia of Sparta rose, mirage-like, as an extreme counterpoint to the creeping softness that fat could represent. By locating fat, fatness and fattening within the interrelated vertical tensions between animal and human, slave and master, feminine and masculine, and European and Asiatic, the Hellenistic world stocked the cultural imagination with vivid stereotypes that would persist in various forms through to the twentieth century.

Early Christianity built upon Hebrew and Hellenistic foundations while adding important new ingredients. It sharpened the agricultural implications of fat, fatness and fattening by radicalizing the animal/human divide and by accentuating the transcendent potential embedded in Platonism. Vertical tensions between different iterations of 'high' and 'low' were retained and reimagined. Plato regretted that most people behave like prey animals who, while indulging their appetites and fattening themselves on food, always look downwards and shun all that is higher. So too would Christians insist that one must transcend animal appetites to seek the heights of truth. One key difference is that among early Christians (and the thinkers who inspired them), fat was closely linked to the heavy, clinging and putrefying filth of the material world, literally weighing down and frustrating the soul's upward trajectory. This pronounced connection between fat and filth was not confined to the patristic era, but was reinforced and refined by medieval theologians who continued to evoke it as ways of materializing their obsession with flesh, sinfulness and decay. Fat was thus located within new vertical tensions between clean and dirty, sacred and profane, and Heaven and Earth. If the Greeks and Romans could look upon fat bodies with some admiration, but often with humour and contempt, Christian writers were fully capable of viewing them with disgust. In so doing, they contributed to the hope of attaining a perfected body that is no body at all, a paradoxically incorporeal body. To one degree or other, such images and ideas would prefigure and structure Western cultural stereotypes about fat people for centuries to come.

FIVE

NOBLE FAT?

Corpulence in the Middle Ages

During the fourth century CE, around the same time that the fat sinners of Antioch were getting a good lashing from Chrysostom's golden tongue, over in the Western Roman Empire Vegetius was writing his influential text on military training and strategy. Addressed to an unknown emperor, the *Epitoma rei militaris* spoke of the importance of discipline and exercise in forging capable soldiers. As the best ones had been trained up from youth, one had to pay careful attention to boys being considered for the soldiering life. Applying the physiognomic insights of the day, Vegetius reflected upon the traits that humans shared with other animals and naturally sought only the noblest qualities. The creatures Vegetius thought best illustrated the difference between noble and ignoble physiognomies were bees, which had a very positive reputation in the ancient world. Not only did these industrious and intelligent little insects possess armies and the capacity to wage war, but their social organization consisted of three tiers occupied by drones, workers and a 'king'. In apian society, it was the drones that were most contemptible, at least when mapped onto human hierarchies. By consuming what other bees produced while doing no work themselves, they fit easily into ancient models of parasitical consumption and status hierarchies. Given that drones consume a great deal, Vegetius warned that any boy with a 'fat, cowardly paunch' most likely possessed shameful drone-like qualities. In addition to possessing modest bellies, would-be soldiers should instead have keen eyes, long fingers, broad chests, muscular shoulders and brawny arms. Their buttocks should be slender, and their calves and feet not 'swollen by surplus fat but firm with hard muscle'.[1]

Saturated as it was with classical values, the *Epitoma rei militaris* would become a widely read manual for the training of medieval knights, the bodies of whom were expected to be aesthetically pleasing as well as hardy and battle-ready. Such ancient ideas were not transmitted wholesale to medieval readers. Rather, a good deal of borrowing, condensing and reordering of available translations over the centuries meant that classical thought was received in a fragmentary and selective manner as it was adjusted to function in a Christian context. Medieval authors could thus pick and choose from a wide array of texts, often abbreviating them as they saw fit.[2] This chapter demonstrates how medieval and early modern elites drew upon classical ideas about the body while adjusting them for their own requirements. After a general discussion of culinary, medical and aesthetic ways of approaching fat, it examines the tensions that surrounded the bodies of medieval kings whose great size was either celebrated or condemned depending upon circumstances. It ends by offering glimpses into late medieval and early modern ways of using corpulence as ways of denoting moral deficiency or monumental importance.

The Fat and the Lean

There are many reasons to believe that the distinction between the fat and the lean marks 'a tension that runs across the medieval body'.[3] Cycles of feast and famine certainly helped to reinforce the symbolism of repletion and privation, especially among the lower orders. Yet bodily fatness was not always associated with dietary fats. What was mainly consumed on 'fat' festival days was meat rather than fats per se, and the kinds of fats one consumed depended upon a number of factors. If the Romans had privileged olive oil as the mark of a civilized diet, the Germanic tribes that would eventually overthrow the Empire shared a marked preference for lard that persisted through to the Middle Ages – especially in northern Europe, where olive oil was generally unavailable. Deemed inappropriate on the numerous meatless days required by the Catholic calendar, lard was replaced by vegetable oils, and finally butter, as the preferred condiment.[4] In fact, through the use of butter and oil, one could consume just as much actual fat in 'lean' times as during periods of abundance.

Gustatory preferences could be framed in moral terms. Those accustomed to sweet-tasting animal fats sometimes failed to understand the Mediterranean appreciation for the pungency of olive oil. Upon a visit to Constantinople, Bishop Liutprando of Cremona found himself repulsed by foods he considered 'vile and obscene, saturated with oil as though they wanted to get drunk on it'.[5] Among the lower orders, whose diet was largely based on cereals, the relative scarcity of tasty fats understandably made them into the stuff of culinary fantasy. Hence the importance of fatness as symbols of plenty during the Mardi Gras (Fat Tuesday) festivities that encouraged an irreverent 'war' between the fatness of Carnival and the leanness of the Lenten austerities set to begin on Ash Wednesday.[6] Hence, too, the abundance of fatty meats and fattened bodies in popular stories of the Land of Cockaigne, a mythical fantasy world full of food and free of labour. So abundantly were fats available in this 'body utopia' that geese and pigs would be roasted in the manner of ancient hunters, rather than cooked in a pot (according to everyday peasant practice) to preserve as much fat as possible.[7]

The symbolic value of fat as a sign of sensual pleasure and abundance, and therefore of the joys of material life, was somewhat mitigated by what physicians had to say about it. On the one hand, animal fats retained their place in the European pharmacopoeia. In the Middle Ages, as in antiquity, they were prescribed as ointments for the treatment of nerve-related issues as well as various aches and pains.[8] On the other hand, medieval and early modern physicians frowned upon dietary fats and warned against consuming them to excess. Many preferred to treat fats more as condiments than as the centrepiece of a meal.[9] Thus the physician-philosopher Moses Maimonides was not only reflecting Jewish dietary rules when he warned against excessive amounts of fat, notably when derived from certain fish and especially from sheep, the fat of which 'is all bad; it surfeits, corrupts the digestion, suppresses the appetite and generates phlegmy humor'.[10] Since at least the fourteenth century, cookbooks recommended prudence in the use of fats, which in France often meant skimming or 'degreasing' sauces before serving them. Even wealthy people in the Middle Ages seem to have consumed less fat than their seventeenth-century counterparts. This was partly due to its relative rarity and expense, but also because medieval gourmandize was less oriented toward fats generally. Recipes for sauces in medieval English,

French and Italian cookbooks called for little or no oil and butter, instead requiring acidic ingredients like wine, vinegar and citrus juice and thickeners like bread, nuts, egg yolks, liver or blood. Thus, for all of the medieval celebrations of the 'fat' over the 'lean', a culinary appreciation of fats (as well as sugar) would not develop until the sixteenth century or so. As we will see, this was around the same time that Europeans began to emphasize gastronomic refinements leading to the development of 'taste' and to express greater discomfort with very corpulent bodies.[11]

Medieval dietetic advice manuals reinforced what was being said in culinary literature, though the genre only began to flower after the Arab translations of ancient texts during the eleventh century.[12] Of special importance to the development of European dietetics was the work of the Persian physician and philosopher Ibn Sīnā, widely known in the West as Avicenna. Translated into Latin in the twelfth century, Avicenna's works provided an important conduit for the diffusion of Greek medical thought throughout Christendom. Avicenna observed how many illnesses occurred when people who go without food during periods of famine are prone to overeat during more fertile times, thus causing themselves many health problems.[13] Moderate exercise was his recommendation for restoring the body's equilibrium and to expel impurities and residues. Avicenna's prescriptions for weight-loss were partly based on health grounds – here he concurred with Aristotle and Galen – but they were also proposed for the sake of appearances. In his view, 'undue thinness and fatness' were less diseases as such than 'disfigurements' of the body, 'conditions in which the beauty of the form of the body is impaired, either in respect of hairiness, colour, odour or form'. It was for these reasons that Avicenna devoted a fuller discussion of weight-loss and weight-gain techniques as part of what he called 'beauty culture' in the fourth book of his *Canon*.[14] Here, in addition to expanding upon the health problems that excess fat brought, he gave advice on how to 'fatten' certain parts of the body (including the hands, nose, prepuce and penis) by rubbing them until they turned red, which he claimed was a way of directing nutrition to body parts that seemed too small.[15]

The impact of Avicenna and other non-Western physicians on European dietetic literature was considerable. In the eleventh century, the Arab monk Constantine the African combined Avicenna with Aristotle to argue that fatness renders the body more vulnerable to disease by blocking the flow of the spirits and reducing the amount of blood, an opinion that would continue to be cited in centuries to come.[16] The most influential medieval health manual, the *Regimen sanitatis Salernitanum*, also built upon Avicenna. Invoking the theory of the four humours that informed medical thinking throughout the Middle Ages, the *Regimen* explained that the particular combination of humours within a person does not in itself breed virtue or vice (though it may give one an inclination to do certain things). People with 'sanguine' complexions – meaning that blood was the predominant humour in their bodies – could tend to be fat, but they were also usually cheerful and kind. Much given 'to their ease, to rest and sloth' and generally tending toward mental dullness, phlegmatics were also 'inclined to be rather fat and square'.[17] Numerous other regimens followed, often with very similar advice about the importance of moderation. Drawing generously upon Avicenna, the physician Nicolaus Falcuccio counselled his readers to 'abhor fat' in his 1484 compendium of contemporary medical knowledge.[18]

While it is true that possessing a fleshy physique could be viewed as partly reflecting one's natural bodily habit, none of this meant that the personal and physical attributes of different complexions were equally valued. As Henri de Mondeville, royal surgeon to Philip the Fair, showed in the fourteenth century, the various qualities connected with complexion were hierarchically arranged, with the moist and soft characteristically appearing in subordinate, albeit complementary, positions that often corresponded to divisions in medieval society. Just as certain parts of the body are soft and fleshy (buttocks, shoulders) while others are solid and hard (bones, sinews, cartilage), so too were individuals characterized according to their occupations and lifestyles as well as their corresponding effects on the body. Those who regularly lived rough and engaged in strenuous bodily exertion counted among the most 'solid' and 'firm' members of society, and naturally included labourers, farmers, sailors and soldiers. If this group presented the most 'masculine' occupations, the soft and fleshy was a more inclusive category populated by 'children, women, eunuchs, phlegmatic or effeminate men, freshwater fishermen, scholars, bourgeois, monks, and all those who spend most of their time in the shade, leading a quiet and leisured life'.[19] In this portrait of the social body, the more familiar feudal hierarchy of priests, knights and labourers was intersected by one that divided groups into hard and soft, manly and womanly. In a way that is not dissimilar to ancient society, medieval fat occupied a subordinate place in a gendered social hierarchy of textures and characters.

The problematic softness of fat was enhanced by its insulating capacities. Here, as in antiquity, the thickness and insensateness of body fat were said to pose material obstacles to intelligence and even morality. Not only was the derisive term 'fathead' first recorded in the Middle Ages, but the thirteenth-century scholar Bartholomew of England contended that the very composition of the human head consisted of little flesh and fat in order to promote 'sharpness of wit and help of understanding'.[20] As the outward appearance of the body was thought to be a faithful reflection of inner character, many looked to physiognomy for tips on how to read these external features.[21] An authoritative guide for deciphering appearance was the *Secretum secretorum*, which appeared in numerous forms around the same time as the *Regimen sanitatis* and which was for centuries mistaken for Aristotle's *Politics*. In this text the famed philosopher teaches Alexander the Great the finer points of reading bodies. As different versions of the *Secretum* show, ancient inferences about character could be achieved through a careful study of physical traits: 'And who þat es fleschy and right fat on face, he es litel wyse, vnbyhofull and lyeing' [And he whose face is fleshy and quite fat is stupid, useless and lying][22] Other versions of the *Secretum* echoed and elaborated upon this view: 'Whos face is flesshly, he is not wise. Importune, slowe, and lyer he is . . . Flesshe in plenté and harde, grosse witte and intellect it shewith.'[23] A man's belly should be 'menely fatte and not grete', recommended another text in this tradition. If it happens to be large then he is most likely 'a fool, without discretion, proud and lecherous'.[24] No less an authority than Albertus Magnus concurred, declaring men with large bellies to be careless, stupid, vain and lustful.[25] Informed by ancient physiognomic knowledge, fatness would continue to denote a range of unflattering personal qualities.

In addition to designating foolishness and immorality, medieval aesthetic standards held that fatness could render the body ugly, even if this was not typically represented in pictorial form.[26] Maintaining that 'appearance should be especially delineated' when seeking to describe individuals in verse, Matthew of Vendôme drew upon Virgil's *Aeneid* to illustrate the difference between beauty and ugliness in women. He praised the beautiful Helen of Troy for possessing a body that narrowed 'at her waist up to the place where / The luscious little belly arises' and a hand 'that does not shake with flabby flesh'. The lovely Helen posed a stark contrast to the noble woman Beroë, who had been possessed by Iris to orchestrate (on behalf of the goddess Juno) the burning of Aeneas' boats on the beach. The fact that Virgil had written nothing about Beroë's appearance was of no concern to Matthew, who decided that such a woman must have been an oozing and putrefying 'disease of nature' with a belly that 'looms with lust'.[27] Matthew had made his point about what features a beautiful woman should possess, but men were also judged according to appearances. The *Book of the Knight of the Tower*, written in the fourteenth century by Geoffrey IV de la Tour Landry to instruct his daughters on manners, included the tale of a ropemaker's wife caught having an affair with a fat prior. Rather than condemning her for infidelity – with a clergyman, no less – the neighbours seemed more disturbed by her lack of taste in selecting a lover. Since she was already blessed with a husband who was 'so fair and good, wise and rich', how could she have ever 'turned her heart to love such a prior, who had such a great belly and was so thick and fat and so dark and so foul of face and so unrefined'?[28]

Rather than an unproblematic prerogative of elite status, then, corpulence fitted uneasily into aristocratic aesthetic and moral standards. Throughout the early Middle Ages, warrior nobles partly displayed their power through the quality and quantity of the food they consumed. The physical strength that was so closely associated with the warrior caste of noblemen, as well as the meat that distinguished noble meals from the mostly grain-based diets of the peasantry, placed great emphasis on the ability to eat to satiety. William Miller reminds us that, when warriors ate to excess, their gluttony was supposed to be driven by a warrior spirit:

> feasts were cast in the form of competitions in drinking and boasting, so that gluttony was enlisted to the cause of courage; the warrior feasted on his loot, the hero delighted in his drinking bouts, but they were not gluttons in the sense that a good meal ranked first among desires.[29]

This robust approach to eating also legitimated a figurative right to 'devour' that expressed in alimentary terms a nobleman's ability to dominate and thus grow fat off others.[30] The social dominance of nobles over commoners was thus predicated on symbolic anthrophagy or 'cannibalism'. Even those aristocrats who had lost touch with their military past could participate in such symbols. Nobles in Lombardy, for example, took great pride in their plump appearance, especially in the face and head, which distinguished them from social inferiors. Some were so proud of their corpulence that they had descriptions of their bodies carved on their tombstones. One nobleman wished to be remembered as having been 'most florid and robust', while another let posterity know that he was 'of admirable shape' when he died.[31] Yet nobles too acknowledged a difference between healthy and excessive corpulence. The tendency to use food as a marker of social distinction could militate against the development of bodies deemed fit for service. Some wealthy Italians grew so large as they aged that they were ashamed to be seen in public, with some too embarrassed even to sit for a portrait.[32] Being overweight in one's youth could also pose problems. In Lombardy, excessive fat was frowned upon in young women from good families, who were instead expected to be pretty and docile. Physical charms became less important as women aged and were busy running the household.[33] And, as we have already seen, boys contemplating the priesthood could be scrutinized for any signs of looseness or lasciviousness that plumpness might suggest.

The body that was mortified in theology was exalted in the warrior aristocracy. For practical reasons, being 'whole of limb' was crucial for those aspiring to knighthood.[34] Whereas a nobility of the spirit or soul was always acknowledged, noble birth or 'blood' remained a favourite way of indicating aristocratic status. Medieval versions of Vegetius' text reminded readers that excess fat designated an ignoble person, and offered a means of distinguishing true knights from wealthy commoners seeking to pass themselves off as aristocrats.[35] In the thirteenth century such language carried with it a more specific social distinction between nobles and commoners, as Chrétien de Troyes made clear in his description of 'big and fat' bourgeois in *Yvain, ou, Le Chevalier au lion*, whose corpulence was a symbol of how cowardly and unfit such men were to bear arms.[36]

Chivalry books reinforced this impression. The Catalan philosopher and theologian Ramon Llull maintained that the true knight would be known by distinctive physical traits. Insisting that only those with 'whole' bodies were fit to become knights, Llull excluded those with 'evil' bodily features:

> A man lame or ouer grete or fatte or that hath any other euyl disposycion in his body, for whiche he may not vse thoffyce of chyualrye, is not suffysaunt to be a knight.[37]

Bodily wholeness was meant to be as pleasing to the eye as it was functional in battle. In addition to symbolizing the cleansing of sins, the baths that prospective knights took in the company of others the night before their dubbing most likely allowed them to display their unblemished bodies.[38] Bodily stereotypes thus marked distinctions between nobles and commoners, both in terms of beauty as well as fighting capacity. Would it be any different for kings?

Fat Kings

Sometimes credited with miraculous healing powers, kings' bodies were considered sacred in the Middle Ages. They were also positioned between competing ideals and interests, some of them built upon classical ideals about moderation. In a book on food written around 530, the Frankish king Theodoric was warned that

> We who trifle with different foods and different delicacies and different drinks must regulate ourselves so that we are not disordered by overindulgence, but that by living moderately we may keep our health.[39]

Classical appeals to moderation found a potent complement in the ancient suspicion that long periods of peace and comfort were antithetical to the warrior virtues that many considered essential for ruling a kingdom. Although a king had an undeniable right to devour as he pleased, the fattening of the royal body could reduce a monarch to an ignoble form of animality and even 'corruption' redolent of organic putrefaction.

The idea that regular campaigns and warfare were good for kings had been posited centuries earlier in Plutarch's *Moralia*. There the admirer of Sparta described how the once valiant King Attalus II of Pergamon had been so 'completely enfeebled by long inactivity and peace' that he suffered the disgrace of being 'actually fattened like a sheep' by his chief minister Philopoemen.⁴⁰ The troubadour Bertran de Born echoed this fear of corruption through too much peace in the twelfth century, a period marked by 'a profound dis-ease with organic change, an association of nutrition and growth with decay'.⁴¹

> War is no noble word, when it's waged without fire and blood for a king or great potentate whom anyone can scorn and call a liar, and he just relaxes and fattens up! A young man who doesn't feed on war soon becomes fat and rotten [*gras e savais*].⁴²

Hence, perhaps, Sir John Mandeville's contempt when his fourteenth-century travels took him to the 'land of the great Chan' (China). Here he encountered rich nobles who lived out their days 'without doing of any deeds of arms, but live evermore thus in ease, as a swine that is fed in sty for to be made fat'.⁴³

What made these warrior ideals somewhat difficult to realize was the fact that overindulging in food and drink was precisely what proper rulers were expected to do. Striking the appropriate balance between these competing images of the monarch was a challenge both for kings and chroniclers alike. Stories about the Frankish king Charlemagne, for example, present conflicting reports about the qualities possessed by the great ruler. While some commented approvingly on Charlemagne's ability to pack away massive amounts of meat per day, his counsellor Alcuin emphasized classical ideas about the well-exercised and harmonious body that avoided all manner of excess and coarseness.⁴⁴ The king's most famous courtier, Einhard, played up these ancient ideals in his flattering portrait, *The Life of Charlemagne* (c. 830). Despite adopting a generally moderate approach to eating and drinking, fuelled partly by his contempt for drunkenness, Einhard's Charlemagne was an avid swimmer and equestrian who could not go for long without food, complaining that religious fasting made him ill. Here was a king with a 'large and powerful' physique marred only by a rather short and thick neck and a belly that 'seemed to stick out'. Happily, though, 'the symmetry of the other parts [of his body] hid these [flaws].'⁴⁵

Whatever Charlemagne's actual eating and exercise habits had been, in medieval France ideals of royal moderation were often honoured in the breach. As the most powerful of nobles, kings were naturally expected to eat ... well, like kings, and many were renowned for putting away astounding amounts of food. So ingrained was this idea that stories were told of nobles who failed to attain the throne due to their dietary *restraint*. One such tale was told after the break-up of Charlemagne's empire following his death. According to Liutprando of Cremona, the real reason the Carolingian dynasty came to an end in 888 was because Guido, the duke of Spoleto who was being considered for the throne, was too frugal an eater to be a proper Frankish king. This opinion of Frankish appetites was registered by others. 'No one who is content with a modest meal can reign over us,' the Archbishop of Metz is said to have declared.[46]

Evidently the last Carolingian emperor, known to history as Charles the Fat (Charles III), had set quite a precedent. But did majestic girth necessarily elicit awe? In Charles's case, being fat may have been his most noteworthy quality. Widely considered a hapless occupant of the throne, he was singularly lacking in martial virtues and good judgement. Repeatedly bending his ear to bad counsel, Charles failed to mount a proper defence against the invading Vikings and thus brought shame upon his army. Some even questioned his sanity. As a young man, Charles had a mystical vision, leading him to declare that he wanted to abandon the world and no longer wished to have intercourse with his wife. (She claimed he made good on this vow, which may explain why Charles left no legitimate heir.) As it was, the troubled king was deposed by his own nobles in 887, and died (most likely murdered) the following year.[47] Whatever one may think of Charles's record as a king, however, it was not a fat man who had acted so ignobly. The corpulence that would be his most distinctive trait developed not long *after* Charles lost power, so that when the disgraced monarch was later dubbed *Karolus pinguis* (no earlier than the twelfth century, it seems) the label was hardly meant as an honour. 'Fat' retroactively – and negatively – characterized his short and pathetic reign.[48] While he was king, it seems, Charles was a fat man trapped in a thinner man's body.

If Charles would not be the last fat king, others who had grown corpulent with age had at least done remarkable things during their younger and leaner years. William the Conqueror had famously invaded Britain before becoming so fat that he decided to go on a diet. Unsurprisingly, the rather counterintuitive regimen he set for himself (bed rest and plenty of alcohol) failed to work, so by the time he died in 1087, William had grown so large that his corpse had to be broken in order to fit into his sarcophagus.[49] The size that William had finally attained was more than would have been thought appropriate for kings, and in the centuries to come the bloated old monarch would be unfavourably contrasted to the young lion who had conquered Britain. Similar problems faced fat kings in Spain. In the tenth century, Sancho I of the kingdom of Léon was so fat he could not mount his horse and even walked with great difficulty. His girth became a political liability when, shortly after ascending the throne, he became involved in a dispute with the Umayyad caliph, who wanted him to honour a truce made with Sancho's predecessor. Rejecting the truce, the caliph attacked Léon and prompted nobles to replace the king. Fleeing to Pamplona, Sancho petitioned the caliph to help him retake his throne, which was only accomplished after Sancho lost weight under the supervision of the Jewish physician Hasdai Ibn Shaprut. Although in 960 a now slimmer Sancho retook the throne with a large Muslim army, history would continue to remember the rejuvenated king as 'the Fat'.[50] Insofar as such imagery drew from a common Hellenistic source, it is not surprising to see that it appeared in the Byzantine world as well as in the Latin West. Chroniclers' depictions of the short reign of John Komnenos, also known as 'the Fat', heaped contempt upon the pot-bellied and sweating usurper who was as greedy as he was 'fat in the head'.[51]

The Capetian dynasty that followed the Carolingian collapse set no records for royal slenderness. Like many Capetian kings, Louis VI (1078–1137) was also a big man. His father Philip I (sometimes called 'the Fat') had been heavy too, but he was also widely seen by chroniclers as weak and ineffective, his appetites for food and sex apparently stronger than his taste for war. In an era when religious zeal and a passion for conquest drove many nobles to perform glorious deeds, Philip instead immersed himself in his own pleasures and pastimes. This included dallying with women much younger and thinner than his wife, Bertha of Holland, whom the corpulent Philip hypocritically repudiated for being too fat. For these and other reasons, the chroniclers of the day were not kind to Philip. William of Malmesbury ridiculed him as a glutton 'belching from his daily surfeit of food', while Orderic Vitalis called him 'indolent, fat, and unfit for war'.[52] Would his son, Louis, fare any better?

Much of what we know about Louis VI comes from his counsellor Suger, abbot of St-Denis, who hoped to enhance the prestige of his abbey by exaggerating the virtues of his lord. Known as 'the Justiciar' and 'the Battler' in his day, Louis was celebrated in Suger's biography as 'the Glorious' (*gloriosus*). Seeking to curry favour with Louis' successors so that his abbey would prosper, Suger fibbed in order to put a positive spin on the king's reign. Perhaps with his subject's future girth in mind, Suger suggested a parallel between the growth of the royal body and the expansion of the realm. We learn that the virtuous young Louis had a handsome and 'graceful' body that was growing so tall that 'his future realm held immediate promise that the kingdom would be honorably enlarged.' Regardless of his size, Louis had an appetite for war that his father lacked. By the time Louis gathered his forces to crush the treacherous counts of Auvergne in 1122, 'his body was heavy, weighed down as it was by burdensome folds of flesh.' Out of these masses of flesh Suger spun a tale of heroic self-transcendence. A lesser man would have buckled under the pressure of such weight, for 'no one else, not even a beggar, would have wanted or been able to ride a horse when hampered by such a dangerously large body.' Were it not for his 'amazing fervor of spirit' Louis might have resigned himself to humiliating immobility, but he overcame both the weight of his body and the protests of his friends. Not only did Louis get back on his horse but he performed arduous tasks in the heat of summer – 'something even young men shrank from'. The indefatigable Louis even 'poked fun at those who could not bear it'.[53]

By the time he was 46, though, Louis had grown so fat that he could no longer mount his steed. Yet while Suger allowed his version of the king to endure some less dignified moments – such as when Louis 'had to be carried through narrow passages in the swamps on the sturdy arms of his men' – for the most part the abbot expressed sycophantic awe at his lord's strength of character. This was particularly evident when the king exacted an awful revenge upon the troublemaking Thomas of Marle, Lord of Coucy, who was notorious for his brutal treatment of peasants. Leading an attack on his enemy's castle, Louis 'summoned amazing zeal and, despite the weight of his body, led his host across steep slopes and along paths blocked by woods, paying no regard to the danger'. Yet not even the mighty Louis could sustain this level of endurance. When the end finally came, it was not because his spirit had wavered. Rather, 'the weight of his fleshy body and the toil of endless tasks had quite beaten down the lord king Louis.'[54]

As one might expect, the enemies of France did not pull their punches when recording the death of a king who seemed just as pathetic as his father. The English chronicler Henry of Huntingdon wondered, 'What can be said of Philip, the French king, and his son Louis, who reigned in our time, whose god was their belly, a deadly enemy indeed?' Henry had some choice things to say about father and son:

> For they ate so much that they lost their strength in fatness [*pinguedine*] and could not stand up. Philip died of fatness [*pinguedine*] long ago. Louis has now also died of fatness [*pinguedine*], while still a young man.[55]

Even French chroniclers seemed to have been disgusted by their lord. When disenchanted clerics later changed Louis' honorific to *grossus*, the new name stuck.[56] Despite Suger's best efforts to glorify the king, then, posterity would know his royal patron as 'Louis the Fat'.

Excess flesh played a role in constructing the reputations of medieval kings, but the meaning of that flesh depended to a great extent on whether contemporaries thought ill or well of them. It also moved the poison pens of foreign enemies seeking any excuse to cast aspersions on their names. Notwithstanding political allegiances that would have tainted any portrait of enemy monarchs, chroniclers were often irked by girth so extreme that it left one incapacitated. In a world where the prowess of knights was closely linked to their horses, being unable to ride or even stand was a potentially damning situation. If feasting was widely seen as a royal prerogative, no one thought that it should distract a king from his political and military duties. This is why the 'empty-headed Frenchman' maligned by William of Malmesbury was also described as 'that tunbelly Louis [*Ludouicum, hominem aqualiculi*], who had been wont to keep his fat self in bed'.[57] Although Louis VI was a far more successful king than his father, his unfortunate sobriquet seems to have been crafted by resentful clerics (the ones who later altered the title of Suger's biography) and reinforced by malicious English chroniclers.

LOUIS VI. dit LE GROS
XXXIX.ᵉ Roy de France,
Mort à l'Abbaïe S.ᵗ Victor en 1137. apres
29 ans de régne.

Celebrated by his adoring biographer as *gloriosus* ('the Glorious'), Louis VI had his honorific changed to *grossus* ('the Fat') by his enemies.

The transformation of 'Louis the Glorious' into 'Louis the Fat' may also reflect historical shifts in expectations about the royal body. The bodies of kings came under closer medical scrutiny as the *regimen sanitatis* genre expanded during the twelfth century. It was during this time that the disappointing Charles III was retroactively dubbed 'Charles the Fat'. Moreover, in the wake of the Black Death of the fourteenth century, physicians became more or less permanent fixtures in princely courts.[58] Ancient analogies between how a man managed his appetites and his ability to govern a city gained a new lease of life. 'A King that cannot rule him in his dyet', warned the English version of the *Regimen sanitatis Salernitanum*, 'will hardly rule his Realme in peace and quiet.'[59] Physiognomic literature also played a role in seeking to curb royal appetites. The various versions of the *Secretum secretorum* were full of health advice implicitly addressed to kings, who were expected to play the role of Alexander the Great receiving the wisdom of Aristotle. We can detect other changes in perceptions of royal fatness throughout this period. If the historian Froissart commented with approval on the formidable meals of the nobleman Gaston de Foix, and drew no link between his regime and eventual death by apoplexy in 1388, disapproval of such excess was becoming more apparent by the late fifteenth century. Not that slenderness had suddenly become de rigueur – excessively thin bodies were never deemed fitting for men or women – but overly corpulent bodies were certainly considered problematic on medical as well as aesthetic grounds. In contrast to Froissart's portrait of Gaston de Foix, Philippe de Commynes' history of King Edward IV of England criticizes the fat monarch, who fled his throne and died of apoplexy without leaving an heir.[60]

None of this put an end to monarchical excess. The thrones of Europe would continue to groan under the weight of fat kings. Yet such corporeal extravagance would remain ambiguous signs of royal privilege. Perhaps the most famous of fat kings, Henry VIII, had been an active sportsman when he was young but gained weight soon after his fall from a horse in 1536. Within four years, Henry's 94-cm (37-in.) waist had expanded to 137 cm (54 in.), as measured by his armourer, and he let his normally close-cropped beard grow out to cover his now prominent jowls.[61] Eventually Henry's weight became such a burden that a mechanical sedan chair was devised to transport him around his various palaces. It was necessary to manage the public impression of Henry's bulk through aesthetic means, thus seeming to transform what some might see as a debilitating mass of flesh into a formidable mountain of strength, an impression somewhat aided by the king's considerable height. Hans Holbein's famous frontal portrait of Henry VIII (1540) discouraged any negative associations between girth and royal power, with its bulky subject defiantly confronting the viewer as a tyrant not to be trifled with.[62] Not everyone was persuaded by this painterly illusion. Overseas, Henry was sometimes known as the

Unable to move about his various palaces without a mechanical sedan chair, the very fat Henry VIII appeared monumental and powerful in the hands of Holbein. Hans Holbein, *Henry VIII*, 1540.

'English Nero',[63] an epithet that rolled his tyrannical reputation into the negative connotations attached to his size and appetites. Unlike other fat monarchs, though, Henry could still be lifted onto his horse to go hawking or to watch his huntsmen round up deer for the slaughter, even if he was too fat to walk or stand on his own.[64] Perhaps this is why no one remembers him as 'Henry the Fat'.

Representing Corpulence

Not long after Henry VIII died, another fat king was profiled in Pierre Boaistuau's popular *Histoires prodigieuses* (1560), 'a sort of Renaissance Ripley's Believe-It-Or-Not' filled with all manner of monsters and bizarre stories.[65] Updating Athenaeus' tale of Dionysius of Heraclea for early modern readers, Boaistuau wrote about a tyrant that he called 'Denis Heracleot', an ancient king who had 'let himself be so carried away by his delicacies [*se laissa si bien trãsporter* [*sic*] *à ses delices*]' that he did nothing all day but eat, drink and sleep. He eventually became 'so fat and monstrous that he no longer dared show himself to people for fear of being mocked and thus remained a recluse'. Some details were altered for late medieval readers – instead of needles, the royal physicians came armed with leeches in an attempt to siphon off 'the humour that had made him fat'[66] – but the overall effect was the same.

The inclusion of Denis Heracleot in the *Histoires prodigieuses* may seem odd. While the fabled king was certainly unusual, he was no wonder of nature like the other creatures depicted in Boaistuau's book. He was, for instance, no match for the armless bat-winged hermaphroditic fish/bird known as the Ravenna Monster that appears elsewhere in Boaistuau's book. Rather than an absolutely singular being, as many other monsters were known to be, Heracleot represented an emerging category of people who were said to have made themselves into monsters through immoral deeds.[67] It was thus riotous living and lack of restraint that caused Heracleot to become 'fat and monstrous' all on his own. Even if he had possessed a humoral predisposition to become overweight, by leading a life of excess Heracleot had recklessly 'let himself' become a monster, thus personifying the perversity of a world out of balance that Boaistuau perceived all around him. Moreover, Boaistuau's withering portrait of Heracleot echoed his related condemnation of those 'gourmands who make a God of their belly'.[68] Growing references to self-made monstrosity may mark a new development in the medical approach to fat, where cautionary examples from the past were regularly deployed to frighten the wayward bodies of the present.[69]

Regardless of the broader import of his comments, Boaistuau made sure to include a woodcut of Denis Heracleot in his book. This, too, was somewhat unusual for the time. In fact, the Western

de gresse que les braceletz de sa femme luy seruoient, d'an-
neaux a ses doigtz, comme les historiens escriuent. Comme

histoire d'un
Roy qui estoit
si gras, qu'il
se faisoit tirer
sa graisse a-
uecques des Sã-
fues.

en semblable ce grand tirant Denis Heraclet se laissa si-
bien transporter a ses delices qu'il s'habitua enfin de ne
faire

In the 16th century the ancient tyrant Dionysius of Heraclea was resurrected as the self-made 'monster' Denis Heracleot. Pierre Boaistuau, *Histoires prodigieuses les plus mémorables* (1560).

tradition features few artistic representations of very fat people prior to the Renaissance. The fat wine steward in Giotto di Bondone's *Wedding at Cana* (1304–6), one of the frescoes he painted for the Cappella Scrovegni, was among the first European depictions of corpulence since ancient times, and it illustrates some of the insights taught by medieval physiognomy. Unaware that Jesus had miraculously turned water into wine, the steward concludes that the bridegroom has departed from convention by saving the best wine for last. With his rotund body mirroring the shape of the jugs around

Giotto's *Wedding at Cana* offered one of the first European depictions of corpulence since ancient times. With his rotund body mirroring the shape of the jugs around him, the incredulous wine steward stands as a grotesquely foolish counterpoint to the faithful (and slender) guests. No merriment is evident in this depiction of the foolish fat man. Giotto di Bondone, *Life of Christ: Marriage at Cana*, 1304–6. Cappella Scrovegni, Padua, Italy.

him, he stands as a grotesquely foolish counterpoint to the faithful and obedient guests. Like other figures of folly painted by Giotto, the fat steward was not meant to be viewed sympathetically. Grotesque bodies were often laughed at freely in the Middle Ages, especially when physical deformity was used to represent vices and villainy. No merriment is evident in this depiction of the foolish fat man. The laughter elicited by such grotesqueness would have been 'neither innocent nor good-natured, but knowing and condemnatory'.[70]

There is a social dimension to these representations that cannot be overlooked. If what is often called the twelfth-century 'renaissance' witnessed a resurgence of ancient ideas about healthy living it was also the time when recommendations about the proper comportment of the body were codified to form a genre explicitly aimed at polishing the manners of elites. It was not simply the fact that doctors began to speak of bodies as 'fortresses' and 'towns'. Rather, just as cities were constructed with walls to separate city-dwellers from peasants, so too were emotional barriers being erected to distinguish increasingly refined urban lifestyles from the coarser habits of the countryside.[71] Such boundaries were at once social and personal, with deviations from what would eventually be called 'civility' increasingly associated with the boorish manners of rural folk. Far from being realistic portrayals of rural life, representations of peasants were often satirical and designed to convey social criticism. Usually painted by and for members of the higher orders, they often flattered the perceived superiority such elites would have felt in relation to country folk, a practice that resembles the ancient delight in depicting slaves as grotesquely misshapen and fat. The literature of the time supports this stereotype, with the Miller in Chaucer's *Canterbury Tales* depicted as extremely stout and boorish.[72] The late medieval woodcuts of Hans Weiditz also reinforced this conceit, revealing how corpulence could be viewed as a telling sign of idleness, immorality and intemperance among the coarse lower orders.[73] Even scenes of peasant revelry often emphasized their tendency toward immoderation in eating and drinking as well as senseless violence, thus painting common folk in unflattering terms.[74]

Social tensions between refined and grotesque bodies were complemented by the war of images that accompanied the Protestant Reformation. Irrespective of ideas about physical beauty, fat members of the clergy were favourite targets of reformist anger, not least because their corpulence was widely viewed as a symbol of the Church's corruption. An early adherent to the reformist ideas of Jan Hus, Petr Chelčický criticized the hypocrisy of fat popes and bishops who lived large while others were starving. He lashed out at the leading members of the Catholic hierarchy, those 'honourable men, who sit in great houses, these purple men, with their beautiful mantles, their high caps, their fat stomachs'.[75] In a gesture common since antiquity, Chelčický condemned corpulence as one among several symptoms of *luxuria* and corruption. The idea that one group fattened itself at the expense of others resounded in a number of domains. For instance, usurers figure among the corpulent sinners damned in the fifteenth-century Last Judgement mural in the Cathedral of Saint Cecilia in Albi, France.[76] Similar claims could even be exploited in order to

In Dürer's depiction of *The Twelve-year-old Jesus in the Temple*, a stout rabbi is astounded by the boy's spiritual wisdom. Building upon biblical motifs, it is as if the insensate 'fatness' of his heart had grown to engulf his entire body. Albrecht Dürer, *The Seven Sorrows of Mary: Twelve-year-old Jesus in the Temple*, c. 1494–7.

In the battle of images that attended the Protestant Reformation, Martin Luther's allies transformed his bulky body into an icon of immovable force. Luther himself saw a difference between 'good' fat that was solid and 'bad' bloating and flabbiness, and even joked that he would 'give the worms a fat doctor to feast on' once he was dead. Lucas Cranach the Elder, *Martin Luther*, 1551.

take swipes against Jews, whose marginal existence in medieval Europe was reinforced through all manner of superstitions and persecutions. The depiction of fat Jewish leaders became a common feature of religious art during the fifteenth and sixteenth centuries. Albrecht Dürer's painting of *The Twelve-year-old Jesus in the Temple* (1497) features a very stout rabbi apparently perplexed by the boy's wisdom, as if the insensate 'fatness' of his heart had grown to engulf his entire body. Such exaggerated features went hand-in-hand with other stock representations of Jews, which often included hooked noses, puffy lips, enlarged mouths and bulging eyes.[77]

Despite these pointed depictions of corpulence, representations of large bodies remained subject to multiple interpretations. If the fat bodies of bishops, popes and Jews could be exploited as commentaries on luxury and vice, stout bodies could still be admired as signs of healthy fullness and monumentality, at least when represented in the right way. This is evident in the case of the religious reformer Martin Luther. Having been slender in his youth, Luther had filled out by the time of the Diet of Augsburg in 1530, ultimately becoming so fat that he was largely immobilized during his later years at Wartburg Castle. Citing the inevitable edibility – and corruptibility – of 'fattened' things, Luther even joked that he would 'give the worms a fat doctor to feast

Early modern representations of peasants were often satirical and designed to flatter the supposed superiority of elites. This resembles the ancient delight in depicting slaves as grotesquely misshapen and fat. Hans Weiditz, *A Fat Man and a Wheelbarrow*, c. 1521.

on' once he was dead.[78] In his writings, however, Luther distinguished 'good' fat from 'bad' fat, drawing the line between what he saw as admirably solid bodies and those that were flabby and bloated. Maintaining that all people would be fattened for their eventual 'slaughter' through death, Luther invoked this old farming image to condemn those who became bloated through feasting and carousing.[79]

Protestant representations of Luther helped to cement the image that many would have of the famed reformer. As Holbein had done

In this rare denigration of Luther's fatness, an anti-Protestant engraving uses the reformer and his wife Katharina von Bora to symbolize the exile of Lutherans from Bohemia after the Battle of the White Mountain in 1620. Eduard Fuchs, *Die karikatur der europäischen völker vom altertum bis zur neuzeit* (1901).

with Henry VIII, Luther's supporters transformed his bulk into an icon of immovable force. Although one late image, in an obvious emulation of Weiditz's 1521 engraving, depicted a very fat Luther carting his beer-swollen belly on a barrow,[80] the overall impression of Luther's monumentality was persuasive and durable. Not even Luther's Catholic enemies, whose frequently chubby bodies were often skewered by his prose, were inclined to use it against him. While happy to depict the heretical reformer as a pig, more often than not they represented his body as slender. As Lyndal Roper proposes in her insightful analysis of Reformation visual polemic:

> so successful had Lutheran propaganda been in presenting Luther's presence as physically powerful that Catholics found it hard to wrench its meaning back to suggest corruption or lassitude.[81]

*

The parallel iconographic traditions that coexisted during the Reformation reveal the instabilities in representing fat bodies that have persisted in the West. Luther was not the only divisive figure of the period to have his physique appropriated for polemical purposes. The Swiss physician, botanist and occultist, Paracelsus, outraged many by rejecting the entire Galenic medical tradition, as well as ancient ideas about the four elements, by arguing instead that the world was primarily composed of salt, sulphur and mercury. In a strategy not unlike

FAMOSO·DOCTOR PARESELSVS.

By depicting Paracelsus as a monumental fat man, the controversial physician's supporters hoped to project his formidable reputation. Paracelsus himself said that dry and muscular bodies are the healthiest, and likened the moist and fat body to 'a field that has become too rich, and is thereby ruined so that the fruits rot too quickly'. After Metsys Quentin, *Portrait présumé du médecin Paracelse*, 1465.

that pursued by Lutherans, the defenders of Paracelsus also waged a war of words and images that included the deliberate representation of their hero as fat. By depicting Paracelsus in monumental terms, they hoped to enhance impressions of his formidable reputation and the credibility of his ideas. For them, fatness signified gravity and power rather than weakness.[82]

While it is unclear how Paracelsus himself felt about being depicted in this way, what the controversial doctor had to say about fat reveals the tension between the monumentality of corpulence and the problems that additional flesh could bring. 'A sound and firm nature consists in a dry body,' Paracelsus wrote, 'not a fat, adipose, and humid one. A dry and muscular body is the best and healthiest.'[83] That corpulence was a moral as well as a medical issue was briefly spelled out in his *Opus paramirum*. In addition to harming the digestion, Paracelsus explained, overeating makes parts of the body 'too rich' (*zugeyl*) and the flesh excessively fat, oily and soft/effeminate (*lind*). Such a body was like

> a field that has become too rich, and is thereby ruined so that the fruits rot too quickly; or like a field that has been spoiled by too much rain so that its fruits rot in it or it manifests its nature in some other way.

This phenomenon, he said, was best understood through the concept of *luxus*, which was freighted with all of the sensual connotations of opulence, indulgence and dissipation conveyed by the Latin term *luxuria*.[84] By making such links between fat bodies and organic overgrowth leading to decay, Paracelsus tapped into a pool of ancient agricultural thinking that remained operative through the Middle Ages. As the next chapter shows, Paracelsus was not alone in thinking about fat with reference to soil, plants and animals.

SIX

THE FAT OF THE LAND
or, Why a Good Cock
Is Never Fat

The phrase 'A good cock is never fat' (*un bon coq n'est jamais gras*) is one of those folksy old sayings whose origins are hard to identify. Although recorded in the early seventeenth century, like most proverbs it was probably in use long before being committed to paper.[1] And, as one might guess, this pearl of wisdom worked on a number of levels, few of which concerned the finer points of roosters. In traditional rural society, the virile man was one whose body retained a moderately rounded shape through vigorous toil and frequent copulation – activities that most assumed would prevent him from becoming fat. Like any other exercise capable of causing fatigue, sexual intercourse involved heat-generating exertion thought to be naturally conducive to weight-loss. Like a rooster among hens, such a man was able to sire offspring, exert dominion over females and children, and maintain his status among male peers. While the fat man may have been capable of signifying enviable levels of prosperity and health, he could just as easily have been associated with laziness, an avoidance of the strenuous work that would ordinarily keep a body trim. In this hard-working culture, as other proverbs tell us, 'a good cock is always thin [*un bon coq, c'est toujours maigre*].' For those who still thought that the *coq* in question really did refer to a rooster, other proverbs made their point in the baldest of terms: 'A working man should not be obese [*Celui qui travaille ne doit être obese*].'[2] Not unlike Vegetius' drones, fat men consumed what other bees produced while doing little or no work themselves.[3]

Proverbial sayings like these are repeated over the centuries because they encapsulate what many consider to be common-sense knowledge about the world. Functioning as 'generationally tested strategies of wisdom', they seem to speak with 'a continuous claim of moral authority and didactic intent'.[4] Proverbs may also migrate from their original location. Indeed, rural ideas about fat and potency resonated in urban contexts long after medical knowledge had largely ceased to draw analogies between the human body and the agricultural world. As late as the 1880s, French doctors were still invoking barnyard wisdom to make a medical point. 'Among obese men the sexual instinct is in general barely developed; some are absolutely impotent,' quipped one. 'A good cock, they say, is never fat.'[5] Rooted in oral traditions, the sources of proverbs are often hard to determine, and oftentimes the directionality of influence is difficult to determine with precision. Does the idea that inspired 'a good cock is never fat' spring from an agricultural context wherein observations about roosters formed a metaphorical basis for thinking about men? Or are they simply rural versions of ideas formulated and disseminated by elites, in this case physicians and their patients interpreting male bodies?

Solving the riddle of which came first, the cock or the man, is not the aim of this chapter. Of more immediate relevance is the question of how European concepts of fat, which had been understood with reference to agricultural ideas since antiquity, continued to be imagined in this way into the eighteenth century. Indeed, agricultural metaphors for explaining fertility and sterility are common in Western culture, and have been invoked to explain a wide variety of phenomena, from sexual reproduction and intellectual training to the problems of abundance and morality. Ancient too was the idea that sexual intercourse is a form of physical exertion that generates heat and, when performed regularly, keeps the weight off. We have already seen how Soranus of Ephesus recommended copulation to fat women as a weight-loss technique. By the seventh century, Isidore of Seville was even claiming that the word 'thinness' (*macies*) derived from 'adultery' (*moechia*) 'because immoderate sexual desire makes people thin'.[6] Insofar as fat has been intimately connected to the ways in which plants and animals have been imagined in our culture, it evokes concepts of increase and excess that are agricultural in origin.

This chapter approaches these issues, quite literally, from the ground up. We know that since antiquity fat has been identified as an oleaginous quality of certain kinds of soil, and that the analogical thinking that facilitated a cultural transcoding of bodies, plants and fields extended to non-human animals as well. The fattening of fields that could result in either fertility or decay was seen as having similar effects on animals, representing, as the Roman concept of *luxuria* suggests, a form of 'overgrowth' that was fraught with moral connotations. This ambiguity is also manifested in proverbs about fat, which are capable of affirming as well as negating its links to fertility in fields as well as in bodies. This agricultural framework even made it possible to imagine the 'fatness' of other lands and peoples through an environmental mindset whose core elements, while updated in the seventeenth century, are also ancient. All of these dimensions are haunted by the disturbing yet durable intersection of femininity and decay that are inescapably bound up with many notions of fertility. The sheer ubiquity of agricultural images made fat a very rich substance to think with and the process of fattening a complicated activity indeed.

'Ripeness is All'

In 1573, the French royal surgeon Ambroise Paré described how the human body functioned as a microcosm of phenomena occurring in the natural world. Thus, while explaining how one can discern such natural developments as sterility and drought in people who have been emaciated by fever, he gave the following

> example of fertility: one recognizes it in those who are fat with large buttocks and paunches, so much so that they are bursting in their skin [*ils creuent en leur peau*] . . . it is necessary for them to remain always lying down or seated, because they cannot carry the great mass of their body.[7]

In stark contrast to the almost skeletal figures that represented scarcity in medieval Europe, the body that Paré conjured up was so lush and ripe that it seemed bound to the earth itself, even to the point of being unable to rise from a recumbent or seated position. It resembles the replete and satiated bodies featured in Pieter Bruegel's *The Land of Cockaigne* (1567), painted just a few years earlier.

What Paré conveyed in this portrait of swollen fertility was more complex than an image of beneficial abundance, although that was

Fatty meats and fattened bodies abounded in popular stories of the Land of Cockaigne. Pieter Brueghel the Elder, *The Land of Cockaigne*, 1567.

certainly present as well. Some degree of plumpness could indeed be taken as a sign of plenitude and health. For instance roundedness could be a criterion for selecting a good wet nurse because it indicated a woman who was full of milk.[8] Whereas moderate fleshiness could betoken health and beauty, though, moralists had long frowned upon bodies so swollen that they seemed about to burst. In addition to denoting bursting or exploding through overfilling or gorging, the French verb *crever* used by Paré refers to the force-feeding of animals in order to fatten them for the slaughter, a fate reinforced by the fact that *crever* also means *to die*. Swollen like overripe fruit, Paré's example of exuberant fertility was in implicit congress with decay and death. It was thus similar to Paracelsus' linkage of fat bodies with over-rich soil and rotting produce. To link fatness to fertility, then, was to locate it along an organic continuum in which life and death, fertility and decomposition, were bound up with each other. When Shakespeare declared in *King Lear* that 'Ripeness is all,' (v.2) then, he suggested that everything on the road to 'ripeness' may be seen as development and immaturity, beyond which lies decline, death and decomposition. Shakespeare was not writing about fat at the time. Nevertheless, his view of ripeness may also be applied to the idea of fat as a borderline concept located on the cusp of fecundity and putrescence.

Evoking ancient ways of defining the human being with reference to the earth and plants, Paré's observation rested upon centuries of accumulated opinions about fat, fertility and decay, a constellation of ideas that Piero Camporesi calls 'excremental superfetation'.[9] The fact that classical perceptions of human bodies had always been cross-fertilized with farming knowledge was not lost on medieval thinkers. Well acquainted with the biblical account of the creation of humankind from soil, they acquired their knowledge of classical agronomy from the fourth-century writings of Palladius.[10] Thinkers like Paracelsus could thus wax lyrical about the potential benefits of decay, whether it took place naturally or through the intervention of human art, 'that is to say, by Alchemy'. Such processes might naturally provoke anxiety because, after all, putrefaction suggests 'the change and death of all things'. Yet because such decay was also 'the first step and commencement of generation' it clearly had a positive dimension as well.[11] Fertile soil is life-giving and beneficial precisely *because* it is composed of greasy and decaying matter, thus achieving the 'fecund putrescence' that is essential to organic process.[12] The ambivalent responses elicited by very fat soil found an analogue in corpulent bodies, as an Anglo-Saxon proverb attributed to the Desert Fathers clearly articulated: 'Just as fat earth [*fætt eorþe*] brings forth that which is hidden in it, so does flesh-fat [*flæs fætt*] produce vice [*leahter*].'[13]

The ambiguous feelings aroused by generation and decay may have been particularly concentrated in the substances often used to improve or 'fatten' insufficiently fertile soil by altering their composition and texture. Especially effective for such purposes was animal dung, sometimes fermented with straw to increase its potency, as well as human faeces or 'night soil' carted in from nearby towns.[14] The logic of this ancient farming technique was self-evident to Paracelsus. The 'quintessence' of a living thing, he wrote, is bound up with its material 'abode', and

> if that dwelling-place be dissolved by putrefaction, then the quintessence is received into that upon which it lies . . . Whence it happens that fields are rendered fat and fertile, not on account of the corruption, but on account of the quintessence existing in the dung.[15]

If soil that had been well-fertilized or 'dunged' was frequently described as 'fat', it was mainly because 'fatness' – suggesting richness and fertility as well as thickness and unctuousness – was thought to be an intrinsic property of faeces that could be transferred to the earth itself. Arguing from a very different scientific tradition, the natural philosopher Francis Bacon had a similar idea in mind when he warned farmers not to leave manure on the ground too long before mixing it into the soil: 'the *Sunne* will draw out much of the *fatnesse* of the *Dung*.'[16]

Bacon's words reflect a worldview that may seem unusual today. 'Modern' links between corpulence and excrement are often explained with reference to industrial capitalism's emphasis on efficiency and profit, an economic model of body and society that promotes *metaphorical* equivalences between fat and shit as forms of surplus or 'waste'.[17] Pre-modern culture offered a much more *literal* perspective. Beyond its medical status as a specific kind of bodily excretion, fat was materially related to forms of excrement that appeared at once fatty and fattening. Paracelsus and Bacon were therefore merely observing what farmers knew from experience: faecal matter is capable of enriching fields through the intrinsic properties linked to its nutritious composition and unctuous consistency. So, just as references to fat soil implied the greasiness of the matter itself, the 'fatness' of excrement was no mere metaphor. Fertile fields, as well as the dung used to improve them, were literally greasy as well as 'rich', which perhaps explains why the concepts of surplus and fatness so often seem to imply one another. Indeed, the agricultural concept of 'richness' seemed to require, as the agronomer Walter Blith insisted, substances bearing the qualities of thickness and 'filth'.[18] Other agricultural authors agreed. One explained that the best way to turn barren clay into fertile soil was to mix in some of the 'greasie, fat and putrefied substances' found around kitchens and wash houses. Since 'there is nothing more better or proper for the ground than mans ordure', one should be sure to include 'the scourings of common Sewers, especially those through which much of mans urine doth pass . . . there is no better manure that can be used for these kind of grounds.'[19]

Even if manure was literally fat, the metaphorical extensions of such imagery are worth pondering. Just as a 'rich' substance is often said to be thick or viscous, and 'rich' land is that which has been 'fattened' with manure, so too could financial riches (for example, gold) be described in terms of the accumulation or distribution of excremental fatness.[20] The Greek diviner Artemidorus had said as much in his second-century BCE dream book, a text that was widely cited in the early modern era. Describing dung as 'a great surplus', he claimed that

> It is a good sign, moreover, if a poor man dreams that he is sleeping on a dunghill. For it means he will acquire many goods and come into the possession of much money.

In actuality dung is only converted into gold when it is carted away from the person, which is why the same excrement, if smeared on the body, portends 'hatred, dissension, and injuries' from someone else.[21] Always ambiguous, such associations were capable of suggesting richness and plenty as well as surfeit and waste. Whatever one may think about psychoanalytic associations between infantile anal eroticism and notions of money as 'filthy lucre', by fostering a connection between the fatness of excrement and the excrementality of fat, agricultural logic offered its own ways of imagining filthy richness and the 'filthy rich'. If it is correct to say that 'the stench of shit lingers where gold sleeps,'[22] then perhaps the stereotyped corpulence of the wealthy subtly resonates with the fabled fat of the land.

The ambiguity of fatness and excrement extended to spiritual matters. Insofar as it involved handling manure that was greasy, smelly and bound up with rotten matter, the act of fattening the land was a dirty job with unavoidably excremental connotations. Dung is, after all, an especially potent vital substance capable of evoking strong reactions, even if the long-term benefits of fattening typically outweighed whatever initial discomfort this might entail. Fat fields were frequently viewed as a sign of the earth's life-giving potential, and Christian writers sometimes encouraged readers to look upon the sufferings they might endure as forms of excrement delivered by a caring God to ensure the development of their souls, much as a farmer might when fertilizing his fields. The English Puritan Jeremiah Burroughs thus likened the deeds committed by wicked men to the manure husbandmen used to render the ground more fruitful. 'God suffers wicked men to gather up all the filth that can be, and cast upon his people, which is but as dung to make fat the soil, the hearts of Gods [sic] people.'[23] After all, as John Bunyan reminded readers a century later, hadn't Christ himself said in one of his parables that he would fertilize the soil to make the barren fig tree grow? 'You know dung is a more warm, more fat, more hearty, and succouring matter than is commonly the place in which trees are planted.'[24] Uttered centuries after Philo and Porphyry, such references to 'fattening' the soul echo some of the distinctions early Christians made between the 'good' fat of the spirit and the debased fat of the flesh.

The fact that readers had to be reminded of the benefits of fat dung suggests that admiration may not have been their initial reaction. Even though European responses to excrement have sharpened since the early modern period, we should not assume that ancient and medieval peoples were unmoved by the sight, scent and feel of shit.[25] Among Christians, the rankness of manure and of overly fertile lands have elicited disgust responses since at least the late second century. Back then, some Christian apologists challenged assumptions about the inherent goodness of the earth by pointing out how defiled it is with excrement and corpses. Such views were not put to rest in the Middle Ages, when concerns about rottenness and excrement continued to provoke alarm among theologians, who were repulsed by the idea that the bodies of believers had first to undergo putrefaction in the ground before being resurrected at the end of time.[26] From its links to putrefaction and muck, fat slipped easily into carnality in general. Claiming that the name 'Gethsemane' refers to a 'vale of fat things' – a low place into which refuse flows to make it 'rich' – Anthony of Padua thought it fitting that Jesus would have been betrayed in a place frequented by those 'who take their ease in the vale of carnal pleasure, besmeared like pigs with the filth of temporal riches'.[27] And, as we have already seen, images of grease, fat and filth were used by medieval theologians to give sinners a preview of what awaited them in the bowels of Hell.

All of this helps to explain why overly fat fields were capable of symbolizing foulness and decay as well as life-sustaining abundance. As William Langland had indicated in *Piers Plowman*, the most fertile fields were those capable of generating excessive and unwanted growth: 'On fat lond ful of donge foulest wedes growth.'[28] So if in his *Ship of Fools* (1494) the Alsatian humanist Sebastian Brant was able to condemn the sin of gluttony without ever mentioning corpulence, he could still invoke the rankness of thick and fatty substances to make a moral point about greed. Men who married older women for their money, he claimed, are like fools who 'seke and grope for the vyle fatnes' under an ass's tale, gathering 'fowle dunge and ordure' as if it were treasure.[29] Such imagery easily rounded back on bodies themselves as others enlisted the less savoury dimensions of fatness and excrement in order to criticize corpulence. The German knight and scholar Ulrich von Hutten criticized sportsmen whose 'entire art consists in fattening themselves up'. In addition to risking an early grave, he insisted, such men let their minds 'lie buried in blood and fat as if in a dung heap . . . incapable of higher things'.[30] Mental and spiritual transcendence were frustrated by flesh and blood, fat and shit.

Medieval and early modern responses to fat, faeces and other vital substances were therefore complex and often contradictory. The agricultural logic that put the bite in Hutten's snarky comment about athletes allowed him to articulate a further dimension of fat and farming: overly corpulent bodies rarely yielded perceptive or subtle minds. Here, too, the ideational roots run to antiquity. In the Greek and Roman eras, teaching and culture were seen through the farming imagery of the sowing of seed, with students frequently likened to 'soil' and the teaching of virtue explicitly associated with cultivation.[31] Such ideas were reinforced by Hebrew and Hellenistic observations about the insensateness of fat as well as the perceptual and even moral insensitivity that sometimes seemed to flow from it, all of which enlisted ancient support for images of the fat person as foolish and even stupid. Matters were not helped when one considers the analogies often drawn between the lethargy and dullness of certain domesticated animals and mental processes perceived as thick, slow and 'gross' (that is, without refinement). Proverbs provided an important conduit for the selective transmission of ancient ideas into medieval and early modern Europe. The English epithet 'fathead' encapsulated the image of a mind encased in insensate thickness, and subsequent proverbs have simply reinforced stereotypes about how fat bodies rarely produce powerful minds. A variation of Galen's old saying about the foolishness of the fat was recorded in French in 1358: 'The full belly will never learn' (*Ja ventre plein n'apprendra*).[32] Similar sayings proliferated in English: 'a belly full of gluttony will never study willingly', 'a gross belly does not produce a refined mind', 'fat bellies make empty skulls', 'fat bodies, lean brains', 'fat paunches have lean pates', and so on.[33]

The agricultural dimensions of fatness pertained to more than plants and soil. If 'ripeness is all,' as Shakespeare put it, it is also the moment when many growing things are considered ready for harvesting and consumption. This highlights the unequal relationship between that which is fattened and those who consume it. A common French term for greasy manure, *l'engrais*, also referred to the act of putting animals to pasture in order to fatten them for slaughter (*mettre à l'engrais, tenir à l'engrais*). In addition to evoking the scent of shit, when viewed from the perspective of animal bodies, fattening also carried a whiff of subordination and violence. Consider the good feelings that would have been conjured up during the summer months in medieval England, a period often known as the *pinguedo* ('time of grease') because this was when the deer were at their fattest and tastiest.[34] It is not difficult to detect the power relations implied in this term. Notwithstanding fantastic tales of the Land of Cockaigne where, among other conveniences, live fish, ducks and chickens freely offered themselves for human consumption, everyone knew that hunters and diners were far more likely to savour the pleasures of the *pinguedo* than the deer themselves. Their role was to grow fat so they could be killed and eaten, which was what was expected to happen to many other animals kept for human consumption.[35] In the agricultural imagination, therefore, the process of fattening indicated an unequal and often unstable relationship in which 'increase' occurred for the benefit of someone else, often at one's own expense.

This unequal relationship applied to humans as well. Even when having grown fat through feasting, an act that under the right circumstances could affirm the mastery of diners over their food, the fattening of humans has never been free of subtle links to animality and violence. We have seen how disparagingly Plato and Seneca wrote of those who fattened themselves out of laziness or overindulgence. In so doing, they suggested, such people revealed their bondage to their own appetites and passions, and perhaps their subjection to the will of others. Given the overarching concerns with mastery and servitude that structured classical thought, it stood to reason that – not unlike sheep who meekly submitted to fattening and slaughter – such complacent persons might actually *deserve* whatever violence was visited upon them. Similes proposing how certain humans can be *like* other animals at other times yielded to scenes of humans being employed *in the place* of beasts. Medieval travellers'

'Ripeness is all.' The fattening of humans has rarely been free of subtle links
to agricultural processes of growth, maturity and decay, all of which point
to the possibility of being consumed by another. The symbolic anthropophagy
so common in the West barely conceals troubling reminders of human edibility.
After Pieter Bruegel the Elder, *Battle between Lent and Carnival*, c. 1600.

tales of cannibalism in far-off lands offered grim reminders that
fattening could also result in being literally consumed. John Mandeville told of merchants on the Island of Lamary (Sumatra) who sold
children who were fattened before being eaten. On the island of
Lammori (Borneo), he added, merchants went from village to village
bearing 'fat men, selling them unto the inhabitants as we sell hogs,
who immediately kill and eat them'.[36] The symbolic anthropophagy
so common in the West – the fact that the dominance of one group
over others could be imagined as a form of devouring – barely conceals these troubling reminders of human animality and edibility.

   This attitude partly explains some of the contempt we have seen
heaped on medieval kings who were too fat to fight, ride or even walk.
The seemingly positive images of wealth, status and power radiated
by elite corpulence were therefore complicated by niggling questions
about the circumstances surrounding such fattening as well as the
purposes that such fattening served. In medieval England, colourful

descriptors like 'great-bellied whoreson' or 'draff-bellied churl' could be hurled as insults precisely because of popular suspicions that the bellies of the rich were swollen with things that had once belonged to the people.[37] The 'devouring' that brought about such worrisome fattening and which haunted medieval conceptions of the social hierarchy was subject to multiple interpretations: as a predatory deed whereby the weak were consumed by the powerful or as mindless feeding that reduced the predator to the level of a dangerous but dumb beast.[38] Hence, perhaps, the Latin parodies produced during the thirteenth century, such as the so-called Money-Gospel, in which the fatness and oiliness of corrupt bishops pose a stark contrast to the slenderness of pious paupers.[39]

Images such as these, we have seen, grew even more intense during the Reformation, when anticlerical images of monks often vacillated from pigs grown fat on excess food and drink to hungry wolves cannibalistically devouring the common folk.[40] As Bruegel's *Battle between Lent and Carnival* (c. 1600) suggests, fatness and fat-tening were, among other things, reminders of human animality, mortality and edibility. Shakespeare's claim that 'ripeness is all' may therefore have some connection to the unpleasant truth disclosed in *Hamlet*: 'We fat all creatures else to fat us, and we fat ourselves for maggots. Your fat king and your lean beggar is but variable service – two dishes but to one table.' (IV.2)

Fat and Infertility

There is another dimension to Ambroise Paré's ambiguous symbol of fat fertility worth exploring. As the surgeon himself knew, associ-ating great corpulence with fertility may have made symbolic sense, but it also contradicted nearly 2,000 years of medical wisdom. Aside from the obstacles to coitus that excess flesh can pose, Paré noted elsewhere, so much blood is expended in creating *la graisse* that the production of semen and menstrual blood is diminished.[41] Just three years after Paré offered his image of organic superfetation, the phy-sician Laurent Joubert published his well-known *Erreurs populaires* (1578) in an effort to dispel common misconceptions about health and illness. Here Joubert contended that it was certainly possible, albeit unusual, for a woman to deliver *nine children at once* provid-ing she was herself quite large – 'the largest size imaginable' – with 'a nice ample womb unencumbered by fat from the parts surrounding it'. Since fat was derived from concocted blood, then, too much of it would prevent such a woman from having 'enough rich blood to run throughout the body . . . to nourish several children at once'. For similar reasons this woman's partner would need to be just as large as she without being 'fat and plump'. Blood not channelled into the production of semen would naturally turn to fat, 'for where there is much fat there is little sperm.'[42] Other physicians concurred. Gesturing towards the contradictory tendencies of proverbs, Louis de Serres contended that the common saying that 'good fat is never attached to bad flesh' (*iamais bonne graisse ne se prend à mauuaise chair*) simply does not hold when it comes to human fertility.[43] To the extent that the ambiguity of fat often generated positive as well as negative proverbs, this author could easily have turned to several other rustic sayings to support his claim, such as 'Fat flesh is flesh of ice' (*Chair graisse, chair de glace*)[44] or 'The fattest is the first to rot' (*Le plus gras est le premier pourri*).[45]

As usual, the roots of such ideas extend to earlier periods. This medical belief in the potential sterility of fat people, originated by the Hippocratic authors and further developed by Aristotle, found a conduit into the Middle Ages through the sixth-century writings of Aetios of Almida.[46] Fat, we have seen, was viewed as a particular concoction of blood that, under other circumstances, might have been turned into semen or breast milk. Its presence in large quantities implied a potential deficit of these other vital substances. One pioneer of medieval physiognomy, Michael Scot, thus declared that men and women who were fat (*pinguis*) but could not purge themselves of excess humours through coitus (such as members of the clergy, at least in theory) naturally fell ill.[47] The Bishop of Paris, William of Auvergne, contended in the thirteenth century that fat men were sexually disadvantaged. Having gathered anecdotal evidence from women who had confided their problems in confession, a reading of Aristotle and Avicenna persuaded William of the significance of these reports.[48] Another avid reader of Aristotle, Thomas Aquinas, had come to the same conclusion, declaring that

> animals of great size, which require much food, have little semen in proportion to the size of their bodies, and generated seldom; in like manner fat men, and for the same reason.[49]

Others proposed that insufficient semen was only part of the problem, pointing out that corpulent men were also more likely to have shorter penises and would thus be unable to sow what little seed they had. Why would this be the case? Albertus Magnus explained that the extra bit of flesh that might have extended the fat man's member had already been deposited elsewhere in the body.[50]

From the uneven endowment of the fat man's body, it was but a short jump to a commentary on his virility. Hildegard of Bingen pulled no punches in her withering depiction of fat men. Naturally cheerful and good-natured, she observed, phlegmatic fat men tend to appreciate women 'in their natural weakness because they are also weak'. Men like this 'do not have the full power to plow the earth because they cannot interact with women the way fruitful men can, but rather are unfruitful'. Insisting that fatness and generative power were hardly synonymous, Hildegard arrived at the only conclusion she could: 'one cannot call them men.'[51] Hers was not an isolated opinion, and the implications of male weakness wrought by corpulence could be serious. In medieval Ireland, at least, a woman could divorce her husband if he was impotent or was so fat that he was incapable of performing intercourse.[52]

This tension between fatness and fertility extended to women as well as men. Medieval explanations for female infertility echoed what physicians had been saying since Hippocratic times. Excess fat could pose an obstacle to conception or block the birth canal to prevent delivery.[53] Prescribed methods for overcoming the problem varied from the potentially pleasant to the downright uncomfortable. Some echoed the ancient advice of Soranus of Ephesus, who had recommended more frequent intercourse to women who needed to lose weight.[54] According to the medical compendium attributed to a female healer called Trotula, though, a fat woman seeking help could look forward to having her body anointed with good wine and cow dung before being made to perspire profusely in a steam bath. By doing this several times a week, she should have lost enough weight to be able to conceive. Other manuals recommended bleeding, sleeping on a hard bed and even altering the woman's emotional state to lose weight: anger, anxiety and sadness were all useful for reducing the fatness of the womb. Infertile fat men could expect similar treatment, though their sweating would take place in a hollowed-out 'grave' dug by the seashore. Here, half-buried in sand during the hottest part of the day, the corpulent could sweat themselves to fatherhood.[55]

Just as they described fertile soil as fat, so too did medieval people imagine the womb as a 'field' in which fertilization took place. Accompanying this metaphor was the notion that, as in agriculture, fertility required the presence of waste products that were essential to the germination of 'seed', an extension of the medieval notion that all generation occurs *ex putri* (from putrefaction).[56] Some twelfth-century medical texts even claimed that the womb was 'nature's field', which functioned as a receptacle for the noxious 'bilge water' that regularly accumulated in a woman's body and thus rendered her fertile.[57] If this was a rather common medieval view of 'profoundly equivocal' female bodies,[58] it exercised a hold on the cultural imagination, at least as long as sexual reproduction continued to be viewed in terms of organic 'generation'. Homologies between soil and bodies would be used to explain fertility for centuries, and the same warnings that applied to farming pertained to women as well. In his *Philosophical Discourse of Earth* (1675), the horticulturist John Evelyn warned that soil that was 'wanton' or 'over-rank (for there may be some too fat, as well as too lean)' had a tendency toward barrenness. Evelyn invited his readers to meditate on how counterintuitive such a statement probably seemed: 'though it seem a Paradox that any Soil should be too rich,' he explained, ''tis yet a Truth indubitable, and holds as well in Plants as Animals, which growing very fat, are seldom prolific.'[59]

To the extent that procreation was often conceptualized through agricultural imagery, it is easy to see how husbandry (referring to the art of farming and the management of household resources) was implicit to the idea of the 'husband' as a cultivator of fields and a sower of 'seed'. Given the supposedly natural impurity of female bodies, 'plowing' such 'fields' was potentially 'dirty' work for any man to perform. So entrenched were such ideas in the cultural imagination that physicians and laypeople alike described the womb as a 'field' well into the eighteenth century:

> Since as all SEEDS do not answer alike in *one Field*, some requiring a Pinguid and Loose *Soil*, others a Lean and Slender *Ground*; so it is With the Womb and the injected SEED.[60]

Once again, agricultural wisdom closely paralleled medical advice:

> that being always best, which is between the two Extreams, and not containing the two different Qualities of soft and hard mix'd, of churlish and mild, of moist and dry; not too unctuous nor too lean.[61]

Even as gynaecological knowledge eventually shed its reliance on agricultural models for conceptualizing reproduction, agronomers would continue to think about soil with references to animal bodies for quite some time. And so, too, would some commentators on human health, such as the Scottish doctor George Cheyne. Writing in the early eighteenth century, Cheyne claimed that the art of fattening bodies that were too thin relied on models given in the wider natural world:

> we must first plump up and extend, and then harden and strengthen. This is the Way of Nature in Vegetation. And thus the Animal Creation, devoid of Reason, rear up their Young.[62]

With or without explicit farming analogies, physicians would continue to view great fatness as being at odds with human and non-human fertility throughout the early modern era and beyond.[63]

The Fat of Other Lands

If the notion of the 'fat of the land' seems rather quaint today, it is partly because our modern urbanized worldview has severed meaningful connections to the agricultural universe within which our predecessors located themselves. As modern soil science increasingly based its findings on chemistry in the nineteenth century, such traditional ideas would come to be seen as relics of a lost world. Almost as a testimony to such changes, in the early 1800s the English philologist Walter Whiter produced a massive etymological study seeking to connect a spectrum of words to concepts derived from ancient relationships with the material world. In this fanciful yet fascinating study, Whiter claims that it is the physical tendencies of 'pudge' (a marshy and muddy lowland) that motivate a number of terms referring to an upward or outward swelling, while the consistency and other properties of pudge (such as its plasticity, stickiness, looseness and softness) structure many others.[64] Whiter may not have realized that the linguistic world he described was already fading away. By the end of the eighteenth century, the adjective 'pudgy', which had indeed indicated the qualities of a marshy lowland, was already being used to describe bodies that were themselves short, chubby and thick. Even as modern culture began to wash its hands of its agricultural heritage, the filthy fatness of the land was smuggled into the vocabulary used to describe corpulent bodies.

In addition to providing ways of thinking about bodies, the fatness of the land was said to have direct implications for the bodies and minds of those who inhabited it. The roots of such thinking are similarly implanted in classical antecedents. The Roman farming authority Columella had considered 'the very best soil' that which had a good combination of the '*pinguis*' and the '*putris*' because 'in producing the most it demands the least, and what it does require is supplied with trifling labour and expense.'[65] The flipside of this image of abundance was the claim that, because they rarely had to labour very intensely to earn their subsistence, people inhabiting such fat lands were more likely to be weak, lazy and cowardly. This is how ancient writers like Arrian and Diodorus Siculus described those inhabiting the astoundingly fertile lands outside of the 'temperate' regions that many Greeks and Romans called home. In his discussion of India, Arrian explained that the great heat and moisture of the environment resulted in extreme fecundity as well as the accelerated development of all living things. Just as fruits were said to ripen and decay there at an unimaginable rate, so too did humans and animals grow, procreate and die at an accelerated pace. So fertile was such land, according to Diodorus, that its inhabitants never had to work very hard to enjoy its fruits. According to classical models of environment and character, such an easy life naturally rendered them soft and complacent. Having circulated widely in the fifteenth century, these ideas contributed to the mental template that Columbus took with him to the Indies, a region that he found 'fertile to an unthinkable degree' and whose seemingly numberless inhabitants were, in his opinion, prolific but short-lived, cowardly and indolent.[66] Fatness could affect character, and did not even have to be inside the body to do so.

So, as the Age of Exploration dawned during the late Middle Ages, Europeans invoked their classical heritage to map the antique geography of softness onto hitherto uncharted regions of the world. These ideas would be systematized with the revival of Hippocratic ideas in the late seventeenth century, which produced a doctrine that refined ancient explanations for human variation based on the interplay of climate, environment and culture.[67] While most of its practitioners steered clear of reducing all of human culture to the effects of climate or the land, environmentalist theory validated a number of long-standing beliefs about the sources of human variation. It extended the Hippocratic explanation for why the Scythians were physically flabby and mentally sluggish as a way of accounting for differences between early modern Europeans and other peoples in the world. This occurred as early as the thirteenth century, when the Flemish explorer William of Rubruck judged Mongol women to be ugly and 'astonishingly fat'.[68] As future chapters will show, he would hardly be the last European to make such observations about certain non-Western peoples.

The revival of Hippocratic ideas was also critical for the formation of what would come to be known as 'the Tropics' in the eighteenth century, a conceptual and geographical space that allowed Westerners to define that which was environmentally as well as culturally alien.[69] When addressing differences in physique, the pioneers of tropical medicine claimed that hot climates were more likely to diminish rather than augment body size, adding that this tendency could be altered through cultural practices. As the physician John Arbuthnot argued, people living in such environments 'are not subject to be fat, for strong Perspiration keeps an Animal from being so', though he hastened to add that exceptions to the rule spring largely from a 'copious Diet and Inactivity'.[70] When people in warm regions grew fat, it was attributed to custom rather than climate, as was sometimes observed in torrid zones like Africa. The same extremes of temperature and humidity that caused the muscles to relax also contributed to such character flaws as timidity, laziness and sensuality. Whether the result of culture or climate, fatness could be seen as emblematic of a 'soft' constitution fostered through specific material conditions. Such environments were thus 'obesogenic' long before this modern term was coined.

One way of understanding this development is to take a brief look at travellers' encounters with Egypt, a land that occupied a special place in European perceptions of fat and flesh. A region of sensuality and excess for the Romans, who told stories of fat tyrants like Ptolemy VII, the home of Philo of Alexandria was imagined as a vast 'land of the body' where the passions were said to dominate the spirit.[71] Writing in the third century, Aelian recorded claims of how Egyptians ascribed to the 'sweet water' of the Nile River the ability to make a person 'grow fat' due to its capacity to help 'build up a mass of flesh'.[72] Early modern encounters with Egypt infused these old images with new life, and seem to have been based on real developments.[73] During his travels in the 1580s, the Venetian botanist Prospero Alpini was struck by how Egyptian women performed the 'art of fattening' by taking warm baths and various drugs as well as by injecting themselves with enemas full of bran, sesame oil and animal fat. Extending classical stereotypes about how softness and indolence reigned supreme in Egypt, Alpini concluded that 'down there' this deliberate cultivation of corpulence reflected a more prevalent 'vice of the flesh' (*carnis vitium*) that had 'invaded the marrow of the people'.[74] Examples of Egyptian sensuality were multiplied in the seventeenth century. Some, like Shakespeare in *Antony and Cleopatra*, reminded readers that this was the feminizing land where Julius Caesar 'Grew fat with feasting' (II.6). In a similar vein, a Dutch travel report updated Egypt's gender-bending reputation by observing that the men of Cairo were so fat that 'they have breasts bigger and thicker than the women.'[75] Egypt was thus a land of flabbiness and effeminacy where, as Hippocrates had said of the Scythians long before, one could scarcely tell men from women.

Perhaps most strikingly, the renowned fatness of Egypt was not restricted to the bodies of its inhabitants. After nearly 2,000 years of lore about the almost magical powers of the Nile, most geographers were well acquainted with the remarkable fecundity of the soil that lined its banks. So rich and fat was this land that, as one French seventeenth-century writer explained, the locals had to 'thin it out [*l'amaigrissent*] by mixing some sand into it'.[76] As was often the case with extreme fecundity, though, the fatness of Egyptian land made Europeans uneasy. The richness of the soil meant that its rank and unctuous qualities could vaporize under high temperatures to permeate the atmosphere. This naturally generated claims for the fatness of the air itself. 'The *Air* of this Country is very hot', complained Patrick Gordon in 1737, 'and generally esteemed extremely unwholesome, being always infected with nauseous Vapours, ascending from the fat and slimy Soil of the Earth.'[77] Geographers also knew that rainfall and melted snow could carry away some of the fatness of the land, thus producing rivers whose water too was 'fat'.[78] This led some travellers to propose that simply drinking the water of the Nile caused ordinary Egyptians to gain weight despite their otherwise modest diet.[79] Greasy fatness thus seemed to be just about everywhere in Egypt: in the land, air and water as well as in bodies. No wonder it would be on the minds of its inhabitants. It was perhaps only a matter of time before traditional wisdom about the cognitive 'thickness' of fat people would be applied to countries where the land seemed to be overly fertile, as if enjoying the bounty of the earth necessarily rendered one 'soft' in mind as well as body. 'A fat Soil produceth a fat Understanding,' John Arbuthnot quipped in a rather obvious play on Galen's famous saying.[80]

Such observations about the fatness of Egypt resonated in claims about other environments outside of the West. For some there was no end to the vices that exorbitant fertility could generate, even when it did not result in barrenness or sterility. Citing prosperity as something that could cause people to turn away from God, one author declared that 'Atheism scarce ever grows but in a fat Soil. The afflicted Person cannot forget God; but the *Prosperity of Fools destroys them.*'[81] People with no need to struggle to earn their subsistence seemed to lack the kind of virtue that came with hardship and labour. 'Exhaustion and labour make man vigilant and virtuous,' claimed the Jesuit historian Jean-Baptiste Du Halde in his study of China. Idleness and earthly delights, on the other hand, give rise to vice: 'Peoples who inhabit fat and fertile lands are usually very voluptuous and not very industrious.'[82] By resurrecting ancient models of climate and culture, proponents of environmentalist theory extended to several non-Western regions of the world classical stereotypes about the softness and effeminacy of peoples who inhabited fat lands. When it came to places outside of the West, then, the fat of the land could yield much more than was expected, and sometimes more than was considered appropriate.

✳

Mobilizing the many connotations that Europeans had attached to agricultural concepts of fertility – from the greasiness of soil and the fatness of manure to the foul vapours that rose from the ground – fat lands offered mixed blessings for those who worked and inhabited them. The same held true for human bodies, where excessive fecundity and overripeness often seemed to promote decay rather than vitality. Perceptions of foreign fertility naturally varied. For some travellers, the extreme fecundity they encountered in faraway lands, particularly in tropical locales, was enough to awaken 'utopian fantasies of sustenance without labour' that invoked any number of mythical antecedents, from the Garden of Eden to the Land of Cockaigne.[83] Yet in other cases such fertility conjured the lingering spectres of *luxuria* and corruption by generating fears of overgrowth in which a once manageable abundance has shifted into self-destructive overdrive. Even if images of the earth as a female body fell out of scientific favour from the sixteenth century onward, it may be impossible to separate these feverish visions of dangerous fecundity from perennial fears of femininity out of control.[84] Depending upon one's perspective, the fat earth could be viewed as a selflessly nurturing mother who gave freely while asking for nothing in return, or as a wanton whore promiscuously offering herself to all comers, infecting them with her voluptuousness and decay while greedily devouring their seed. Those subscribing to this view would have agreed with Herodotus that 'Soft lands breed soft men; wondrous fruits of the earth and valiant warriors grow not from the same soil.'[85] As Hippocrates himself had put it, 'rest and slackness are food for cowardice.'[86]

We may therefore detect in old ideas about the fat of the land some key ingredients of an early modern preoccupation with strong, firm and moderately proportioned bodies. Since in the agricultural imagination the act of fattening diminished even as it increased, there was something oddly compelling about harsh environments that forced their inhabitants to eke out a meagre existence that would leave their bodies lean, hard and virtuous. To persist with the gender metaphor often applied to the soil, some of the most outspoken proponents of classical virtue preferred land whose benefits required more 'masculine' techniques. The inhabitants of Thomas More's imaginary island of Utopia, which he described in 1516, are healthy, strong and virtuous partly because the earth is not overly fertile and the climate somewhat harsh, requiring them to remain industrious and resourceful without being slavishly consigned to endless toil.[87] As steeped as he was in classical thought, it is perhaps not surprising to learn that More had Sparta in mind when describing his utopia.

By the eighteenth century, this rugged warrior ideal would circulate as part of the Neoclassicism that marked the age. The Spartan model was central to the thought of that influential proponent of environmental theory, Montesquieu, who echoed Herodotus by writing that 'The barrenness of the earth renders men industrious, sober, inured to hardship, courageous, and fit for war.' Such hardy and virtuous men 'are obliged to procure by labour what the earth refuses to bestow spontaneously'. Worse off were those people for whom the good earth offered its bounty without requiring endless toil: 'The fertility of a country gives ease, effeminacy, and a certain fondness for the preservation of life.'[88] By being connected up with concepts of material well-being and happiness, the fat of the land could facilitate the moral flabbiness that many Europeans viewed with ambivalence and often attributed to non-Western lands, a topic that will be explored later in the book. How the supposed virtues of hardness and even discomfort informed misgivings about fat is the focus of the next chapter.

SEVEN

SPARTAN MIRAGES
Utopian Bodies and the
Challenges of Modernity

I n 1602, the Dominican priest Tommaso Campanella imagined
a utopian society in which fat people would eventually be eliminated. His 'City of the Sun' was a Platonic republic of virtue,
properly moralized through an injection of Christian piety and
Spartan hardness, where the inhabitants breed according to the
principles applied to animals. Not only do men and women participate naked in public games 'in the manner of the ancient Greeks',
but all practise the military arts in order to prevent indolence and
complacency. They also present their naked bodies before magistrates charged with deciding which couples should be paired to
produce the most attractive children. In this eugenic model of society, Campanella explained that the very fat and very thin are paired
with one another 'so as to avoid extremes in their offspring'. Through
such reproductive intervention the solar city would gradually breed
immoderate bodies out of existence, thus creating a society whose
beautiful inhabitants could expect to live for at least a century.[1]

Neither utopian dreaming, nor the notions of human perfectibility that accompanied them, were unusual in the early modern era.
It was during this time that fears generated by natural catastrophes
(such as fires and storms) and supernatural phenomena (like magic
and witchcraft) 'nurtured the ideal of the healthy, invulnerable,
strong and long-lived body'.[2] Indeed, a renewed appreciation for
classical ideas and a growing focus on secular matters encouraged
interest in the prolongation of health and vitality well beyond what
was normally expected under given social conditions. Beginning in
the sixteenth century one sees the emergence of health manuals,
such as Luigi Cornaro's well-known *Discourses on the Sober Life*

(1563), teaching people how to live for well over a hundred years. It's not surprising that some would imagine societies that took deliberate steps to ensure the health of citizens, even if it meant promoting intrusive government control that may strike our eyes as 'the vision of an early surveillance state'.[3] Indeed, a few decades before Campanella described his perfectly administered world, the philosopher Nicolò Vito di Gozze had already proposed that cities should close their gates to fat people and carefully monitor the bodies of the young. Arguing that every effort should be made to instill healthy habits in children, he warned that those who were not weaned at an early age (eighteen months for girls, two years for boys) risked becoming fat and stupid as they grew older. Seeking to revive what he claimed was an old Spartan custom, Gozze recommended that children who were still too fleshy by the age of fourteen should be exiled.[4]

While such extreme practices were never enacted, the fantasy of taking harsh measures against the corpulent is noteworthy. Nostalgia for lost worlds of physical, moral and martial virtue are certainly traceable to tales of the Spartans, whose iron utopia was predicated on the regular monitoring of bodies for signs of softness and corruption. Fat men, so the story went, could be punished or even banished, while fat slaves were routinely executed and their masters fined. To be sure, not everyone was a fan of Spartan harshness. Plenty of critics over the centuries have frowned on that society's contempt for culture, commerce and comfort. The humanist Lorenzo Valla, to take one example, ridiculed the Spartans for their peculiar attitude towards pleasure: 'they were doubly foolish in this, because they defrauded their own natures, and because they were inclined towards death.'[5] Yet many commentators over the centuries have been impressed by this apparent commitment to virtue, virility and fitness that seems to have been lost in societies that had given themselves over to luxury. Such disagreements about what constituted a properly 'human' life reflect a resurgence in the early modern period of the 'Spartan mirage', that haze of myths, half-truths and misunderstandings that has generated polarized accounts of what life was really like in that warrior state and, more crucially, whether any of it could or should be adopted by non-Spartans. While periodic admiration for Sparta was registered during the Middle Ages, the vision that had once fascinated Xenophon and Plutarch reappeared in the early modern era as Europeans identified themselves ever more closely with what they understood as their classical heritage. This may be why serious theorists of utopia, ancient as well as modern, often borrowed ingredients from Sparta while rejecting fantastic worlds devoted to sensual pleasure, notably the medieval Land of Cockaigne.[6]

Around the same time that Gozze was imagining an ancient precedent for expelling fat children from the city, the French were building their own bridge to a lost world of virtue. For this they drew upon the Greek geographer Strabo, who reported on what the historian Ephorus of Cyme had to say about the Gauls centuries before. Supposedly being 'great admirers of the Greeks', the Gauls were careful 'not to become fat or big-bellied, and that if any young man exceeds the measure of a girdle, he is punished'.[7] When this claim reappeared in the early seventeenth century, it was cited as one reason why the French tended to be more slender than other European peoples.[8] A similar search for a pagan golden age was underway in Germany. There Ulrich von Hutten condemned the gluttony and decadence of his fifteenth-century countrymen, whose daily repasts were 'dripping with fat' as their bodies grew ever plumper. Just as French critics of luxury fantasized about the hardiness of the Gauls, Hutten looked to ancient Germanic tribes for lessons in strength and simplicity.[9]

Numerous studies have shown how the early modern era imposed new rules on the proper size and shape of the body, one effect of which was to stigmatize corpulence as a deviation from emerging aesthetic ideals.[10] By roaming rather freely across several centuries and cultures, this chapter complements these findings by elaborating a different approach to this shift in European attitudes. It examines how a renewed interest in classical virtue, which was sometimes accompanied by a professed admiration for 'Spartan' austerity, accelerated pre-existing misgivings about emotional and corporeal 'looseness' and 'softness' that would have significant consequences for perceptions of fatness, especially in light of the validation of material comfort and consumerism that was also taking place during this time. After outlining the broad contours of the 'culture of tightness' that developed in the sixteenth century and the emphases on bodily control and appearance that it entailed, the chapter shows that fatness posed a challenge that was as emotional as it was aesthetic. It supports this claim by examining the shifting fat/happiness relationship between the Middle Ages and the eighteenth century. It then demonstrates how the risks of material happiness were reflected in political commentaries about how a modern acceptance of 'luxury' threatened to make the body politic itself bloated and unhealthy. The common denominator of all these concerns was a belief in the prophylactic value of hardship and even pain that could inure one against the encroaching flabbiness of modern life. Despite the expansion of consumer pleasures made possible by modernity, 'happiness' did not depend on abandoning oneself to the satisfaction of material desires, but on a willingness to expose oneself to privations designed to heal and elevate. No pain, they say, no gain.

A Culture of Tightness

'Tightening marks modernity.' With this phrase, Georges Vigarello aptly sums up the various processes of constriction and strengthening that accelerated in several overlapping domains of early modern culture.[11] The phrase conveys much truth. It is widely acknowledged that social transformations gave rise to many new developments during the sixteenth century with regard to physical appearance and a new emphasis on the individual self, both as an aesthetic object and a subject of self-control. A much more elaborate concern with physical appearance, inspired in part by the new forms of sociability being promulgated in court life, offered elites new opportunities for personal display as well as an acute sensitivity to the opinions of others. While aspects of this concern with appearance may be found in earlier times, what had changed by the sixteenth century were the minuteness of detail and the refinement of techniques for achieving beauty and reading the body. New injunctions about correct posture, along with more restrictive clothing and prosthetic aids to help achieve it, reinforced associations between physical and moral rectitude, which in turn received further support from emerging beauty ideals that drew attention to the height and upper parts of the female body, especially the face. An increase in individual autonomy was thus crafted out of greater personal constraint as beauty was gradually described as an 'achievement' and modernity came to define itself through the numerous ways in which it fostered attempts to constrict and enclose the body.[12] The culture of tightening also imposed new distinctions between city and country, polish and pollution, that increasingly drove a wedge between the dirt and muck of agricultural realities and the 'clean' bodies of 'civilized' urban-dwelling elites.

As apt as the term is, though, 'tightening' is not the only hallmark of modernity. Insofar as it also gave rise to a culture of luxury consumption on increasingly larger scales, modernity is at the same time marked by the opposite qualities, namely sensuality and self-indulgence potentially leading to laxity and softness. Promoting looseness as well as constraint, modernity creates conditions in which individuals find themselves pulled in different directions. On the one hand, they are encouraged to seek out material comforts and indulgences while, on the other, exhorted to rein in their appetites and to exercise self-control. As is evident from the neo-liberalism of our own day, a dialectic of tightening and loosening marks a central paradox of modernity's impact on the body and its pleasures. If ours is indeed a 'culture of bulimia', its sources are much older than the twentieth century. As we will see below, attention to the bodily exterior depended upon some corresponding assumptions about the passions, emotions and habits, especially since these new constraints emerged during a period that saw the growing acceptance of material comfort and sensual pleasures.

If modernity is to some extent a culture of tightness, it is also a culture of lightness. 'The modern body', as Steven Connor rightly notes, 'inhabits and seeks ethereality.'[13] The rise of gastronomy and gourmandize during the early modern era illustrates an interplay between indulgence and restraint while also charting a course whereby elites aspired to rise above animality. This trajectory is evident in the gradual elevation of the concept of 'taste', which shifted during the seventeenth century from a grossly material and bestial sense to the sign of an almost spiritual form of discernment worthy of cultured elites.[14] The purification of the sense of taste was well suited for the culinary revolution of the eighteenth century. One of the chief aims of *la nouvelle cuisine* that emerged at the time was to make 'food lighter, cleansing it from all harmful materials, which, cooks thought, would make food healthier, as it would become easier to digest'.[15] This purification and even spiritualization of food required disconnecting it from its links to earthiness itself. Contrasts were drawn between traditional eaters whose bodies were weighed down by coarse and earthy food, and modern diners who thrived on the refined 'essences' that the new cuisine made possible. Although not explicitly concerned with corpulence, the new cuisine also sought to improve the bodies that consumed it. The refinement of food made digestion easier, thus freeing the modern eater from those 'animal spirits' that digestive problems generated. As one modern commentator has observed: 'The nouvelle cuisine could satisfy the eater's physical tastes and needs while it liberated him from his body.'[16] Even the notion of a culinary 'delicacy' included assumptions of lightness and ethereality that could seemingly be transferred to the body.[17] 'Hence, more vigour and agility in bodies,' promised one writer, 'more liveliness and fire in the imagination, more breadth and strength in the genius, more delicacy and finesse in our taste.'[18] This paved the way for a more fully developed notion of gastronomy, which by the early nineteenth century elevated the refined eater above all those who seemed to be driven by mere appetite. Animals 'feed', as Brillat-Savarin would famously put it, but civilized people 'eat'.[19]

During the early modern era, conduct at the table became a special focus of attention of etiquette manuals seeking to distance civilized elites from the coarser aspects of animal life, both in terms of the quantity they ate as well as the manner in which they dined. The action and noises of the stomach were particularly circumscribed as conduct manuals sought to erase the process of digestion from polite society.[20] Books on dietetics had become fashionable, and while they didn't obsess over moderate plumpness, they did warn of the dangers of great fatness. Diets of the sixteenth and seventeenth centuries recommended reducing the quantity of food being consumed, with the prescription that one select meats that dry out the body. Animals whose flesh was fatty and greasy were specifically discouraged as physicians tended 'to read danger at the slightest sign of goo or grease'.[21] While the aversion to grease will be explored in more detail in Chapter Eight, similar advice appeared in household medical manuals. This popular genre offered an eclectic mix of recipes and advice that allowed literate gentlewomen to manage the health and well-being of the men and children in their care.[22] If being fat was capable of signifying prosperity and power, the process and corporeal effects of fattening continued to evoke disreputable images of animality that were signified, in part, by the perceived loss of control over the appetites. Alongside the development of gastronomic discernment, the systematic inculcation of table manners reflected a long-term process of deanimalizing the body of the gourmand.[23]

New words came into usage during this period. Referring both to aesthetic as well as health concerns, the fifteenth-century French term *embonpoint* denoted an equilibrium between the extremes of slenderness and fatness. It referred to the moderately plump condition of those who were more or less 'well-made'. The sixteenth-century elaboration of the medical concept of *obésité* (from the Latin *obesitas*, which would find its English equivalent a century later) referred to the state of '*excès d'embonpoint*'.[24] Noting that fatness was detrimental to health, beauty, virility, fertility and intelligence, physicians drew liberally from ancient and contemporary knowledge to frame 'obesity' as a disease.[25] The rise of a new terminology was accompanied by important shifts in the medical model of the body, which was imagined less in the fluidic terms of the four humours than with reference to the firmness or slackness of nerve and muscle fibres. Modernity was marked by movement as well as purification, or, as it is perhaps better put, purification-through-movement. Echoing ancient assumptions that great amounts of fat were not really part of the body proper, early modern gymnastics was conceived as a process of purging from oneself all that is unnecessary, including excess fat as well as bad humours, to reveal 'the pure grain' of the healthy body concealed beneath such 'chaff'.[26] These developments in medicine and gymnastics added more complexity and urgency to the kinds of moral and physical problems that had been linked to consumption since ancient times. Taken together, they contributed to the rather durable notion that modern 'civilization' is an inherently ambiguous phenomenon that destroys as it creates, subtracts as it adds, and may be at the root of many of the physical and emotional problems summed up in the oft-cited 'diseases of civilization' that would be noted with growing trepidation from the seventeenth century onward.[27]

Early modern art engaged with many of these issues. While there is no room here to delve deeply into visual culture, Renaissance painters revelled in depicting youthful and energetic bodies, sometimes as hopeful glimpses of the afterlife or as wishful thinking about the here and now. Lucas Cranach the elder's *The Fountain of Youth* (1546), for instance, shows older women with greying, sagging bodies dipping into a swimming pool to emerge as pink, shapely and beautiful young women who are greeted and then, after dressing themselves, wined and dined by appreciative courtiers. While the

In keeping with early Christian ideas, some Renaissance painters projected
Hellenistic aesthetic ideals of balance and proportion onto their image of the
afterlife. In this scene from Luca Signorelli's fresco in the Capella Nova, the
dead rise at the end of time to receive new flesh, emerging from the earth with
strikingly fit and youthful physiques. Luca Signorelli, *Resurrection of the Flesh*,
1499–1502. Cappella Nuova, Umbria, Italy.

Fountain of Youth could be regretfully dismissed as a mere dream,
the Christian faithful could look forward to the resurrection of
bodies at the end of time. When depicting the afterlife, references
to classical aesthetic ideas were not unprecedented. As we have seen,
even if Christian authors offered sketchy information about what

the perfected resurrection body would look like, there is evidence that they projected Hellenistic aesthetic ideals of balance and promotion onto their image of the afterlife. A vivid Renaissance example is Luca Signorelli's fresco in the Cappella Nuova in the cathedral of Orvieto, which depicts the resurrection of the flesh in striking detail. Skeletons line up to receive new flesh and emerge from the earth with strikingly fit and youthful physiques.[28] Just as Augustine and Aquinas had reassured everyone centuries before, the resurrection body would be beautiful, whole and well-proportioned, never ugly, disabled or fat.

Whether the product of rejuvenation or resurrection, these idealized bodies perhaps reflect the mainstream of Renaissance aesthetic visions of corporeality. While such bodies may fall short of our own contemporary expectations of beauty, few of these would have been considered particularly fat at the time. The Flemish painter Peter Paul Rubens was unusual in the attention he devoted to fleshy bodies, especially those of women, which seemed to represent 'the energy of life' in ways that explored excess and ambiguity.[29] For all of the fleshiness that dominates his canvases, though, Rubens was just as enthralled by Spartan austerity and fitness as his counterparts elsewhere in Europe. He, too, proposed that the ancients stood in closer proximity to natural beauty than the degenerate moderns of his own day, whose physical deterioration mirrored their intellectual decadence. Rubens cited bad habits as the main reason for the corporeal decline of modern men. 'The principal cause of the difference between men of our age and the ancients', he wrote, 'is the sloth and lack of exercise of those living; indeed, [today] one eats and drinks, exercising no care for the body.' Things were far better in ancient times, when 'everyone exercised daily and strenuously in palaestras and gymnasiums.'[30] Approvingly citing the Spartan code that threatened fat men with banishment, Rubens regretted that so many modern people had fat paunches and scrawny limbs bearing little resemblance to the splendid specimens of ancient times.[31]

Rubens had different standards for female bodies, which were traditionally considered to be naturally fleshier than those of males. Although he would later be criticized for showing rather too much preference for female flesh, Rubens was not under any impression that the bodies he painted were unduly fat, or at least not in ways that violated gender norms. Rather, he explained that female proportions would ideally be 'weaker and smaller', for when it comes to the perfection of forms 'woman holds the second rung after man'. Even if fleshier by nature, the female should nevertheless display moderation in all her aspects, being 'neither too thin nor too scrawny, neither too big nor too fat, but a moderate embonpoint, according to the model of antique statues'. Rubens thus maintained that a woman's hips and thighs should be 'large and ample', her breasts smoothly separated so they 'project moderately from the chest'. The skin of her stomach 'should not be loose, nor should the stomach sag, but [it should be] soft and with a smooth and flowing contour'. Since nothing about the female form should allow it to be confused with the male, all efforts must be made to avoid the appearance of stiffness or musculature. In general, a female body should resemble a circle: 'round, delicate and supple, and altogether opposed to the robust and masculine form' (which, incidentally, should approximate a cube).[32] Extra flesh enhanced rather than diminished women's appeal and further separated them from the kinds of bodies that men should possess. Thus, far from uncritically extolling the virtues of fleshiness or representing a lost cultural preference for fat, it may be more accurate to say that Rubens displays 'an obscure and personal taste for the luxuriance of flesh while recalling . . . the neoclassical will for thinness'.[33]

Insofar as it is capable of symbolizing superfluity, fatness was criticized in other areas of European culture. For instance, a new firmness was being recommended in literary style as well. Here, too, correspondences were routinely drawn between the tautness of one's writing and the condition of the authorial body. None of this was really all that new, though. Metaphors of male and female bodies have pervaded discussions of literary and oratorical styles in Roman times, and such metaphors continued to gender the ways in which 'good' and 'bad' style was evaluated. Following the classical model articulated most clearly by Quintilian, neo-Stoic writers like Justus Lipsius argued that a 'masculine' style was one marked by sinews (*nervi*) and thus by vigour, force and strength. An 'effeminate' style was, by contrast, *enervis* (enervated) or *factum* (broken, impotent). The virile and the sinewy were thus contrasted to the effeminate, the slack and the bloated. As Quintilian had claimed centuries before, literary style had everything to do with bodily condition.[34]

The fleshy goddesses in Rubens's *Three Graces* would come under fire a century later for their lack of 'grace'. Peter Paul Rubens, *The Three Graces*, c. 1635.

Such distinctions, along with the inevitable connections between literary style and material bodies, could be applied to writers of the time. In his book *Timber, or, Discoveries Made upon Men and Matter* (1640), Ben Jonson, too, argued for a plainer writing style unencumbered by the superfluity he observed all around him. 'Language most shews a man,' he declared; 'speak, that I may see thee.' Jonson objected to verbose poetry that seemed 'wanton' and 'fleshy' and which, through sheer excess, risked growing 'fat and corpulent . . . full of suet and tallow'. This sharp call for poetry that was lean and spare, a recurring tendency in Western literary history, would return to haunt Jonson as he grew more corpulent with age. By then his enemies were quick to turn Jonson's own ideas against him, alleging that the immoderate lifestyle and ample proportions of 'decaying Ben' were now evident in his bloated poetic style. Even Jonson's defenders manifested a classically oriented aversion to fat when they drew distinctions between the poet's 'grotesque' body and those inner qualities which they represented as chaste, clean and pure. Jonson's friends acknowledged their hero's physical decay, but, much as the defenders of pudgy Socrates had done in Athens, ended up insisting that it's what's inside that counts.[35]

'Laugh and Grow Fat'

Proverbs, as the last chapter explained, endure partly because they are thought to convey common-sense knowledge about the world. Yet sometimes the knowledge being conveyed is itself complex and even contradictory, or, at the very least, context-specific. 'Laugh and grow fat' is another old saying to consider, in this case implying a relationship between mirthful happiness and the process of weight gain. There are several ways for us to understand why such a proverb would have made sense. Digital research into metaphors in the English language reveals a strong correlation between words for wealth and corresponding bodily and emotional states of fatness and happiness. Poverty, on the other hand, invokes the contrasting metaphors of thinness and unhappiness.[36] Along with related sayings like 'the heart's mirth does make the face fair' or 'laughter is the best medicine,' proverbs about fatness and happiness turned on the logic of humoral medicine that envisioned fat as a concoction of food that had been 'cooked' in the stomach. Most importantly, humoralism maintained that people possessing phlegmatic complexions were more or less cheerful individuals who were naturally prone to be fleshier than others. The same model encouraged the idea that thin persons were more or less 'consuming' themselves partly due to their own humoral dispositions (in the sense that fat is melted by heat) and the state of their emotions. People who had lost a lot of weight were said to have been 'withered', 'drained' or 'eaten away' by cares and worries.[37] If moderate plumpness thus signified health and contentment, in culinary terms fat was considered to be a highly pleasing substance to eat. French peasants, for instance, perceived a natural fit between fat and happiness: their largely grain-based diet transformed fats into a rare luxury that enticed the senses and fired the imagination. Meats were boiled, as they had been in Roman times, to extract as much fat as possible, and 'fat soup' (*la soupe grasse*) was a festival dish served in several provinces. In some regions, to have lips shining with grease after a good meal signified intense gustatory enjoyment and *joie de vivre*. Medieval tales of the Land of Cockaigne helped to cement these cultural associations between fats, fatness and a sense of material well-being.[38] And, as we have seen, the agricultural imagination fostered the idea that fat lands may yield things that bring sensual pleasure and happiness.

Ever since the Middle Ages, then, fats and fatness were linked to happiness in ways that made medical as well as common sense. The philosopher-physician Avicenna had helped to lay the conceptual groundwork for such ideas by maintaining that plumpness and thinness depended to some extent on a person's emotional state. 'Great joy makes the body bloom with health,' he declared, adding that some degree of fatness was evidence of 'flourishing'. Like most physicians who preached the virtues of moderation, Avicenna recognized that there was such a thing as flourishing too much, at least insofar as an overflowing of contentment generates 'too much' fleshiness. To compensate for such situations, Avicenna saw some medical benefit in measured doses of worry and sadness that, while potentially fatal for the very thin, would be 'useful for those who need to lose a few pounds'.[39]

Emotional wellbeing was closely connected to lifestyle. With its attention to air, nutrition, movement, sleep, evacuation and the emotions, the medical doctrine of the six 'non-naturals' validated the idea that moderation in nutrition should correspond to temperance in relation to the 'passions of the soul', just as religious morality typically argued that material well-being was a poor substitute for the far greater happiness waiting for people in Heaven. This advice proved influential throughout Latin Christendom. In time, fertility experts were recommending that corpulent women wishing to have children should be deliberately moved to anger, anxiety and sadness as methods of reducing the fatness of their wombs.[40]

Acting upon emotions as a method of altering the body was also recommended outside of reproductive health circles. The humanist Petrarch sketched the relationship between fat and the emotions in his *Remedies for Fortune Fair and Foul* (1365). Gently dismissing the notion that growing fat as one aged needed to be cause for alarm, Petrarch insisted that someone truly wishing to shed unwanted flesh must 'arise by force of quick wit and reduce your weight. Drive it away with busy striving; engage in many difficult projects to exercise mind and body, and avoid all pleasures.' This meant committing oneself to a regimen that carefully avoided ordinary comforts:

> Banish repose; thrive on work; disdain desires; hate idleness; love to worry about things; forget about ease; espouse harsh discipline; enjoy what is difficult; and insist on being continually moderate in food, drink, reclining, and rest, and sleep briefly and lightly.[41]

By demanding a conscious distancing of oneself from those habits and experiences that rendered one complacent and soft, weight loss required a methodical cultivation of self-denial and discomfort in order to occur. Shedding fat was as much a state of mind as a matter of diet and exercise.

This idea that powerful emotions could cause one to gain or lose weight remained alive and well throughout the early modern era, and was believed to hold true regardless of humoral complexion. Acknowledging that phlegmatic persons were likely to be fatter than others, in *The Castel of Helth* (1534) Thomas Elyot declared that joy or 'gladnesse of harte' prolongs the life and 'fatteth the bodye that is leane with troubles'.[42] Laurent Joubert expanded upon this idea a few decades later by observing that those slender people

> who are by nature choleric, when they give themselves up to rest, without worry and without sadness, and if they eat well and take good care of themselves, easily become fat, and lose their natural slenderness.[43]

Ambroise Paré agreed, stating that moderate joy fattens and enlarges the body in salutary ways,[44] while Giovanni Battista Della Porta associated the 'fatness of flesh that is caused by blood' with kindness, merriment, song, laughter and love. If there was a kind of 'lightness' to certain heavy people, he proposed, it was mainly because their very blood is 'airy'.[45]

But there was a flipside to fat happiness that continued to cause concern. Those who are content with what they already have, it was sometimes held, will rarely seek to achieve more, and happiness of a merely material sort could breed stupidity. This is why, with a nod to the Roman author Plutarch, Shakespeare's Julius Caesar famously said that he preferred to be surrounded by advisors who were fat rather than thin. Being largely complacent and lazy, fat people are less likely to engage in conspiracies, whereas men like Cassius have 'a lean and hungry look; / He thinks too much: such men are dangerous.' (*Julius Caesar*, 1.2) In addition to reflecting the proverbial stupidity of the corpulent, this perspective was in general agreement with contemporary understandings of melancholia, a form of depression that typically afflicted scholars whose bodies were usually dried out and emaciated rather than moist and fleshy. This is why Joubert could observe in his *Treatise on Laughter* that cold and dry melancholics 'laugh the least' and 'scarcely ever become fat'.[46] And if Della Porta had looked kindly upon 'fatness of flesh that is caused by blood', he also taught readers to interpret 'the big and fat neck, and the fleshy belly, one that is big, soft, and pendulous' as signs of 'a heavy and stupid' person.[47]

This distinction between fat happiness and slender melancholia invites us to rethink the stability of a saying like 'laugh and grow fat' in light of the contradictory tendencies of proverbs. As attractive as they might seem, the benefits of becoming fat and happy could be offset if people also believed that 'fat bellies make empty skulls'. This might be viewed as a problem in a culture that was increasingly placing a premium on education and intellect as paths to success. This is why, in learned circles, melancholia was a rather good malady from which to suffer, functioning as a sort of badge of honour that affirmed intelligence as well as the seriousness that seemed to accompany it.[48] Moreover, as described above, the culture of tightness was accompanied by a transformation of manners that sought to constrain emotional displays in ways that called even the virtue of spontaneous laughter into question. As Mikhail Bakhtin has famously shown, the popular 'grotesque body' that was often celebrated during Carnival, with its large belly and gaping mouth, stood in stark contrast to the much more regulated and 'closed' bodily ideal emphasized by the emerging bourgeoisie. An important by-product of this development was the 'degradation' of raucous laughter that was underway in the sixteenth century as bourgeois 'seriousness' increasingly became the rule in European societies.[49]

The unrestrained belly-laughing associated with commoners was what well-mannered elites were encouraged to avoid in their ever more measured and restrained world. The fantastically gluttonous Land of Cockaigne could not stand as a model for the corporeal utopias being imagined in the early modern period.

We must be wary of exaggerating the changes that were taking place during this period, many of which were already underway in the Middle Ages. Nor should we turn a blind eye to the uneven and incomplete ways in which these changes unfolded. To see some of the mixed messages that were being transmitted about fatness and happiness, we may briefly consider early modern dream books. These texts counselled elites on how to make sense of the troubling images and transformations that could occur while the conscious mind slept. Joseph's famous interpretation of Pharaoh's dream in the Book of Genesis (the one where dreaming of seven fat and seven lean cattle portended, respectively, seven years of plenty and famine) was widely repeated in this literature, and the same logic applied to dreams of fat people as well. A sixteenth-century example of the genre attested to the generally auspicious nature of fat as a dream symbol. Dreaming of a man with a fat face or belly, or to imagine oneself as fat, signified good things like friendship, joy and riches.[50]

So far, so good. Just as fat fields could promise beneficial increase and abundance, to dream of oneself as fat augured well for future wealth and happiness. Yet the same fleshiness that foretold such good things could generate problems elsewhere. It is worth considering these passages on dream interpretation alongside the short physiognomic treatises that were often appended to such manuals. Building upon ancient techniques for reading the body, interest in interpreting external signs for corresponding character traits acquired new importance as Europeans became more oriented towards the visual. Becoming fat in a dream could indeed mean that one 'will enjoy riches' and fine clothes, as one seventeenth-century English text maintained. Readers had only to turn to the book's later sections to find out what people might think if one actually became very fat. Featuring analyses reminiscent of the medieval *Secretum secretorum* texts, there we learn that people with good memories have bodies whose upper parts are 'small, comly, well-shap'd, proportionable, well-flesh'd, but not fat, for where they are corpulent, it is a signe the party is stupid and forgetful'. Fatness could also be a sign of intemperateness, for people with this trait were distinguished by being 'wide-mouth'd, soft and big-belly'd, hanging down'.[51] A French text aimed at the diversion of elites made a similar point, describing people with large bellies as 'prying, fools, arrogant, bawdy', and someone with a fat face as 'an ignorant man much given to sensual pleasure'. Material well-being was a good thing, no doubt. But, when pushed to excess, the glowing contentment that moderate corpulence might signify could become 'evidence of a dazed and forgetful man'.[52] Ancient physiognomic wisdom about the inverse relationship between fatness and intelligence had not only been updated during the Middle Ages, but it was still being cited in the seventeenth century and beyond.[53]

So, was it better to be fat and happy (and risk being perceived as a coarse, lazy and stupid sensualist) or lean and hungry (but potentially more refined, clever and industrious)? By the eighteenth century – when, as we will see, the notion of earthly 'happiness' experienced a dramatic rise in value – elites would have been forgiven for having been somewhat confused. Many Britons would have looked to that influential arbiter of manners, Lord Chesterfield, who drily confirmed that fatness and stupidity 'are looked upon as such inseparable companions, that they are used as synonymous terms'.[54] Since adjusting oneself to the opinions of others was paramount in Chesterfield's sociable world, his widely read letters to his son combined the connotations of 'polishing' and 'policing' that were integral to achieving the ideal of politeness. Insofar as becoming fat is 'troublesome, unwholesome, and ungraceful', Chesterfield maintained that it was better for his naturally plump son to exercise more and even feign illness rather than indulge in the rich cuisine being thrust upon him in Paris.[55] That self-control might deprive him of pleasure was irrelevant. 'Real happiness' was qualitatively different from the 'immediate and indiscriminate gratification of a passion, or appetite'.[56] The best advice Chesterfield could offer his son was the second-century recommendation of the satirist Juvenal:

Mens sana in corpora sano [a sound mind in a sound body], is the truest description of human happiness; I think you have them both at present; take care to keep them; it is in your power to do it.[57]

The Fat of the Body Politic

Human happiness, which had never been understood as consisting entirely of material well-being or the satisfaction of animal appetites, was defined as partly based on constraint, an effect of the moderation that had been promoted as integral to the good life since antiquity. Indeed, a tension between organic life and the 'good life' is a recurring feature of Western culture. And, of course, moderation never amounted to a wholesale rejection of pleasure. It rather encouraged taking enjoyment in life while retaining respect for the requirements of health, beauty and morality.[58] Yet if the concept of luxury was often vilified by the classical-influenced republicans of the Renaissance, it underwent a profound transformation by the time of the Enlightenment. Whereas Aristotle viewed the condition of 'human flourishing' as representing a life without any deficiency, one in which all conceivable desires have been satisfied, theorists began to question whether an earthly life without desires was preferable or even conceivable. The philosopher David Hume defended desires because they spur one toward actions designed to satisfy them and are thus an important antidote to indolence. He also had some choice words for those who glorified ancient *askesis* (self-discipline). Sparta may have been powerful because it lacked commerce and luxury, but it was also a brutal society committed to constant warfare. It lacked the refined 'softness' that a more 'civilized' culture would have offered. Political economist Adam Smith concurred, seeing in 'opulence' and 'ease of body' proof of a positive social condition. Although physicians and gymnastics instructors of the time might beg to differ, both authors maintained that the 'martial spirit', and therefore male bellicosity, are not necessarily diminished by this softening of life.[59]

Changes were also taking place in material culture. This was the period during which Western societies began to embrace the idea of *comfort* as a physically pleasing relationship between the body and its immediate physical environment. This development reflected a new validation of earthly pleasures that included the search for consumer goods as well as culinary treats.[60] Widespread support for consumerism did not occur overnight, nor would the victory ever be quite complete. Lingering associations between masculinity and bellicosity would ensure a conflicted relationship between manhood and consumerism to the present. Rather than a simple shift from a classical-republican critique of luxury to a wholehearted endorsement of consumption, then, it is more useful to highlight the tensions and ambivalence that haunted both sides of these debates.[61] Even amid the apparent victory of consumerism, such tensions would remain embedded in Western societies from this point onward. They may explain our tendency to vacillate between the competing pressures to indulge our desires through consumption and curb them as a technique of self-mastery. The eighteenth century was when many of these issues became debated. Naturally, then, corpulence

> fell at the center of the tensions and contradictions of a society divided between the calls for moderation formulated within the culture of politeness and the interests and passions inscribed in the ethics of trade and consumption.[62]

Some of these tensions could be dramatized in the art world. The celebration of classical bodies that emerged during the Renaissance reached its fullest expression in the eighteenth century. During this time, influential aesthetes like Johann Winckelmann cast any deviations from their physical ideal as sources of disgust. Like Rubens before him, Winckelmann claimed that the beautiful and harmonious bodies of Greek sculpture were accurate reflections of the steps the Greeks took to create healthy and beautiful children: 'These exercises gave the bodies of the Greeks the strong and manly contours which the masters then imparted to their statues without any exaggeration or excess.'[63] Winckelmann's rules for depicting the body echo some of the recommendations that ancient physiognomy made about noble physical traits. Although the face still carried the burden of representing a person's character, slender buttocks and a flat belly were also important. The stomach, the sounds of which were unwelcome at the dinner table, was now expected to be inconspicuous in art as well. 'Even in male figures', Winckelmann noted, 'the abdomen is the same as in a person after a sweet sleep, and after healthy digestion – that is, *without belly*, and of the sort physiologists consider an indication of a long life.' The fit and muscular body Winckelmann celebrated was a softly smooth and seamless surface, pristinely free of organs, blood, belly, excrement or anything else to remind viewers of the embarrassing messiness of organic life.[64]

The Neoclassical love affair with beautiful naked forms has sometimes been described as a renewed appreciation of the body in Western art. This is certainly true when we consider how medieval art often downplayed the human. Yet, as with the neo-Platonic celebration of the ideal that prevailed during the Renaissance, the 'body' being appreciated here had little in common with the imperfect vessels that people actually possessed. As the case of Winckelmann suggests, it was the embarrassingly organic features of bodies that aesthetic ideals often sought to push out of sight, especially those revolving around eating, sexuality and excretion, but also those redolent of decay and death.[65] Similar purification projects, we have seen, were underway in gastronomy and dietetics. To be 'civilized' meant being upright and moral, capable of mastering one's emotions and, through an array of techniques for personal displaying, of managing the impressions one made on others. But it also meant a more pronounced withdrawal from the disconcerting aspects of embodied existence. Charting the history of aesthetic disgust, Winfried Menninghaus sees in Neoclassical art the beginnings of a mindset that still operates today:

> this body subsumed to aesthetic illusion, with its normative youthfulness, its smooth skin free of blemish, its slender-athletic elasticity and nonobscene nudity, anticipates a now-predominant regulation of the body, its sleekest forms emerging from the world of advertising, cosmetics, and – as analagon [*sic*] of the antique gymnasia so enthusiastically evoked by Winckelmann – the fitness center with its various machines.[66]

In this cultivation of appreciation for idealized forms, one also sees a corresponding devaluation of the ordinary as well as a flight from the messiness of the mundane. Contemporary observers noted with increasing alarm that health, beauty and morality seemed to have declined sharply from the standards laid down in classical times. A prominent worshipper of such ideals, Winckelmann regretted that the men of his own day deviated so much from the statues he admired. 'The most beautiful body of one of us would probably no more resemble the most beautiful Greek body than Iphicles resembled his [half-]brother Hercules,' he lamented.[67] The aesthetic deviation that fatness signified pointed mainly to a problem of character. Even

Considered by Winckelmann a perfect example of classical sculpture, the Apollo Belvedere possessed an ideal body whose 'abdomen is the same as in a person after a sweet sleep, and after healthy digestion – that is, *without belly*, and of the sort physiologists consider an indication of a long life'. Apollo Belvedere, 120–140 CE, Roman copy of a lost bronze original from 350–325 BCE.

the English politician William Hay, who in the 1750s championed disabled people and wrote passionately about the primacy of character and civility over beauty or ugliness, agreed that 'a prominent Belly' was a more reasonable object of ridicule than any inborn physical trait. Such a protuberance was, after all, 'generally the Effect of Intemperance, and of Man's own Creation' rather than the result of nature.[68] If fatness could be seen as a form of disability, it was, as in Boaistuau's view of Denis Heracleot's monstrosity, something one brought upon oneself.

Lamenting the decline of virtue and character amid the unfolding consumer revolution, critics of luxury sometimes evoked corpulence as a way of envisioning the body politic degenerating from the firmness of virtue to the flabbiness of vice. Amid the fascination with classical values that dominated this period, it is not surprising to see ancient exemplars enlisted in discussions about fat, especially when the medical rationale for doing so wasn't entirely clear. For instance, the *Encyclopédie* article on '*Obésité*' reminded readers, for no apparent reason, that the Spartans 'could not suffer such massive embonpoint' among the young and imposed strict regimens to keep them fit.[69] The author of this article, the luxury-hating chevalier Louis de Jaucourt, may have approved of the spirit of such measures, for elsewhere he declared that the very name 'Sparta' naturally called to mind 'the greatest virtues' of all Greek city-states.[70] For similarly mysterious reasons, the anonymous author of the article on 'Corpulence' felt compelled to mention what an 'infamy' excess flesh represented in the eyes of the Spartans.[71]

The cultural imagination of collective bodies often mirrored observations of personal bodies. Classical republicans who continued to distrust commerce and luxury despite the rise of consumption sometimes described the body politic as if it were caught in a spiral of corruption. The resolutely pro-Spartan Jean-Jacques Rousseau linked fat and fatness to the soft sensuality of Paris, which posed a stark contrast to the rustic hardness he celebrated in countries like Corsica and Poland. Far beyond the personal body, fat was for Rousseau a matter of national import. 'I regard finance as the fat [*la graisse*] of the body politic,' he claimed, 'fat which, when clogged up in certain muscular tissues, overburdens the body with *un embonpoint inutile*, and makes it heavy rather than strong.'[72] Empires that expanded too rapidly and indiscriminately were particularly at risk, especially if it meant the importation of foreign luxuries into the metropole itself. Claims that once-glorious Rome had eventually collapsed as a result of luxurious effeminacy were widely taken for granted, and some likened the vast size of the empire to a decadent and bloated body. As another *philosophe* claimed, by adopting the decadent habits of the lands Rome had conquered (namely Egypt and India), the empire quickly became bloated with 'the embonpoint of luxury, a disease that heralds the decline of strength. This great empire fell under its own weight.'[73]

Enlightenment critiques of corpulence echoed those that the Romans made when they reflected on the vast and unwieldy size of their empire as well as the moral vices that such expansion seemed to promote. Yet the use of corporeal language to describe entire nations should not distract us from the very literal ways in which medicine was employed in the social projects of the Enlightenment.[74] In his eugenic plans to 'perfect the human species', Charles-Augustin Vandermonde contended in 1756 that, like excessive slenderness, '*trop d'embonpoint*' needed to be avoided if one was going to produce ideal children. Not only was being too fat unattractive, but 'men and women of this type [*complexion*] are usually sterile, or little disposed to generation.'[75] Nearly twenty years later, in an influential text on health in relation to marriage, the Jesuit author Joseph-Adrien Lelarge de Lignac presented a rather damning assessment of the man with a phlegmatic, or what was increasingly called 'pituitous' temperament. Owing to excess moisture in his body everything about such a man announced to others his 'weakness of Nature'. Yet the phlegmatic man was even more problematic than that. Given that his 'body is feeble, and incapable of supporting heavy labour', Lignac proposed an environmental approach to the formation of tempera-ments: 'the man of this constitution is not in Nature, since it is so very rare in the country,' where life demands more exertion.[76] Those who were fat could only be abject creatures of the city – just like melancholics, whose bookish and sedentary lifestyles also fostered constitutional peculiarities.

Lignac also questioned the intelligence and virility of fat men, whose inability to generate physical force was matched by their intel-lectual weakness (such men 'are incapable of producing masterpieces which announce genius') and lack of moral power. Unable to resist or even understand strong sensations, such a soft and malleable man is the plaything of inner and outer forces, and 'willingly receives the impression that they give him'. This was no man, as Hildegard of Bingen had claimed centuries before. Lignac stated:

> He is a charge, perhaps, to Nature; for she has not scattered men on the earth with the germ of melancholy, and of pituity – Depravation of morals! Luxury! Effeminacy! Behold your work!

For Lignac, the 'ordinary causes of the abundance of pituity' (that is, the phlegmatic/pituitous temperament described above) are eating too much rich food, drinking too much alcohol, too much repose and sleep. Echoing Hildegard's feminizing critique of the phlegmatic, he suggested that men who were 'flabby, soft and covered in fat' were not really capable of reproducing anyway:

too weak for extracting his subsistence from the bosom of the earth, too weak for daring to attempt to serve his country with weapons in his hands, who is a bad labourer and a bad soldier, can [such a man] be a good husband?

Just in case sterility wasn't a quick enough solution to the problem of excessive corpulence, Lignac had another idea. Echoing the policy that Campanella had imagined for his City of the Sun, he recommended the eugenic coupling of the fat and the lean so that both extremes would eventually be eliminated.[77]

✳

What is called 'modernity' is characterized by ambiguity and paradox. A culture of tightness as well as lightness, modernity promotes the virtues of self-control while creating the conditions for indulgence and excess. While supposedly embodying the new, modernity nevertheless raids the past for many of its models. The lingering appeal of antiquity in the history of fat is a case in point. The closing section of the previous chapter offered glimpses into how latter-day 'Spartans' like Thomas More and Montesquieu sang the praises of toil and hardship as opposed to the corruption that very fat land could yield. This is the same period that scholars usually identify as initiating a distinctly 'modern' contempt for corpulence, and one can see why. Aside from the Spartans, one would be hard pressed to find joking, much less serious, recommendations for the elimination of fat people from society prior to the sixteenth century. Modernity did not invent stereotypes about fat people, but it surely sharpened them.

The changes taking place at this time were therefore critical for the creation of modern stereotypes about fat. The Spartan mirage was one of those ancient ideas that were 'reborn' during the Renaissance, receiving a new lease on life that would persist throughout the modern era.[78] One of the central features of this mirage – that the Spartans valued fitness and virtue so much that they expelled fat men from society – would prove especially compelling among those who would seek to regenerate Western culture as it became more accepting of material pleasures. The socially meliorist and frankly eugenic proposals of some eighteenth-century French authors may partly explain this fascination with eradicating 'unfit' bodies. Claiming that 'too much fatness destroys beauty', the polemical physician

Antoine Le Camus railed against corpulence in his campaign to reform the bodies and minds of women, condemning it as a source of 'disgust' as well as a symptom of weakness, stupidity and even barrenness.[79] Although stopping short of recommending the expulsion of fat people, Le Camus could not help admiring how 'this wise nation' Sparta used to punish the fat because such persons were suspected of having 'little prudence or understanding'.[80]

Within a few decades, the French were happily expelling some of their more decadent 'fat' people. The collapse of the Bastille in 1789 unleashed a torrent of claims that the regenerated (male) citizen was fast becoming fit and hard like the Spartans or the ancient Gauls, scornful of luxury and poised to subject France to a new 'regime', in the double sense of political order and orderly lifestyle. If one cannot say that fatness was singled out as a problematic corporeal trait among the general population, it circulated as a powerful symbol of the accumulated wealth of the clergy (to be reclaimed, as one cartoon promised, by a 'patriotic fat remover'), of the 'parasitical' and bloated aristocrat ('the man who has fattened himself by starving the people') and of the 'imbecile' and 'impotent' 'pig-king' Louis XVI ('a fat mass of flesh who eats, who drinks, but who is limp').[81] As European

ah! Le maudit animal, il m'a tant gêné pour s'engraisser, il est si gras, qu'il en en est Ladre, je reviens du marché, je ne sais plus qu'en faire.

The plump King Louis XVI was regularly likened to a pig in the nasty rhetoric of the French Revolution. Carl de Vinck and Michel Hennin, 'Ah! That damned animal . . .', 1791.

During the French Revolution aristocrats and clergy exceeded the new 'national level' in terms of bodies and characters. *Le Niveau Nationale*, 1790.

societies sought pathways to the future through an imaginative recuperation of the past, the perceived decadence of the present was condemned through the mutually reinforcing images of corruption, deformity, animality, effeminacy and fatness. According to this narrative, the future would be truly human – virtuous, muscular and beautiful. As the next chapter shows, it would also be graceful and clean.

EIGHT

GREASE AND GRACE
The Disenchantment of Fat?

O ne night in 1731, Cornelia de Bandi burst into flames. When the 62-year-old Italian countess was found the next morning, her head and torso had been reduced to ash and grease. Only her arms and legs remained intact. After examining what was left of her body, a local physician concluded, in a report cited years later, that the conflagration 'was caused in her entrails' by the variety of combustible materials to be found there, including alcohol and fat, 'an oily liquid . . . of an easily combustible nature'.[1] An early instance of what would come to be known as 'spontaneous human combustion', de Bandi was one of many cases later studied by Pierre-Aimé Lair. If there was a common denominator to these otherwise unexplained phenomena, Lair concluded, it was the fact that most of them involved corpulent older women with a penchant for drink, thus combining fat and alcohol in a literally explosive mix. In addition to the fuel that excess body fat provided, which was rendered even more combustible when 'penetrated by alcoholic substances', surplus fat was said to create higher levels of hydrogen, thus making the body especially flammable. Lair concluded:

> Thus there is no cause for surprise that old women, who are in general fatter and more given to drunkenness, and who are often motionless like inanimate masses, during the moment of intoxication, should experience the effects of combustion.[2]

Even though William Wadd, a famous proponent of English weight loss, would count it among the 'grievous incidents' fat people might have to face, erupting into flames has rarely been cited as a reason why someone should seek to thin down.[3] In fact, by the time Lair published his findings, the list of health problems associated with corpulence had already grown expansive and complex. Just about any of them seemed far more likely to occur than explosion. What is most relevant about the de Bandi case is the way in which fat was discussed. Whatever Lair might have thought about fat old ladies who drank too much, in his report fat is about little more than the chemicals that comprised it and the properties that rendered them combustible. Scientifically breaking down the stuff of life into its components was part of a more general process of quantification that gained momentum during the seventeenth century to become pervasive in the eighteenth and nineteenth.

It was also during this time that agricultural metaphors ceased to inform medical views of the body. Mechanistic ideas gradually eclipsed the organicism that had characterized Western views of nature since antiquity. The language of the body began to shift from the model of an organism to that of a machine whose energy was generated from internal combustion. Age-old descriptions of pro-creation as 'generation' were increasingly replaced with a focus on 'reproduction', and digestion was rethought in terms of a chemical process rather than the 'concoction' of food in the 'cauldron' of the stomach.[4] Even the food that bodies needed to survive was becoming purified of its connections to the land – as we have seen, *la nouvelle cuisine* inaugurated 'the self-consciously modern art of stripping food of earthiness'.[5] This was also the period during which corpulence underwent a process of quantification and medicalization that would eventually contribute to our present views of 'obesity' as a disease.[6] Older ideas about fatness and mirth were reconceptualized in more mechanistic terms. The physician Thomas Short maintained that cheerful people tended to be corpulent because laughter, which he likened to a convulsion, mechanically squeezed oil from the blood into the fat vesicles.[7] Such mechanistic and quantitative explanations would only gain momentum in the years to come. With the development of height and weight tables in the nineteenth century, the stage was set for the further development of ideas about metabolism, nutritional requirements and eventually the Body Mass Index of our own time. And, of course, this process paved the way for the now ubiquitous bathroom scale.

The famed proponent of English weight loss, William Wadd, counted bursting into flames among the 'grievous incidents' fat people might have to face. William Wadd, *Comments on Corpulency* (1829), illustrated by A. M. Broadley, 1901.

The widening net of quantification and medicalization is an important feature of the history of diets and dieting. But quantification cannot fully account for the stigmatization of corpulence that had been steadily gaining ground in the West. The feelings of disgust that fat would come to elicit are not caused by having a particular belt size, weighing a certain amount or consuming more than the recommended daily allowance of fats or carbohydrates. The issues addressed in this chapter unfold in the midst of a perceptual shift from a time when human fat was viewed as imbued with vitality and seen as being capable of almost magical healing properties to a more 'modern' situation in which its physical properties became the target of greater scrutiny and growing cause for alarm. It is tempting to view this transformation as a 'disenchantment' of fat, but this assumes that we are dealing with the scientific unmasking of something magical. The more appropriate term is the less felicitous 'devivification', the draining of life from a substance that would in time come to be (erroneously) viewed by many as little more than dead weight and dirty waste. Just as the rise of soil science chipped away at traditional concepts of the fatness of the land, modern chemistry effectively toppled human fat from its place in the Western pharmacopoeia and cultural imagination.[8]

But more profound changes were taking place as Westerners sharpened their already sensitive reactions to fat and grease. Probing the materiality of fat during this transitional period reveals that the growing containment and closure of bodies that many scholars have observed was not only a matter of visuality, but part of a developing kinaesthetic that contributed to the lived experience of containment and closure. A withdrawal from corpulence in bodily frame marched in stride with an accelerating repugnance toward fat and grease as morally and hygienically problematic substances that one could feel and smell as well as see. Growing intolerance for various forms of fat reflects a sensory transformation of the white European elite habitus in which tactile and visual impressions reinforced one another.[9] The qualities of greasiness, softness and flabbiness take on considerable importance in understanding how fat stereotypes unfolded in the modern period, particularly when many of these were applied to the bodies of colonial peoples in a variety of countries. Grease was becoming antithetical to grace. Before we come to that, though, we must return to the early modern era.

Harvesting Human Fat

Whether procured from plant, animal or human sources, in one form or another fat has been an important element in the European pharmacopoeia since ancient times. For reasons that are not quite clear, a medicinal interest in human fat was especially pronounced in the sixteenth and seventeenth centuries. In 1543, the physician Andreas Vesalius instructed anatomists who boiled bones for the study of skeletons to carefully collect the layer of fat 'for the benefit of the masses, who ascribe to it a considerable efficacy in obliterating scars and fostering the growth of nerves and tendons'.[10] Vesalius knew what he was talking about. At the time, human fat was widely considered – and not just by 'the masses' – to be efficacious in healing wounds, and was sometimes harvested from the recently deceased. In October 1601, after a particularly bloody battle during the siege of Ostend, Dutch surgeons descended upon the battlefield to return with 'bags full of human fat', presumably to treat their own soldiers' wounds.[11]

If the fat of warriors was efficacious, that of executed criminals was easier to lay one's hands on. What was called 'poor sinner's fat' was rendered from the bodies of the recently executed and used to treat sprains, broken bones and arthritis. Beyond such uses, human fat was also prescribed as a painkiller or to treat sciatica and rheumatism, while dead men's sweat was collected for the treatment of haemorrhoids.[12] Until the mid-eighteenth century, executioners in the city of Munich, who often prescribed and administered home-made remedies from the corpses of their doomed clients, had a lucrative trade in the fat they delivered to physicians by the pound.[13] Knowing what would become of their corpses was a source of great anguish for the condemned, many of whom believed in the Christian doctrine of the resurrection of bodies and were not consoled by the thought that their fat, flesh, blood and bones might be parcelled out for the benefit of others.[14] Still, business was business, and against the wishes of donors executioners continued to supply fat, blood and other body parts to those willing to buy them. And it wasn't just ordinary people buying such things. The wise druggist kept large supplies of human fat (*Axungia hominis*) on hand alongside numerous other solids and liquids derived from human corpses, a class of *materia medica* known as 'mummy'.[15] If fortune smiled on the fat trade when the rate of executions increased, it would have been positively beaming during the Terror days of the French Revolution. According to some reports, certain Parisian butchers started offering their customers an exciting new item: *graisse de guillotiné*, supposedly procured from the corpses of the freshly executed.[16]

What was it about human fat that made it so sought after? And what was so special about the fat of slain criminals in particular? The practice no doubt echoes the Catholic cult of holy relics, whereby saints were considered to be fully present in their bodies after death, as well as in the objects they touched. We have already encountered stories of saints exuding aromatic or healing oils from their incorruptible bodies. Yet this mystical appreciation only explains so much, and, needless to say, most executed criminals were no saints. Rather, the use of fat for medical purposes was perceived as a *natural* rather than magical practice, and thus based on assumptions about the physical properties of the substance itself.[17] Despite the apparent obsolescence of many of these beliefs, the claim that fat could heal wounds was not misguided. Physicians today know that adipose tissue is highly 'angiogenic', meaning that it promotes the growth of new blood vessels from pre-existing ones.[18] Early modern doctors knew this too. The Paracelsan physician Robert Fludd appealed to personal experience for the efficacy of human fat:

> Againe, that the Oyle of Mans Fat is a great appeaser of the Gout and other Dolours, and a healer of Wounds, and a present dryer vp of all manner of Excoriations; often experience hath taught, as well my Masters as my selfe.[19]

Thus early modern people may have used fat in this way simply because it seemed to work. The reasons they gave for *why* it worked seem less persuasive to most modern readers. According to Paracelsus and his followers, some of the vital force of the human being lingered in the body after death. This vitality, they contended, was strongest in the bodies of healthy young men who had died violently, especially – as in the case of an execution – when death came so swiftly that the life force had no time to evacuate the body. The provenance of this insight is uncertain, and even Paracelsus admitted to having received much of his medical knowledge from executioners trading

Axunge hominis, or human fat, was a popular remedy from the 16th century through the 18th century. Two apothecary vessels, *c.* 17th or 18th century.

in such substances. Nevertheless, the use of human fat remained widespread among lay people and doctors alike, even among more orthodox Galenic physicians.[20]

This well-known trafficking in human fat inevitably gave rise to fears that the precious matter might be harvested in less legitimate ways, perhaps for nefarious purposes. This fear was made plain in Spanish encounters in the New World. The soldier and chronicler Bernal Díaz del Castillo recorded how, following his first battle with the Tlascans in the Andes, he opened up the body of a plump slain Indian to dress his soldiers' wounds with the dead man's burned fat, and that in subsequent battles more Indian fat was used to heal wounded Spaniards. This was standard medical procedure among the conquistadors, another of whom – Hernando de Soto – was also said to have used Indian fat as a medicine. Yet harvesting fat was a boon for sailors too. Before leading the expedition that would bring down the Aztec Empire, Hernán Cortés supposedly caulked thirteen boats using the fat of the dead. Insofar as they too ascribed great powers to fat, the native population was understandably terrified by such behaviour. In the Andes, rumours that the Spanish were exporting boatloads of fat back to Spain for medical purposes prompted the largest native rebellion of the first two hundred years of Spanish rule.[21] So durably entrenched did this fear become that, to the present day, Andeans tell stories about a bogeyman called the *pishtaco* (often depicted as a white man) who harvests Indian fat for medical and cannibalistic purposes.[22] According to the missionary Jean-Baptiste Labat, similar concerns caused alarm among Africans who had been sold into slavery. Upon disembarking in America, the frightened captives told each other, their fat and marrow would be extracted and melted to make oil for the Europeans.[23]

Anthropophagy of one form or other is a recurring theme in discussions of non-Western fat and fattening. Echoing Mandeville's medieval account of the sale of fat men in Borneo, indigenous peoples were sometimes said to castrate their enemies so they could be fattened for eating. In such stories, the horror of animalization was facilitated by the indignity of emasculation. After capturing their enemies, John Bulwer claimed, 'Cannibals who live neare the Equator . . . many times geld them, and so fat them up for slaughter as we do Capon.'[24] Sometimes it was the fat of the fallen that was prized. Father Labat claimed that Caribbean natives would typically dry and smoke the flesh of a slain enemy and 'fill gourds with his fat' as 'a trophy & mark of their victory and valour'.[25] By the 1800s, stories of fat theft began to appear in reports on Australian Aboriginals.

Concerns about the illicit harvesting of fat were not only by-products of colonial violence. Back in Europe, allegations of unauthorized fat extraction cropped up in numerous contexts. In a tradition extending back into the Middle Ages, especially in Germanic cultures, many thieves believed that their nocturnal pilfering would go unnoticed if they burned a candle made of human fat or crafted from the fingers of dead babies. As long as these 'thieves' candles' burned, it was said, burglars acquired powers of invisibility while homeowners would remain blissfully asleep. So powerful was this belief that in the sixteenth and seventeenth centuries several thieves were convicted of murdering people just to make such candles.[26] How ironic, then, that the murderers' own fat would probably have been parcelled off after their executions, to be used in medicines and other concoctions.

Thieves were not the only bugbears reputed to steal human fat for their dirty deeds. As the examples above demonstrate, allegations of fat theft were also methods of demonstrating how one group literally or figuratively 'devoured' another. Indeed, one of the things that troubled the sleep of condemned men was the thought that their fat, blood and bones might be used for the purposes of witch-craft.[27] Criminals were not the only ones at risk, for baby fat too was thought to possess powerful properties. In one fifteenth-century case, witches in northern Italy were said to have admitted to stran-gling infants for their fat, which they mixed with the venom of toads and other creatures to make an ointment that would cause an ago-nizing death to those who touched it.[28] It was also taken for granted that witches cooked up a powerful ointment 'composed of the fat of children they had murdered' that gave them the power of flight.[29] 'I had a dagger: what did I with that?' declares a witch in one of Ben Jonson's early masques: 'Kill'd an infant, to have his fat.'[30] Such beliefs were dramatized in plays as well. 'Here, take this unbaptised brat,' instructs Hecate in Thomas Middleton's *The Witch* (1615); 'Boil it well, preserve the fat: / You know 'tis precious to transfer / Our 'nointed flesh into the air.'[31]

Evidently witches swapped recipes with werewolves, who were also said to be on the prowl for the fat of children in order to concoct the dreadful unguent that turned men into beasts.[32] As there was an imaginative link between supernatural beasts who preyed on people and wealthy humans who 'devoured' common folk in everyday life,

Stories of fat-stealing witches circulated widely in early modern Europe.
In this detail from the title page of Peter Binsfeld's *Tractatus de Confessionibus Maleficorum et Sagarum* (1591), a witch boils a baby for its fat while two others appear to be servicing Satan and one of his more dapper demons.

actual collaboration between the two groups was entirely thinkable. In 1747, a great fear gripped the small Alpine community of Primarette, where rumours circulated that lords and/or clerics connected with the local glassworks had sent werewolves to procure the fat and flesh of children for use in glassmaking.[33] As tales of witches and werewolves became the stuff of legend, the monstrosity of ordinary humans was thrown into relief. When rampaging Catholics killed French Huguenots on St Bartholomew's Day in 1572, it was rumoured that their fat had been extracted and sold at public auction.[34] The next time large amounts of French fat were taken was during the French Revolution, and not just the kind sold by enterprising butchers. When pro-revolutionary troops were sent to quell the revolt in the western region of the Vendée, the soldiers supposedly created a makeshift rendering facility to extract the fat of 150 rebellious women. Casks of their fat were later sold in Nantes to appreciative citizens who found it 'a thousand times more pleasing than lard'.[35]

That human fat would be a mainstay in European pharmacies is thus not all that surprising. Yet the fact that druggists kept supplies of human fat and other body parts on hand does not mean the practice always had the seal of approval of doctors, many of whom had long argued that there was nothing special about human as opposed to any other kind of fat. In fact, by the mid-eighteenth century professional medical interest in human fat had already started to wane. 'At present', wrote the physician John Hill, 'we are grown wise enough to know, that the Virtues ascribed to the Parts of the human Body are all either imaginary, or such as may be found in other animal Substances.'[36] Such disapproval was compounded by a growing competition between doctors and executioners for access to dead bodies, the result being that the procuring of corpses was eventually taken out of the hands of executioners altogether.

Despite these changes, it took more than the frowning of a few doctors to stamp out the clandestine trafficking in human fat. A thriving fat trade had been reportedly operating for years out of the dissecting theatres of Paris. Its eventual discovery in the early nineteenth century was kept quiet for fear of alarming the public. Before being caught red-handed by the police agents who had been tipped off to their activities, medical assistants connected to various dissecting rooms had joined forces with their counterparts at the Faculty of Medicine to bring the fat to the people. They were hardly discreet about their activities, which seem to have been well known to everyone except the faculty administrators. Police raids revealed that at least four of the entrepreneurs had been storing the stuff at home. One was caught with massive amounts of it in his apartment. Another, presumably lacking more suitable containers, had filled two decorative sandstone fountains with purloined fat. While a fair amount was sold to medical charlatans and used to grease the wheels of medical carts, it was the city's enamellists and fake pearl-makers who benefited most from this trade, thinking that they were receiving fat procured from horses or dogs. Or so they said.[37]

The vital properties that seemed inherent in human fat, and which fostered anxieties about real and imagined beings that threatened to steal this substance from the body, persisted in the popular imagination throughout the eighteenth and nineteenth centuries. By 1828, a French physician was lamenting that common people remained enthralled to 'the most ridiculous prejudices' exploited by charlatans.[38] Yet among elites such properties were also being systematically demystified and denied through a number of developments that not only aimed at devivifying the stuff of life but also connected it more closely to processes of immorality, filth and putrefaction. Some of these changes, as we have seen, were medical and scientific, leading to new discoveries about the chemical composition of fats, as well as more overtly mechanistic views of the body and nutrition, that would further develop in the nineteenth century. Other developments were closely linked to shifts in morality and social class that reflected changes in the sensoria of white elites. Indeed, many came to view the practice of using human body parts as medicine as simply 'disgusting' and sought to distance the medical profession from practices that were coming to be viewed as barbaric and irrational.[39] As the next section shows, the vital qualities that made fat so coveted as a medical ingredient were also in a state of tension with its manifestation as sweat and grease. Extending aesthetic and moral ideas developed in the Renaissance, grease was entering into a more complicated relationship with 'grace'.

Grease and Grace

As a material substance, fat has always held an ambiguous status as both a carrier of vitality and a locus of decay. Yet the unfavourable connotations of the word 'greasy' seem to have accelerated around the mid-sixteenth century, notably in northern Europe, where religious reformers condemned the use of holy oil in Catholic rites. It was also around this time that the word 'smear' began to acquire connotations of dishonesty and untrustworthiness, eventually becoming a metaphor for describing the tarnishing of one's reputation. 'By the beginning of the seventeenth century,' Steven Connor notes, 'the disapproval in the word had curdled unmistakably into disgust.'[40] Protestants had no monopoly on this emotion. Even among Catholics, grease and fat signified sensuality and materialism, and were commonly cited in religious texts as material symbols of high living as well as moral and corporeal corruption. In her story cycle *The Heptameron* (1560), Marguerite de Navarre invoked biblical references to the insensateness of adipose tissue to criticize carnal individuals (*les charnelz*) who are 'too encased in their fat [*graisse*]' to know whether or not they even have a soul.[41] Drawing upon the rich imagery that circulated around the sin of gluttony, other moralists invoked the full spectrum of concerns that fat could evoke, from ugliness, filth and decay to health problems and beast-like servility. In addition to causing the stomach to revolt against the soul as well as the rest of the body, wrote one author, culinary delicacies should be avoided because they 'render the body flabby and effeminate [*lache et effeminé*]' and 'fill it with a mass of excrement [*d'un amas d'ordure*]', eventually transforming it into 'a source of corruption and decay'. It may be legitimate to fatten birds because they are destined to become human food, this author opined, but a person should never 'fill oneself with fat like these animals', not least because *la graisse* is a 'superfluity' that causes many physical problems while doing nothing beneficial for the body itself.[42]

The well-mannered body, as the last chapter explained, was elevated above the crude habits and gestures demonstrated by the lower animals. Noteworthy here is the vertical tension, inherited from late antiquity and persisting through the Middle Ages, between those who strive for 'higher' values and those seemingly content to wallow in the immanence of materiality. Hence, the glutton was one unable to 'raise the spirit' higher than his or her mouth, and instead 'only thinks of growing fat'.[43] In Protestant Germany, the Latin poet Helius Eobanus Hessus Christianized pagan authority to explain those whose diets prevented them from transcending corporeality:

'as Galen says, "a mind choking on fat and blood is incapable of discerning anything divine."'[44]

It is thus easy to see how fat, especially when viewed in terms of 'grease', could be treated as the virtual opposite of the recently minted term 'grace'. Emerging out of the seventeenth century and closely related to aesthetic ideas, grace referred to a positive set of qualities ranging from reputation (favour, good will, good opinion, credit) and morality (virtue, honesty, integrity) to physical appearance (beauty, comeliness, handsomeness) and behaviour (decorum).[45] By the mid-eighteenth century, grace was being defined as 'pleasingness itself' and linked to specific forms of movement and virtue. Movement was essential, for there can be 'no Grace without motion', as one commentator observed. According to a growing number of art critics, the robust nudes of Rubens notably lacked such qualities. Described as 'the greatest and most general Misleader of our Judgments', [sic] Rubens had foolishly depicted women as they actually appeared in the Netherlands rather than according to loftier aesthetic standards. 'His very *Graces* are all fat,' it was said, and thus not really graceful at all.[46]

Grease and grace also divided women along lines of class and morality. Indeed, the elision of fat with animality, sin and corruption was materialized in kitchen grease and the low-born women who collected and sold it. For centuries, the greasy drippings and other effluvia collected from the kitchens of elites were peddled on the streets of European cities, destined either for soap-makers, tallow chandlers or, more likely, the tables of the poor. Such foul 'kitchen-stuff' was colloquially linked to the figure of the kitchen wench or any female domestic servant whose 'greasy' sexuality aroused illicit desire as well as moralizing alarm.[47] The plump kitchen wench Nell in Shakespeare's *Comedy of Errors* (III.2) is a case in point. This 'very beastly creature' promised to make a 'fat marriage' because she herself was 'all grease', from her tallow-drenched clothes and grimy face to a body that was spherical 'like a globe; I could find out countries in her'. The fatness of the kitchen wench was readily linked to her 'dirty' demeanour and 'filthy' sexuality, all of which were as greasily alluring as they were potentially repulsive. Although not a kitchen wench, a similarly equivocal figure is cut by Ursula, the sweating pig-woman in Ben Jonson's *Bartholomew Fair* (1614). Described as a 'walking Sow of Tallow . . . An Inspir'd Vessel of Kitchin-stuff' whose body is fit to grease the wheels and axles of coaches, Ursula's sexuality threatens to drown a man in thick, greasy matter: 'Is she your Quagmire . . . is this your bog? . . . 'Twere like falling into a whole Shire of Butter.'[48]

Fat's connection to sensuality was, of course, not unique to this period. Indeed, to 'get greased' had been a metaphor for intercourse at least since the time of the medieval fabliaux.[49] Images of slippery, engulfing sensuality may also alert us to the practical uses of oil and other unguents for sexual purposes during this period. When infused with certain herbs they had heating qualities that elicited desire and heightened pleasure, and when used as lubricants they assisted vaginal or anal intercourse.[50] It is perhaps no wonder that in England the dubious-sounding remedy known as 'oil of man', the recipe for which called for the melted fat of criminals, was also a slang expression for semen, 'an oyle which women should not (unlawfully) tast of'.[51] The potentially rotten carnality of grease and fat extended to popular speech, where those who uttered obscenities in the seventeenth century were said to 'talk fat' (*parler Gras*) or to speak in/with a 'fat tongue' (*la langue Grasse*).[52]

We cannot separate a growing aversion to grease from the perceptual changes taking place among elites. Among the nobility and bourgeoisie, wiping the grease from one's fingers with a napkin or cloth (rather than licking them clean) was considered a habit worth instilling in boys as part of their overall education in civility.[53] Grease was also associated with sweat, a bodily secretion closely linked to urine and blood but which was also thought to contain quantities of fat as well. As a form of excrement whose periodic evacuation from the body helped to ensure good health, sweat was an equivocal fluid capable of eliciting feelings of shame and contamination.[54] Uneasiness about sweating increasingly demanded that one change clothes on a more regular basis than before. In a culture where people avoided excessive contact with water, especially the immersion of the whole body, clean white linen acted like a sponge that, by removing oily substances from the skin, allowed sweat to be excreted more readily. Aversion to grease was also an education in sensibility in which repugnance toward the oily and dirty diminished tolerance for wearing sweaty garments. Encouraged by the high status that pristine white linen had achieved, the power of whiteness to signify cleanliness and status had become irrefutable by the seventeenth century.[55]

Nor was this a passing obsession. Well into the nineteenth century, long before full-body bathing became a norm of personal hygiene, being 'clean' meant wearing clothes that were free of grease, dirt and odour.[56]

This distaste for grease and the things it connoted throws into relief some of the problems posed by the very corpulent, whose fat was often explained as the accumulation of excremental bodily fluids.[57] English travellers to tropical climates sometimes reported that the extreme temperatures caused their fat to 'melt' and accumulate inside of their bodies rather than being released through perspiration, an alarming condition resembling what we might call 'heat stroke' today.[58] Under ordinary conditions their sweat would flow freely, and throughout the seventeenth century corpulent people were lampooned in terms of the sweat and oil that rendered them 'leaky' when compared to the more properly contained bodies that elites aspired to achieve.[59] This leakiness was an issue partly because very fat bodies were said to 'abound with many crude and superfluous humours', as the physician Tobias Venner put it.[60] To be fat was to be more predisposed than others to an embarrassing overflowing of one's boundaries, and by habitually soiling his or her clothes the fat person risked compromising the imagined purity of whiteness. The contempt heaped upon Shakespeare's Falstaff is consonant with such concerns, and shows that repeated references to him as a 'greasy knight' and 'this whale, with so many tuns of oil in his belly' (*The Merry Wives of Windsor*, ii.1) pertain to issues that cannot be reduced to size and shape. Being 'as subject to heat as butter; a man of continual dissolution and thaw' (*MWW*, iii.5), Falstaff himself expressed concern that his enemies 'would melt me out of my fat drop by drop, and liquor fishermen's boots with me' (iv.5). Henry iv's recommendations to Falstaff thus fit well with the times: 'Make less thy body hence, and more thy grace' (*Henry iv, Part ii*, v.5).

The problems of sweat and grease were further complicated by their durable connection to ideas about superfluity, putrefaction and immorality.[61] Early advocates of gymnastics encouraged the idea that, through vigorous movements, ordinary bodies could be purified of gross and encumbering substances. Laurent Joubert, we have seen, proposed that through the sweat of exertion one could eliminate 'an abundant mass of soft flesh [*viande molle*] that is as useless as it is superfluous', thus stripping away all unnecessary 'chaff' to reveal 'the pure grain' of the healthy body.[62] For Francis Bacon, such substances

The association between fat and sweat was well-established by the time Mr Jacob
Powell, Butcher of Stebbing, died in 1754. 'Remarkable for his uncommon Bulk
& Size', the 40-stone/560-lb Powell 'was carried by sixteen Men to his Grave'.
Despite the wonder that stories of Powell and other famous fat men generated,
Powell was likened to Falstaff (in Shakespeare's *Henry IV*) and subjected to some
jesting animalization: 'Thy Native Essex may now truly say / Death has not struck
so fat a Calf to Day'. William Wadd, *Comments on Corpulency* (1829), illustrated by
A. M. Broadley, 1901.

were bound up with decay. Just as all forms of excrement are 'the refuse and putrefactions of nourishment', Bacon explained, so too are 'things that are fat or sweet' to be considered 'aptest to putrify'.[63]

When we consider the work of the Scottish doctor George Cheyne, who in the early eighteenth century became famous for his reducing diet, we must recall that his bodily ideal was a largely spiritual one that required the purgation of excess humours and other superfluities. Framing his analyses within his Christian background, Cheyne viewed such excrescences as the natural by-product of life in a fallen world in which 'We see Luxury, inordinate Leachery, Riot and Laziness, first incrassat [fatten], then inflame, and at last mortify and putrify human and animal Bodies.' Against the downward tug of all things rotten, Cheyne recommended practices that would 'lighten, enliven and volatize' encrusted bodies, namely 'Abstinence, a low and cool Regimen, Exercise and Air'.[64] The kind of bodywork Cheyne imagined suggests the intervention of a sculptor or tradesman perfecting an ideally ethereal object rendered gross through the accumulation of a kind of sediment. All human learning, culture and labour must ultimately be devoted to

> *fileing* off, *melting* away, and *scraping* down, those Chains, and Crust superinduced upon them; and are only removing *Super-fluities*, reducing *Excrescences*, and rendering the gross *Patchwork* super-induced on our spiritual Body, pliant, supple and correspondent, with the least Resistance to it; that the *Creation Body* may be at Liberty to extend and disincumber [*sic*] itself.[65]

Thus Cheyne could declare that 'the gross ruinous *Planet* we inhabit' has covered over the 'original *aethereal* Vehicle' of the human soul.[66] If Cheyne saw materiality as a weighty and filthy burden for the soul to bear, less otherworldly authors made similar points. Commenting on the threat that great fatness posed to health and beauty, Antoine Le Camus also explained that this gross substance generated stupidity through the downward pressure it imposed upon the mind: 'The soul is oppressed by the enormous weight of this material, and all the functions of the understanding languish so much that all brilliance is removed from the mind.'[67] Rotten, heavy and filthy, fat may have been imbued with vitality but remained an obstacle to many forms of transcendence.

The alchemy capable of transmuting such base material emerged from the same demands for purity that condemned it. Of particular concern were foul odours, which counted among the most telling signs of the coarse materiality that so vexed Cheyne and Le Camus. Up until the time that strong scents began to be distrusted in the early nineteenth century, the wealthy had been trying since the Middle Ages to mask the odour of decay with the heavy-handed use of powders, perfumes and other aromatics.[68] Rather startling, then, is the extent to which, when transformed into fragrant balms and ointments, otherwise corruptible fat could be used to *conceal* the odour of decay and even to preserve or restore youthfulness. Thus elites would frequently make use of pomades, which consisted of scented animal fat worn on the head and absorbed into the hair and scalp.[69] Unfortunately such applications also rendered the complexion especially greasy, and women who employed them often had to avoid hot places lest their faces begin to 'melt' in embarrassing ways.[70]

Beyond its role in covering up foul odours, fat was also a mainstay of cosmetics and skincare. To promote a more youthful appearance, one could use pomade, a cream made from animal fat or vegetable oil that promised to clean, lighten and moisturize the hands and face. Those wishing to have softer hands could sleep wearing gloves 'that had been' dipped in fat.[71] Finally, the scent of decay could also be washed away with another fat-based product, soap, high-quality versions of which began to be imported into England from the Castile region of Spain during the late sixteenth century. Considered a household necessity by the mid-seventeenth century, soap's importance to elite and middle-class culture would continue to grow throughout the modern era.[72]

Such alchemy was necessarily incomplete. If fats drawn from animal and vegetable sources could perform cleansing and beautifying functions, personal grease and fat continued to be closely linked to putrefaction. Anatomists preferred to dissect corpses that were relatively fresh and not very fat, partly because excess adipose tissue made it difficult for them to separate the parts they wished to dissect, but also because 'it greatly accelerates the decomposition [*la pourriture*] of the Cadaver'.[73] Gravediggers also attested to the inherently putrefying tendency of fat. Concerned that the rotting corpses in the cemeteries of Paris were emitting noxious miasmas that contaminated the air, in the late 1770s the government began the task of relocating the bodies. The men who exhumed some of these from large common graves in the cemetery of the Innocents discovered cadavers that were in more or less good condition, except for their surprising transformation into a gelatinous, greyish-white mass they compared to soft white cheese but ended up calling 'fat' (*gras*). Early analyses of this widely reported phenomenon, subsequently known as adipocere or *gras des cimetières*, proposed that bodies that had been already 'overloaded with fat' in life tended to pass more easily into this state after death.[74] Perhaps the more disturbing speculation was that muscle could turn to fat even before death, and that within five years of burial *all bodies* were susceptible to having their skin, organs and muscles turn to fat.[75] Even though chemists would later describe this transformation of matter into a soap-like substance as *saponification*, around 1800 becoming fat seemed like the way of all flesh.[76]

Partly inspired by a renewed awareness of 'the precarious nature of organic life', anxieties about the ineradicable presence of decay within life promoted among the upper classes 'a permanent monitoring of the dissolution of individuals and the self'.[77] Along with concern about the odour that such substances produced, vigilance about greasy sweat underscored the anxiety experienced by the upper-class individual who 'was unable to *fix* – that is the crucial term – or control the elements which composed him'.[78] Always already in a state of flux, the ripening or overripe body was a palpable reminder of processes that frustrated attempts at achieving self-mastery. Sweat that accumulated in the armpits, genitals or buttocks was not only said to 'inflame' those areas, but was liable to be reabsorbed by the body, thereby 'disposing the humours to putrefaction'. An argument in favour of the localized cleaning that the recent innovation of the bidet could provide, observations like this also spoke to the potential health risks posed by sweat.[79] Like 'so many common sewers to a city', warned one physician, the 'excretory ducts' of the skin were meant 'to carry off redundant humours, which retained, must turn to putrid filth and nastiness'. This was why failure to regularly wipe away 'greasy, clammy' sweat could cause itching and blemishes as well as 'stench and putrefactions'. The same author explained that warm baths were most effective in opening the pores and releasing this excrement from the body, even though afterwards some might find 'a gross fat substance' floating on the top of the bathwater in such quantities that it is 'capable of being collected like fat upon broth'.[80]

The immoderate consumption of dietary fats did not improve this situation. If some proposed that the putrefaction had already begun simply by eating too many animal products, their views of fat remained quite similar. 'We debauch in fat and butter beyond what any stomach can thoroughly digest,' pronounced Dr William Grant. Such substances easily became 'rancid' in the body:

> they frequently find their way into the vessels, mix with the blood, are deposited in different parts of our body, and make us fat, and bloated, and big-bellied; then they stagnate and corrupt, breed scurvy, gout, and other diseases.[81]

This was the reason why authoritative sources like the *Encyclopédie* proposed that 'excessive embonpoint can be corrected through stomach purges' occasioned by bouts of diarrhoea,[82] and why – up to the present, in fact – some would insist that constipation was a *cause* of weight gain. In this respect, we may detect echoes of traditional agricultural thinking within such 'enlightened' medical linkages between fat, excrement, decay and dirt in general. A recoil from fat seems to pace a more generalized aversion to excrement. Insofar as both stood as reminders of human connections to organic life, they were substances that have been typically disavowed in bourgeois culture.[83]

Such repeated links between fat and decay encouraged the idea that corpulence was itself a kind of putrefaction. This is why Antoine Le Camus could declare that 'excessive embonpoint corrupts/rots beauty [*gâte la beauté*]'.[84] Thus when the Scottish physiologist Malcolm Flemyng described corpulence as resulting from noxious oily fluids (including sweat, urine and faeces) that had not been properly evacuated from the body, he fitted broadly into the general perspectives of his day. Somewhat more novel was his recommendation that fat people should use soap – internally, as a liquid, paste or pill – because of its properties as a mild diuretic and dissolver of oil. Flemyng's approach to corpulence reflected the emergence of a more modern medical attitude that separated corpulence out from other dietetic concerns. Yet his unorthodox treatment connected medical thought with the wider culture that perceived an intimate relationship between cleanliness, health and morality. Just as soap could restore filthy linen to 'cleanness, sweetness, and whiteness' – the sort of thing elites were already doing to ensure that their clothes were spotless – Flemyng assured readers that it could also be used for cleansing the fat from within.[85] This also revealed the paradoxical role that fat played in the cultural imagination. In many respects, fat was seen as a kind of filth that accumulated within the body. Armed with soap, however, one could fight fat with fat, a practice that was widely recommended well into the nineteenth century. In the 1820s, William Wadd was spreading the news of a man whose corpulence was 'perfectly cured' by using Castile soap for a mere six years.[86] That soap was used to clean middle-class bodies, inside and out, reinforced the subtle but growing alignment of moderately proportioned bodies with cleanliness, morality and whiteness.

This last term, *whiteness*, has received minimal treatment in historical scholarship on fat, even though intimations of it appear throughout the discourses of grease and corpulence traced in this chapter. In the colonial imagination, the loaded term 'grease' conjured up 'the clinging filth of savagery, the grime of uncontained bodies and unsavory associations'. The lascivious connotations of the greasy were widespread, especially among Evangelical Christians who used it to describe a troubling 'stickiness' that marked 'a body that refused to separate itself from the world'. Grease was, in a very real sense, the opposite of Grace.[87] Although this conflation of grease with racial otherness developed in the eighteenth century to be most fully formed in the imperialist discourses of the nineteenth, we have already caught glimpses of it in Alpini's report on Egyptian women who used oils and fatty foods to enhance their corpulence.[88]

The 'fatness' of non-Western lands that we encountered in Chapter Six was further enriched by repeated references to the bodies and habits of their inhabitants. Indeed, describing moments where the encounter with non-Western peoples elicits disgust appears to have been 'a textual convention of the travelogues and proto-ethnographies that proliferated in the seventeenth century'.[89] Links between greasiness and non-white populations accelerated amid seventeenth-century reports of native peoples smearing their bodies with fat and eating foul-smelling fatty meats.[90] If French missionaries in North America commented approvingly on the athletic physiques of native males, sometimes with favourable comparisons to classical models, the indigenous healers who smeared their bodies with pitch were culturally tarred with the interlinked imagery of grease, filth, sexuality and femininity.[91]

Early travellers in Africa commented frequently upon the natives' unexpected use of animal fat, the viscous and malodorous qualities of which seemed to amplify the revulsion elicited by the physical ugliness Europeans invariably observed. The German explorer Peter Kolb remarked on this practice among the Khoikhoi (widely known as 'Hottentots'), who smeared their bodies with butter and sheep's fat, mixed with soot, to darken their appearance and protect themselves from the sun. Despite his disgust at this practice, Kolb was unusual in the relativistic stance he adopted toward unfamiliar customs.[92] Conceding that this was a reasonable way of coping with the harsh environment, Kolb noted that otherwise 'the continual excessive Heats would, in all Probability, exhaust and destroy them.'[93]

No pragmatic explanation for the practice exonerated these people from being a source of disgust. Kolb's tolerance was not matched by Gottfried Lessing, whose garish (and widely cited) portrait of Hottentots combined images of dripping and rotten fat with other traits Europeans considered ugly, from flat noses and flabby breasts to the entrails they sometimes draped over their bodies. Lessing considered this a useful way of throwing the superiority of classical beauty into relief. In 1766 he challenged his readers to 'think of this as an object of an ardent, reverent, tender love; let one hear this uttered in the exalted language of gravity and admiration and refrain from laughter!'[94] As we will see, within a few decades grease smeared on the outside of non-white bodies would come to be materially and morally associated with the fat that swelled from within. This would become a matter of taste that prompted Europeans to re-evaluate what they might once have considered beautiful and graceful.

✳

The modern development of disgust towards corpulence must be viewed against the backdrop of growing intolerance for 'dirt' in general as well as 'the metaphysical anxiety engendered by the advance of putrefaction to the very depths of being'.[95] As we have seen, whether in the form of grease from meals or sweat from the body, fat represented a form of contamination that threatened to undermine the fetishized 'whiteness' of Western bodies. The physiologist Anthelme Richerand gathered these strands in 1807. Writing about the 'fatty oil' [*huile grasse*] secreted from the pores that prevents the skin from drying out, he noted that this 'adipose substance, with which the skin is anointed, is abundant and fetid in some persons'. This foul substance was, for instance, 'more copious in the African negroes, as if Nature had been anxious to guard against the too rapid desiccation, by the burning atmosphere of tropical climates'. Not only was this internal secretion complemented by 'the tallow, the fat, and the disgusting substances with which the Caffres and the Hottentots anoint their body', but it was directly linked to body fat. 'It is this humour which soils our linen,' Richerand explained, adding that 'I know several [presumably white] people overloaded with fat' who sweat copiously when their bodies are 'heated by the slightest exertion. They all grease their linen in less than twenty-four hours.'[96]

As we will see, this link between fat and grease – and the opposition of both to 'grace' – persisted into the nineteenth century. Always on a diet and involved in one exercise regimen or another, the poet Lord Byron ruefully counted himself among the greasy fat people described by Richerand. His widely cited quip that 'fat is an oily dropsy' was thus based on more than the great poet's fertile imagination.[97] Fat was a concept that allowed for conceptual slippages from dirtiness and decay to the complex realm populated by the subhuman. Even when fatness was linked to the now fading notion of a phlegmatic temperament, such a person's body was still 'characterized by a soft doughtiness of the whole surface [and] by the animality of its fleshy and ponderous countenance'.[98]

A related withdrawal from greasy fat was taking place in the domestic interior as well. By the 1830s, growing numbers of middle-class British women began to recoil from kitchen work as dirty, coarse and contaminating, and gladly entrusted the cleaning of these greasy 'nether regions' of their homes to hired cooks.[99] This is why cooks were warned to conceal the tub of kitchen-stuff, 'an evil which exists in every kitchen', from the sensitive eyes of the mistress of the house.[100] The 'evil' of filthy grease slipped easily into matters of morality and trustworthiness. Among the popular orders of nineteenth-century Paris, the terms 'fat' (*gras, graisse*) and 'oil' (*huile*) functioned as ambiguous metaphors for money and financial success.[101] Accompanying the rise of soap as a 'yardstick of civilization' was a pronounced distaste for those who fell short of evolving standards of cleanliness, morality and humanity. By the end of the century, British soap manufacturers would be gratuitously using racial imagery to market their products to anxious bourgeois people across the world, drawing none-too-subtle connections between the filth they wiped from their bodies and the 'great unwashed' both at home and abroad.[102] And what of fat people themselves? In the United States those attending the annual Fat Man's Ball in St Louis were colourfully described by a local newspaper as 'Living Grease'.[103] The Jacksonian health reformer and vegetarian advocate, William Alcott, would go even further, condemning the stuff of life as a 'disgusting' excremental substance unbefitting a human being. 'Let us leave it to the swine and other kindred quadrupeds, to dispose of gross half poisonous matter, by converting it into, or burying it in fat.'[104]

A pronounced distrust of grease and fat, as well as all of their ambiguous connotations, was becoming a hallmark of an elite identity that predicated itself on the synonymous and nearly interchangeable 'human' ideals of cleanliness, morality and whiteness. What linked fat white people to black Africans was the rancidness of their sweat, and both groups were coming to mark a deviation from the clean, polished and contained bodies that 'civilized' people aspired to possess. Manifested as sweat, adipose tissue or even cooking oil, fat emerged in the nineteenth century as a powerful yardstick of savagery. In the form of soap or pomade, though, fat could be redeemed as a promoter of purity and grace, thus attesting to its lingering alchemical potential. 'Nations are so much the more brutal and rude', declared an American writer at the beginning of the nineteenth century, 'the more voracious they are, the more disgusting and nauseous things they live on, the more raw and unprepared meats or carrion they devour, and, lastly, the greater avidity they have for pure fat or animal oils.' That overindulgence in fat would produce disgustingly bloated bodies was a logical extension of such a claim. As one 1804 article had it:

> All the nations of southern Asia regard obesity as the height of beauty, and in order to acquire it they drink melted butter, or other oleaginous liquors. This taste and conceit the Hindoos have adopted from the Mongolian nations of southern Asia.[105]

From the malodorous sweat of Africans and the oily fare of Indians to the grease stains of Richerand's husky buddies, the materiality of fat signalled the abject nature of other races as well as the repressed animality and mortality of bourgeois whites themselves.

It also materialized the principle of incorporation – a seemingly cross-cultural assumption that 'you are what you eat' – that made it possible to link the bodies and morals of 'savage' peoples to the gross and filthy victuals they consumed.[106] As the next chapter shows, the fat that had been observed mainly on the skin became viewed as integral to many non-white bodies and became even more distanced from European perceptions of what their own bodies should look like.

NINE

SAVAGE DESIRES
'Primitive' Fat and 'Civilized' Slenderness

When travelling to Athens in the opening years of the nineteenth century, the Irish painter Edward Dodwell was not amused by what he found. Like many cultured white men travelling to Greece, he had hoped to encounter women whose bodies approximated the 'sylph-like forms' and 'airy elegance' that 'enrapture the beholder in [classical] statues'. Instead of animated museum pieces worthy of his refined sensibility, Dodwell was confronted by the rude spectacle of actual women. In addition to their unpleasantly pale complexions, these deviations from his aesthetic ideal suffered from 'premature corpulence' brought on by a hot climate and indolent lifestyles. What really irked Dodwell was the fact that their fatness was for modern Greeks more 'an object of desire than aversion'. Back in the good old days of antiquity, Dodwell and many others had been taught, women 'did not attempt to fascinate by the ponderous magnitude of their dimensions, but on the contrary took every method to prevent corpulence'.[1] Variations of Dodwell's complaint were not uncommon in the nineteenth century. The usual explanation for the collapse of classical beauty in modern Athens was that, over many centuries, the culture had succumbed to the influence of its Turkish neighbours, often described as a sensual and fat-loving people with no appreciation for beauty, much less learning or morality.[2] This is why, as another author noted, a woman with moderate proportions like the Medici Venus 'would find few clients' were she offered alongside the many fat prostitutes available in a city like Constantinople.[3]

At the heart of Dodwell's concerns was the rhetorical question Prospero Alpini had asked centuries earlier about Egyptian fattening practices: 'Can one desire anything more shameful than obesity [*obaesitate*] acquired through the wicked vice of the flesh and of unchecked sensuality?'[4] Echoes of Alpini's question became more audible as the Age of Exploration gave way to the rise of overseas empires, the same period in which European elites grew increasingly suspicious of fat in its other forms. In addition to reports on how various indigenous peoples relished fatty foods, inhabited disturbingly fecund landscapes, smeared grease on their bodies, or cut fat from their enemies' corpses, by the late eighteenth century a growing number of authors observed that many of the world's peoples profoundly admired fat and would, if they had the means, seek to make themselves as large as possible. Insofar as it literally seemed to incarnate all of the other ways in which the problems of fat could be imagined, the deliberate and even forced fattening of non-white bodies mobilized a wide spectrum of Western misgivings about this ambiguous substance. The grease of fat, in other words, was inconsistent with the grace of Greece.

The role of non-Western cultures in the formation of Western stereotypes about fat is unusual in discussions of the nineteenth century. Historical treatments of Victorian dieting usually focus on the medicalization of 'obesity' made possible by the quantification of bodily states in relation to biomedical norms and their relationship to the needs of states. The medicalization of fatness went hand-in-glove with its quantification, which grew out of the rise of chemical medicine in the sixteenth century to become more fully developed around 1800. Although by this time many elements of the ancient humoral model of the body had been discarded, some of its core ingredients were retained and reworked in references to individual temperaments. Important, too, is the rise of statistical bases for determining the proper weight of the 'normal' person, which would gain more momentum in the twentieth century. So, too, would ways of promoting the dietary health of the industrial workforce, and the eventual development of the field of nutrition and the widespread circulation of the calorie as a unit of measure. Such changes contributed to a biopolitical understanding of bodies as quasi-mechanical entities capable of being managed by the state and made to function efficiently in the economy. There is now a fairly substantial body of scholarship addressing these important developments, most of which focuses primarily on developments within the West itself.[5]

As the main focus of this book is not on dieting and nutrition, though, this chapter takes a different approach to the Victorian era. By peering at nineteenth-century discussions of fat through a colonial lens, it reveals the imperial and racial subtext to our contemporary tendencies to demonize corpulence. It argues that, whether understood as a sexual yearning for very fleshy bodies or a wish to become fat oneself, references to an illicit desire for fleshiness on the part of certain cultures allowed white Westerners to disconnect their own growing corpulence from any sort of cultural approval of fat. While allowing for congenital factors in the etiology of corpulence, this ethno-medical discourse suggested that when 'civilized' white people became overweight it was either the result of factors beyond their control (such as climate or heredity) or of lapses of willpower (overindulgence and/or lack of exercise). Thus, as the gastronome Jean Anthelme Brillat-Savarin put it in the 1820s, when 'civilized' people become fat it is 'almost always due to our own fault'.[6] It was not because they saw anything beautiful or desirable in fatness, and certainly not because they willed such a thing for themselves or for others. The modern West thus revived and radicalized the Graeco-Roman belief that deliberately fattening oneself or one's children 'belonged to the sphere of the strange and exotic'.[7] In so doing, it ensured that race and ethnicity would be central to characterizations of bodies and bodily practices that fell outside of an increasingly restrictive norm.

This focus on race also helped to widen the focus of anti-fat sentiments. Brillat-Savarin may have written disparagingly of his own belly as an 'enemy', but growing opposition to fatness was beginning to cohere more densely around the white female body. Having long represented an obstacle to the virility of men because it could signify a lack of industry and a cowardly clinging to life, through the course of the nineteenth century, fatness was becoming more consistently condemned as antithetical to the beauty and morality of women, who were held up as models of the 'civilized' purity and proportion that the Western aesthetic tradition was supposed to embody. It was roughly during this period, then, that the burden of anti-fat sentiments began to fall more heavily upon girls and women whose bodies seemed to fall short of the 'civilized' white ideal. The problem, however, was that desires for excess flesh also seemed to proliferate within the West itself, and by the end of the nineteenth century disgust at the 'savagery' of those who professed a love of fat would be mobilized against whites who failed to live up to the values of their own culture. If Western societies partly saw themselves by reflecting upon the colonial 'others' who populated empire, what loomed before their eyes in the nineteenth century was often constructed out of greasy fat.

Empires of Fat

It is widely known that, in many world cultures, fatness has been deliberately cultivated as a means of storing up the forces of life and reproduction that become desirable signs of fertility, strength and status. European encounters with such attitudes played a significant role in shaping their views of the 'civilized' white body. Indeed, empire provided countertypes against which models of white manhood and womanhood could be measured, usually by drawing attention to physical extremes that threw into relief the 'moderate' bodies that whites were supposed to possess. Yet the early nineteenth century was a transitional phase in European perceptions of non-Western bodies. Just a few decades earlier, it was not uncommon to find discussions of female beauty couched in relativist language emphasizing cultural variations in what constituted the ideal form. When the physician Pierre Roussel described excess embonpoint as being contrary to beauty, for example, he hastened to add (with a reference to Prospero Alpini's report on Egypt tucked away in a footnote) that he was only referring to 'conventional ideas . . . received among us'.[8] By 1800 much of this high-minded relativism was falling away as deviations from the Western standard were increasingly described as 'disgusting' and the desires that fired them disparaged as baffling and even unnatural. This was not simply a matter of the ethnocentric judgement of non-Western tastes. As one beauty expert of the period opined, Rubens could have been one of the greatest painters in the world had he not evinced this 'strange taste which deforms [*dénature*] his finest works'.[9] Although these seemingly incommensurate passions were explained with reference to climate, culture and, in time, the concept of race, the idea that many non-Western cultures deeply admired fat bodies would remain intact through the twentieth century.

Much could be written about how Europeans engaged with those cultures that seemed inordinately attached to corpulence in the

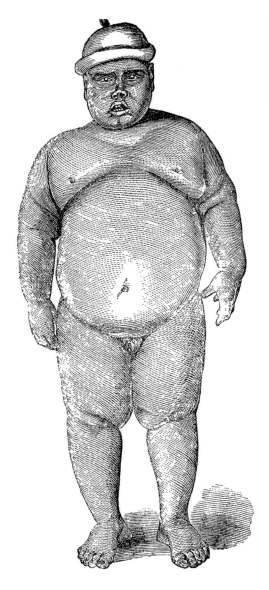

Shakarm, the 'Fat Boy' of Bombay. W. G. Don, 'Remarkable Case of Obesity in a Hindoo Boy Aged Twelve', *The Lancet*, 1859.

nineteenth century. At various times, the Chinese, Turks, Australian Aborigines, Eskimos, and especially Africans, were all described with reference to fatness. For the British, the problem was especially note-worthy on the Indian subcontinent. In addition to the slight bodies of 'effeminate Bengalis' and the well-built physiques of the 'martial races' observed by colonizers after mid-century, the 'monstrous' cor-pulence of upper-caste Hindus frequently generated comments from travellers, ethnographers and physicians.[10] Dispelling suspicions that normally vegetarian Brahmins might have been sneaking meat to achieve such 'rotundity of corporation', the physician James Johnson assured his readers that 'all is accomplished by *ghee* [clarified butter] and indolence!'[11] The *Imperial Dictionary* of 1859 explained exactly what 'indolence' meant to the colonizers. From the Latin *indolentia*, it meant 'freedom from pain' but also something more than mere idleness or an 'indisposition to labour'. 'Indolence, like laziness, implies a constitutional or habitual love of ease; idleness does not.' To be indolent was to be 'listless; sluggish; indulging in ease . . . Free from pain; as an indolent tumour'.[12]

Indian corpulence was not only grounded in the sluggishness of indolence. When the British served up their impressions of subcontinental fatness, their comments often came swimming in grease and laced with animality. This allowed a variety of travellers to record encounters with 'a fat, oily Bengalee Babu',[13] to remark on the 'increased oiliness and obesity which always mark the prosperous native',[14] or to declare Indians generally to be an 'easy, oily people . . . [who] get fat when they feed well, with the certainty of a pig or a goose'.[15] This posed challenges to the sensory and affective habitus of British elites. In railway carriages the sensory effect was heightened since, 'being often fat, the natives perspire very freely . . . which intensifies the [unpleasant olfactory] effect of the anointment [rubbed on their skin].'[16] Greasy fat also stained the pages of literary works. Alexander Allardyce's novel *The City of Sunshine* (1877) describes the wealthy proprietor of a spirits shop as 'a bull-headed, frog-necked Hindoo, whose obese and greasy person was the fitting envelope of a bloated and slippery moral nature'.[17] And we cannot neglect Rudyard Kipling's vividly viscous impressions of Calcutta in the evening. Kipling's prose slides easily from visions of immorality, stench and decay to the spectacle of vicious corpulence. The insalubrious 'dark' parts of this 'city of dreadful night' are a form of 'muck' that visitors do not so much enter as 'dive into'. The Calcutta night itself is 'greasy', the air 'heavy with a faint, sour stench', and its inhabitants 'ruined' by the sweltering heat of Bengal. Indeed, the very soil of Bengal was 'fat and greasy with good living, and the wealth of the bodies of innumerable dead things'. Rather than offer relief from this oppressive oiliness, the city's brothels instead proffered repulsive figures of greasy sensuality. While it was possible to encounter a slender 'Dainty Iniquity' in such places, Kipling conceded, a Calcutta whorehouse was more likely to offer a 'Fat Vice' whom the locals consider to be "'a monstrous well-preserved woman". On this point, as on some others, the races will agree to differ."[18]

Such observations about subcontinental fatness may seem counterintuitive, especially when one considers the high rates of malnutrition in many parts of India. But fat is not something containable in simple references to body shape. What was at stake in these reports was less the empirical evidence of widespread corpulence than the assumption that what was considered desirable for elites necessarily fired the passions of everyone else. If high-caste Indians deliberately became corpulent, it stood to reason that fatness must be considered a very positive thing among the populace as a whole. Ordinary people, it was assumed, must also harbour a desire to become fat, but simply cannot do so under their current impoverished conditions. This assumption was backed up by reports claiming that even the peasantry thought that becoming 'fat is a distinction' while suggesting that 'better government would ameliorate the condition of this people.'[19] Others detected a love of fat in Indian religious culture, noting how the faithful prostrate themselves before 'the most monstrous and hideous deformities imaginable', thus seeming to 'deify' corpulence and ugliness generally.[20] By dismissing the deity Ganesha as a 'belly-god', Christian missionaries enlisted an ancient epithet to propose that here was a god truly made in the idealized self-image of the people. Although obviously not referring to the god's distinctive elephantine head, one author wrote that 'If Ganesha stood he would be the very image of many fat, rupee-worshipping Baniyas [members of the merchant and money-lending caste], to be seen all over India.'[21] Through such logic, one could generalize about the innermost desires of entire populations while accounting for the emaciated and starving bodies that often struck the eyes of observers. With the means and opportunity, ethnographers and popularizers seemed to conclude, all would become fat, and that was the problem.

Indian society offered many opportunities for British observers to contemplate the moral problems that a love of corpulence might denote. In the European colonial imagination, however, Africa was the region most consistently and disparagingly linked to fat. The earliest sources may be medieval in origin. In the early fourteenth century, the Dominican missionary Jordan Catala of Sévérac had negatively appraised East African bodies as 'very black, pot-bellied, fat, but short; having thick lips and squab nose, overhanging forehead, and hideous countenances'.[22] Non-Europeans had made similar observations about African bodies, but in tellingly different terms. The fourteenth-century Moroccan traveller Ibn Battuta approvingly acknowledged a preference for very fat women among the women of the nomadic Berber tribe known as the Bardama:

> They are the most perfectly beautiful of women and have the most elegant figures; they are pure white and very fat. I have not seen in the country any who are as fat. They feed on cow's milk and pounded millet, which they drink, mixed with water, uncooked, night and morning.[23]

As we have seen in the case of Alpini, European reactions to African fattening practices were more negative, and the combination of fascination and revulsion that such local customs provoked grew more common as European explorers ventured further into Africa towards the end of the eighteenth century.

For some it was the deliberate and forced fattening of girls that was most arresting. One widely circulating account came from the Scottish explorer Mungo Park when he travelled among the Moors in the late 1790s. Corroborating earlier French reports of Moorish customs,[24] Park marvelled at how

> gracefulness of figure and motion, and a countenance enlivened by expression, are by no means essential points in their standard [of female beauty]; with them corpulence and beauty appear to be terms nearly synonymous.

What Park described as a 'prevalent taste for unwieldiness of bulk' compelled mothers to feed their daughters copious amounts of couscous and camel milk so that they might one day achieve the desired body size that would make them fit for marriage:

> A woman of even moderate pretensions, must be one who cannot walk without a slave under each arm to support her, and a perfect beauty is a load for a camel.[25]

The Frenchman René Caillié found nothing to admire in such aesthetic views when he explored the nearby Brakna region in the 1820s. 'The Moors have no interest in beauty of form or mind,' he bluntly concluded; rather 'what is a defect for us is an attraction for them.' Among the most widely cited aspects of Caillié's account were details about how girls were deliberately fattened, even being pinched, beaten and tormented if they failed to consume massive amounts of food so they could become 'enormous' by the age of twelve.[26]

The information in Park and Caillié's reports was widely cited and reproduced throughout the nineteenth century. In the person of Saartjie Baartman, though, metropolitan Europeans could witness African corpulence at first hand. Taken from her home in southern Africa, Baartman was exhibited in Britain and France as the 'Hottentot Venus' from 1810 until her death in 1815.[27] Scholars have rightly pointed out the nexus of race and sexuality involved in the public displays of Baartman's body in the early nineteenth century, but have afforded less attention to the role this 'savage' played in mediating European perceptions of fat. In fact Baartman's large buttocks were popularly seen as a sign of corpulence rather than steatopygia, and in addition to being encouraged to gawk at her body spectators were invited to touch and prod her behind.[28] That fatness was among the main sources of her fascination was not lost on William Wadd, who took the opportunity in his *Cursory Remarks on Corpulence* to illustrate the 'disgusting excess' favoured by unrefined societies by reminding readers that they 'lately had a specimen [of it] in the Venus Sartjie'.[29] No doubt one could derive sensual pleasure from such a body, opined the philosopher Victor Cousin, but pleasure of that sort could never be a standard for measuring true beauty, such as one would find in the Medici Venus.[30] The Hottentot Venus would cast a long shadow over nineteenth- and early twentieth-century perceptions of fatness and civilization, leaving many to echo the sentiments of Robert Chambers, who recalled how this 'poor wretched woman' possessed 'an intensely ugly figure, distorted beyond all European notions of beauty'.[31]

Whether cited as evidence of sexual desire or social status, the esteem that great corpulence could command in Africa and other countries was perplexing to European eyewitnesses. Many were wont to associate fattening with lesser forms of animality. 'If obesity is to be considered as a sign of royalty,' wrote the Swedish explorer

Charles Andersson of his meeting with the king of Ondonga, 'then Nangaro was "every inch a king".' In this sarcastic report, Andersson saw in Nangaro none of the majesty or regal bearing he expected of European monarchs. What he found instead was

> the most ungainly and unwieldy figure we had ever seen. His walk resembled rather the waddling of a duck than the firm and easy gait which we are wont to associate with royalty.

Taken from her home in southern Africa, Saartjie Baartman was exhibited in Britain and France as the 'Hottentot Venus' from 1810 until her death in 1815. 'Love and beauty – Sartjee the Hottentot Venus', *c.* 1810.

Likening Nangaro to a duck rather than a lion, the traditional symbol of European royalty, invoked the ancient tendency to associate the very fat with livestock and therefore with subjection rather than mastery, foolishness rather than *gravitas*. The addition of porcine imagery completed this denigrating portrait. Speculating on why such a man had been chosen to be king in the first place, Andersson supposed it had something to do with the people's need to find males with a natural tendency toward corpulence or, 'more commonly, fattening them for the dignity as we fatten pigs'.[32]

One may detect here echoes of ancient contempt for the fat Ptolemies of Egypt or for Dionysius of Heraclea/Denis Heracleot. What applied to fat African kings was easily extended to other corpulent local notables. During his travels along the Niger River, the Belgian geographer Adolphe Burdo expressed jaw-dropping wonder that

> any people, however barbarous, could find grace [*du charme*] in this monstrous deformity, but such is the case. Some of the women weigh four hundred pounds! And these are the favourites of kings and potentates! One can scarcely believe one's eyes and ears.

Burdo was particularly appalled by the appearance of a tribal oracle named Agimi, whose body evoked for him associations with vegetality as well as animality. With a face that 'was flabby, like over-ripe fruit [*lâchée, comme blette*]', Agimi crawled from her hut on all fours, perhaps, Burdo speculated, because her weight made her incapable of walking or standing. When combined with her 'over-ripe' face, this beast-like prostration prompted Burdo to conclude that 'nothing about her justified the veneration with which she is regarded. To me she was simply a monster.'[33] It had been established a century earlier that 'There is no Grace without motion,'[34] which is one reason why Agimi's way of getting around seemed like an affront to female comportment as well as human uprightness.

Thanks to these and other travel reports, Africa and Africans would become closely linked with fat in European travel and ethnographic reports. When they weren't writing about how corpulent Africans could be, travellers criticized the general 'softness' and indolence of their character. This, they thought, resulted in a lack of willpower that many saw as a cause of weight gain itself. Missionaries made similar observations. While they tended to sharpen the perceived link between excess 'flesh' and sexuality, they sometimes echoed the apostle Paul by accusing this or that tribe of being 'belly-slaves' or of worshipping their bellies as their god.[35] Such claims no doubt encouraged some pro-slavery ideologues in the United States to maintain that black people overeat 'like children' and 'often gorge themselves with fat meat'.[36] Others even managed to find corpulence regardless of physique by decrying the lack of enterprise and 'obesity of mind' they detected among African pastoral peoples.[37] Such generalizations could also be extended to all black people who, like most Indians, were thought to have fat on their minds even when their bodies were thin. As usual, classical ideals were trotted out in order to underscore the 'disgusting' nature of such tastes:

> The Greeks praised the slender and graceful figure – the Moors prize fatness to obesity; and their women are fatted for marriage as our turkeys are for Thanksgiving or Christmas.[38]

It is thus fair to say that the English clergyman and traveller Sabine Baring-Gould was playing upon a common formula when he pompously opined that 'While the European spirit has achieved such ideals as the Madonna of Raphael . . . the negro has set no other type of beauty before his mind than obesity.'[39]

Overseas and Overweight

Even with these brief glimpses into the colonial world, we can see how expansively 'fat' was imagined in the nineteenth century. In addition to something amassed inside the body, fat was rubbed onto its surface and folded into food. Fat did not even have to be material in order to be active: it fired the imaginations of the undernourished, and even existed metaphorically to describe the insensate stupidity ('obesity of mind') of this or that population. As we saw in Chapter Eight, in some cases fat was such a prized substance that it was stolen from the body. This is why, when they weren't being accused of killing boys 'for the sake of their fat, with which to bait their fish-hooks',[40] Australian Aborigines were said to be so obsessed with the stuff that they lived in fear of having enemy sorcerers and warriors steal kidney fat from their bodies.[41] Since such claims unfolded against the backdrop of growing anxieties about corpulence within the West itself, the colonial imagination played a critical role in the denigration of fat as antithetical to Western ideals of beauty and desire.

If all of this greasy talk connecting fatness and savagery seems a bit rich in light of Europe's own (admittedly, hushed-up) history of medicinal cannibalism, it reveals how much had changed in a relatively short period of time. After all, it was not so long before that the French and British had been swapping stories about how witches, werewolves and revolutionaries were stealing fat from the bodies of innocents. Yet even as human fat fell out of medical favour and tales of fat-stealing bogeys tapered off, Europeans became more concerned about the fat that was swelling inside their increasingly well-fed and sedentary bodies. But this did not occur immediately, and for the first half of the century corpulence among middle-class men was tolerated, indeed encouraged, as a kind of proof of status and even of civilization. This appreciation for elite male fat rested on the assumption that financial success was a mark of a bourgeois masculinity that did not depend upon vigorous bodily performance in order to be credible. In his well-known *Physiologie du goût* (1825), Brillat-Savarin offered a mixed appraisal of the relationship between corpulence, gender and civilization. Conceding that eating and drinking to excess was a human trait that united the civilized and 'savage' worlds, he proposed that what *les sauvages* did out of sheer appetite was in the 'civilized' world conducted in the rarefied circles of fine dining and connoisseurship.[42] Thus, despite mounting medical warnings about the health risks of gaining too much weight, male elites might still tolerate corpulence as a happy indication of their status. 'Savages' might devour their food like animals – after all, both of them 'feed' (*se repaissent*) rather than 'eat' (*mange*) – but only the civilized have the means and discernment allowing them to eat well and grow fat.[43]

This opinion would have resonated among those portly bourgeois who embraced their swelling paunches as proof of worldly success. Although they had a lot to say about how women should appear, bourgeois men on both sides of the Channel seemed less concerned that their own bodies deviated from classical standards of health and beauty. These were the days when a fat man might have been 'congratulated on the portliness of his corporation, and the goodly rubicundity of his visage'.[44] This is why the British-born Unitarian minister Henry Giles could famously declare in 1850 that

> There is something cordial in a fat man, everybody likes him, and he likes everybody. Food does a fat man good; it clings to him; it fructifies upon him; he swells nobly out, and fills a generous space in life.

Organic imagery vied with mechanical metaphors in Giles's depiction of the happy fat man, who 'has an abundance of rich juices' even as 'the hinges of his system are well oiled; the springs of his being are noiseless.'[45]

This complacent portrait of happy fat men should not be exaggerated, for it was certainly fading by the time Giles sketched it. If successful men appreciated rotundity as proof of 'civilization', their ample proportions were also subject to criticism on medical, moral and aesthetic grounds. For one thing, it could interfere with locomotion in ways that diminished the capacity of gentlemen to demonstrate their status through strolling the streets of the city. Thus did Honoré de Balzac and other writers offer their withering critiques of bourgeois corpulence.[46] Similar criticisms were evident across the Atlantic. American writers claimed that such fatness represented 'an inversion of the order of nature' and that it was 'not the genteel thing'.[47] Beyond aesthetic matters, excessive fatness also retained its connections to foolishness and insensateness. Too much *graisse* and flesh would only end up 'blunting physical sensitivity, [and] weakening the moral faculties', pronounced the author of a French medical pamphlet.[48] No doubt fatness was able to indicate a certain level of status and power in middle-aged men, but this did not prevent some from saying that such a successful person had nevertheless been 'thickened and animalized by excess'.[49]

Fatness was also beginning to indicate the possible slippage from civilized whiteness into some lesser stage of human development. Contrary to Brillat's claims that *les sauvages* did not know corpulence, by mid-century the importance of fatness for non-Western peoples had become quite well known. For some it had become a veritable marker of backwardness. The palaeontologist Marcel de Serres was heard holding forth on the 'functional and organic degradation in proportion as we descend from the Caucasian to the inferior races', and the correlation of human progress with the shrinking of the belly. 'The effect of civilization', Serres claimed,

> appears to consist in diminishing the capacity of the abdomen, which in the vegetative and animal lives of savages and barbarians attains a considerable size. The Chinese, American Indians, the African tribes, and many others, are all remarkable for corpulence.

While a 'moderate' physique remained the ideal for much of the century, Serres insisted that slenderness, not corpulence, was the true yardstick of civilization. The bodies as well as the 'vegetative and animal lives of savages and barbarians' proved it.[50] It would take several decades for the link between slenderness and civilization to become common sense. Nevertheless, by the 1880s many would have concurred with the feminist and anti-vivisectionist Anna Kingsford that 'Almost all active, inventive, and conquering races are of lean habit, while inert and meditative nations exhibit a tendency to obesity.'[51] Claims like this would persist for the next century.

Not all cases of corpulence were explained with reference to 'primitive' preferences and habits. Environmental factors counted as well. Long before Americans seized the title, the English were considered the fattest people in the Western world, an accomplishment generally attributed to the cold and moist climate of the island nation as well as the commercial success that encouraged elites to eat more and exercise less. At the time many saw this as a very positive thing. If the portly figure of John Bull conveyed a happy sense of English prosperity, real fat men, such as the 317-kg (700-lb) Daniel Lambert, loomed large in the national imagination as well as in the minds of foreign visitors.[52] Since the days of the Hippocratic authors, environment has often been viewed as exercising a major impact on the relative weight and size of the body, as well as the moral character of peoples. It was therefore easy to accept English corpulence as an effect of the cool and moist environment of the British Isles. Other environmental phenomena contributed to fatness as well. For years it was believed that butchers were especially prone to corpulence, not only because their diets relied heavily on meat, but because they continuously ingested minuscule bits of flesh (known as 'putrid effluvia') tossed up into the air as they worked.[53]

This literally 'fleshy' atmosphere would result in correspondingly beefy bodies, although the meaning of the resulting bulk was open to interpretation. Sometimes caricatured as clumsy and stupid (qualities that were also attached to the corpulent in other manual professions), butchers could also be admired for their rough natures and physical bulk. Not unlike John Bull, they could for a time effectively serve as symbols of English manhood and prosperity.[54] This ambiguity regarding male corpulence persisted throughout the nineteenth century, providing a rather tense back-story to colonial engagements with fat overseas.

Related to such claims were misgivings about the consumption that accompanied British commercial power and the rapid expansion of its empire after the Napoleonic wars.[55] One critic likened the expansion of British influence to a body that, much like the empires of old, had 'grown great, or rather unnaturally bloated from commerce, and then . . . sunk beneath their unwieldy corpulence'.[56] British anxieties about fatness were thus played out within a colonial frame in which facetious references to classical beauty and vice often shifted to derisive comments about non-Western habits. Fat Britons thus fitted uneasily into the aesthetic and moral standards of their own culture. For instance, the late eighteenth-century figure of the nabob, a man of modest origins who made his fortune in India before triumphantly returning home, was frequently lampooned as having acquired 'Oriental' proclivities while overseas. These included cultivating a prominent belly as well as a penchant for gluttony and lasciviousness. The cultural discrediting of the nabob was complete by the time team sports rose to prominence around mid-century, after which time the iconic British male began to be represented less as the fleshy John Bull than as the well-built sportsman.[57]

Growing references to the inherent superiority of British manhood, most of which praised muscularity while frowning upon flabbiness, were matched by attempts to impose similar standards upon the native troops charged with enforcing colonial rule by promoting, among other things, team sports and dieting. This is how the British could help to 'elevate' the Indians. Worried about the prevalence of weight gain among the Cavalry Native Officers, in 1870 the army doctor Joshua Duke penned a small book promoting William Banting's popular weight-loss plan. Duke revealed that, while writing this book, he was often warned not to expect many results,

Long before Americans seized the title, the English were considered the fattest people in the Western world. Foreign visitors often hoped to spy a legendary fat man, such as the 700-lb Daniel Lambert. *Daniel Lambert, Weighing Almost Forty Stone, c.* 1800.

though. Insofar as the battle against fat required much 'firmness and determination', he was told that such an ambitious project 'never can be carried out by natives of this country'.⁵⁸

The only problem with Duke's plan to slim down the natives was that the colonizers couldn't quite keep the weight off either. A certain 'Modern Pythagorean' experienced a trip to Calcutta as having been 'thrown, as it were, upon a new world' where the simple act of walking was

> quite abolished. You will see great, fat, unwieldy Europeans, carried through the streets, not in carriages but in palanquins, and not by horses or bullocks, but on the shoulders of men.[59]

A mid-century travel memoir warned that an Englishwoman hoping to preserve her beauty in India would need to keep busy to beat off the 'demon of ennui'. Otherwise she would succumb to the nefarious influence of the land itself:

> Yielding to the influences of climate, and the evil suggestions of domestics, who are ever about her person, she falls a victim to indolent habits and coarse indulgences – the sylphlike form and delicate features which distinguished the youth of her arrival, are rapidly exchanged for an exterior of which obesity and swarthiness are the prominent characteristics, and the bottle and the hookah become frequent and offensive companions.[60]

So intuitive was this link between India and fattening that one woman simply listed 'going to India' as the 'proximate cause' of her corpulence.[61]

The fate of British soldiers in India was perhaps even more worrisome. Acknowledging that among natives a paunch was considered an 'effect of good living' and thus a most desirable trait, physicians warned of the 'lazy habits' that 'are apt to be induced' among Europeans in India because 'it is almost impossible to exert the bodily or mental faculties when oppressed by the intense heat which prevails for many months.'[62] These habits seemed to increase with status, for both natives and Europeans were said to grow fatter as they moved into the higher ranks of the officer corps. So, when a British officer described how a young man of his acquaintance arrived in India as 'a fine, healthy, good-looking young man' only to become 'fat and bloated' over time, he was recounting what had become a common experience.[63] Such concerns grew more intense after the Indian Rebellion of 1857 raised questions about the state of British imperial power. One would-be whistle-blower purporting to reveal the 'truth about the Indian army and its officers' described how lax conditions encouraged many officers [to] take it so easy that, what with eating, drinking, punkah, and bed, they become ... so corpulent that their English relations would never recognise them.[64]

The fat colonial Briton had become such a stock figure that when Joshua Duke revised his weight-loss book in 1885, he had to account for this troubling situation. Reflecting the wisdom of more 'matured experience', what had once been pitched to the native population was now primarily directed to the fat colonizers themselves. 'Is it possible that the Englishman has altered, or that the sturdiness and doggedness of a race has in any degree been influenced by external and foreign influences?' Duke wondered ominously. 'It would indeed be terrible to think so.'[65]

'The African Style of Beauty'

Fears that exposure to non-Western cultures could have a deleterious effect on the white male body fitted well into the more widespread anxieties about degeneration that circulated at the end of the nineteenth century. Similar concerns about the decline of white womanhood were also expressed. Placed in a contradictory and largely unrealizable position, women were typically caught between competing demands to remain morally pure while appealing to male fantasies, a tension that was played out in their own bodies. While middle-class women have often been uneasily positioned between competing expectations, it was during the nineteenth century that the focus of female beauty shifted to accentuate the 'lower' parts of the body, especially the breasts and hips, which naturally transformed these zones into sites of seduction as well as apprehension. Accentuated through the use of corsets that tightened the waist, for much of the nineteenth century fleshy protrusions about the bosom and buttocks were considered desirable features of a woman's body. This 'selective flesh control' made the creation of a pleasingly rounded silhouette a more central goal than slenderness per se, though the constriction of the waist anticipated the more rigorous thinness that would be imposed on women by the 1920s.[66]

How, and whether, to use the corset were subjects of some disagreement. If the 'thick-waisted' woman deviated from most standards of female beauty, doubts were cast on the morality of those who laced their corsets too tightly or who failed to wear one at all. If many doctors condemned its use on health grounds, the bottom line was that fleshiness in the 'right' places was to be maintained through some combination of orthopaedic devices and lifestyle choices. There was a fine line between too much and too little flesh. Agreeing that some degree of embonpoint in women was 'universally agreeable', William Wadd insisted that 'this taste is carried to a disgusting excess in proportion as refinement has made less progress in any society.'[67] The British physician Robert Verity proposed that the march of civilization would eventually improve 'the proportion and quality of the constituent structures of which the human body is composed' and 'transform the gross succulent body of the peasant-woman to the fine-grained nervous tissue of the high-bred lady'.[68] This was standard advice in the nineteenth century, especially in France, where female beauty was often a source of national pride. As always, moderation had to be observed when it came to women's physiques. 'If excessive thinness is hideous,' warned one beauty expert, 'excessive embonpoint is disgusting.'[69]

Even as female beauty was being located at some midpoint between the hideous and the disgusting, the common association between fatness and sensuality could make corpulence seem alluring as well as dangerous. This prompted concerns that 'primitive' tastes were beginning to impress themselves on European sensibilities. Not long after the Hottentot Venus became a fixture in the cultural imagination, worried critics sought to clear up any confusion people might have about what 'true' beauty was. An anonymous British book of 1825 titled *The Art of Beauty* commanded women to watch their weight rather than subscribe to 'the African style of beauty'.[70] Despite warnings about the baffling tastes of other cultures, though, the world beyond the West remained available as a source of female beauty tips. Where else would a very thin woman seeking to gain a few pounds turn for advice than to the tantalizingly exotic seraglios of Turkey? In order to cultivate that 'enormous embonpoint which renders them so precious in the eyes of Asia's polygamous men', it was here that such 'indolent creatures' were pampered with warm baths and massages, fed a steady diet of rice and jellied meats, and passed their days 'in places filled with perfumes and flowers' freed of 'every passion, every troubling emotion'.[71] Even when numerous authors criticized the ways in which 'Oriental' women were fattened like livestock in

FIG. 102.—TURKISH LADY
The more obese the more admired are the ladies of the harem

The fattening practices of the Turkish harem were widely recommended to those Western women who, finding themselves too thin, wished to gain weight. Image from A. H. Keyne, *The World's People* (1909).

order to whet male appetites, few beauty writers failed to mention such practices when it came to gaining weight. Fattening regimens required girls and women to engage in habits (such as regular bathing) that at the time smacked of immorality and unhealthiness. Expected to maintain a certain degree of plumpness, 'neither too much nor too little', women's bodies were uneasily positioned between the chaste contours of classical models and the exotic sensuality of the harem.[72]

It is difficult to gauge the impact of such images on practice. Dieting would not become a mass obsession for several more decades, and research into the diaries of American girls of the period suggests that appearance had not yet eclipsed morality as the core aim of girls' lives.[73] Yet, as early as 1835, French parents and teachers were being warned that plump girls were foolishly taking thinness as the epitome of beauty. By succumbing to this 'fatal prejudice', one doctor warned, these girls were destroying their health so they can 'arrive at a skeletal state, the most disgraceful state of all'.[74] Others took aim at changes in fashion that seemed to reflect the opposite desire to copy 'primitive' predilections for fat. The bustle, a bundled framework of cloth worn below the waist to prevent a woman's dress from dragging on the ground, was often said to reflect a perverse desire to emulate Saartjie Baartman's 'natural bustle', and gave rise to claims that European aesthetic standards had degenerated from the Venus of antiquity to the Hottentot Venus.[75] Conventional boundaries between the beautiful and the ugly also seemed to be under threat in popular culture. Travelling 'freak shows' exhibiting fat ladies as well as various 'primitive' peoples emphasized physical differences that might reinforce middle-class norms, but they also fuelled anxieties that spectators might not be able to tell the difference between beauty and deformity. Some worried that such confusion might collapse all distinctions between the beautiful and the ugly, healthy and diseased, civilized and savage.[76]

If aesthetic issues were prominent in these anti-fat discourses, concerns about female agency and humanity also animated those who objected to the forced fattening of non-Western girls. In addition to the frequently voiced claim that excess fat 'corrupts' beauty, readers were reminded that, when encumbered by fat, 'the soul is oppressed by the enormous weight of the substance'. Corpulence thus impairs 'all the functions of the understanding'.[77] Acknowledging subtle connections between desire and power, several commentators proposed that the pleasure Asian and African men took in excessively fat females thinly concealed their tyrannical wish to dominate them. Variations on the claim that 'Oriental ladies are fattened for matrimony, as we of this Western world fatten pigs for the market'[78] were made throughout the century, as were complaints about how the bodies of such women were rendered sensual, indolent and vain because their flesh had been 'nourished at the expense of their souls'.[79] The French writer Paul Belouino thus remarked that force-feeding slave girls in certain Arab countries represented a desire 'to shackle the liberty of women under the burden of excessive embonpoint' that was strikingly similar to the Chinese practice of foot binding.[80] Others pointed out the perverse logic that transformed 'the most excessive embonpoint, and the perpetual imprisonment that encourages it, into principles of honour, wisdom, and good taste'.[81] Despite the ways in which Western beauty ideals constrained female bodies through dieting, corsetry and other sartorial technologies, compulsory fattening was cast as a crippling animalization that rendered women immobile and stupid as well as unappealing. Voicing their objections to what may have seemed like 'Oriental despotism', some insisted that respect for women partly depended upon release from this fleshy imprisonment. 'When birds endure captivity they get fat. Such are the prisoners of the Orient.'[82]

This depiction of fattening as a form of subjection and even imprisonment not only invoked ancient ideas about how domesticated animals and Asiatic tyrants were 'enslaved' by their fat. It also reinforced impressions that fatness was a kind of 'invasion' of the body whose resistance required willpower and determination. Representations of fat as an alien 'invader' of the civilized white body were common from the mid-nineteenth century onward. In his wildly popular *Letter on Corpulence*, the diet reformer William Banting defended his repeated use of the word 'parasite' to describe the effects of adipose on the body: 'if fat is not an insidious creeping enemy, I do not know what is.'[83] The struggle pitted the willpower of females against their own bodies as well as the weight of the world. If 'obesity' now represented what a French physician called 'the enemy of feminine beauty (in the West, at least)', then the act of deterring this 'invasion' was tantamount to repelling from the civilized self the creeping savagery that fat represented.[84] Female agency, at least in relation to the adoption of beauty standards, was to some extent articulated in relation to this enemy within. In such imagery, we can catch glimpses of what would become commonplace by the early twentieth century. By 1901, Ella Fletcher was telling readers that the first thing a woman should ask herself when she becomes conscious of her weight is: 'Shall I allow this encroaching master to overcome me? Am I not strong enough to assert my freedom of will?'[85] The same question might have been on the minds of imprisoned suffragists who, having gone on hunger strikes in 1917, were force-fed with a tube three times a day while being held down on a bed, naked, by male warders. Under such conditions 'leanness and abstinence had taken on a new, sometimes heroic seriousness.'[86] Advocated by proponents of women's rights as ways of making female bodies healthy and strong, weight-loss techniques enhanced female agency even as they promoted submission to aesthetic ideals.[87]

The inescapable volume and weight of real bodies seemed to mitigate the rather ethereal image of femininity that was common in the Victorian era. As numerous scholars have shown, appeals to female self-control were predicated on the age-old assumption that girls and women are fundamentally dominated by the downward tug of their fleshy natures. When we factor in lingering claims that excessive fatness could produce barrenness rather than fertility, as well as already heightened anxieties about greasy substances redolent of filth, decay and illicit desires, we find more ingredients for attempts to control female corporeality. Encouraged by Neoclassical and Romantic aesthetics, a number of artists approached true beauty as something disconnected from the facts of organic existence. For John Ruskin, to take an extreme example, the discovery that real women have pubic hair that was never depicted on the Greek statues he adored elicited a wave of disgust so powerful that he was unable to have sex with his own wife (instead he cultivated a chaste appreciation of the bodies of pubescent girls).[88] This rather disembodied view of female beauty was also reflected in the nineteenth-century 'cult of invalidism' that prized representations of women as weak, sickly and even near death, all of which emphasized the triumph of a spiritual rather than earthly ideal.[89]

Such apparent disembodiment could inspire fantasies of flight as well as collapse. Around mid-century, the Italian ballerina Marie Taglioni astounded audiences by dancing on her tiptoes (*en pointe*), which gave the impression of sylphlike weightlessness. Here was a living example of the 'sylph-like forms' that Edward Dodwell had failed to find in modern Athens. Transformed into a world-renowned symbol of feminine ethereality who 'appeared to transcend the material condition of humanity',[90] Taglioni set the standard for the kind of light, non-fat bodies considered essential for ballerinas to possess.[91] Whether or not all of this amounts to a 'Victorian culture of anorexia', there is no doubt that, as beauty was increasingly conceived of as an achievement, and therefore an act of planning and willpower, women were being expected to monitor their bodies like never before.[92] Control over fat would become a central strategy in this wider campaign, the aims of which were never skin deep.

Associations between female fleshiness and immorality facilitated further links between corpulence and 'savage' desires overseas. In an apparent extension of what took place in the seraglio, prostitutes, both within the West as well as abroad, were commonly said to grow very fat due to warm baths as well as the sedentary and overindulgent lives they led.[93] Ruling out the usual explanations given for the 'excessive obesity' of prostitutes (hot baths, mercurial preparations and so on), late in the century the Italian criminologist Cesare Lombroso instead speculated that this propensity was due to the 'animal' lives they led and was 'perhaps of atavistic origin'. Lest anyone doubt this rather sweeping proposal, Lombroso had recourse to women whose fatness had already been explained in this way. 'Hottentot, African and Abyssinian women when rich and idle grow enormously fat,' he observed, and here too 'the reason of the pheno-menon is atavistic.' But fatness like this was never purely foreign. Lombroso turned to Europe for his final piece of 'evidence', observ-ing that 'in prisons and asylums for the insane, the female lunatics are far more often exaggeratedly fat than the men.'[94] Through this diagnostic chain of associations, immoral women were readily linked to primitives overseas and the insane at home, their unfitness for inclusion in 'civilized' society conspicuously evident in their bodies. Fatness, in other words, was primitive and animal, perhaps even criminal. A middle-class white woman would have to be mad to let herself become that way.

Savage desires for female fat were at the heart of a book by the American writer Henry Finck. Expanding upon the centrality of fat to sexual desire among the 'uncivilized and Oriental races', Finck maintained that such predilections were less examples of love or beauty than of sheer lust.[95] The proper appreciation of beauty, he wrote, is 'an entirely different thing from the predilection for fat and other coarse exaggerations of sexuality which inspire lust instead of love'.[96] Citing anthropological writings in an age when racial theory had largely eclipsed environmental models, Finck argued that Hotten-tot men feel no love or affection for women whatsoever, but are, in a purely materialist way, interested solely in the process of fattening them up. 'What a Hottentot "regards" in a woman is Fat,' Finck maintained; 'Sentiment is out of the question'.[97] Australian Aborigines proved far worse offenders when it came to mistreating women. The 'fact' that an Aborigine 'has been known to bait his fish-hook with his own child when no other meat was at hand' was ample evidence of the twisted emotions of such people.[98] Aboriginal women were just as bad as the men, though they were driven by crudely pragmatic,

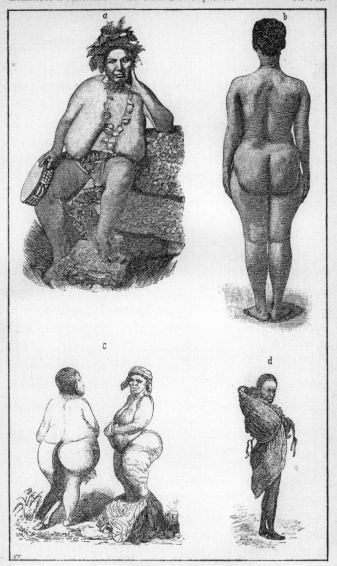

POLISARCIA IN ABISSINA.
CUSCINETTO POSTERIORE IN AFRICANE.

a) Ballerina o prostituta Abissina (Ploss) (tipo di polisarcia africana). — *b)* Ottentotta con cuscinetto posteriore (Ploss). — *c¹*) Donna Bongo (Schweinfurth). — *c²*) Donna Koranna con cuscinetto posteriore e ipertrofia delle natiche e delle coscie (Ploss). — *d)* Donna selvaggia che porta un bambino sul dorso, come in tutti i popoli primitivi (Ploss).

Polisarcia in Abissina, in Cesare Lombroso and G. Ferrero, *La Donna delinquente: La prostituta e la donna normale* (Turin, 1893).

utilitarian concerns rather than lust. What passes for 'taste' in such women is also what compels Aboriginal men to 'anoint themselves with grease and ochre' to make themselves look fatter and therefore more important.[99]

Despite the overall nastiness of these analyses, this crucial distinction whereby desire was associated with base sensuality rather than a lofty aesthetic sense allowed Finck to draw startling links between 'primitive love' among non-whites and men of the 'civilized' world. Not only is fatness 'the criterion of feminine attractiveness' in other cultures, but it also holds true for 'coarse men (i.e., most men) even in Europe and America to this day'.[100] While Finck says little more about 'most men' in the West – and nothing about fat men – he clearly considers the masses at home to be just as 'primitive' as indigenous populations. Women's fashion seems to cater to such types when it is not being inspired by the lowest sorts of women:

> The object of the modern wasp waist (in the minds of the class of females who, strange to say, are allowed by respectable women to set the fashion for them) is to grossly exaggerate the bust and the hips, and it is for the same reason that barbarian and Oriental girls are fattened for the marriage market.

As with the 'Hindoos' who also idealized women with slender waists and large breasts, here too the 'appeal is to the appetite, not to the esthetic sense'.[101] Here was a disturbing eruption of the 'savage' within Western civilization, a sort of Indianization of white bodies that bode ill for the future of the race. If even the conventional wasp-waisted woman of the nineteenth century was too fat, then what Finck had in mind was something thinner still. He would get his wish about twenty years later, and this hyper-thin ideal would look nothing like the Medici Venus that had served as the model of female beauty for much of the century.

*

By the close of the nineteenth century, a desire for fatness had become so closely associated with non-Western cultures that it was possible to chart an evolutionary curve from 'primitive' corpulence to 'civilized' slenderness based on observations of the various peoples of the world. Since the attainment of a relatively moderate physique was perceived as a by-product of the civilizing process, Joshua Duke was able to claim, in one breathtaking sentence, that the mission to civilize the Indian subcontinent was analogous to the personal project of weight loss: 'The corpulent [man] like the Indian has a long journey before him.'[102] The fat Indian was thus doubly challenged. This loosely evolutionary perspective received considerable support from archaeological discoveries of Palaeolithic figurines depicting rotund women, which were often dubbed 'Venuses' with the same sarcasm heaped upon Saartjie Baartman decades earlier. The French archaeologist Édouard Piette almost certainly had Baartman in mind when he dubbed his most famous find the 'Venus of Brassempouy'. Upon discovering figurines with slender bodies and flat stomachs, Piette speculated on the existence of 'two human races' during the Palaeolithic era, one fat and hairy and the other thin and hairless, who hated one another. The antipathy between fat and thin had now become primordial. Apparently echoing Marcel de Serres' ascending curve from primitive fatness to civilized slenderness, Piette's letters describe a gradual transition from an 'old fat-hipped race' to a modest and slender one that was 'more civilized than the other' and which ended up conquering it. Piette concluded that his discoveries confirmed the suspicion of anthropologists that female Bushmen (whose physiques supposedly resembled those of the figurines) were in fact the 'oldest known race' whose 'fatty protuberances' evoke 'the most ancient appearance of humans in our regions'.[103] Most telling was the fact that such 'fatty races [*les races adipeuses*] are everywhere on the path to extinction, despite the taste of the Negroes and even the Berbers for opulent forms.'[104] From an evolutionary perspective, extinction was thus one way of removing excess fat from the world. The even more famous 1908 discovery of another 'Venus' figurine near Willendorf, Austria, only reinforced this assumed cultural evolution from fatness to thinness, and hardened the contrast between 'perverse' primitive desire and the refinements of Western aesthetic judgement.[105]

The colonial discourses that helped shape the fat imaginary encouraged white elites to see the appreciation of fat and fatness as evidence of animalistic and 'primitive' impulses more appropriate to 'savage' than 'civilized' societies. With actual human fat now long gone from the Western pharmacopoeia, doctors and pharmacists could look back with wonder at the earlier days of medicine when fat was prized for its vital and healing properties. Even if something marketed as 'poor sinner's fat' was still being sold in the Netherlands in the early twentieth century, the mindset that drove people to fall for such quackery was considered not merely dated but downright backward. This sort of thing was widely associated with the 'cannibals' overseas who, everyone knew, were often the same peoples who had a taste for fat bodies.[106] This cluster of associations generated questions about the meanings of fat in the twentieth century. What civilized person would want to look that way? Who would want others to look that way? And what kind of person could experience anything other than disgust for such bodies? The discourses that generated such questions also aimed to act upon desire itself, that of males as well as females, to construct an image of the fat person – greasy and filthy, ugly and bestial – as sexually unappealing and unloveable on just about any level. To employ crudely the imagery of a bygone era, the ground for future cruelties had been fattened and made fertile by the shit people were saying about the stuff of life.

TEN

BODILY UTOPIANISM
Modern Dreams of
Transcendence

"Oh, look, look!" They spoke in low, scared voices. "Whatever is the matter with her? Why is she so fat?'" Such were the questions whispered by the ageing but still slim and beautiful elites in Aldous Huxley's *Brave New World* (1932). They had just encountered Linda, who had recently returned from the Savage Reservation, where she had been sent years earlier to give birth to her son, John. The reasons for their discomfort were understandable. In a society where technology had made it possible to extend youthfulness beyond the biological norm, it stood to reason that they had 'never seen a face that was not youthful and taut-skinned, a body that had ceased to be slim and upright'. Older than Linda by roughly twenty years, these 'moribund sexagenarians had the appearance of childish girls. At 44, Linda seemed, by contrast, a monster of flaccid and distorted senility.'[1]

An exaggeration of contemporary cultural trends for didactic purposes, the future projected in *Brave New World* gathers some of the corporeal fantasies that, in one form or another, have been articulated throughout Western culture. The nightmare that Huxley portrayed was a caricature of the utopian desires he saw manifested all around him: for youth, health, beauty and performance with few limitations, in a world where illness, ugliness and ageing were coming to be managed by new technologies. As an unsightly sign of age and perhaps sickness – troubling reminders of human finitude but also inescapable facts of organic existence – fatness was but one of the many aspects of 'life' that a technological utopia would attempt to engineer out of existence. This wish for a more or less fat-free world, at least for elites, is hardly novel. As previous chapters have shown, visions of an earthly society or heavenly afterlife inhabited by perfected human forms have inspired health reformers and religious believers for millennia. Adjusted to match seventeenth-century expectations, would Linda's ageing and flabby body have seemed any less out of place had it appeared among the fit denizens of Campanella's City of the Sun? While the *means* for achieving the ideal body were very different in that 'vision of an early surveillance state',[2] the future that Huxley feared placed a similar premium on youthfulness and longevity, as well as on the eventual elimination of non-normative bodies among the elite.

There is a distinctly modern dimension to such fat intolerance, at least when approached in terms of body size and shape. Historians agree that many of the core ingredients of our contemporary anti-fat prejudices had already fallen into place by the time *Brave New World* appeared. By then, bodily ideals within the West had become slenderer than ever before. With scientific advances from the mid-nineteenth century placing food and other commodities within the reach of larger numbers of people, the plumpness that had once symbolized middle-class social privilege lost much of its prestige. As fat bodies became increasingly commonplace, in the social hierarchy they were depressingly 'common'. With fatness gradually becoming more associated with lower-class and non-white bodies,

> external signs of wealth [were] displaced into other forms of consumption, [and] the cult of the thin, healthy, sportive, performing and ascetic body dominate[d] in the hierarchy of representations.[3]

While the habit of ridiculing fat people seems to have been on the rise throughout the nineteenth century, this tendency was exacerbated by the expanding culture of advertising and mass consumption.[4] The visual focus of this culture is obvious. Along with European cinema, Hollywood played a memorable role in an ensemble cast. Just as the silver screen projected images of ideal bodies around the world, motion-picture fan magazines shared with the masses the reducing diets and fitness regimens of the stars.[5]

The early twentieth century is a useful site for contemplating our current views of fat. As Georges Vigarello quite rightly states, the 'body of the 1920s is quite simply the herald of today's body.'[6] Henceforth, the Western image of corpulent bodies would represent an 'aesthetic threat and a health risk' tied to twentieth-century concepts of bodies as consumable objects on display as well as medical problems that would, in time, place burdens on healthcare systems.[7] Having been described as a life-shortening and disfiguring disease since the sixteenth century, 'obesity' became even more vocally denounced by doctors as the harbinger of sickness, disability, old age and death. Demands that people curb their appetites while adopting healthy diet and exercise regimes transformed the body into something that had to be regularly managed through sheer acts of willpower. All of this reflects the paradoxes of a mass society that encourages consumption while simultaneously demanding greater self-control. This self-control, in a further paradox, requires purchasing fitness products and services that are part of the same consumer society credited with producing fatness.[8] These trends would develop more fully in the decades to come. With the rise of neo-liberalism in the 1970s, as well as the attendant 'culture of bulimia' that coupled compulsory consumption with an equally insistent demand for self-discipline, fatness would become one of the most recognizable emblems of a loss of personal control and a social fall from grace.[9] Even if its cultural roots are much deeper than this, our current disgust with fat has its most immediate conditions of possibility in the early twentieth century.

But do these developments adequately address why responses to fat bodies became so visceral and nasty, as if their very existence posed a threat of contamination? Building upon centuries of accumulated misgivings about grease and corpulence, especially as these clashed with evolving ideas about cleanliness, whiteness and civilization, modern disgust about (and fear of becoming) fat may reflect aspirations that are more utopian and transcendent than is usually thought. The word 'utopian' is here used in its most basic sense. As defined by Ruth Levitas, the 'essence of utopia seems to be desire – the desire for a different, better way of being'.[10] She proposes that the sources of what some may call a utopian 'impulse' lie in

> the human experience of a sense of hunger, loss and lack: a deep sense that something's missing . . . Everything that reaches to a transformed existence is, in this sense, utopian.

In this more or less 'existential' definition, utopia is not a concept that depends upon representations of alternative or perfected worlds.

Rather it 'occurs as an embedded element in a wide range of human practice and culture'. This is why Levitas can maintain that 'contemporary culture is saturated with utopianism, even (or especially) where there is no figurative representation of an alternative world'.[11]

The family resemblance between utopian and religious wishes is fairly obvious. Both seem to have sources in the ambiguity of embodiment. Much as utopian hope may be grounded in the lived experience of incompleteness – including the universal human grappling with pain, illness, ageing and death – religion's central concept of 'transcendence' may also be said to be 'anchored in the relative indeterminacy of our embodied existential condition'.[12] Moreover, just as the concept of utopia does not require actual hope for alternative worlds in order to be expressed, transcendence need not be conflated with belief in divine beings or otherworldly realities. Indeed, rather than seeking to surmount the body altogether, this reflects Western culture's recurring tendency to make use of the body as a vehicle for surmounting the limitations of the body. Insofar as there may be plausible links between utopian and religious figurations and the kind of magical thinking that structures disgust – an emotion in which, we will recall, 'we take the measure of the disjunction between how the world actually works and how we would like it to be'[13] – it is reasonable to see modern anti-fat attitudes as expressing a tendency towards bodily or corporeal utopianism and a desire for transcendence. If we define 'corporeal utopianism' as culturally inflected wishes for different (and, one assumes, better) forms of embodiment, specifically those that resist the degenerative forces of the environment and are less subject to the exigencies of organic life, then we can see how fat and fatness might emerge as unwelcome reminders of the limits of such wishes. The flight from fat and fatness is an effect of the pursuit of 'perfect health', which amounts to visions of a 'new utopia', if not a new 'eco-bioreligion'.[14]

Varieties of corporeal utopianism are evident throughout history, not least in attempts to explore and maximize human perfectibility and in ongoing attempts to extend human life, even to the point of defeating death.[15] We have seen examples of related aspirations in previous chapters. Hopes to overcome the limitations of ordinary embodiment could also inspire new plans for organizing society. Some argue that Western culture has for centuries manifested a utopian drive to control the body through the biopower of the state, to make those bodies reproductive, productive, disciplined, fit, homogeneous, normalized, or any other desirable set of traits, whether it is through a direct physical intervention or through the indirect training of citizens to instill self-regulatory practices.[16]

Others have tracked the rise and fall of a 'utopian' attempt to create working bodies that would not succumb to fatigue, a dream buoyed up well into the twentieth century by attempts to maximize the machine-like capacities of workers. The science of labour, which achieved its apotheosis in the Fordism and Taylorism of the 1920s and '30s, sought to actualize 'the daydream of the late nineteenth-century middle classes – a body without fatigue'.[17] These machinelike bodies, it was hoped, would be pushed beyond ordinary human capacities so as to never grow tired or require much rest, a fantasy to some extent converted into twentieth-century athletics' dreams of unlimited performance.[18]

Insofar as the ambiguities of embodiment are often experienced on a deeply personal level, not all of these utopian or transcendent desires are entirely reducible to social pressure, as countless personal projects for maximizing health and extending longevity make clear. Dietary reforms and exercise programmes have been central to these projects as individuals have sought to live longer, healthier lives. In many cases, moreover, these body projects may be experienced as empowering and even emancipating. Yet insofar as such techniques of the self are always enmeshed in social contexts, the management of diet and exercise has also dovetailed with political and economic agendas. From the mid-nineteenth century onward, nutritional intervention into the diet of workers aimed at promoting efficiency and performance while curtailing the body's natural tendency to dissolution and decay.[19] It is therefore unsurprising that nutritionists also sought to institute a kind of 'utopia' in which the 'perfect human diet' would be developed to provide 'salvation' for all.[20] That the idea of utopia would eventually become individualized with the advent of neo-liberalism at the end of the twentieth century does not diminish the persistence of this yearning for experiences that might overcome the limits of ordinary embodiment. Diet and fitness regimes may energize collectives, but they can just as easily offer paths to more personal forms of transcendence. There is thus a 'dialectic' that operates 'between the external trim of the fitness frame (the embodied performance of normative body ideals) and the internal one (self-competition and involvement)'.[21] While the following discussion engages more with discourse than lived experience, the latter is important for understanding the benefits and attractions of health and fitness.

A slippage between ideas about health and 'salvation' is commonplace and enduring. It is also quite old. Ancient visitors to the sanctuary of the Greek healing god, Asclepius, left inscriptions indicating that 'salvation' (*soteria*) for them resided in the restoration of bodily health on earth rather than in the afterlife.[22] Modern discourses of weight loss and exercise are also replete with images of purification and transcendence, uplifting and overcoming, all of which imply processes of conversion and redemption, whether earthly or spiritual. The British exercise guru Thomas Inch was just one among many who insisted that exercising to lose weight was the key to 'physical salvation'.[23] The corpulent physique was a 'fallen' body in need of redemption. The transcendent aspirations of corporeal utopianism become evident when we consider how often the slender and fit bodies of the twentieth century are captured photographically while airborne or in the act of thrusting upward, momentarily freeing themselves of gravity as they seem to press toward hitherto unimagined heights. With the advent of aviation, humans would literally begin to take flight, and it would not be long before bodies would be even more explicitly likened to streamlined machines and sleek animal bodies efficiently moving through space.[24] To rise above all manner of constraints – earth, creatureliness, primitivity, tradition, history, ageing and even death itself: such are the somatechnical hopes that fuelled the bodily dreams and ideals of the modern world. Having come to be more closely linked to greasy and filthy substances, bestial habits, and lower-class as well as non-white populations, fat, fatness and fattening were readily cast as obstacles to be overcome on the path to personal, if not collective, regeneration.

By exploring the utopian and transcendent yearnings that have informed some of the body cultures of the early twentieth century, this chapter argues that more pronounced ideas about slender and muscular bodies unfolded at the juncture of several developments. Manifested in a variety of domains, from modernist art and literature to athletics and high-performance sports, as well as shifting ideas about beauty, health and ageing, anti-fat prejudice accelerated as part of a generalized cultural yearning for forms of transcendence. Frustration with the messy limitations of conventional physicality – as well as an ever-expanding set of challenges posed by the conventions and institutional structures of modernity – encouraged people to dream of alternative forms of embodiment. While such dreams have antecedents in previous centuries, the twentieth century offered the tantalizing technological possibility of bringing them closer to reality. While some of these visions were expressed in the more overtly utopian projects of communism and fascism, this chapter focuses on how mainstream body aspirations reflected these overt dreams of creating perfect worlds. After exploring how the challenges of modern life evoked yearnings for corporeal utopianism, it examines cases where ideals of lightness flowed into demands for efficiency and how many of these developments impacted ideas about women's transcendence as part of the progressive aspirations of modern feminism. As previous chapters illustrate, the conceptual ingredients of these developments have a very long history. Early twentieth-century culture thus crystallized centuries of Western misgivings about fat, fatness and fattening, gradually marshalling and weaponizing them for our current 'war on obesity'. What follows is a necessarily compact and selective discussion of a complicated knot of concerns that structures some of our current views of fat.

Modernity and Transcendence

Insistence on the modernity of our present-day fat prejudices is widespread and, in some respects, well founded. There is ample evidence that an already limited tolerance for fat and fatness diminished at an uneven pace throughout the modern era, even if there is some lack of consensus on what constitutes 'modernity' and when this supposedly distinct period began. Without delving into the quandary created by questions of definition and periodization, it is tempting to transpose social theorist Zygmunt Bauman's contrast between 'heavy' and 'light' modernity to the history of body ideals. Our current phase of lipophobia, which emerged in full force during the 1970s, does seem to coincide with the end of an era characterized by territorial expansion, mining, industrialization, large machines and 'hardware' of every sort. As opposed to this 'heavy' modernity that had been developing since the age of empire and industrialization, our present moment manifests a clear preference for lightness, movement, fluidity and instantaneity. 'Giant industrial plants and corpulent bodies have had their day,' Bauman remarks. 'Once they bore witness to their owners' power and might; now they presage defeat in the next round of acceleration and so signal impotence.'[25]

This is something appealing about this explanation. It is true that what Bauman calls 'light modernity' places a premium on speed, fluidity and ephemerality, all of which have been contrasted with the heaviness of tradition, history and, of course, the body itself. Yet speed, fluidity and ephemerality have been part of the experience of urban modernity at least since the mid-nineteenth century. Moreover, as we have seen, the heavy bodies of elites never offered unequivocal evidence of status and power. It was precisely during the imperial era that the corpulence of some indigenous and colonized peoples became a reliable countertype to an emergent ideal of 'civilized' moderation and muscularity. Distinctions between 'heavy' and 'light' modernity can be only unevenly mapped onto fat and thin bodily ideals.

It is possible to approach the relationship between fatness and modernity in other ways. A commonsense way of thinking about the modern, at least in temporal terms, is to assume a radical break with the past and a futural orientation for our thought and actions. But the modern is also something that is *lived*. Susan Stanford Friedman proposes a working definition of 'modernity' that takes experience as its core:

> The velocity, acceleration, and dynamism of shattering change across a wide spectrum of societal institutions are key components of modernity as I see it – change that interweaves the cultural, economic, political, religious, familial, sexual, aesthetic, technological, and so forth, and can move in both utopic and dystopic directions.[26]

What is not often acknowledged in views of modernity-as-novelty is the extent to which models from the distant past get recycled as examples for living in the present and future. This reaching backwards is often done with an eye towards overcoming aspects of modern life that strike observers as unhealthy or immoral. The persistence of the Spartan mirage in Western culture is a case in point, as are related claims that our ancient or even prehistoric ancestors held the keys to healthy and moral living.

The historian Roger Griffin has sought to account for this strange braiding of old and new in many forms of modernism. Griffin claims that lurking behind what many scholars see as a bewildering array of modernisms – be they aesthetic or social and political in nature – is 'a common matrix' that may be 'usefully seen as the search for transcendence and regeneration' that is itself a variation of the archaic human myth of rebirth, or what he calls 'palingenesis'.[27] The 'New Man' often imagined in modern times is quite often an implicitly male being requiring some rejuvenated form of 'New Woman' as his partner and breeder. Thus the regeneration promised by many modernist social programmes often entailed a restoration of trad-itional gender roles – the (re)creation of 'real' men and women – in a social order that believes it has jettisoned the degenerative elements of modernity while still remaining recognizably modern. This is evident in some of the most self-consciously utopian political and social movements of the twentieth century. Although there is no space to investigate them here, both the *homo sovieticus* imagined in Russia after 1917 and the 'anthropological revolution' proposed by fascist theorists in 1920s Italy may be viewed as pronounced extensions of this deeply ingrained modern response to modernity's excesses.[28] Revolution, regeneration and rejuvenation often presuppose a future that has been reconnected to the most healthy and admirable models of the past. In this sense, as Lynda Nead proposes, modernity may be 'imagined as pleated or crumpled time, drawing together past, present and future into constant and unexpected relations and the product of a multiplicity of historical eras'.[29]

Expressing 'the desire for a different, better way of being', a range of broadly utopian wishes were widespread during the early twentieth century, not least as responses to the experience of modernity as crisis and discontinuity. The claim that Western societies at the end of the nineteenth century saw themselves in the throes of decadence and degeneration is irrefutable, as is the fact that many individuals and groups engaged in projects aiming at regeneration of one form or other. Regeneration implied rejuvenation, and thus an attempt to recapture youthful energy and beauty in the face of processes of decline. In the United States during the 1980s, for instance, a widespread yearning for regeneration – for rebirth that was variously spiritual, moral, and physical – penetrated public life, inspiring movements and policies that formed the foundation for American society in the twentieth century.[30]

It is not coincidental that the body would form the basis for all manner of regenerations, in the United States and elsewhere:

> As the public world outside the self becomes diffuse, distant, governed by institutions we cannot control or even influence, the body remains important as an arena we can actually control – or we think we can. It becomes a domain of self-expression, a field for developing one's own set of cultural meanings, and a source, quite naturally, of anxiety.[31]

If the body became central to twentieth- and twenty-first-century culture, it is partly because the often-disorienting experience of modernity transformed it into a deceptively stable site for meaning and transformation, personally as well as collectively.

A longing for rebirth or transcendence, which has often been framed as a kind of salvation from a decadent or degenerate world, is implicit in many forms of the modern. Insofar as the body became the locus of personal and social transformation, it was here that tensions between degeneration and regeneration were played out, whether in esoteric and countercultural philosophies or within more conventional scientific frameworks.[32] For many, the apotheosis of the catastrophe of modernity was the First World War, and the unprecedented carnage it produced was a powerful catalyst for the celebration of new bodily ideals that proliferated in the following decades. Aside from the millions killed or missing in action, wounded and disfigured soldiers returned from the trenches as living embodiments of the fears of the able-bodied. The restoration of corporeal wholeness after the war was accompanied by a 'spiritual' yearning that, whether expressed through conventional Judaeo-Christian categories or any number of 'pagan' ideas and images, expressed desires for something more than the grossly material.[33] This yearning was for a kind of disembodied 'will' that nevertheless required the performance of the body in order to actualize itself, instantiating the perennial and paradoxical tendency to employ the body to transcend corporeality.

Fat had no place in the forms of corporeal wholeness that the Great War seemed to inspire. A rather explicit denigration of fat, understood literally as well as metaphorically, is evident in certain forms of aesthetic modernism, which may be seen as 'the expressive dimension of modernity'.[34] To be sure, 'modernism' is itself a loose and imprecise category. But much of the painting and architecture as well as the poetry and literature that merits this label displays contempt for the ornate, superfluous and 'feminine', positing instead forms and lines that have been purified, hardened and masculinized. The Italian Futurists famously epitomized this 'virile' move to purge poetic language of its Victorian superfluity, cutting away 'the flab of adjectives and other emasculating parts of speech'.[35] A similar modernist impulse to eliminate the superfluous and inefficient took place soon afterwards in the cultural rhetoric surrounding 'streamlining', a concept developed in industrial design and extended to thinking about the size, shape and eugenic worth of individual bodies. Like an animal or object moving swiftly through a stream of fluid, cars, buses, aeroplanes and even human bodies were to be engineered so as to maximize efficiency while minimizing all that might cause friction or the backward tug of 'drag'.[36]

Despite its claims to have broken with the past and dispensed with history, modern art has often raided antiquity as well as non-Western cultures for its models. After all, the Greeks and Romans seemed to worship muscular hardness as well, and modern notions of beauty have not completely dispensed with classical antecedents. Historian Ana Carden-Coyne is perhaps the most authoritative guide to the physical and symbolic reconstruction of bodies after the First World War. With this war sometimes imagined as a collective sacrifice that would 'purge the world of its moral miasma', classical aesthetics played an important role in the cleansing process that aimed at the elevation of bodies as well as morals.[37] Such uses of classicism are examples of a 'cultural nostalgia', defined as 'partly a longing for, or an idealizing of, the past, and partly a need to make productive use of the past through cultural practices'. In the 1920s and '30s, slenderness became 'the visible display of modern "ultra-civilization"' to the extent that swollen and misshapen bodies were increasingly described as throwbacks to earlier ways of life.[38] Classical models that had been put to effective use in the physical culture movement, and which had gained momentum from the 1880s onward,

Classical models continue to haunt modern bodies. Peggy Bacon, 'Antique Beauty', 1933.

returned with renewed vigour after the war as 'utopian visions of the classical past and the modern future' merged.[39] Statues and monuments commemorating the carnage made use of classical motifs to project images of 'masculine beauty frozen in a timeless vortex' and offering 'the fantasy of eternal renewal, and the avoidance of death'.[40] The classical style's formal sterility worked well alongside some versions of the modernist style, making it seem 'clean' and thus available for new conceptions of hygiene.[41] Even if the more hedonistic post-war culture promoted comfort and pleasure over sacrifice, neo-classical ideals remained as an ingredient in the demonization of fat that followed.[42]

Whether in the form of avant-garde experiments or neo-classical revivals, modern ideas about the body were vernacularized in – perhaps even abetted by – emerging ideals about the sportive and fit body. In athletics and other forms of physical culture, the aim was less to transcend the body per se than to create one that offered the appearance, and even the sensation, of transcendence. This is why some enlisted stock images of the human body as a kind of machine while downplaying its troubling organic qualities. In this way, the ideal body could be imagined as streamlined and efficient, much like the vehicles and appliances being produced by industry. This forward-looking vision of machine-like bodies presented fatness as a form of 'drag' and 'waste' that diminished speed, efficiency and productivity. 'Streamline your figure' was the 1930s advice of Sylvia of Hollywood, fitness trainer to the stars. Since weight gain was partly linked to undigested food and other residues, one had to purge the system by way of colonic irrigation before beginning any kind of weight-loss plan. 'It's like changing the oil in a car,' Sylvia explained; 'they drain out the old worn oil and sediment before putting in the new.'[43] As effects of 'pleated or crumpled time', modern concepts of hygiene, as well as emerging ideals of hairlessness, were based at once on the sanitized 'skin' of modern vehicles and the smooth and sterile contours of classical statuary.[44] Even classical ballet displayed bodies that evoked 'the arresting beauty of a finished airplane, where every detail, as well as the general effect, expresses one supreme object – that of speed'.[45] A slender body was now a modern body, as readers were reminded even in the most mundane magazine advertisements. As a 1932 ad for Sun-Maid proclaimed, the fact that raisins burn fat 'will mean much in the lives of modern women who wish to remain modern'.[46]

In their efforts to whip ordinary citizens into shape for the greater good, proponents of physical culture were animated by

a problem of *too much body*, or at least too much of the wrong kind of body ... [They] saw their mission as that of reining in the overwhelming presence of a body in excess.[47]

As perhaps the most conspicuous sign of this 'excessive' flesh, fatness was one of the conditions that physical culturists and sporting enthusiasts insisted upon overcoming. The explosion of skiing culture in the twentieth century captured some of these aspirations. The German enthusiast Carl Luther claimed that Alpine skiing was particularly attractive to modern people 'because we live faster and must demonstrate greater resistance – because we do not wish to age, but rather to remain young, fresh, and slender'.[48] Some even propose that modernist culture, broadly construed, is informed by an 'anorexic aesthetic' predicated on a rejection of all that the 'feminine' seems to represent in Western culture. This mobilized a chain of associations that we have encountered repeatedly in previous chapters: 'Femininity is interchangeable with softness; softness is represented by bodily fat; and all of these things – femininity, softness, and fat – are "disgusting"... Anorexia is a reaction to pervasive cultural symbols related to femininity.'[49] If the skeletal appearance of anorexic bodies is one (albeit extreme) response to the 'femininity' of corpulence, we must remember that bone is not the only 'other' of fat. The hard muscles promoted by physical culture are a central leitmotif of modernity, and many who have fled the seemingly corrupting softness of fat have sought refuge within their deceptively reassuring firmness.

Animality remained a potent point of reference in the twentieth century, with some animals, as usual, attracting more respect than others. For instance, it remained possible to identify oneself with noble lions and sleek greyhounds that possessed praiseworthy traits that could flatter a person. As always, though, having one's body or behaviour likened to 'lower' animals was most degrading. The continuing slippage between racialization and this kind of animalization cannot be ignored. As we have seen, the colonial world played an essential role in throwing into relief the kinds of regenerated bodies that white Westerners aspired to possess. By the early twentieth century, it was taken for granted that a preference for fatness, whether in oneself or in others, reflected a kind of primitive desire that was out of step with the purportedly loftier aesthetic sensibilities of the Western world.[50] This is why authors like Henry Finck could claim how 'savage' it was when supposedly 'civilized' people manifested a preference for fleshy bodies. When the demand for slenderness became more pronounced in the 1920s, by which time physical reformers were promoting a transnational rejuvenation of Western

"Garn! I told you it wasn't a whale!"

The animalization of fat people persisted in post-war Britain, as this postcard from the late 1940s/early 1950s shows.

civilization, Finck channelled his racialized disgust for fat into a weight-loss book entitled *Girth Control*. Reminding readers of those places in the world 'where beauty means fat', he pointedly compared certain 'American women of our day' to the 'much admired dusky wonders of obesity' overseas.[51]

The continuing animalization of 'backward' colonial peoples only served to strengthen the 'civilized' white person's shaky claim to represent the truly human. So common was this animalization of non-white fat that Franz Fanon felt compelled to address it decades later. 'When the colonist speaks of the colonized he uses zoological terms,' Fanon pointed out, a practice that typically evoked 'obese bodies that no longer resemble anything'.[52] Tacitly informing the racialization of fatness was the closely related problem of fattening, which evoked perennial misgivings about docile animals fed for the benefit of others. Raising the prospect of becoming fattened and subordinate 'beasts', like certain people overseas were said to be, was one way of shaming whites into weight-loss regimes. As French fitness guru Georges Hébert declared, only 'certain sedentary domestic animals and gluttons present traces of adiposity' as well as those 'oriental peoples' whose taste for fat female bodies evinces 'a complete aberration of the aesthetic sense'.[53] Durable links between fatness and status facilitated the equally entrenched association between animalization and feminization. Aside from signifying disgusting aesthetic and sexual tastes, fattening remained an issue of gendered power relations. Drawing direct analogies between 'the obese man and the animal being fattened for the kill [*l'animal à l'engrais*]', the physician Francis Heckel described the fat man as 'a monster ill-adapted to his human function'. Insofar as the act of fattening constitutes beauty only among pigs, sheep and cows, it was completely at odds with masculinity. 'Fat devirilizes and emasculates.'[54] Far from being consigned to the dustbin of history, ancient tropes connecting fat with animality, docility and femininity continued to structure modern perceptions of bodies well into the twentieth century, and beyond.

Lightness and Performance

Twentieth-century bodies were not simply imagined as being ideally slender or muscular. Rather, obsessions with health, beauty and performance were bound up with the verticalizing tendencies that have marked Western dualisms since antiquity.[55] All of this promoted corporeal ideals that were meant to be *experienced* as well as represented. While one can identify a cultural infatuation with ethereality and immateriality long before physical lightness was being methodically measured on a scale, by the end of the nineteenth century such qualities had become connected to the technological concept of efficiency that informed many aspects of Western culture. Hillel Schwartz reminds us that it was the 'pursuit of a *sensation* of lightness'[56] that, by producing a 'kinesthetic ideal of energy without volume', wove a 'knot of relationships' between gluttony and fatness, fatness and inefficiency, and inefficiency and lack of energy.[57] This point accounts for the fast, lithe and streamlined bodies promoted during the 1930s, whose movement through space was meant to be rapid and efficient.[58] Insofar as bodies were imaginatively aligned with a range of technologies, we may view the steps we take to preserve, extend or recapture youth as further efforts at 'immobilizing time'. But such lightness was not meant to suggest aimless drifting at the mercy of random atmospheric conditions. Rather, if the weak bodies and minds of the late nineteenth century were widely viewed as being passive reactors to external stimuli, then the new self of the modern age would assert itself in more agentic ways, affirming the supremacy of individual spirit or 'will' over the menacing immanence of materiality.[59] This is why 'in the visual iconography of 20th-century body culture, perhaps no other visual topos more directly connoted the *modern* body than that of the jump.'[60] To understand why fatness came to be such an affront to twentieth-century sensibilities, we must address the cultural and existential meanings of 'gravity' in a world where the virtues of lightness and overcoming were so frequently celebrated.

In 1930 Lucky Strike ran a series of ads suggesting that smoking could prevent one from gaining weight, often contrasting the beauty and sportive fitness of the smoker to his or her less impressive 'future shadow'. Here the streamlined body of a white male diver soars above his less aerodynamic 'shadow'.

Efficient movement, whether vertical or lateral, was essential in the early skirmishes that would spark our current 'war on obesity'. This, too, was in contrast to observations made about the world outside of the West. As we have seen, many accounts of African fatness were not restricted to the 'disgusting' spectacle they offered, but revolved around the incapacitation it seemed to impose upon women as well as men. This incarcerating fatness enforced a kind of inertia or 'indolence' that frustrated the ability to put the will's commands into action. Given the period's emphasis on speed, efficiency and performance, fat bodies did not look as if they could *move* in ways considered appropriate for a fast-paced modern world. The demand for efficiency underscores the extent to which discrimination against fat people was not reducible to perceived deviations from aesthetic ideals. Every step the fat man took, noted that apostle of American efficiency Luther Gulick, is 'a costly drain upon his energy'.[61] This was especially true in the workplace. 'There is increasing competition in business and a growing demand for effective service,' declared the politician and homeopathic physician Royal S. Copeland. He continued:

> In the shop, the office, the home – wherever men and women work – the rivalries of modern life demand health and vigor. In this contest fat folks are handicapped.[62]

The desire for speed, efficiency and the ability to move in restricted spaces encouraged employers not to hire fat people for sales positions: 'There isn't enough room for them back of the counter,' Paul Henry Nystrom complained in his popular *Economics of Retailing*. 'They don't move quickly enough.'[63] As other claims from the period suggest, fat's age-old link with mental and physical slowness had become grounds for discrimination in employment.

If modern urban life generated heightened expectations about physical performance that demanded free, efficient and effective movement, then excess fat could be viewed as an encasing and encumbering substance that hindered motility. That ordinary everyday movement may not have *actually* been impeded by a person's corpulence was less important than the common assumption that fat bodies *could not possibly* move quickly and efficiently. Whereas the corpulent body was certainly not the only presumed effect (or cause) of idleness and fatigue, its presence was a reminder of the body's limited capacity to transcend its own organicity or to resolve the paradoxes of modernity. Hence numerous references in health and fitness manuals to fatness as a 'handicap'.[64] Resonating with ancient claims that large amounts of fat could immobilize and even suffocate bodies, the corporeal utopianism of the twentieth century shunted corpulence more conspicuously into the category of disability, which had become increasingly visible following the carnage of the First World War. Evoking situations in which the fragile and precarious nature of all embodiment is foregrounded, the fat body – like the disabled body – would come to represent 'a tear in our being that reveals its open-endedness, its incompleteness, its precariousness'.[65]

Modern sports dramatized the twentieth-century dream of bodily transcendence through the application of *askesis* or self-discipline. If it is impossible to approach the athletic renaissance of the period without noting its explicit contempt for fat, one should not seek the vertical aspirations of modern bodies only in literal postures and movements. Not all athletic performances require lightness, or actual leaps into the air. Boxing, bodybuilding and football were just some of the activities where muscularity and weight had practical value. Even when sportive bodies seem 'heavy' and remain more or less close to the earth, their speed and agility – as in the case of runners – make them seemingly free of the friction that contact with the ground would create. Mass culture's growing fascination with all manner of record-breaking performances attests to an interest in overcoming expectations, moving beyond hitherto accepted ideas about what human bodies can do. *Forward* movement in the service of athletic achievement is at the same time *upward* movement. It plots trajectories of vertical transcendence over that which lies beneath, an ever-widening field of the 'low' populated by all things animal, savage, feminine and degenerate. Within this world of fluid movement and streamlined efficiency, fat represented a *downward* as well as a *backward* form of 'drag'. If there is a secular form of 'salvation' in such transcendent practices, notes Peter Sloterdijk, it is because 'the extreme athlete is raised aloft as the spiritually empty counterpart of the saint.'[66]

The vertical trajectory of these practices and prescriptions is evident in many of the period's discourses on diet and nutrition. Such discourses were often scientific and quantitative, with the new term 'calorie' mobilized to encourage people to curb their appetites by

Fig. 78. — Abêtissement de l'expression de la physionomie déterminé par l'engraissement. Aspect et profil porcins.

In an era when swans and greyhounds inspired industrial designers and physical culturists with their sleek and streamlined physiques, fat bodies remained tied to the 'wrong' sort of animality. In a popular dieting book, one French physician felt the need to illustrate 'The dumbing down [animalization] of physiognomic expression as a result of fattening. A porcine look and profile.' Francis Heckel, *Maigrir: pourquoi? comment?* (Paris, 1930).

choosing not to eat more than what was needed for health.[67] It was modern civilization's inherent tendency to drive people to excess that made counting calories essential.[68] Approaching the consuming body as a kind of machine did not at all rule out the search for 'higher' values. Rather, the rapid expansion of the calorie, along with the related recommendation to seek out healthy foods without much regard to taste, helped to align healthy choices with moral judgement. In this way, a growing obsession with counting calories is 'a good example of modern nutrition functioning as an empirical science *and* a spiritual discipline'.[69]

Moreover, since eating remained a source of pleasure as well as anxiety, this entailed the further humanizing of an activity that people shared with non-human animals. This often meant denigrating organic life in favour of another, more exalted ideal. Appeals for more elevated approaches to eating were widespread. 'Living to eat is debasing life to its lowest terms, on a plane with mere animal life,' health and beauty writer Ella Adelia Fletcher argued at the dawn

'Movement is life.' Suggesting that transcendence was within the reach of ordinary women as well as trained dancers, the 'Famous leap by Peggy St. Lo' became the logo for the Women's League of Health and Beauty. By 1939 the League boasted 170,000 members in Britain, Australia, Canada and Hong Kong.

of the century, 'and the man or woman who does this often fails to evince even the instinct and discretion with which the higher order of beasts control their appetites'.[70] The contempt that the spiritually inclined Fletcher had for 'mere animal life' was shared by educators who spoke of elevating the body above decay and animality towards a kind of divinity. 'Learning and science are beginning to hear the divine call of the stomach,' declared William M. Beardshear, president of the National Educational Association, 'to displace its satiety with purity of flesh and its putrefaction with purity of soul.' Despite being a United Brethren minister, the bodily 'divinity' Beardshear invoked was rooted in classical mythology and proper English values rather than Christian imagery:

> A stomach's god shall no longer be Silenus . . . but the goddess Hygeia; its emperor no longer [the Roman emperor] Vitellius, but the empress Victoria; its animal not the pig but the exalted man.[71]

Even if the quest for transcendence did not need to assume conventional religious forms, it is no surprise that many Christian movements have accorded an almost sacred status to the health and 'purity' of the body. This is particularly evident in the United States. Since the early nineteenth century, white, middle-class Protestants have promoted dietetic and fitness regimens promising varying degrees of bodily health and perfection. Protestants involved with the New Thought movement often engaged in fasting and exercise as ways of creating spiritualized bodies that could be less corruptible, less subject to the 'gross' sensual demands of the flesh. In some cases, these perfected bodies were even believed capable of achieving physical immortality. The 'spirit bodies' that some of them imagined promised more reassuring forms of embodiment than ever-disappointing 'natural bodies'.[72] As Marie Griffith persuasively shows, such vertical tendencies would be readily secularized in the decades to come:

> Dogged optimism in a kind of mechanized etherealization of the flesh – as in the typical affirmation, 'I am growing lighter and lighter each day . . . My food is assimilating properly, all waste is being carried off and I am growing better in every way' – represents one of the most unshakable themes running through American diet culture.[73]

Implicit to the insistence that bodies should externally conform to aesthetic standards was the assumption that, in so doing, individuals would share a sensory experience of energy and buoyancy. Dieting and exercise were thus meant to effect profound changes throughout the sensorium. Given that buoyancy was an emotional as well as kinaesthetic ideal, weight-loss charted a path towards all manner of levity. If the 'sluggish' fat body was at odds with efficiency, which Thomas Inch dubbed 'the watchword of to-day', within just a few days of following an exercise and dietary regimen one would begin 'to feel such an immediate benefit, a lightness in movement; even thought speeds up; you feel more youthful and brighter'.[74] Youthful fitness promised happiness as well as beauty; bodily efficiency was emotional as well as motoric. Indeed, there was enjoyment as well as sacrifice to be found in vigorous exercise regimens. Bodywork itself was presented as the inherently pleasurable, indeed euphoric, activity, that it can often be. Even the act of fasting could be promoted partly for the sensual gratification it supposedly made possible.[75] Thus did the sensual and 'animal' gratification associated with corpulence yield to the 'higher' delights wrought through diet and exercise.

The slender, muscled physique that came to dominate the visual imagination of the early twentieth century did not only indicate an ability to sculpt the body in accordance with reigning aesthetic ideals. Of course, it accomplished this as well, but it is worth remembering that aesthetic ideals have never been skin deep. Rather these were bodies meant to *enact* as well as display an inner quantum of energy, and so supported a principle of performance – and thus able-bodiedness – that was just as critical for the transformation of physiques. As mentioned above, nothing was more at odds with this accelerated society than the ponderous body that portended disability and decay. An 1892 ad for Marienbad Reduction Pills could sagely chide the world-weary that the 'burden of life is heavy enough without the added burden of superfluous flesh'.[76] Within a few decades it was life itself that needed to become dynamic and light. 'Movement is life. Stillness is the attribute of death,' declared Mary Bagot Stack, founder of the Women's League of Health and Beauty, echoing a 1920 German gymnastic manual. 'A body without movement is like the stagnant pool: it collects the weeds of disease which will finally kill it.'[77] Here, too, it was upward movement that was being celebrated.

In this fast-paced world, fat bodies seemed to afford only sluggish-ness and torpor; they 'cannot give joy and pride'.[78] Evoking qualities that were a mainstay of colonial descriptions of native peoples, one author noted that the corpulent 'not only become physically indolent, but they often become mentally lazy' as well.[79] As such, they were incapable of eliciting respect, much less love. 'Everybody likes a fat man,' insisted one writer in defiance of the received wisdom of the day. They are especially loved by wives since a

> fat husband, placid, good-natured, liberal, is much easier to live with, day in and day out, than a thin, nervous, worried husband who plays golf for fear of losing his figure.[80]

Claims like these were destined to attract scorn at a time when male 'domestication' was sometimes likened to emasculation, and when the phrase 'nobody loves a fat man' had become a veritable proverb.[81] Fat women might be 'hard to tolerate', maintained one fitness writer, but 'it is absolutely impossible to look at an obese man without a feeling of disgust.'[82] It was no wonder that good-natured fat men would be relished by wives, snorted Leonard Williams, for these are just the kind of submissive males that women adore. Don't be fooled if a woman seems to take pride in her man's swelling body 'as a

'Nobody loves a fat man' remained a proverb in American English through the 1950s. Elmer Wheeler, *The Fat Boy's Book* (New York, 1950).

farmer takes in his well-fed animals', for she probably has darker motives for fattening him up. 'She realizes by a sort of hereditary sex instinct that a fat man is easy-going, yielding, uncritical; stupid in fact.' Those women for whom this was not a purely instinctual reflex could consult Shakespeare to learn how Caesar wisely preferred to surround himself with the corpulent: 'All tyrants know that they are safe with fat men, and the domestic tyrant is no exception.'[83] Physicians like Williams provided medical confirmation of the old claim that fattening amounted to bondage, subordination and thus feminization. Such dramatic images easily lent themselves to fictional elaboration. 'I'm in love,' confessed the fat narrator of Henri Béraud's novel *Le Martyre de l'obèse*; 'that's what makes everyone laugh.' Winner of the Prix Goncourt before being adapted into a popular 1926 film, Béraud's story presented corpulence as a painful and unhappy ordeal, a kind of 'martydom'.[84]

While the idea of a loveable fat person was being ridiculed in medicine, literature and film, others chipped away at whatever was left of the link between fatness and happiness. The popular saying about fatness and love, one author quipped, 'could be read more correctly, "Nobody loves a fat man (or a fat woman) less than he does himself."'[85] Physicians and psychologists were ready to support such ideas. 'The old dictum of "Laugh and grow fat" should not be taken too seriously,' sniffed a British doctor, who observed:

> The fat person, as a rule, avoids effort, mental and physical, his critical faculties are dulled, and a tendency to laugh rather than to grumble shows his bias towards taking the easier path.[86]

Popularized psychoanalysis reinforced the notion that fatness was evidence of unhappiness. Hilde Bruch proposed that the dynamic of the family circle was partly enabled by emotionally charged food that symbolized love, sometimes even becoming love's veritable substitute. If to feed is to show love, and to eat is to accept and acknowledge that love, then food could serve as one of love's surrogates.[87] Disseminated in popular culture through the many articles she wrote for women's magazines, Bruch's views on fat and love dominated the psychological landscape in the 1940s and '50s. *Life* magazine popularized these ideas by declaring that

As for obesity, its usual cause is overeating, but overeating is interpreted as an act whereby the gourmand compensates for some inner deprivation or frustration.[88]

Fatness might refer to sensual pleasure, of course. But, as Lord Chesterfield had declared centuries earlier, it could never be a sign of 'true' happiness. 'One is happy or unhappy depending upon one's weight,' reported Henry Béraud's fictional martyr of obesity.[89]

The decades to come offered only more elaborate versions of claims like these. Officially discredited, yet persistently appealing, updated versions of the ancient 'science' of physiognomy lived on as ways of reading external bodily signs for evidence of inner qualities. By the 1940s, William H. Sheldon's famous characterological typology of male bodies was warmly received by the American public, especially by gym teachers ready and willing to press their young charges into neat categories.[90] Seeking to demonstrate the connection between physique and character, Sheldon linked the chubby 'endomorphic' body type to the 'viscerotonic' temperament. The latter was marked by a love of food, comfort and sociability, an aversion to pain and effort, a tendency toward emotional display, and

> a certain flabbiness or lack of intensity in the mental and moral outlook . . . a dull, vegetable-like quality [and] lack of purpose beyond the elementary biological purposes.

Rather than demonstrating action and solidity, a male like this 'gives off the general impression of soft metal'.[91] Thanks to such efforts, by mid-century the idea that fat boys displayed 'inadequate masculine physique' and a 'feminine' character was well established.[92]

However variably they were imagined, men and women of the period were often encouraged to enact a modern transcendence of the problems of modernity, even if the achievement of the toned and slender body required modern technologies in order to be actualized. This entailed a celebration of whiteness as synonymous with muscular fitness, aesthetic appeal and efficient performance. Mental and physical regeneration was often performed against beliefs that the future of the white 'race' was at stake. Far from these being entirely new developments, the discourse of degeneration that gave rise to modern eugenics exhibits an 'ideological continuity' with the ideals of human perfectibility proposed in the eighteenth century.[93] Classical bodies, traditionally celebrated because they supposedly conveyed an aesthetic ideal shorn of any corrupting sensuality, were now becoming eroticized as fatness slipped further into abjection. The ideal of eugenic purity was a matter of cleanliness as well as a lack of adulteration. Some proponents of eugenics saw fatness as a largely hereditary defect ('a dysgenic factor') and, for the good of the race,

MAUVAIS PRÉTEXTE

— Tu ne pourras pas me dire que c'est pour le Père Noël... ?

The unlovability of fat men and women was loudly pronounced in the 1920s and '30s. 'You can't tell me that these are for Father Christmas . . . ?', Georges Léonnec, 'Mauvais Prétexte', *La Vie parisienne* (1926).

discouraged marrying fat people without first checking their family history. Echoing eugenic advice from the seventeenth and eighteenth centuries, they recommended that those who did choose to marry the fat should make sure they were themselves slender, with the idea that corpulence would eventually be bred away.[94] In many cases, though, the eugenic problem of corpulence sorted itself out because, perhaps due to diminished libido, 'in general, those predisposed to corpulence are therefore less inclined to marriage.'[95] Given this climate of contempt, it is tempting to interpret the proverb 'nobody loves a fat man' as having a prescriptive aim rather than merely descriptive meaning.

Located in the modern celebration of movement and speed is a corresponding wish for stasis, a freezing or overcoming of organic time, and thus a certain resistance to the cycle of 'life' itself. Modern bodies would therefore be youthful bodies, and the passage of time seemingly sacrificed on the altar of speed. This was the unrealizable wish expressed by Carl Luther, and his words, cited above, merit repeating: 'we do not wish to age, but rather to remain young, fresh, and slender.'[96] Implicit in the celebration of youthfulness is the framing of biological ageing as an inevitable process of decline with its own physical and emotional problems. Independently of regular reminders that fatness is a kind of disease, associations of corpulence with ageing reinforced its links to decline and death. To be sure, warnings that fatness contributed to ageing and shortened one's life have been articulated since antiquity, but such assumptions acquired a new urgency by the twentieth century, where corpulence was deemed 'one of the first indices of senility'.[97] By then, British as well as American life insurance companies had come to view 'obesity' as a risk factor.[98] It was during roughly the same period that the concept of middle age began to develop, throwing into relief long-standing links between youth, health and beauty. At some point between the early 1900s and 1935, 'the decline theory of life' developed to create the lived sense that, as one ages, one finds oneself locked within a process of decay that inevitably ends in death.[99] The emergence of middle age as a period of decline was particularly problematic for women, for whom ageing could mean a diminishment of physical attractiveness as well as the loss of a maternal role.[100] The phrase 'fat and forty' came into circulation, not simply due to its alliterative appeal, but because corpulence was quickly becoming a sign of

physical decline and a harbinger of death itself. The British eugeni-
cist Caleb Saleeby bristled at the closely related phrase 'too old at
forty' that had become popular early in the century, but he saw the
reasons behind it. Whereas the 'hale and mentally alert centenarian
should really be a commonplace', he felt, all too often people who
reach the age of fifty or sixty have gained so much weight and are
beset by so many other ailments that 'the distinctively *human* life has
really expired. They scarcely do more than cumber the ground.'[101]

Seemingly exempted from the category of the human, if one
takes Saleeby seriously, fatness worked against the era's insistence on
young, efficient and able bodies. Luther Gulick wrote disparagingly
of how the 'fat, clumsy, unsightly bodies' of middle-aged businessmen
showed 'every degree of dilapidation and inefficiency'.[102] Shifting
between mechanical and organic imagery, Leonard Williams wrote
with concern of how 'a machine intended to last for 120 years, shows
serious signs of wear at 50 years of age' while maintaining that 'the
ordinary man begins to "rot" at 30 years of age, and when he reaches
50 the sinister process is in full swing.'[103] This litany of morbid associations was recounted elsewhere. '*A fat adult is always degenerating
or sick*,' declared one popular nutrition text,[104] while a beauty manual
predicted that a person who passes fifty and does not curb his or her
appetite might in fact be 'committing slow suicide'.[105] That the process of midlife decline always ended in death was repeatedly
underscored, almost as if youth was a state that could be indefinitely
extended:

> When you learn to measure overweight in terms of increased
> prospect of early death and to measure normal weight, or less,
> in terms of increased prospect of long life, you will hesitate no
> longer.[106]

Here, too, fatness seemed to pull one backward as well as downward.
The only thing fat seemed to accelerate was the way in which one's
appearance marked one's current location in the life course. 'To grow
fat is to age a little,' Armand Hemmerdinger cautioned French readers, but ageing only portended the ultimate dread: 'To age is to die a
little.'[107] As fatness came laden with intimations of decline and mortality, diet and fitness culture promoted the fantasy of freezing time
in a modern world predicated on movement, weightlessness and

eternal youth. In the face of such aspirations, the fact that the stuff of life had always been a troubling reminder of mortality achieved even greater importance. 'Fat is fatal.'[108]

The stuff of life was fast becoming the stuff of death. For some, it had never really been alive anyway – 'virtually dead tissue' is how one best-selling diet book described it.[109] 'Fat cells are scarcely more

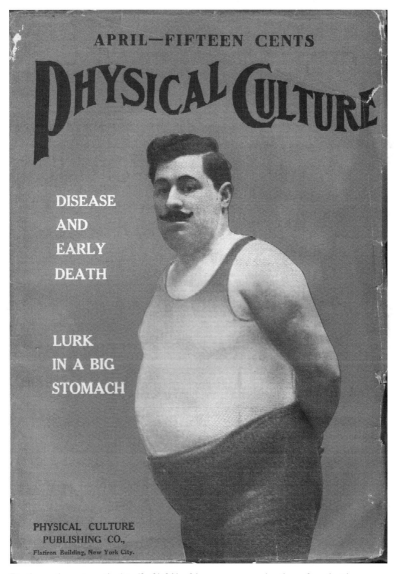

By the 20th century the 'stuff of life' had become more closely and explicitly connected to disease and death. *Physical Culture* (April 1909).

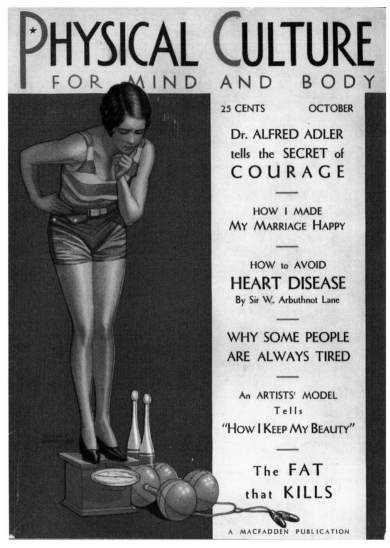

'The Fat that Kills', *Physical Culture* (October 1930).

worthy to be called alive than the cells which compose our visible nails or hair,' opined Saleeby. Considering that fat is 'in no sense part of the living tissue of the body', the corpulent middle-aged man was in effect carrying around a lot of dead matter: 'his muscle cells, including those of his heart, will degenerate, die, and become replaced by lifeless oil or fat.'[110] When present in large amounts, this dead substance disturbed the operations of the human machine, preventing efficient locomotion as well as internally 'clogging the wheels which should run smoothly, and hindering the important organs from performing their functions as they should'.[111] Images of fat as inefficient and dead 'waste' invited further comparisons to filth and excrement. This fed into a growing tendency, already underway in the nineteenth century, to purge the inner body of traces of the food that passed into it from the outside. With constipation sometimes listed as a cause of corpulence, particularly insofar as it produced 'toxic' effluvia that built up in the body, many Americans and Britons sought to lose weight by way of laxatives and high-fibre diets.[112] As the continuing appeal of colonic irrigation and other forms of internal cleansing suggests, the eighteenth-century notion that corpulence is caused by unexcreted filth has proven hard to shake. Worse than dead matter, fat has once again become shit.

Female Transcendence

Savage and dirty, if not a portent of sickness, disability, old age and death, fat now weighed more explicitly and heavily on existential matters than ever before. It may be useful to consider briefly how the impact of such developments worked in relation to women's bodies as well as the rise of feminism. Feminisms of most forms qualify as 'utopian' in the broad sense employed here: 'the desire for a different, better way of being'.[113] Whereas conventional wisdom maintains that women have typically borne the brunt of anti-fat stigma, historical work on modern weight-loss texts suggests that, even in the early twentieth century, it was often males who were exhorted to slim down.[114] The fat man's historically shaky grasp on virility was further diminished as images of muscular manhood came to predominate in the sporting, physical culture and bodybuilding movements.[115] Fat women were considered problematic in different but related ways. Suggesting the anti-modern potential of illness and idleness, fatness located women in another aesthetic and moral register. The emergent female aesthetic of the 1920s was dynamic as well as slender. Beauty implied energy, lightness and movement; fatness suggested inertia and stagnation.[116] The image of heavy immobility that had characterized women in the Victorian era was gradually replaced by an appreciation for the body in motion, dynamically engaged in its projects and adapted to the accelerated pace of life that characterized modernity.[117] Of course, the true weight of lightness would be felt once the slender ideal became de rigueur for girls and women, but the aspirations and dreams that motivated it tapped into ideals of agency and autonomy as well as appearance.[118]

Fat was a feminist issue, mainly as something to be combated. The abdication of agency that fat represented was especially condemned among female reformers, who encouraged women to exercise even greater control over their appetites and their figures. Like all physical traits considered beautiful, slenderness conveyed moral qualities that suggested a conquest of the self through willpower alone, at least as it pertained to exercise and dietary discretion. The tight grip on the body that was once exercised by the corset, for example, was now replaced by what health reformer Bess Mensendieck called a 'muscle corset', a purely 'natural' accessory crafted and applied by the woman herself.[119] In a world in which 'the body becomes its own corset', a pronounced emphasis on willpower in beauty culture placed responsibility for personal appearance firmly on the shoulders of individuals.[120] There was thus not much to be done for those people for whom 'gourmandize gains the upper hand over pleasing the opposite sex [*la coquetterie*].'[121] The idea that one must 'suffer' for beauty reinforced this idea of appearance as an achievement, so that if one became fat everyone knew where to place the blame: 'One doesn't merely acquire a belly,' went one French slogan, 'one accepts it.'[122] The 'softness' that was once considered an essential and desirable 'feminine' trait was a potential liability for the self-possessed modern woman. 'Don't be soft with yourself,' barked Sylvia of Hollywood. 'You've got to go after that figure with bull-dog determination! Nobody can give you a lovely figure but yourself. I'm telling you *how* to do it, *but you must do it*.'[123] It took a firm character to have a hard body.

Attesting to the residue of agricultural thinking within a modern frame, Western culture continued to see in the act of fattening evidence of subjection and eventual consumption, whether for alimentary, sexual or political purposes. As a French beauty guide pointed out, in non-Western cultures some people would grow and sell women 'like livestock, more or less according to their good health, their resistance to fatigue, or even – O blasphemy! – the quality of their fat'.[124] This perennial alignment of fattening with livestock elicited warnings from physicians as well. When pondering corpulence, warned Armand Hemmerdinger, one should not confuse the perspective of the cook for that of the bird. Citing the inevitable fate of geese as well as pigs, female readers were reminded that the 'breeder considers the beast to be "in good form" [*en bon point*] when it is fat enough to be killed'.[125] We have seen how, in the nineteenth century, it was often claimed that excess fat 'corrupts' female beauty. But readers were also reminded yet again that, when encumbered by fat, 'the soul is oppressed by the enormous weight of the substance' and thus impairs 'all the functions of the understanding'.[126] Still considered a material obstacle to perception and cognition, fat's gross materiality weighed down the soul or mind that was supposed to take flight. Female agency and emancipation were among the things promoted by those authors who objected to the forced fattening of non-Western girls as brutal subjection.

To some extent, then, fat, fatness and fattening were at odds with the aims of modern feminism. Rather than allowing themselves to be reduced to an ignoble level, women were encouraged to transcend their status as domesticated creatures to lay claim to their full potential as human beings. Many advocates for women's rights shared the idea that female fatness represented a kind of domestic servitude that needed to be overcome. For those pressing for women's voting rights, the battle was not simply about beauty and appearance, but the qualities they hoped their slender bodies might convey. Female 'weakness' was thus literally man-made, and capable of being reversed through self-discipline and physical fitness.[127] What was needed was not flabby sentimentality or weakness, but courage, resolve and willpower. Such traits could be dramatized when imprisoned suffragists went on hunger strikes and had to resist both their own hunger pangs and the force-feeding they might have to endure by ostensibly well-meaning male authorities.[128] What women applied to themselves should pertain as well to their children. Writing against the French practice of 'puericulture', which celebrated the plumpness of babies, Hemmerdinger retorted that 'The value of a pig is measured according to weight, not that of a child.'[129] Feminist body culture, to speak in broad terms, was often subject to the same vertical tensions inherited from the past and accelerated in the modern era. For many women seeking to rise above the domestic bondage to which a sexist culture consigned them, weight appeared as a burden that kept them down.

The tension between fatness and feminism was dramatized in the work of philosopher Simone de Beauvoir. In *The Second Sex*,

Beauvoir writes of a male cultural demand that women 'represent the flesh [*la chair*] purely for its own sake', the 'most naïve form' of which is 'the Hottentot ideal' along with the 'taste of Orientals for fat women'. In her view, such abundant flesh was 'an aimless fact', an 'absurd richness', an 'unnecessary, gratuitous blooming' that was demanded even in Western society where it was meant to be domesticated, as in the case of women's breasts and hips. Subjected to paralyzing clothing and the 'rules of propriety', the Hollywood starlet was just as petrified and incapacitated as the foot-bound Chinese woman.[130] Modern times had at least offered the possibility for change. Although by the 1940s the hyper-slender boyishness of 1920s fashions had receded, Beauvoir was relieved to see that 'at least the overopulent ideal of past centuries has not returned.' Aware of the persistent power of the male gaze to reduce girls and women to mere objects, de Beauvoir conceded that if the female body is still 'asked to be flesh', it is at least done with some discretion: 'it is to be slender and not loaded with fat [*graisse*]; muscular, supple, strong, it is bound to suggest transcendence.'[131]

Often criticized for holding a negative view of the female body, Beauvoir's perspective on fat was firmly located within the broader currents of the day. In her opinion, the new beauty demands made of women facilitated rather than hindered their strength and agency, and thus their capacity to overcome their existential situation:

> Modern aesthetic concepts permit her to combine beauty and activity: she has a right to trained muscles, she refuses the invasion of fat [*l'envahissement de la graisse*]; in physical culture she finds self-affirmation as subject and in a measure frees herself from her contingent flesh.

Not losing sight of the ambiguous nature of women's engagement with such projects, she added that, in some cases, this apparent 'liberation easily falls back into dependence'. Indeed, certain women – Beauvoir terms them 'frigid or frustrated', though she may also have been thinking about those suffering from anorexia – will recoil at 'the depreciation that all living growth entails' and 'endeavour to preserve themselves as others preserve furniture or canned food'. Instilled with 'a horror of life itself', women who recoil from 'all living growth' end up becoming 'enemies of their own existence and hostile to others'.[132]

As the prospect of an anorexic recoiling from 'life' darkens this heroic image of female agency, one wonders whether Beauvoir was aware of Ludwig Binswanger's now famous psychological assessment of 'Ellen West', published in 1944. This was a controversial case study of a pseudonymous Swiss woman who ultimately committed suicide after suffering for years from a fear of growing fat. Binswanger saw West's fear of corpulence as

> a concretization of a severe existential dread, the dread of the 'degenerating life,' of withering, drying up, moldering, rotting, becoming a husk, eroding, being buried alive, whereby the world of the self becomes a tomb, a mere hole. Part of this is the fear of putting on fat and turning into material. It is the 'earth-heaviness' which 'pulls her down,' and what she dreads is this being-pulled-down.[133]

The West case has often been cited by feminist scholars as a tragic instance of anorexia, though Binswanger rejected this diagnosis in favour of what he called polymorphous schizophrenia. The specific diagnosis is perhaps less important. Connected as they are to organic processes, the vicissitudes of embodiment seem to have prompted West to freeze her ideal body image rather than reconcile herself to change over time. Unable to adapt to the 'turbulence that character-izes our lived bodily experience', notes philosopher Gail Weiss, in her 'desire to be an ethereal or "fleshless" body', West opted to annihilate the flesh she despised.[134] Without minimizing the very personal dimensions of West's suffering, the distinction she drew between an earthbound 'tomb-world' and an 'ethereal world' of lightness resonates as a tragic echo of a larger cultural development. By choosing death, West settled on a very final way of transcending the stuff of life.

✳

Whether or not Simone de Beauvoir was aware of Binswanger's analysis of Ellen West, the form of immanence he described would also have been attributed by many to animals as well as certain 'primitive' peoples who were also inappropriate models for liberated women to emulate. For Beauvoir, the challenge of fatness was partly related to appearance but pointed to other concerns as well, some of which evoked the ambiguities of embodied life.[135] If it is true that a 'masculinist ontology' permeates Beauvoir's concept of female transcendence,[136] a similar ontology has structured perceptions of fat, fatness and fattening for much of Western history. Indeed, such images have haunted various forms of feminism since at least the early twentieth century and help explain why many feminists today express uneasiness about fat activism. Amy Erdman Farrell rightly observes that

> to the extent that feminism means claiming a place of equality and resisting the position of 'other,' it is no wonder that feminists have had a peculiar relationship to weight – both recognizing the way ideas about weight get wielded against women but also wanting to resist the stigma of 'weak willed' and 'primitive' that fatness connotes.[137]

The second-wave feminist Germaine Greer was certainly of this mind in 1970, around the time when the war on fat really heated up:

> Historically we may see that all repressed, indolent people have been fat, that eunuchs tend to fatten like bullocks, and so we need not be surprised to find that the male preference for cuddlesome women persists.[138]

As was the case with castrated animals destined for the chop, fatness was a fleshy reminder of the diminished and disempowered status of the 'eunuch', male or female.

Extending and reworking aspects of the cultural imagination of fat whose sources are traceable to antiquity, the early twentieth century promoted the 'civilized' white body as that which was ideally clean, smooth and light, efficiently quantifiable and predictable, with traces of the organic or animal removed or pushed out of sight and mind. It is not an exaggeration to treat such developments as broadly 'utopian' or to suggest that they have been pursued with an almost 'religious' fervour. To imagine bodies as efficient, streamlined and machinelike is to indulge in a fantasy of temporary transcendence of the messiness of organic life and of the fragile creatureliness that humans share with non-human animals. Streamlined machines are smooth, dry, sleek and clean. With proper maintenance they perform efficiently and may endure. Though made of metal and therefore weighty, their power and speed allow them to resist the downward pull of gravity. Hard and dry like bones, smooth, clean and metallic bodies do not elicit disgust. Alongside these ideals, or implicit within them, are closely related fantasies of purity – of food, hygiene, sexuality, race, and so on. The violence with which modern disgust at fat is often manifested seems aimed at driving the inconvenient aspects of embodied life out of existence. In this sense, it confirms the claim that the 'aim of utopias, to a greater or lesser extent, is to eliminate real people'.[139]

CONCLUSION

Purity, Lightness and the Weight of History

T
wo thousand years since the death of Jesus, Christians still disagree about what their bodies might look like in Heaven. One churchgoer in Broken Arrow, Oklahoma, is 'confident she is going to heaven. What scares her is the possibility that she'll show up 30 pounds overweight and stay that way forever.' Her 'secret hope' is that 'when she walks through the pearly gates the weight will "disappear" to be remembered no more.' Another member of the congregation, 'a mom who is in marathon shape', wants to take her current body with her. 'I haven't worked this hard on my body only to have it taken away once I die,' she maintains. Nor does she want Heaven to look like 'every mall in the u.s. where half the people are so big they have a hard time moving around'. A third woman, 'a substantially overweight church member who says she carries around enough extra pounds "to form another small human"', hopes for a more diverse and inclusive afterlife. While preferring to retain her current physique, her vision of Heaven is marked by a liberating lightness and enhanced mobility: 'she looks forward to "zooming around heaven in a big, impressive body".'[1] Disagreements about body size and shape notwithstanding, all three women expect Heaven to be a more or less weightless and timeless experience.

Most versions of Christianity promise bodily resurrection and eternal life, but the defeat of death has little to do with 'life' as it is organically experienced. Accounts vary of exactly what the resurrection body will be like, but it will surely be free of the limitations and weaknesses of bodies as they are actually lived. In keeping with what Augustine promised, there is to be no fat in Heaven, nor any of the other offending substances, processes or mutations associated with organic existence.[2] Nor is there to be any form of disability or ageing. This disconnection between the bodies that humans actually possess and those they might like to have is not uniquely Christian. Aside from being located in an otherworldly realm, the perfect bodies that will supposedly populate Heaven bear a more than passing resemblance to the bodies that are celebrated, if not sought after, here on Earth. And those idealized bodies, it is widely affirmed today, cannot be fat either.

If Christian beauty ideals are therefore laden with 'worldly' values, the secular quest for perfection manifests certain 'spiritual' tendencies, for lack of a better word.[3] Not only was the quest for slenderness being described as a kind of 'religion' by the late 1960s, but secular weight-loss programmes often organized themselves as quasi-religious institutions, even in the absence of any explicit or conventional religious orientation. As people became engaged in cycles of praise, confession and atonement, losing weight was even more overtly cast as a process of 'cleansing' and 'purifying' bodies and souls of the 'sin' that fat seemed to represent.[4] In recent years, the collective quest for transcendence has gone online, as research into Internet support groups for overeaters shows. Whether they emphasize the quest for cleanliness, purity and abstinence, as do religious support groups, or disgust with the self that is common among secular groups, all are concerned about cleanliness and filth, purity and impurity.[5] Secular fitness practices thus dovetail with certain forms of Protestantism, collectively amounting to 'a devotional project aimed at bodily perfectibility' achieved through 'a kind of mechanized etherealization of the flesh'.[6] A 'religion of lightness' is how some describe the belief system of modern culture, and not just in relation to bodies, food and fitness:

> Lightness is our artifice, our urban invention. It does not lack models: the bubble, the balloon, the cloud, the wind. But also the bird, the angel, the aviator . . . and the saint.[7]

Nor does it lack companions, for lightness often requires the pursuit of purity as well.

As fascinating and important as these developments are, it would require a second book to examine them with the precision and depth that they merit. Rather than probe our present anxieties about embodiment in detail, the aim of this book has been to show that these anxieties have sources that are to some extent rooted in the distant past. Despite tracing the emergence of negative stereotypes about fat people over time, though, it has not proposed an unbroken cultural or emotional continuity across obviously diverse historical periods and places. But it has insisted that there is more to fat than fatness, and that by probing these other dimensions we may be able to understand the complex ways in which disgust towards corpulence operates in our world. By briefly casting an eye over developments since the 1970s, which is when our current obsessions with fat and slenderness really took off, this book's closing pages sketch in very broad terms the persistence and extension of historical developments into our disgusted present. It is safe to say that contemporary beauty, diet and fitness cultures have extended and radicalized the transcendent and utopian dreams that have circulated in the West since the early 1900s. Numerous studies have convincingly demonstrated the often-disastrous effects that the modern cult of appearance has had on the perception of bodies, especially female ones. Yet despite the obvious focus on appearances, fat, fatness and fattening continue to be visceral as well as visible phenomena.

✳

Understood literally or figuratively, 'trimming the fat' is a core tenet of neo-liberalism, a now widely entrenched political and economic theory that emphasizes individualism and free enterprise (as well as free trade, unrestricted markets and private property rights) as keys to human well-being. With its emphasis on renewing and radicalizing eighteenth-century liberal ideals of self-reliance, willpower and risk-taking, neo-liberalism generally distrusts the state's regulatory interference with individual liberties and personal responsibility.[8] In economic and somatic terms, neo-liberalism is a prime example of the technocratic 'light modernity' described by Zygmunt Bauman. What amounts to the 'managerial equivalent of liposuction' functions as a strategy for carrying out the tasks of 'slimming, downsizing, phasing out, closing down or selling out some units because they are not effective enough'.[9] It is telling that French sociologists see this technocratic world as striving to be *dégraissé* – literally 'degreased' or 'defatted', but also figuratively streamlined, cleaned and dried.[10]

This is an extension and acceleration of the trends towards mechanical efficiency that developed more than a century ago, and which are considered by many to be worth celebrating. Regardless of the disastrous human costs that it often incurs, neo-liberalism's most powerful and vocal proponents often treat it as 'a *utopian* project to realize a theoretical design for the reorganization of international capitalism'.[11] Such a utopian project demands a corresponding corporeal utopianism that has taken the form of a 'coercive healthism', the roots of which extend at least as far back as the nineteenth century.[12] The self-control that coercive healthism demands is paradoxically located within an aggressively consumerist society, creating a 'culture of bulimia' in which the excesses of more or less compulsory consumption are supposedly 'fixed' by the equally compulsory consumption of weight-loss programmes and products. Individuals who gain weight in such a culture appear as 'failed citizens' unable or unwilling to manage their appetites in an 'active' way.[13] For all of its emphasis on personal freedom, then, neo-liberalism demands that individuals subject themselves to a 'governmentality of girth'.[14]

Eating, which always entails some degree of ambivalence, has no doubt become more complicated in foodscapes dominated by agribusiness, battery farms, chemical additives, agricultural pesticides and fast food. Today there are any number of diets that one may follow, each promising specific benefits to those with enough time, money and willpower to follow them. Whether historically verifiable or nostalgically imagined, models from the past remain important to how one conceptualizes eating practices. Many diets locate themselves within recognizable narratives that depict the present as a falling away from some original, virtuous and healthy past. The locations of these lost worlds may be imagined as the prehistoric cave, the Garden of Eden, the pre-colonial paradise or the pre-industrial world.[15] All may qualify as 'utopian' in the broad sense used in this book. Thus we can approach the Palaeolithic or 'Palaeo' diet as an attempt to create an 'embodied utopia' by a return to an imagined past. Such imagined pasts are often anchored to imagined places. Conjuring images of 'a purely European, Graeco-Roman and Western Mediterranean' characterized by the wisdom of 'ancient' traditions, the Mediterranean Diet evokes ideals that are as utopian as they are ethnocentrically nostalgic.[16] The narratives of the Slow Food Movement, as well as the Locavore trend, also combine longing for lost times and places with forward-looking proposals for healthy living in the present and future.[17] The fact that 'utopia' is literally a 'non-place' is unimportant. As in many modern food utopias, 'the *place* of the promised paradise is actually the *body* of the dieter as the body brokers between mythic history and utopian future.'[18]

The utopian project of degreasing the world takes a more literal turn as we follow fat into the neo-liberal body itself. Research into people's experiences with different kinds of food reveals considerable anxiety about what greasy and fatty substances are capable of doing to the body. In many ways, such lipophobia pivots on the notion that 'you are what you eat' – in this case, the tacit belief that 'eating fat makes one fat.'[19] This phrase arguably encapsulates two related intuitions: that eating fatty foods may cause one to grow fatter, and that such foods have the capacity to alter or transform a person's bodily substance. To 'become fat' is thus to become larger and softer, but also to literally incorporate the qualities attributed to the abject substance itself. In one study, 'good' foods are not only classified as 'light', 'cool', 'cleansing' and 'useful', but are said to have the power to 'open' and 'aerate' the body while generating internal feelings of equilibrium, clarity and lightness. 'Bad' foods, especially fats and red meat, are 'useless' forms of 'surplus' that produce sensations of indigestion, 'heaviness', 'stagnation' and even 'pollution' and 'parasitism'. In the latter cases, sensations of 'invasion' come to the fore, as if the body is capable of being 'possessed' by the food it ingests. One respondent to Chrstine Durif-Bruckert's ethnography of French eating anxieties even insists that eating fatty foods is less disturbing than the idea that, after being ingested, such substances would be 'in contact with me on the inside'.[20]

This lingering sense that bodies may be inhabited by fat – and that excess fat is not part of the 'real' body – is evident in fitness culture, where people are implored to 'melt' or 'burn off' their fat, wiping it away as if it doesn't really belong to them at all. At least one gym instructor in the United Kingdom has been known to smear greasy food on a mannequin and 'then ask members to visualize what their bodies would look like if their dietary intake was similarly visible'.[21] As research in other countries confirms, then, grease and fat are frequently aligned with the 'dark', 'slimy' and 'dirty' as well as the 'unhealthy'.[22] Fat continues to be something that can be read geographically as well. The attractions of bodily cleanliness and lightness are often matched by an aversion to clutter and mess in the home.[23] Some authors imagine the home as a kind of body that needs to be 'unstuffed', 'distressed' and even 'detoxed'.[24] Others go so far as to allege links between clutter at home ('hoarding') and excess body fat.[25] A reduction of commodity consumption is thus likened to weight loss. 'Food is fuel, nothing more,' declares one of the self-professed 'Minimalists' who seek to 'help people live more meaningful lives with less'.[26] The Minimalist guide to life often reads like so many footnotes to Zygmunt Bauman: 'Lean body and fitness to move, light dress and sneakers, cellular telephones (invented for the use of the nomad who needs to be "constantly in touch"), portable or disposable belongings – are the prime cultural tokens of the era of instantaneity.'[27] Too heavy to be light, too maxi to be minimal, the fat body is emblematic of what such trends seek to avoid. As a method of achieving the semblance of lightness in body and world, ritualized purification may be the 'dominant ideology' of our time.

Promising a slimmer and lighter silhouette designed to be pleasing to the eye, dieting is also a quasi-spiritual or magical act in which body, soul and world are purified.[28] Refusing to eat aims at something similar, especially in the case of girls and women. Since at least the nineteenth century, they have been particularly subjected to demands to become fit and slender in a culture that also demands indulgence. Anorexia has usually been described as a pathological response to the beauty ideals circulating in Western culture, and thus as a disorder rooted in the hegemonic impact of the visual. Yet fear of fat, in the narrow sense of acquiring 'too much' flesh that violates dominant models of beauty, may not only be what drives people with anorexia to refrain from eating. Without discounting the distorted body images that beauty ideals create for girls and women, ethnographic research reveals that many are often less obsessed with thinness per se than with an avoidance of fats (corporeal and noncorporeal) that they associate with impurity and contamination. If anorexia aims at achieving a state of being 'clean, pure, and empty',[29] then fat is a problem less because it seems to produce a certain physique than because fatty substances lend properties to foods that give them the 'ability to move and seep into the cracks of one's body'.[30] One of the women with anorexia who spoke with Megan Warin was not only anxious about the 'dirty' feeling she experienced when coming into contact with butter, but so concerned about oily substances being absorbed through her skin and congealing in her body that she stopped using hand creams, wouldn't wash her hair with shampoo or use lip balm to moisten her lips. Her rationale at the time was: 'Well, where does it go? It disappears into your body, and then what?'[31]

Fat marks the presence of otherness, within the person as well as the outside world. As corpulence became more closely connected to lower-class and non-white bodies, perceptions of fatness, as well as the experience of ingesting fats and carbohydrates, were registered differently as one moved up the social ladder. As a French study showed, such perceptions were visceral as well as visual early on. When people were asked how they felt after eating a rich meal full of starches and fats, responses varied according to socio-economic level, with agricultural and manual labourers likely to report sensations of being 'full' or of 'regaining strength'. A white-collar professional eating such a meal was more likely to report feelings of 'heaviness', 'nausea', 'drowsiness' and the sensation of being 'weighed down'.[32] Such differences were central to the distinctive strategies of the bourgeoisie, who had long prided themselves on their refined sensibility. They had been predisposed to see in the lower classes a kind of 'congenital coarseness', thus exhibiting a 'class racism which associates the populace with everything heavy, thick and fat'.[33] Insofar as 'obesity' today is quite often associated with racial/ethnic minorities as well as the poor and marginalized, the disgust that it so often elicits retains aspects of the 'ideological' sort that refers to status and is closely related to contempt. As a form of bodily difference that has played a role in the histories of slavery and empire, fatness continues to be connected with non-white populations, thus further strengthening the durable link between slenderness and whiteness as dual markers of 'civilization'.[34]

The widespread animalization of corpulent people only enhances disgust. To characterize fat as a form of 'blubber' or to depict fat people as whales, pigs, cows and so on, reveals the persistent tendency to invoke certain animals as ways of denigrating individuals whose behaviour and status appear to be 'low' and less-than-human.[35] This often takes the form of self-animalization, where failure to conquer one's appetites can make one seem as if a person has lost control in a bestial way. Even the militantly pro-animal People for the Ethical

Treatment of Animals (PETA) exploited fears of animality to evoke fat shame. 'Save the whales' declared one PETA billboard in Jacksonville, Florida, before public complaints led to it being taken down: 'Lose the blubber: go vegetarian.'[36] If in this case it was the female body that needed to avoid being animalized, in other cases it is the 'bestial' masses. The persistent animalization of lower-class fatness is explicit in Greg Critser's ironically condescending analysis of how fat and class intersect in neo-liberal America. Slender white elites benefit from the seeming docility of the fatter lower classes, whose consumption reduces the possibility of their demanding real social change. In the process, such people are reduced to the level of domesticated animals: 'fat people do not threaten our way of life; their angers entombed in flesh, they are slowed, they are softened, they are *fed*.'[37]

The dieting and fitness culture that exploded in the 1970s, and which would come to dominate our world, has always had its critics. The sheer oppressiveness of it all prompted the journalist Raoul Mille to defy the trend by entitling his memoir *Fat and Happy to Be So*. As Mille famously quipped, 'We obese people know we are mortal.'[38] It was the others who seemed to imagine themselves otherwise. Mille's point is apt. Within a culture seemingly committed to overcoming the limitations of ordinary embodiment, it may be unfair to accuse vegans, vegetarians and animal-rights activists of engaging in a 'denial of death'[39] or of allowing their food choices to express 'discomfort not just with our animality, but with the animals' animality, too'.[40] As social psychologists have amply demonstrated, 'denial' and 'discomfort' are widespread and probably inescapable responses to reminders of mortality and animality.[41] Insofar as it is categorized as a disease, and one with a strong likelihood of causing an early death, 'obesity' is capable of instilling anxieties about collapse and dissolution that are common to other forms of illness.[42] Seeking to cut through the trappings of contemporary nutritionism and healthism, the dietician Michelle Allison thus seizes upon an important point:

> Forgetting about death is the *entire point* of food culture ... Diet culture and its variations, such as clean eating, are cultural structures we have built to attempt to transcend our animality.[43]

It is, nevertheless, inadequate to propose that disgust at fat is simply a reaction to mortality. Death may elicit fear, we have seen, but not disgust. Extreme responses to fat may shed light on the ordinary. Ethnographic work shows that the fasting practices of people with anorexia involve a 'disconnection from life itself'[44] in which food is treated as that which opposes the dream of becoming 'a being without a body'.[45] In so doing, they display a recoil from the messiness of organic existence that 'normal' people manifest in less dramatic ways. Insofar as the object of anorexic dread may be more visceral than a conventional focus on appearances is prepared to acknowledge, there is 'no real boundary' between people suffering from anorexia and those whose quest for lightness and purity stops short of self-starvation.[46] Sharing anorexia's focus on the etherealization of flesh, what is called 'orthorexia' is an obsession with healthy eating that seems more or less fashionable today, at least to varying degrees. Some even characterize our neo-liberal world as an 'orthorexic society'.[47] Not only is the obsession with healthy eating grounded in magical thinking about food, but in some cases it even perceives physical reality as a kind of enemy, 'especially when it involves feeing one's stomach or tiredness after a meal' or even the gustatory pleasure of eating itself.[48] Diets ostensibly aimed at forestalling death may result in lifestyles that treat 'life' as a problem. We may all be encouraged to *eat* organic, but not because we are entirely comfortable *being* organic.

While our current situation is surely distinct from that of the early 1900s, what was true a century ago seems even more relevant today: the body remains a deceptively stable platform for the performance of identities in a world that has become increasingly threatening and uncontrollable.[49] The fact that the body may seem *available* for the enactment and experience of identity in an uncertain world does not mean that the body is ever up to the task. Bodies are composed of substances and subject to processes over which we have little or no control. They are susceptible to illness and injury; they grow old and suffer various forms of disability; they die and decompose, in the process giving rise to new life. Thus, if 'self-control' is really the common denominator of neo-liberal bodily ideals, as is often claimed, then what one seeks to control is not some immaterial 'self', but bodily phenomena that are less subject to, if not altogether beyond, conscious manipulation. Although modern technological innovations seek to promote longevity and eliminate a myriad of biological imperfections, for now we still find ourselves unable to master the materials that comprise us. Beneath many modern dreams of efficiency, performance, omnipotence and invulnerability is 'the sense that our mere mortality is something shameful, something we need to hide or, better yet, to transcend altogether'.[50] Neo-liberal disgust about 'obesity' thus reflects the futility of such projects, manifested by 'the unwelcome intrusion into public discourse of that shameful and stubbornly illiberal aspect of human life: the body'.[51]

This book has approached this development by acknowledging, but also looking beyond the emphases on health and beauty that are the focus of other studies. Approaching stereotypes about corpulence in terms of fat, fatness and fattening, it has proposed that the building blocks of our contemporary anti-fat imagery have some of their sources in the distant past, long before the 'war on obesity' was declared. Noting that the modern world promotes fantasies of bodies capable of transcending the limitations of bodily life, it has employed the problem of disgust as its conceptual springboard. In addition to being widely viewed as an emotion that has more to do with tactility than visuality, disgust is animated by almost magical thinking that wards off certain realities about human embodiment. Among these realities is our condition as vulnerable and finite creatures subject to organic processes that involve birth and growth as well as decline and death. Whether expressed in the metaphysical claims of philosophers or the otherworldly hopes of the religious, the impossible wish to overcome the body's most disappointing and unreliable aspects is a recurring feature of Western culture. If we accept that disgust is an emotion in which we 'take the measure of the disjunction between how the world actually works and how we would like it to be',[52] it is not at all surprising to see that disgust about fat reached a fever pitch around the same time that Western culture engaged in more openly transcendent and utopian ideas about the body.

The stuff of life, then, remains a problem. Writing of our modern attraction to machinelike efficiency and dreams of transcending the organic body, philosopher Michael Hauskeller reminds us that

> Living things rise and decline. They come into existence and go out of existence. That is why we wish for a form of existence that is not life, at least not life as we know it.

The desire to change physical traits thus springs less from dissatis-faction with specific aspects of our bodies than the fact that 'we are unhappy with the body as such'.[53] 'Life' is therefore a potential source of ambivalence because living beings do not remain vital and healthy. Because things grow old and decay, life eventually reveals its intrin-sic softness and fragility. Life is a mixed blessing precisely because – for us – it ends. From this perspective, fat is an especially insistent reminder of a corporeality that many would prefer to overcome.[54] Alongside the aesthetic stigma that fatness generates, to reject fat is not only to recoil from a specific form of the body considered dis-pleasing or unhealthy. It is also part of a more basic ambiguity about embodiment that may be manifested in numerous ways. To live this ambiguity often means setting such facts aside or, more likely, pro-jecting our discomfort onto others. In so doing we neglect the fact that embodiment is a state of becoming-in-the-world-with-others who are as vulnerable and finite as we are.[55]

The question, then, is not *whether* certain stereotypes about fat have persisted in various forms over time, but why. Perhaps the 'stickiness' of fat pertains to ideas and emotions as well as bodies and substances.[56] To ask what remains of the past is not only to enquire into how the past shapes our present. It also means asking which parts of history *we refuse to forget*, which ideas and ideals we resur-rect and invoke as a means of transforming or lamenting our present. Whether repeated out of habit or custom, or simply because we don't know how to do things differently, the past does not impress itself upon the present in any direct or unavoidable way. Alternatives are possible.[57] It is we who raid the past to find pathways to the future. We are the ones who participate in the weaponizing of history so it can be wielded at others. In some respects, then, it may be the weight of history, more than the burden of flesh, that encumbers us the most.

REFERENCES

All translations are the author's own unless otherwise stated.

Introduction

1 Acknowledging that 'fat', 'fatness' and 'corpulence' are imperfect solutions to the problem of stigmatizing and pathologizing terms like 'obesity', I nevertheless follow the usage of scholars like R. Longhurst, 'Fat Bodies: Developing Geographical Research Agendas', *Progress in Human Geography*, XXIX/3 (2005), pp. 247–59; L. F. Monaghan, *Men and the War on Obesity: A Sociological Study* (London, 2008); and A. C. Saguy, *What's Wrong with Fat?* (New York, 2013), p. 7. My occasional use of 'overweight' is meant to convey the impressions of various periods. When it appears, 'obesity' reflects the terms of original or translated source material.

2 For example, see J. L. Fikkan and E. D. Rothblum, 'Is Fat a Feminist Issue? Exploring the Gendered Nature of Weight Bias', *Sex Roles*, LXVI (2012), pp. 575–92; L. Berlant, 'Slow Death (Sovereignty, Obesity, Lateral Agency)', *Critical Inquiry*, XXXIII/4 (2007), pp. 754–80; S. Strings, 'Obese Black Women as "Social Dead Weight": Reinventing the "Diseased Black Woman"', *Signs*, XLI/1 (2015), pp. 107–30; V. Swami et al., 'The Attractive Female Body Weight and Female Body Dissatisfaction in 26 Countries across 10 World Regions: Results of the International Body Project I', *Personality and Social Psychology Bulletin*, XXXVI/3 (2010), pp. 309–25.

3 L. Fraser, 'The Inner Corset: A Brief History of Fat in the United States', in *The Fat Studies Reader*, ed. E. Rothblum and S. Solovay (New York, 2009), pp. 11–14; P. Rogers, 'Fat Is a Fictional Issue: The Novel and the Rise of Weight-Watching', in *Historicizing Fat in Anglo-American Culture*, ed. E. Levy-Navarro (Columbus, OH, 2010), pp. 19–39.

4 E. Levy-Navarro, *The Culture of Obesity in Early and Late Modernity* (Basingstoke, 2008), p. 37.

5 G. Eknoyan, 'A History of Obesity, or How What Was Good Became Ugly and Then Bad', *Advances in Chronic Kidney Disease*, XIII/4 (2006),

pp. 421–7. For a recent popular iteration of this narrative, see S. Tara, *The Secret Life of Fat* (New York, 2017).

6 M. Douglas, *Purity and Danger: An Analysis of the Concepts of Pollution and Taboo* (New York, 1966). See also Kristeva's concept of 'abjection', a well-known extension of Douglas's model. J. Kristeva, *Powers of Horror*, trans. L. S. Oudiez (New York, 1982). For a critique of these related accounts of 'impurity', see R. Duschinsky, 'Abjection and Self-identity: Towards a Revised Account of Purity and Impurity', *Sociological Review*, LXI/4 (2013), pp. 709–27; and 'Ideal and Unsullied: Purity, Subjectivity and Social Power', *Subjectivity*, IV/2 (2011), pp. 147–67.

7 J. E. Braziel and K. LeBesco, eds, *Bodies Out of Bounds: Fatness and Transgression* (Berkeley, CA, 2001).

8 See M. Warin, 'Material Feminism, Obesity Science and the Limits of Discursive Critique', *Body and Society*, XXI/4 (2015), p. 61.

9 On the importance of conceptual frames, see Saguy, *What's Wrong with Fat?*

10 O.J.T. Harris and J. Robb, 'Multiple Ontologies of the Problem of the Body in History', *American Anthropologist*, CXIV/4 (2012), pp. 668–79.

11 In one of the most important theoretical discussions of fat embodiment, Samantha Murray reminds us that 'perception is a mode of bodily being-in-the-world that is constitutive of this being, and is not (and can never be) confined to the "visual"'. S. Murray, *The 'Fat' Female Body* (Basingstoke, 2008), p. 149.

12 M. M. Lelwica, *Shameful Bodies: Religion and the Culture of Physical Improvement* (London, 2017), p. 46. The 'visceral' may be defined in terms of 'the sensations, moods and ways of being that emerge from our sensory engagement with the material and discursive environments in which we live'. R. Longhurst, L. Johnston and E. Ho, 'A Visceral Approach: Cooking "at Home" with Migrant Women in Hamilton, New Zealand', *Transactions of the Institute of British Geographers*, XXXIV/3 (2009), p. 334.

13 A. E. Farrell, *Fat Shame: Stigma and the Fat Body in American Culture* (New York, 2011), pp. 127–30.

14 J. C. Oates, *Middle Age: A Romance* (New York, 2001), pp. 350–51.

15 S. Lawler, 'Disgusted Subjects: The Making of Middle-class Identities', *The Sociological Review*, LIII/3 (2005), p. 442.

16 R. M. Puhl and C. A. Heuer, 'The Stigma of Obesity: A Review and Update', *Obesity*, XVII/5 (2009), pp. 941–64.

17 P. Campos, *The Obesity Myth: Why America's Obsession with Weight Is Hazardous to Your Health* (New York, 2004), p. xxiv; see also p. 67. On the role of emotion in responses to fatness, see also A. Phillipson, 'Re-reading "Lipoliteracy": Putting Emotions to Work in Fat Studies Scholarship', *Fat Studies*, II/1 (2013), pp. 70–86.

18 C. S. Crandall, A. Nierman and M. Hebl, 'Anti-fat Prejudice', in *Handbook of Prejudice, Stereotyping, and Discrimination*, ed. T. D. Nelson (New York, 2009), pp. 469–87; C. S. Crandall, 'Prejudice against Fat People: Ideology and Self-interest', *Journal of Personality and Social Psychology*, LXVI/5 (1994), pp. 882–94.

19 M. Nussbaum, *Hiding from Humanity: Disgust, Shame, and the Law* (Princeton, NJ, 2004), p. 92. See also C. E. Forth, 'Fat and Disgust; or, The Problem of "Life in the Wrong Place"', in *Le Dégoût: Histoire, langage, politique et esthétique d'une émotion plurielle*, ed. M. Delville, A. Norris and V. von Hoffmann (Liège, 2015), pp. 41–60. When certain 'visual sensations' seem to provoke disgust, it may be understood as 'a fear resulting from an anticipation of [tactile] perception'. C. Margat, 'Phénoménologie du dégoût: Inventaire des définitions', *Ethnologie française*, XLI/1 (2011), p. 18.

20 P. Rozin, J. Haidt and C. R. McCauley, 'Disgust', in *Handbook of Emotions*, ed. M. Lewis, J. M. Haviland-Jones and L. Feldman Barrett, 3rd edn (New York, 2008), p. 761.

21 Nussbaum, *Hiding*, pp. 89–90.

22 C. McGinn, *The Meaning of Disgust* (Oxford, 2011), p. 181.

23 G. Bataille, *The Accursed Share*, vols II and III, trans. R. Hurley (New York, 1991), p. 81. The philosopher Aurel Kolnai maintains that 'the emphatic, obtrusive, and excessive manifestation of life as such tends to arouse disgust.' By 'life', Kolnai means the 'swollen overloadedness of vitality or of what is organic, as opposed to norm, direction, and plan of life, framework'. A. Kolnai, *On Disgust*, ed. B. Smith and C. Korsmeyer (Chicago, IL, 2004), pp. 102, 72.

24 'Life' here is similar to Gilles Deleuze's notion of 'a' life, an 'a-subjective' indeterminate vitality not bound up with human projects, except that it includes the negativity observed by Jane Bennett: 'Sometimes a life is experienced less as beatitude and more as terror, less as the plentitude of the virtual and more as a radically meaningless void.' Bennett, *Vibrant Matter: A Political Ecology of Things* (Durham, NC, 2010), p. 54. Rosi Braidotti corroborates the personal affront that such non-human 'life' may represent: 'Too bad that the relentless generative powers of death require the suppression of that which is the nearest and dearest to me, namely myself, my own vital being-there. For the narcissistic human subject, as psychoanalysis teaches us, it is unthinkable that Life should go on without my being there.' Braidotti, *The Posthuman* (Cambridge, 2013), p. 121.

25 W. I. Miller, *The Anatomy of Disgust* (Cambridge, MA, 1997), p. 40.

26 The idea that fat, oil and related substances can be collectively construed as the 'stuff of life' is borrowed from R. B. Onians, *The Origins of European Thought about the Body, the Mind, the Soul, the World, Time, and Fate* (Cambridge, 1951), p. 109.

27 Miller, *Anatomy*, p. xiv.

28 Kolnai, *On Disgust*, p. 62.

29 Rozin, Haidt and McCauley, 'Disgust', p. 761. Certain researchers propose that, from the perspective of evolutionary biology and the biomedical view of 'obesity' as a disease, the sight of fat bodies may trigger the human capacity to detect pathogens. They maintain that disgust at fat stems in part from 'evolved psychological mechanisms for disease-avoidance "hitch-hiking" on perceptions of modern individuals'. D. K. Lieberman, J. L. Tybur and J. D. Latner, 'Disgust Sensitivity, Obesity Stigma, and Gender: Contamination Psychology Predicts

Weight Bias for Women, not Men', *Obesity*, xx/9 (2012), p. 1804. See also D. Kelly, *Yuck! The Nature and Moral Significance of Disgust* (Cambridge, MA, 2011).

30 Poor hygiene comprised one of the six factors of the original Fat Phobia Scale, a fifty-question tool that was later shortened to the fourteen-question F-Scale. B. E. Robinson, J. G. Bacon and J. O'Reilly, 'Fat Phobia: Measuring, Understanding, and Changing Anti-fat Attitudes', *International Journal of Eating Disorders*, XIV/4 (1993), pp. 467–80; J. G. Bacon, K. E. Scheltema and B. E. Robinson, 'Fat Phobia Scale Revisited: The Short Form', *International Journal of Obesity*, XXV/2 (2001), pp. 252–7.

31 Margrit Shildrick proposes 'the notion of intercorporeality as the fundamental structure of being-in-the-world – or rather, as I prefer to put it, becoming-in-the-world'. Shildrick, *Dangerous Discourses of Disability, Subjectivity and Sexuality* (Basingstoke, 2009), p. 24.

32 E. Probyn, *Carnal Appetites: FoodSexIdentities* (London, 2000), p. 12.

33 L. Kent, 'Fighting Abjection: Representing Fat Women', in Braziel and LeBesco, *Bodies Out of Bounds*, p. 135. For philosophical discussions organized chronologically, see J.E.H. Smith, ed., *Embodiment: A History* (Oxford, 2017).

34 M. Bloch, *Prey into Hunter: The Politics of Religious Experience* (Cambridge, 1992), p. 3.

35 M. Foucault, 'Utopian Body', in *Sensorium: Embodied Experience, Technology, and Contemporary Art*, ed. C. A. Jones (Cambridge, MA, 2006), p. 229.

36 Looking as far back as antiquity we see that, rather than an unequivocally 'good' habit of the body, fatness was an ambiguous bodily state that 'spills over conceptual binary boundaries and functions much like a cultural trickster, connecting with both life and death'. S. E. Hill, *Eating to Excess: The Meaning of Gluttony and the Fat Body in the Ancient World* (Santa Barbara, CA, 2011), p. 13.

37 The most notable book-length historical works include H. Schwartz, *Never Satisfied: A Cultural History of Diets, Fantasies and Fat* (New York, 1986); P. N. Stearns, *Fat History: Bodies and Beauty in the Modern West* (New York, 1997); S. L. Gilman, *Fat Boys: A Thin Book* (Lincoln, NE, 2004); S. L. Gilman, *Fat: A Cultural History of Obesity* (Cambridge, 2008); G. Vigarello, *The Metamorphoses of Fat: A History of Obesity*, trans. C. J. Delogu (New York, 2013); Hill, *Eating to Excess*; and Farrell, *Fat Shame*.

38 S. Bordo, *Unbearable Weight: Feminism, Western Culture, and the Body* (Berkeley, CA, 1993); Farrell, *Fat Shame*, pp. 59–81.

39 One might describe this as a cultural *imaginaire* relating to fat, or a 'fat imaginary'. J.-P. Corbeau, 'L'Imaginaire associé à divers types de consommation de gras et les perceptions de leurs qualités', in *Agro-Alimentaire: Une économie de la qualité*, ed. F. Nicolas and E. Valceschini (Paris, 1995), pp. 93–103.

40 A. Meneley, 'Oleo-Signs and Quali-Signs: The Qualities of Olive Oil', *Ethnos*, LXXIII/3 (2008), pp. 305.

41 To borrow Sara Ahmed's terms, the 'stickiness' of certain elements within our cultural imagination of fat is '*an effect of the histories of contact*

between bodies, objects, and signs [emphasis in original]', but it is also the effect of a performative repetition through which relations between bodies, objects and signs may be reproduced. S. Ahmed, *The Cultural Politics of Emotion* (London, 2015), pp. 90–91.

42 N. Boivin, 'Mind over Matter? Collapsing the Mind–Matter Dichotomy in Material Culture Studies', in *Rethinking Materiality: The Engagement of Mind with the Material World*, ed. E. DeMarrais, C. Gosden and C. Renfrew (Cambridge, 2004), pp. 63–71.

43 Claude Lévi-Strauss, *Totemism*, trans. R. Needham (London, 1991), p. 89.

1 The Stuff of Life: Thinking and Doing with Fat

1 C. M. Pond, *The Fats of Life* (Cambridge, 1998), p. 1.

2 C. D. Georgiou and D. W. Deamer, 'Lipids as Universal Biomarkers of Extraterrestrial Life', *Astrobiology*, XIV/6 (2014), pp. 541–9.

3 M. Ben-Dor et al., 'Man the Fat Hunter: The Demise of *Homo erectus* and the Emergence of a New Hominin Lineage in the Middle Pleistocene (ca. 400 kyr) Levant', *PLOS ONE*, VI/12 (2011), p. 9.

4 J. D. Speth, *The Paleoanthropology and Archaeology of Big-Game Hunting: Protein, Fat, or Politics?* (New York, 2010), p. 87.

5 A. Mateos, 'Meat and Fat: Intensive Exploitation Strategies in the Upper Palaeolithic Approached from Bone Fracturing Analysis', in *The Zooarchaeology of Fats, Oils, Milk and Dairying*, ed. J. Mulville and A. K. Outram (Oxford, 2005), p. 157.

6 C. Leray, *Dietary Lipids for Healthy Brain Function* (London, 2017), p. 3. 'The intriguing fact that Neanderthals had brains no smaller but much less innovative than those times' modern humans may be explained by mutations related to the lipid metabolism.' T. C. Erren and M. Erren, 'Can Fat Explain the Human Brain's Big Bang Evolution? – Horrobin's Leads for Comparative and Functional Genomics', *Prostaglandins, Leukotrienes and Essential Fatty Acids*, LXX/4 (2004), p. 346.

7 M. C. Bourne, *Food Texture and Viscosity* (San Diego, CA, 2002).

8 C. A. Running, B. A. Craig and R. D. Mattes, 'Oleogustus: The Unique Taste of Fat', *Chemical Senses*, XL (2015), pp. 507–17; see also E. Dransfield, 'The Taste of Fat', *Meat Science*, LXXX/1 (2008), pp. 37–42.

9 A. Drewnowski and E. Almiron-Roig, 'Human Perceptions and Preferences for Fat-rich Foods', in *Fat Detection: Taste, Texture, and Post Ingestive Effects*, ed. J.-P. Montmayeur and J. le Coutre (Boca Raton, FL, 2010), p. 274.

10 Jane Bennett, *Vibrant Matter: A Political Ecology of Things* (Durham, NC, 2010), p. 40; see also pp. 41–3. For a more complex approach to the 'agency' of fats, see S. Abrahamsson, F. Bertoni, A. Mol and R. Ibáñez Martín, 'Living with Omega-3: New Materialism and Enduring Concerns', *Environment and Planning D: Society and Space*, XXX/1 (2015), pp. 4–19.

11 J. E. Oliver, *Fat Politics: The Real Story behind America's Obesity Epidemic* (New York, 2006), pp. 132–8; see also V. Duffy and L. Bartoshuk, 'Sensory Factors in Feeding', in *Why We Eat What We Eat*, ed. E. D. Capaldi (Washington, DC, 1996), pp. 145–71.

12 Y. Manabe, S. Matsumura and T. Fushiki, 'Preference for High-fat Food in Animals', in *Fat Detection*, ed. Montmayer and le Coutre, pp. 243–64.

13 W. I. Miller, *The Anatomy of Disgust* (Cambridge, MA, 1997), p. 122.

14 Ben-Dor, 'Use of Animal Fat as a Symbol of Health in Traditional Societies Suggests Humans May Be Well Adapted to Its Consumption', *Journal of Evolution and Health*, I/1 (2015), pp. 1–30.

15 M. Gimbutas, *The Language of the Goddess* (San Francisco, CA, 1989), p. 141.

16 R. A. Joyce, *Ancient Bodies, Ancient Lives: Sex, Gender, and Archaeology* (London, 2008).

17 L. McDermott, 'Self-representation in Upper Paleolithic Female Figurines', *Current Anthropology*, XXXVII/2 (1996), pp. 227–75.

18 D. W. Bailey, 'Figurines of Old Europe', in *The Lost World of Old Europe: The Danube Valley, 5000–3500 BC*, ed. D. W. Anthony (Princeton, NJ, 2009), p. 122.

19 D. W. Bailey, *Prehistoric Figurines: Representation and Corporeality in the Neolithic* (London, 2005), p. 165–6.

20 W. Keane, 'Signs Are Not the Garb of Meaning: On the Social Analysis of Material Things', in *Materiality*, ed. D. Miller (Durham, NC, 2005), pp. 182–205; C. E. Forth, 'The Qualities of Fat: Bodies, History, and Materiality', *Journal of Material Culture*, XVIII/2 (2013), pp. 135–54; I. Hodder, *Entangled: An Archaeology of the Relationships between Humans and Things* (Oxford, 2012); R. Colls, 'Materialising Bodily Matter: Intra-action and the Embodiment of "Fat"', *Geoforum*, XXXVIII (2007), pp. 353–65. Arguing that the very act of naming something is to bring it into being in specific ways, Sara Ahmed concedes that 'To name something as disgusting is not to make something out of nothing.' Ahmed, *Cultural Politics*, p. 93.

21 N. Boivin, 'Mind over Matter? Collapsing the Mind–Matter Dichotomy in Material Culture Studies', in *Rethinking Materiality: The Engagement of Mind with the Material World*, ed. E. DeMarrais, C. Gosden and C. Renfrew (Cambridge, 2004), p. 64.

22 S. E. Hill, *Eating to Excess: The Meaning of Gluttony and the Fat Body in the Ancient World* (Santa Barbara, CA, 2011), p. 13.

23 M. Warin, *Abject Relations: Everyday Worlds of Anorexia* (New Brunswick, NJ, 2009), p. 121.

24 'Oils and fats refer to a large and diverse group of chemical compounds that do not easily dissolve in water. There is no strict distinction between oils and fats; fats usually refer to materials like wax, lard, and butter that are solid at room temperature, whereas oils like olive oil and fish oil are liquid. As is well known, butter can melt upon heating and olive oil solidify by freezing.' O. G. Mouritsen, *Life – as a Matter of Fat: The Emerging Science of Lipidomics* (Berlin, 2002), p. 23.

25 S. de Beaune and R. White, 'Les Lampes du Paléolithique', *Pour la science*, 187 (1993), pp. 62–9; S. A. de Beaune, 'Les Techniques d'éclairage paléolithiques: Un bilan', *Paléo*, XII/12 (2000), pp. 19–27.

26 A. Meneley, 'Oleo-Signs and Quali-Signs: The Qualities of Olive Oil', *Ethnos*, LXXIII/3 (2008), p. 312; S. Connor, *The Book of Skin* (Ithaca, NY, 2004), pp. 180, 190.

27 M. Bille and T. F. Sørensen, 'An Anthropology of Luminosity:
    The Agency of Light', *Journal of Material Culture*, xii/3 (2007),
    pp. 263–84; see also M. C. Taylor, *Refiguring the Spiritual: Beuys,
    Barney, Turrell, Goldsworthy* (New York, 2012), p. 16.

28 Connor, *Book of Skin*, p. 179; J. A. Kelhoffer, 'John the Baptist's "Wild
    Honey" and "Honey" in Antiquity', *Greek, Roman, and Byzantine
    Studies*, xlv (2005), pp. 59–73.

29 [Pseudo-]Aristotle, *Problems*, vol. i, trans. W. S. Hett (Cambridge, ma,
    1953).

30 Aristotle, *On Length and Shortness of Life*, trans. G.R.T. Ross, in
    The Complete Works of Aristotle, ed. Jonathon Barnes, (Princeton, nj, 1984),
    vol. i, p. 5; Aristotle, *History of Animals*, trans. A. W. Thompson, in
    Complete Works, p. 66.

31 V. Smith, *Clean: A History of Personal Hygiene and Purity* (Oxford, 2007),
    p. 15.

32 On *le visqueux*, see J.-P. Sartre, *Being and Nothingness*, trans.
    H. E. Barnes (New York, 1993), pp. 604–12. According to Maurice
    Merleau-Ponty, translations of the language of one sense into
    another are integral to the condition of embodiment generally.
    Merleau-Ponty, *Phenomenology of Perception*, trans. C. Smith
    (London, 1962), pp. 104, 132.

33 Y. Bilu, 'Pondering the "Princes of Oil": New Light on an Old
    Phenomenon', *Journal of Anthropological Research*, xxxvii/3 (1981), pp.
    269–78; A. Winitzer, 'The Divine Presence and Its Interpretation in Early
    Mesopotamian Divination', in *Divination and Interpretation of Signs in
    the Ancient World*, ed. Amar Annus (Chicago, il, 2010), pp. 177–97.

34 M. Arad, *Roots and Patterns: Hebrew Morpho-syntax* (Dordrecht, 2007),
    p. 66. Here Arad continues: 'Crucially, the root does not specify the
    precise nature of that material. It is a potentiality, which may be
    incarnated in many possible ways. In different nominal environments,
    the root may create words such as *šemen* (oil), *šamenet* (cream) or *šuman*
    (fat), all of which share the property of being a fatty substance, but are
    obviously different types of substance.'

35 H. A. Hoffner, Jr, 'Oil in Hittite Texts', *Biblical Archaeologist*, lviii/2
    (1995), pp. 108–14.

36 H. Ringgren, 'Semen', in *Theological Dictionary of the Old Testament*,
    ed. G. J. Botterweck, H. Ringgren and H.-J. Fabry, trans. D. E. Green
    and D. W. Stott (Grand Rapids, mi, 2006), vol. xv, pp. 249–53;
    B. D. Sommer, *The Bodies of God and the World of Ancient Israel*
    (Cambridge, 2009), p. 49; J. M. Baumgarten, 'Liquids and Susceptibility
    to Defilement in New 4Q Texts', *Jewish Quarterly Review*, lxxxv/1–2
    (1994), pp. 91–101.

37 A. Marx, *Les Systèmes sacrificiels de l'Ancien Testament* (Leiden, 2005),
    p. 87.

38 All subsequent in-text Bible quotations refer to M. D. Coogan, ed.,
    The New Oxford Annotated Bible (Oxford, 2007).

39 D. Kellermann, '*kelāyôt*', in *Theological Dictionary of the Old Testament*, ed.
    G. J. Botterweck, H. Ringgren and H.-J. Fabry, trans. D. E. Green
    (Grand Rapids, mi, 1995), vol. vii, pp. 175–82.

40 'Bavli Berakhot', *The Babylonian Talmud*, trans. J. Neusner et al. (Peabody, MA, 2005), ch. 1, 1:2, 11.4.P.

41 Hesiod, *Theogony, Works and Days, Shield*, trans. Α. N. Athanassakis (Baltimore, MD, 1991), pp. 28, 84.

42 F. T. van Straten, *Hiera Kala: Images of Animal Sacrifice in Archaic and Classical Greece* (Leiden, 1995), p. 125.

43 R. B. Onians, *The Origins of European Thought about the Body, the Mind, the Soul, the World, Time, and Fate* (Cambridge, 1951), p. 279.

44 A. Clements, 'Divine Scents and Presence', in *Smell and the Ancient Senses*, ed. M. Bradley (London, 2015), pp. 46–59.

45 J. Wilkins, *The Boastful Chef: The Discourse of Food in Ancient Greek Comedy* (Oxford, 2000), p. 70; Athenaeus, *The Learned Banqueters*, 3.125c–f, vol. II, trans. S. D. Olson (Cambridge, MA, 2006), pp. 96–8; G. E. McCracken, trans., *The Case against the Pagans* by Arnobius of Sicca (New York, 1949), p. 605n.

46 M. Corbier, 'Le Statut ambigu de la viande à Rome', *Dialogues d'histoire ancienne*, XV/2 (1989), pp. 107–58.

47 B. Leyerle, 'Monastic Formation and Christian Practice: Food in the Desert', in *Educating People of Faith: Exploring the History of Jewish and Christian Communities*, ed. J. van Engen (Grand Rapids, MI, 2004), pp. 85–112; Philo, *The Special Laws*, IV, in *Philo*, trans. F. H. Colson (Cambridge, MA, 1939), vol. VIII, pp. 69–71, 85–7.

48 When Robyn Longhurst invited scholars 'to write fat bodies *geographically*', she may not have realized that the same could be done with fat itself. R. Longhurst, 'Fat Bodies: Developing Geographical Research Agendas', *Progress in Human Geography*, XXIX/3 (2005), p. 256.

49 Varro, *Rerum rusticarum libritres*, in *Roman Farm Management: The Treatises of Cato and Varro Done into English, with Notes of Modern Instances by a Virginia Farmer*, trans. and ed. Fairfax Harrison (New York, 1918), p. 90.

50 Theophrastus, *An Enquiry into Plants*, trans. A. Hort (Cambridge, MA, 1916), vol. II, p. 179.

51 Varro, *Économie rurale*, trans. J. Heurgon (Paris, 1978), p. 32.

52 Virgil, *Georgics*, in *Virgil: Eclogues, Georgics, Aeneid I–VI*, , trans. H. R. Fairclough (Cambridge, MA, 1978), vol. I, pp. 132–3.

53 Columella, *On Agriculture*, trans. H. Boyd (Cambridge, MA, 1960), vol. I, p. 121.

54 I. D. Bull et al., 'Muck 'n' Molecules: Organic Geochemical   Methods for Detecting Ancient Manuring', *Antiquity*, 73 (1999), pp. 86–96; I. A. Simpson et al., 'Lipid Biomarkers of Manuring Practice in Relict Anthropogenic Soils', *The Holocene*, IX (1999), pp. 223–9. Observing what may be a modern echo of these ancient ideas, my colleague John Younger recalls seeing a rural man in Greece pouring leftover cooking oil into the soil around a tree. What 'fattens' the soil is literally fat.

55 G. Münderlein, 'Chelebh', in *Theological Dictionary of the Old Testament*, ed. G. J. Botterweck and H. Ringgren, trans. D. E. Green (Grand Rapids, MI, 1980), vol. IV, pp. 396–7.

56 Quoted with slight adjustments from I. Dershowitz, 'A Land Flowing with Fat and Honey', *Vetus Testamentum*, LX (2010), pp. 172–6.

57 F. García Martínez and E.J.C. Tigchelaar, eds, *The Dead Sea Scrolls Study Edition* (Leiden, 1999), p. 343.

58 Terry Brown and Keri Brown, *Biomolecular Archaeology: An Introduction* (Malden, MA, 2011), p. 54.

59 R. P. Evershed et al., 'New Criteria for the Identification of Animal Fats Preserved in Archaeological Pottery', *Naturwissenschaften*, LXXXIV (1997), p. 402.

60 See J. Scurlock, *Sourcebook for Ancient Mesopotamian Medicine* (Atlanta, GA, 2014); M. Serpico and R. White, 'Oil, Fat and Wax', in *Ancient Egyptian Materials and Technology*, ed. P. T. Nicolson and I. Shaw (Cambridge, 2000), pp. 390–429.

61 Dioscorides, *De materia medica*, trans. L. Y. Beck (Hildesheim, 2005), pp. 103, 110, 120–21.

62 *Soranus' Gynecology*, trans. O. Temkin (Baltimore, MD, 1991), pp. 221, 223.

63 Pliny the Elder, *Natural History*, trans. W.H.S. Jones (Cambridge, MA, 2006), vol. VIII, pp. 136–8. Wild boars were a source of fascination for Greeks and Romans, who enjoyed the excitement and danger of hunting them. As such, boar hunting was symbolically connected to 'broader notions of heroism, courage, and initiation'. M. MacKinnon, 'Hunting', in *The Oxford Handbook of Animals in Classical Thought and Life*, ed. G. L. Campbell (Oxford, 2014), p. 206.

64 Pliny, *Natural History*, vol. VIII, p. 101; G. Maio, 'The Metaphorical and Mythical Use of the Kidney in Antiquity', *American Journal of Nephrology*, XIX/2 (1999), pp. 101–6.

65 M. Montanari, *Medieval Tastes: Food, Cooking, and the Table*, trans. B. A. Brombert (New York, 2015), p. 91.

66 On sympathetic magic see C. Nemeroff and P. Rozin, 'The Makings of the Magical Mind: The Nature and Function of Sympathetic Magical Thinking', in *Imagining the Impossible: Magical, Scientific, and Religious Thinking in Children*, ed. K. S. Rosengren, C. N. Johnson and P. L. Harris (Cambridge, 2000), pp. 1–34.

67 Dioscorides, *De materia medica*, p. 120.

68 Pliny, *Natural History*, vol. VIII, p. 101.

69 Ibid., p. 63.

70 H. D. Betz, *The Greek Magical Papryi in Translation* (Chicago, IL, 1986), pp. 9, 63–4, 92.

71 J. F. Borghouts, ed., 'The Magical Texts of Papyrus Leiden I 348', *Oudheidkd Meded Rijksmus Oudheiden Leiden*, LI (1970), pp. 1–248.

72 A. Magnus, *The Book of Secrets*, ed. M. R. Best and F. H. Brightman (York Beach, ME, 1999), p. 102.

73 M. M. Lee, 'Body-modification in Classical Greece', in *Bodies and Boundaries in Graeco-Roman Antiquity*, ed. T. Fögen and M. M. Lee (New York, 2009), p. 157; J.-P. Vernant, *Mortals and Immortals: Collected Essays* (Princeton, NJ, 1991).

74 D. Sansone, *Greek Athletics and the Genesis of Sport* (Berkeley, CA, 1992), p. 102.

75 Artemidorus, *Interpretation of Dreams: Oneirocritica*, trans. R. J. White (Torrance, CA, 1990), p. 67.

76 Theophrastus of Eresus, *On Sweat, On Dizziness and On Fatigue*, ed. W. W. Fortenbraugh, R. W. Sharples and M. G. Sollenberger (Leiden, 2003).

77 Dioscorides, *De materia medica*, pp. 25–33, 116–21; S. G. Miller, *Arete: Greek Sports from Ancient Sources* (Berkeley, CA, 2004), pp. 18, 218.

78 Onians, *Origins*, p. 210.

79 S. E. Mullins, 'Myroblytes: Miraculous Oil in Medieval Europe' (PhD dissertation, Georgetown University, 2017).

80 Quoted in R. Kaster, *Emotion, Restraint, and Community in Ancient Rome* (Oxford, 2005), p. 108.

81 Quoted in G. G. Fagan, *Bathing in Public in the Roman World* (Ann Arbor, MI, 1999), p. 188.

82 Miller, *Arete*, pp. 18, 218; Dioscorides, *De materia medica*, pp. 25–33, 116–21.

83 J. P. Toner, *Leisure and Ancient Rome* (Cambridge, 1995), p. 51.

84 A. Bowie, 'Oil in Ancient Greece and Rome', in *The Oil of Gladness: Anointing in the Christian Tradition*, ed. M. Dudley and G. Rowell (London, 1993), pp. 26–34.

85 Plutarch, *Moralia*, trans. F. C. Babbitt (Cambridge, MA, 1961), vol. III, p. 139.

86 C. Laes, 'Writing the History of Fatness and Thinness in Graeco-Roman Antiquity', *Medicina nei secoli: Arte e scienza*, XXVIII/2 (2016), p. 605.

87 Arguing that the disgust response is primarily linked to 'spoiled or decaying matter', some social psychologists propose that certain soft and/or viscous textures serve as reminders of rot and decay, independently of explicit 'reminders of livingness/animalness'. Y. Martins and P. Pliner, '"Ugh! That's Disgusting!": Identification of the Characteristics of Foods Underlying Rejections Based on Disgust', *Appetite*, XLVI (2006), p. 82. See also L. H. Kushner, 'Food for Thought: The Role of Texture in the Disgust Response' (doctoral dissertation, American University, Washington, DC, 2011).

88 C. W. Bynum, *The Resurrection of the Body in Western Christianity, 200–1336* (New York, 1995), p. 221; G. Tétart, *Le Sang des fleurs: Une anthropologie de l'abeille et du miel* (Paris, 2004), p. 231.

89 This connection has been theorized by J. E. Braziel, 'Sex and Fat Chics: Deterritorializing the Fat Female Body', in *Bodies Out of Bounds: Fatness and Transgression*, ed. J. E. Braziel and K. LeBesco (Berkeley, CA, 2001), pp. 237–41.

90 A. E. Hanson, 'Conception, Gestation, and the Origin of Female Nature in the *Corpus Hippocraticum*', *Helios*, XIX/1–2 (1992), pp. 48, 51–2.

91 L. Dean-Jones, 'The Cultural Construct of the Female Body in Classical Greek Science', in *Sex and Difference in Ancient Greece and Rome*, ed. M. Golden and P. Toohey (Edinburgh, 2003), pp. 188–9.

92 Macrobius, *Saturnalia*, trans. R. A. Kaster (Cambridge, MA, 2011), vol. III, pp. 214–15.

93 *Soranus' Gynecology*, pp. 19, 29.

94 T. G. Parkin, *Old Age in the Roman World* (Baltimore, MD, 2003), p. 197.

95 Although ageing was often presented as a process of drying out, in antique comedy old age could be represented by corpulence as well as thinness. Laes, 'Writing the History', p. 608.

96 Quoted in C. Chandezon, V. Dasen and J. Wilgaux, 'Dream Interpretation, Physiognomy, Body Divination', in *A Companion to Greek and Roman Sexualities*, ed. T. K. Hubbard (Oxford, 2014), p. 304.

97 Hippocrates, *Airs, Waters, Places*, in *Hippocrates*, trans. W.H.S. Jones (Cambridge, MA, 1957), vol. I, p. 137.

98 S. Kuriyama, *The Expressiveness of the Body and the Divergence of Greek and Chinese Medicine* (New York, 1999).

99 E. Dench, 'Austerity, Excess, Success, and Failure in Hellenistic and Early Imperial Italy', in *Parchments of Gender: Deciphering the Bodies of Antiquity*, ed. M. Wyke (Oxford, 1998), pp. 126–7.

100 Herodotus, *Histories*, trans. A. D. Godley (Cambridge, MA, 1969), vol. IV, p. 301.

101 Kuriyama, *Expressiveness*.

102 P. Bourdieu, *Masculine Domination*, trans. R. Nice (Stanford, CA, 2001), p. 12.

103 Connor, *Book of Skin*, p. 180.

104 P. Cramer, *Baptism and Change in the Early Middle Ages, c. 200–c. 1150* (New York, 1993), pp. 212–13.

105 Meneley, 'Oleo-Signs and Quali-Signs', p. 305.

106 Keane, 'Signs Are Not the Garb of Meaning', p. 194.

2 Fertile Ambiguities: The Agricultural Imagination

1 O.J.T. Harris and J. Robb, 'The Body in History: A Concluding Essay', in *The Body in History: Europe from the Paleolithic to the Future*, ed. J. Robb and O.J.T. Harris (Cambridge, 2013), p. 214.

2 M. Bloch, *Prey into Hunter: The Politics of Religious Experience* (Cambridge, 1992), p. 3.

3 S. E. Hill, *Eating to Excess: The Meaning of Gluttony and the Fat Body in the Ancient World* (Santa Barbara, CA, 2011), p. 41.

4 C. W. Bynum, *The Resurrection of the Body in Western Christianity, 200–1336* (New York, 1995), p. 113.

5 J. Dollimore, *Death, Desire and Loss in Western Culture* (New York, 1998), p. xiii.

6 For example, see P. J. Brown and M. Konner, 'An Anthropological Perspective on Obesity', *Annals of the New York Academy of Sciences*, CDXCIX/1 (1987), pp. 29–46; J.-P. warnier, *The Pot-King: The Body and Technologies of Power* (Leiden, 2007); R. Popenoe, *Feeding Desire: Fatness, Beauty, and Sexuality among a Saharan People* (New York, 2004); B. Shore, 'Mana and Tapu', in *Developments in Polynesian Ethnology*, ed. A. Howard and R. Borofsky (Honolulu, HI, 1989), pp. 137–73; S. Walentowitz, 'Women of Great Weight: Fatness, Reproduction and Gender Dynamics in Tuareg Society', in *Fatness and the Maternal Body: Women's Experiences of Corporeality and the Shaping of Social Policy*, ed. M. Unnithan-Kumar and S. Tremayne (New York, 2011), pp. 71–97.

7 C. Saint-Germain 'Animal Fat in the Cultural World of the Native Peoples of Northeastern America', in *The Zooarchaeology of Fats, Oils, Milk and Dairying*, ed. J. Mulville and A. K. Outram (Oxford, 2005), p. 108.

8 Popenoe, *Feeding Desire*, pp. 43–4.

9 H. McDonald, 'The Fats of Life', *Australian Aboriginal Studies*, 2 (2003), pp. 53–61; A. P. Elkin, *Aboriginal Men of High Degree*, 2nd edn (New York, 1978), pp. 30–32, 50–52, 75–82.

10 J. W. Bastien, 'Qollahuaya-Andean Body Concepts: A Topographical-Hydraulic Model of Physiology', *American Anthropologist*, LXXXVII/3 (1985), pp. 595–611; A. Orta, 'Syncretic Subjects and Body Politics: Doubleness, Personhood, and Aymara Catechists', *American Ethnologist*, XXVI/4 (1999), pp. 864–89; L. Crandon-Malamud, *From the Fat of Our Souls: Social Change, Political Process, and Medical Pluralism in Bolivia* (Berkeley, CA, 1993), p. 120; A. Canessa, 'Fear and Loathing on the Kharisiri Trail: Alterity and Identity in the Andes', *Journal of the Royal Anthropological Institute*, VI/4 (2000), pp. 705–20.

11 J. Carsten, 'Substance and Relationality: Blood in Contexts', *Annual Review of Anthropology*, XL/1 (2011), p. 20; E. Leach, 'Anthropological Aspects of Language: Animal Categories and Verbal Abuse', *Anthrozoös*, XX/3 (1989), p. 156.

12 Leach, ibid.

13 P. Lemonnier, 'Fertility among the Anga of Papua New Guinea: A Conspicuous Absence', in *Population, Reproduction and Fertility in Melanesia*, ed. S. J. Ulijaszek (Oxford, 2006), pp. 218–38; M. Janowski, 'Masculinity, Potency and Pig Fat: The Kelabit of Sarawak', in The *Fat of the Land: Proceedings of the Oxford Symposium on Food and Cookery 2002*, ed. H. Walker (Bristol, 2002), pp. 130–42; Canessa, 'Fear and Loathing', p. 713.

14 F. J. P. Poole, 'The Ritual Forging of Identity: Aspects of Person and Self in Bimin-Kuskusmin Male Initiation', in *Rituals of Manhood: Male Initiation in Papua New Guinea*, ed. G. Herdt (Berkeley, CA, 1982), pp. 122–3.

15 Warnier, *Pot-King*, pp. 115–17.

16 M. Strathern, *Property, Substance and Effect: Anthropological Essays on Persons and Things* (London, 1999), pp. 45–63.

17 E. J. Sobo, 'The Sweetness of Fat: Health, Procreation, and Sociability in Rural Jamaica', in *Food and Culture: A Reader*, ed. C. Counihan and P. van Esterik (New York, 1997), pp. 260–1.

18 Columella, *On Agriculture*, trans. H. Boyd (Cambridge, MA, 1960), vol. I, pp. 306–7.

19 V. Winiwarter, 'Soils in Ancient Roman Agriculture: Analytical Approaches to Invisible Properties', in *Shifting Boundaries of the Real: Making the Invisible Visible*, ed. H. Nowotnyand and M. Weiss (Zürich, 2000), pp. 137–56.

20 H. von Staden, 'Women and Dirt', *Helios*, XIX/1/2 (1992), p. 9.

21 Columella, *On Agriculture*, vol. I, pp. 110–11.

22 G. Tétart, *Le Sang des fleurs: Une anthropologie de l'abeille et du miel* (Paris, 2004), pp. 109–10.

23 M. J. Schiefsky, *Hippocrates, On Ancient Medicine* (Leiden, 2005).

24 L. Kronenberg, *Allegories of Farming from Greece and Rome* (Cambridge, 2009).

25 M. de Vaan, *Etymological Dictionary of Latin and the Other Italic Languages* (Leiden, 2008), p. 493.

26 E. Gowers, *The Loaded Table: Representations of Food in Roman Literature* (Oxford, 1996); M. Génaux, 'Social Sciences and the Evolving Concept

of Corruption', *Crime, Law and Social Change*, XLII/1 (2004), pp. 13–24. The root *luxus* means sprained and dislocated, but has origins in the idea of the 'bent'. De Vaan, *Etymological Dictionary*, p. 356.

27 Classical culture also described the womb as a hearth or a jar as well as a field. H. King, *Hippocrates' Woman: Reading the Female Body in Ancient Greece* (London, 1998), pp. 33–5.

28 B. K. Ager, 'Roman Agricultural Magic' (doctoral dissertation, University of Michigan, 2010), pp. 188, 199.

29 Pliny the Elder, *Natural History*, trans. H. Rackham (Cambridge, MA, 1983), vol. III, p. 145.

30 Ibid., vol. III, p. 35.

31 Ibid., vol. III, pp. 139–41.

32 Ibid., vol. III, p. 81.

33 Ibid., vol. III, p. 573.

34 Ibid., vol. III, p. 145.

35 F. Héretier-Augé, 'Étude comparée des sociétés africaines', *Annuaire du Collège de France: Résumé des cours et travaux 1989–1990* (Paris, 1991), p. 507.

36 Tétart, *Le Sang des fleurs*, p. 55; see also N. Vialles, *Animal to Edible*, trans. J. A. Underwood (Cambridge, 1994), pp. 128–9.

37 Aristotle, *On the Parts of Animals*, trans. J. G. Lennox (Oxford, 2001), p. 26.

38 'And further it seems that fat people, men and women alike, are less fertile than those who are not fat, the reason being that when the body is too well fed, the effect of concoction upon the residue is to turn it into fat.' Aristotle, *Generation of Animals*, 725b: 29, trans. A. L. Peck (Cambridge, MA, 1943), pp. 85–6.

39 Pliny, *Natural History*, vol. III, p. 567.

40 Pliny, *Natural History*, trans. H. Rackham (Cambridge, MA, 1971), vol. V, p. 153.

41 R. E. Frisch, *Female Fertility and the Body-Fat Connection* (Chicago, IL, 2002), pp. 1, 7, 19–20.

42 D. Lupton, *Food, the Body and the Self* (London, 1996), p. 3.

43 E. Probyn, *Carnal Appetites: FoodSexIdentities* (London, 2000).

44 C. Hénault, 'Eating beyond Certainties', in *From Polysemy to Semantic Change: Towards a Typology of Lexical Semantic Associations*, ed. M. Vanhove (Amsterdam, 2008), p. 297.

45 Ibid., p. 293.

46 A. Beardsworth and T. Keil, *Sociology on the Menu: An Invitation to the Study of Food and Society* (London, 1997), p. 153.

47 I. S. Gilhus, *Animals, Gods and Humans: Changing Attitudes to Animals in Greek, Roman and Early Christian Ideas* (London, 2006), p. 40.

48 Aristotle, *History of Animals*, in *The Complete Works of Aristotle*, ed. Jonathon Barnes, trans. A. W. Thompson (Princeton, NJ, 1984), vol. I, pp. 6–7.

49 D. Price and O. Bar-Yosef, 'The Origins of Agriculture: New Data, New Ideas. An Introduction to Supplement 4', *Current Anthropology*, LII/S4 (2011), pp. S163–74.

50 Robb and Harris, *The Body in History*, p. 56.

51 Gilhus, *Animals, Gods and Humans*, pp. 48–9.

52 J. E. Salisbury, *The Beast Within: Animals in the Middle Ages* (New York, 1994), p. 132.

53 K. Thomas, *Man and the Natural World: Changing Attitudes in England, 1500–1800* (Oxford, 1983), p. 46.

54 Salisbury, *Beast Within*, p. 15.

55 Vialles, *Animal to Edible*, pp. 128–9; G. Ekroth, 'Castration, Cult and Agriculture: Perspectives on Greek Animal Sacrifice', *Opuscula*, VII (2014), pp. 153–74.

56 Varro, *De re rustica*, trans. W. D. Hooper and H. B. Ash (Cambridge, MA, 1934), pp. 481–2.

57 Vialles, *Animal to Edible*, pp. 128–9.

58 M. Horstmanshoff, 'Who Is the True Eunuch? Medical and Religious Ideas about Eunuchs and Castration in the Works of Clement of Alexandria', in *From Athens to Jerusalem: Medicine in Hellenized Jewish Lore and in Early Christian Literature*, ed. S. Kottek and M. Horstmanshoff (Rotterdam, 2000), p. 103.

59 Philosopher Peter Sloterdijk maintains that 'humans are inescapably subject to vertical tensions, in all periods and all cultural areas.' P. Sloterdijk, *You Must Change Your Life: On Anthropotechnics*, trans. W. Hoban (Cambridge, 2013), pp. 12–13.

60 Elizabeth Grosz notes that Western 'philosophy has established itself on the foundations of a profound somatophobia'. E. Grosz, *Volatile Bodies: Toward a Corporeal Feminism* (Bloomington, IN, 1994), p. 5.

61 Plato, *The Republic*, trans. T. Griffith (Cambridge, 2000), p. 305.

62 Plato, *The Laws*, trans. T. L. Pangle (New York, 1980), pp. 196–7.

63 Seneca, *Ad lucilium epistulae morales*, trans. R. M. Gummere (Cambridge, MA, 1979), vol. III, pp. 412–13

64 Athenaeus, *The Learned Banqueters*, trans. S. D. Olson (Cambridge, MA, 2006), vol. I, p. 541.

65 M. Foucault, *The Use of Pleasure*, trans. R. Hurley (New York, 1990), p. 84.

66 C. Laes, 'Writing the History of Fatness and Thinness in Graeco-Roman Antiquity', *Medicina nei secoli: Arte e scienza*, XXVIII/2 (2016), p. 592.

67 S. E. Phang, *Roman Military Service: Ideologies of Discipline in the Late Republic and Early Principate* (Cambridge, 2008), p. 35. Something resembling ideological disgust seems to have been operative among the Greeks as well.

68 M. Bell, *Hard Feelings: The Moral Psychology of Contempt* (Oxford, 2013), p. 52; W. I. Miller, *The Anatomy of Disgust* (Cambridge, MA, 1997), p. 43.

69 Some of these interpretations are glossed in J. K. Aitken, 'Fat Eglon', in *Studies on the Text and Versions of the Hebrew Bible in Honour of Robert Gordon*, ed. G. Khan and D. Lipton (Leiden, 2012), pp. 141–54; S. L. Gilman, *Fat Boys: A Thin Book* (Lincoln, NE, 2004), pp. 45–6.

70 Hill, *Eating to Excess*, pp. 32–4; B. L. Selavan, 'From Healthily Stout to Disgusting Decay: The Fat Context of Judges 3:12–30' (2016), unpublished manuscript. Gilman, *Fat Boys*, pp. 45–6.

71 C. Avramescu, *An Intellectual History of Cannibalism*, trans. A. I. Blythe (Princeton, NJ, 2009).

72 Aristotle, *On the Parts of Animals*, p. 26.

73 Pliny, *Natural History*, vol. III, p. 567.

74 Aelian, *On the Characteristics of Animals*, trans. A. F. Scholfield (Cambridge, MA, 1958), vol. I, p. III.

75 K. Karila-Cohen, 'Les Gourmands grecs sont-ils bien en chair?' in *Le Corps du gourmand d'Héraclès à Alexandre le Bienheureux*, ed. K. Karila-Cohen and F. Quellier (Rennes, 2012), pp. 131–2.

76 Pliny, *Natural History*, vol. III, p. 567.

77 Athenaeus, *The Learned Banqueters*, vol. VI, p. 189. As we will see in the next chapter, Dionysius' status as an 'Asiatic' reinforced the curiosity that the tyrant would have been to Greeks and Romans.

78 Aelian, *Historical Miscellany*, trans. N. G. Wilson (Cambridge, MA, 1997), pp. 291–3l.

79 Athenaeus, *Learned Banqueters*, vol. VI, pp. 189–91.

80 Aristotle, *Physiognomics*, in *Minor Works*, trans. W. S. Hett (Cambridge, MA, 1936), pp. 118–19

81 D. Martin, *The Corinthian Body* (New Haven, CT, 1995).

82 Aristotle, *Physiognomics*, p. 1.

83 Pliny, *Natural History*, vol. III, p. 559.

84 J. Wilgaux, 'Gourmands et gloutons dans les sources physiognomiques antiques', in *Le Corps du gourmand*, ed. Karila-Cohen and Quellier, pp. 32–3.

85 Terence, *The Eunuch*, in *The Comedies*, trans. P. Brown (Oxford, 2006), pp. 166–7; A. Curry, 'The gladiator diet', *Archaeology*, LXI/6 (2008), https://archive.archaeology.org/0811/abstracts/gladiator.html.

86 C. Fischler, *L'Homnivore: Le goût, la cuisine et le corps* (Paris, 2001), p. 313.

87 M. Plaza, *The Function of Humour in Roman Verse Satire: Laughing and Lying* (Oxford, 2006).

88 Galen, 'Thrasybulus (On Whether Hygiene belongs to Medicine or Gymnastics)', in *Hygiene*, trans. I. Johnston (Cambridge, MA, 2018), vol. II, p. 341.

89 This occurs because certain 'messenger chemicals released by the body when we are full can also stimulate the areas of the brain responsible for tiredness'. G. Enders, *Gut: The Inside Story of Our Body's Most Underrated Organ*, trans. D. Shaw (Vancouver, 2015), p. 43.

90 Hippocrates, *Airs, Waters, Places*, in *Hippocrates*, trans. W.H.S. Jones (Cambridge, MA, 1957), p. 137.

91 Quoted in Plaza, *Function of Humour*, p. 94.

92 'The Greek term used [by Lucian], *pacheis*, which means literally "thick", or "fat", carries connotations of both wealth and stupidity when used metaphorically of persons.' M. W. Dickie, *Magic and Magicians in the Greco-Roman World* (London, 2001), pp. 216, n. 343; Lucian, *Alexander the False Prophet*, in Lucian, trans. A. M. Harmon (Cambridge, MA, 1961), vol. IV, p. 187.

93 Hill, *Eating to Excess*, p. 32; S. S. Kottek, 'On Health and Obesity in Talmudic and Midrashic Lore', *Israeli Journal of Medical Sciences*, XXXII/6 (1996), pp. 509–10; H. Ringgren, 'Semen', in *Theological Dictionary of the Old Testament*, ed. G. J. Botterweck, H. Ringgren and H.-J. Fabry, trans. D. E. Green and D. W. Stott (Grand Rapids, MI, 2006), vol. XV, pp. 249–53; J. L. Berquist, *Controlling Corporeality: The Body and the Household in Ancient Israel* (New Brunswick, NJ, 2002), pp. 18–26.

94 D. E. Hartley, *The Wisdom Background and Parabolic Implications of Isaiah 6:9–10 in the Synoptics* (New York, 2006), p. 141.

3 Ancient Appetites: Luxury and the Geography of Softness

1 Xenophon, *Conversations of Socrates*, trans. H. Tredennick and R. Waterfield (London, 1990), p. 233.
2 Cicero, *De fato*, in *De oratore, book III: De fato; Paradoxa stoicorum; De partitione oratoria*, trans. H. Rackham (Cambridge, MA, 1948), pp. 203–5. See also D. R. McLean, 'The Socratic Corpus: Socrates and Physiognomy', in *Socrates from Antiquity to the Enlightenment*, ed. M. Trapp (London, 2007), p. 66. The case of Socrates would recur in future centuries as proof that one could rise above physical shortcomings.
3 On the concept of the 'status shield', see A. R. Hochschild, *The Managed Heart: Commercialization of Human Feeling*, 2nd edn (Berkeley, CA, 2012), p. 163.
4 Plato, *The Republic*, trans. T. Griffith (Cambridge, 2000), pp. 55, 97.
5 N. Loraux, 'Herakles: The Super-Male and the Feminine', in *Before Sexuality: The Construction of Erotic Experience in the Ancient Greek World*, ed. D. M. Halperin, J. J. Winkler and F. I. Zeitlin (Princeton, NJ, 1990), p. 31; G. Sissa, *Greek Virginity*, trans. A. Goldhammer (Cambridge, MA, 1990), p. 65.
6 J. N. Adams, *The Latin Sexual Vocabulary* (Baltimore, MD, 1982), pp. 100, 138–41. Many thanks to A. Corbeill for further translation advice.
7 W. I. Miller, 'Gluttony', *Representations*, 60 (1997), p. 95.
8 A. Booth, 'The Age for Reclining and Its Attendant Perils', in *Dining in a Classical Context*, ed. W. J. Slater (Ann Arbor, MI, 1991), p. 105.
9 Hippocrates, *Aphorisms*, 2.4, in *Hippocrates*, trans. W.H.S. Jones (Cambridge, MA, 1959), vol. IV, p. 109.
10 S. L. Gilman, *Fat Boys: A Thin Book* (Lincoln, NE, 2004), pp. 35–7.
11 G. Vigarello, *The Metamorphoses of Fat: A History of Obesity*, trans. C. J. Delogu (New York, 2013), pp. 12–14.
12 S. E. Hill, *Eating to Excess: The Meaning of Gluttony and the Fat Body in the Ancient World* (Santa Barbara, CA, 2011), pp. 66–74.
13 Hippocrates, *Aphorisms*, 2.44, in *Hippocrates*, trans. W.H.S. Jones (Cambridge, MA, 1959), vol. IV, p. 119.
14 I. Weiler, 'Inverted *Kalokagathia*', in *Representing the Body of the Slave*, ed. T. Weidemann and J. Gardner (London, 2002), pp. 11–12.
15 Caelius Aurelianus [Soranus of Ephesus], *On Acute Diseases and On Chronic Diseases*, trans. I. E. Drabkin (Chicago, IL, 1950), pp. 992–3. This work, the Greek original of which is now lost, is available only in the fifth-century Latin translation made by Caelius Aurelianus.
16 Galen, *Hygiene*, trans. H. E. Sigerist (Springfield, IL, 1951), p. 20.
17 S. Kuriyama, *The Expressiveness of the Body and the Divergence of Greek and Chinese Medicine* (New York, 1999), pp. 206–17.
18 Celsus, *De medicina*, trans. W. G. Spencer (Cambridge, MA, 1935), vol. I, p. 89.
19 Ibid., p. 97.

20 Ibid., p. 57. On the problem of excessive thinness see G. Nisbet, 'A Sickness of Discourse: The Vanishing Syndrome of Leptosune', *Greece and Rome*, L/2 (2003), pp. 191–205.

21 Kuriyama, *Expressiveness*, pp. 144, 146.

22 Aristotle, *Physiognomics*, pp. 93, 99–101, 115–17; Kuriyama, *Expressiveness*, p. 134.

23 A. Stewart, *Greek Sculpture: An Exploration* (New Haven, CT, 1990), vol. I, pp. 75–6.

24 J. Wilkins, *The Boastful Chef: The Discourse of Food in Ancient Greek Comedy* (Oxford, 2000), p. 27.

25 Aristophanes, *Frogs*, in *The Complete Plays*, trans. P. Roche (New York, 2005), p. 589; K. Bergdolt, *Wellbeing: A Cultural History of Healthy Living*, trans. J. Dewhurst (Cambridge, 2008), pp. 16, 35.

26 K. Clark, *The Nude: A Study in Ideal Form* (Princeton, NJ, 1956), pp. 23–4.

27 Plato, *Gorgias*, trans. T. Irwin (Oxford, 1979), p. 97.

28 N. A. Hudson, 'Food in Roman Satire', in *Satire and Society in Ancient Rome*, ed. S. H. Braund (Exeter, 1989), p. 86; K. O. Sandnes, *Belly and Body in the Pauline Epistles* (Cambridge, 2002), pp. 63–4; Hill, *Eating to Excess*, pp. 81–102.

29 T. Morgan, *Popular Morality in the Early Roman Empire* (Cambridge, 2007), p. 73.

30 Sandnes, *Belly and Body*, pp. 149–50.

31 Plutarch, *Lives*, trans. B. Perrin (Cambridge, MA, 1914), vol. I, p. 233.

32 Plutarch, *Moralia*, trans. F. C. Babbitt (Cambridge, MA, 1961), vol. III, p. 139.

33 F. Ollier, *Le Mirage spartiate: Étude sur l'idéalisation de Sparte dans l'antiquité grecque de l'origine jusqu'aux cyniques* (Paris, 1933).

34 E. J. Gilchrest, *Revelation 21–22 in Light of Jewish and Greco-Roman Utopianism* (Leiden, 2013), p. 15. The very idea of 'a people whose response to stimuli is the very opposite of what human nature would seem to dictate' has captivated the Western imagination. S. B. Pomeroy et al., *Ancient Greece: A Political, Social, and Cultural History* (Oxford, 1999), p. 157.

35 R. Hawley, 'The Dynamics of Beauty in Classical Greece', in *Changing Bodies, Changing Meanings: Studies on the Human Body in Antiquity*, ed. Dominic Montserrat (London, 1998), p. 39.

36 Athenaeus, *The Learned Banqueters*, trans. S. D. Olson (Cambridge, MA, 2006), vol. VI, pp. 195–7.

37 P. Cartledge, *Sparta and Lakonia: A Regional History, 1300–362 BC*, 2nd edn (London, 2002), p. 305.

38 A. Corbeill, *Controlling Laughter: Political Humor in the Late Roman Republic* (Princeton, NJ, 1996), pp. 139–43.

39 A. Rousselle, *Porneia: On Desire and the Body in Antiquity*, trans. F. Pheasant (Oxford, 1988), p. 8.

40 A. Dalby, *Empire of Pleasures: Luxuries and Indulgence in the Roman World* (New York, 2000), p. 266; R. M. Schneider, 'Image and Empire: The Shaping of Augustan Rome', in *Conceiving the Empire: China and Rome Compared*, ed. F.-H. Mutschler and A. Mittag (Oxford, 2008), p. 285.

41 R.R.R. Smith, 'The Public Image of Licinius I: Portrait Sculpture and Imperial Ideology in the Early Fourth Century', *Journal of Roman Studies*, LXXXVI (1997), pp. 191–2.

42 S. E. Phang, *Roman Military Service: Ideologies of Discipline in the Late Republic and Early Principate* (Cambridge, 2008), pp. 264–6.

43 L. M. Meskell and R. A. Joyce, *Embodied Lives: Figuring Ancient Maya and Egyptian Experience* (New York, 2003), p. 53.

44 Z. Hawass, 'The Search for Hatshepsut and the Discovery of Her Mummy', www.guardians.net, June 2007.

45 J. F. Nunn, *Ancient Egyptian Medicine* (Norman, OK, 2002), p. 82; J. P. Alcock, *Food in the Ancient World* (Westport, CT, 2006), p. 232; K. R. Weeks, 'The *Anatomical* Knowledge of the *Ancient Egyptians* and the Representation of the Human Figure in Egyptian Art' (doctoral dissertation, Yale University, 1970).

46 Dalby, *Empire*, p. 263.

47 See *The Eunuch*, in *Terence: The Comedies*, trans. P. Brown (Oxford, 2006), pp. 166–7. In this play Chaerea describes his sixteen-year-old girlfriend as having 'a new sort of look' because her flesh is 'firm and juicy'.

48 Martial, *Epigrams*, trans. D.R.S. Bailey (Cambridge, MA, 1993), vol. III, pp. 82–3.

49 Rousselle, *Porneia*, pp. 35–6, 42, 44; *Soranus' Gynecology*, trans. O. Temkin (Baltimore, MD, 1991), p. 29.

50 H. Sancisi-Weerenburg, 'Persian Food: Stereotypes and Political Identity', in *Food in Antiquity*, ed. J. Wilkins, D. Harvey and M. Dobson (Exeter, 1995), p. 298.

51 A. Stewart, *Faces of Power: Alexander's Image and Hellenistic Politics* (Berkeley, CA, 1993), pp. 143–4.

52 Hippocrates, *Airs, Waters, Places*, trans. W.H.S. Jones (Cambridge, MA, 1923), vol. I, pp. 123–37.

53 Ibid.

54 Kuriyama, *Expressiveness*, pp. 137, 142.

55 M. Heath, 'Aristotle on Natural Slavery', *Phronesis*, LIII (2008), pp. 243–70.

56 See D. Montserrat, *Sex and Society in Graeco-Roman Egypt* (New York, 1996), p. 56; J. A. Glancy, *Slavery in Early Christianity* (Oxford, 2002), p. 10.

57 G. Cambiano, 'Aristotle and the Anonymous Opponents of Slavery', in *Classical Slavery*, ed. M. I. Finley (London, 1987), p. 27.

58 B. Fehr, 'Entertainers at the *Symposion*: The *akletoi* in the Archaic Period', in Sympotica: *A Symposium on the Symposion*, ed. O. Murray (Oxford, 1990), pp. 185–95.

59 *The Book of Xanthos the Philosopher and Aesop, His Slave, concerning the Course of His Life*, trans. L. M. Wills in his *The Quest of the Historical Gospel* (London, 1997), p. 181; Weiler, 'Inverted *Kalokagathia*', p. 16.

60 Weiler, 'Inverted *Kalokagathia*', p. 14.

61 Clark, *The Nude*, p. 10, fig. 7: Etruscan tomb. Il Obeso. Tarquinia. See also *Treasures from Tuscany: The Etruscan Legacy* (Edinburgh, 2004), pp. 129, 134–5.

62 Catullus referred to '*pinguis Umber et obesus Etruscus*'. Quoted in
G. D. Farney, *Ethnic Identity and Aristocratic Competition in Republican
Rome* (Cambridge, 2007), p. 139.

63 Quoted in A. Richlin, 'Gender and Rhetoric: Producing Manhood
in the Schools', in *Roman Eloquence: Rhetoric in Society and Literature*,
ed. W. J. Dominik (London, 1997), p. 84.

64 Quoted ibid., p. 87.

65 Athenaeus, *Learned Banqueters*, vol. VI, p. 191.

66 S. L. Alger, 'The Power of Excess: Royal Incest and the Ptolemaic
Dynasty', *Anthropologica*, XLVIII/2 (2006), p. 177.

67 Athenaeus, *Learned Banqueters*, vol. VI, pp. 193–4.

68 Glancy, *Slavery*, pp. 72–3.

69 Seneca, *Letters from a Stoic*, trans. R. Campbell (London, 2004), p. 95.

70 Ibid., p. 221.

71 Seneca, *Ad lucilium epistulae morales*, trans. R. M. Gummere
(Cambridge, MA, 1979), vol. III, p. 69.

72 E. Gowers, *The Loaded Table: Representations of Food in Roman Literature*
(Oxford, 1996), p. 2.

73 Juvenal, *Satires*, in *Juvenal and Persius*, trans. S. M. Braund (Cambridge,
MA, 2004), p. 143.

74 Gowers, *Loaded Table*, pp. 119, 180–88.

75 J. Goddard, 'The Tyrant at Table', in *Reflections of Nero: Culture, History,
and Representation*, ed. J. Elsner and J. Masters (Chapel Hill, NC, 1994),
pp. 67–82.

76 V. E. Grimm, 'On Food and the Body', in *A Companion to the Roman
Empire*, ed. D. S. Potter (Oxford, 2006), pp. 357–8.

77 Suetonius, *The Lives of the Twelve Caesars*, trans. J. Rolfe (Cambridge,
MA, 1914), p. 64.

78 E. R. Varner, *Mutilation and Transformation: Damnatio Memoriae and
Roman Imperial Portraiture* (Leiden, 2004), p. 49.

79 Suetonius, *The Lives of the Twelve Caesars*, p. 181.

80 T. Barton, 'The Inventio of Nero: Suetonius', in *Reflections*, ed. Elsner
and Masters, p. 57.

81 Grimm, 'On Food', pp. 357–8.

82 Cornelius Tacitus, *The Histories*, trans. W. H. Fyfe (Oxford, 1999), vol. II,
p. 98.

83 Suetonius, *Lives of Galba, Otho and Vitellius*, trans. D. Shorter
(Warminster, 1993), p. 91.

84 Ibid., p. 97.

85 On Vitellius' pot-belly as a sign of a tyrannical personality, see R. Ash,
Ordering Anarchy: Armies and Leaders in Tacitus' Histories (Ann Arbor,
MI, 1999), pp. 101–2.

86 M. Bradley, 'Obesity, Corpulence and Emaciation in Roman Art', *Papers
of the British School at Rome*, LXXIX (2011), p. 3.

4 Christian Corpulence: The Belly and What Lies Beneath

1 Quoted in P. W. van der Horst, *Hellenism–Judaism–Christianity: Essays
on Their Interaction* (Leuven, 1998), p. 158.

2 Ibid., p. 159.

3 R.R.R. Smith, 'The Public Image of Licinius I: Portrait Sculpture and Imperial Ideology in the Early Fourth Century', *Journal of Roman Studies*, LXXXVI (1997), pp. 191–2, quote on p 193. In official portraits and coins the emperors Balbinus (*c.* 165–238), Galerius (*c.* 260–311) and Licinius (*c.* 250–325) all depicted themselves as corpulent.

4 'Elagabalus', in *Historia Augusta*, trans. D. Magie (Cambridge, MA, 1924), vol. II, p. 163.

5 Y. Peleg, *Orientalism and the Hebrew Imagination* (Ithaca, NY, 2005), p. 65.

6 S. E. Phang, *Roman Military Service: Ideologies of Discipline in the Late Republic and Early Principate* (Cambridge, 2008), p. 35.

7 N. Shupak, *Where Can Wisdom Be Found? The Sage's Language in the Bible and in Ancient Egyptian Literature* (Fribourg, 1993), pp. 292–7.

8 K. O. Sandnes, *Belly and Body in the Pauline Epistles* (Cambridge, 2002), p. 43.

9 Philo, *Questions and Answers on Exodus*, trans. R. Marcus (Cambridge, MA, 1953), p. 53.

10 Philo, *The Special Laws,* trans. F. H. Colson (Cambridge, MA, 1939), vol. VIII, pp. 69–71, 85–7.

11 Philo, 'On the Posterity of Cain and his Exile', in *Philo*, trans. F. H. Colson and G. H. Whitaker (Cambridge, MA, 1994), vol. II, pp. 397–9.

12 G. Clark, 'Fattening the Soul: Christian Asceticism and Porphyry on Abstinence', in *Studia Patristica*, ed. M. F. Wiles and E. J. Yarnold (Leuven, 2001), vol. XXXV, p. 42.

13 Porphyry, *On Abstinence from Killing Animals*, trans. G. Clark (London, 2000), p. 49.

14 Ibid., p. xx.

15 Philo, *Allegorical Interpretation,* trans. F. H. Colson and G. H Whitaker (Cambridge, MA, 1929), vol. III, p. 393; Philo, *On Husbandry*, trans. F. H. Colson and G. H. Whitaker (Cambridge, MA, 1930), p. 127.

16 Athenaeus, *The Learned Banqueters*, trans. S. D. Olson (Cambridge, MA, 2006), vol. I, p. 529.

17 Ibid., vol. II, p. 53.

18 Sandnes, *Belly and Body*, p. 51.

19 Ibid., pp. 13, 149–51, 153, 167.

20 D. Boyarin, *Carnal Israel: Reading Sex in Talmudic Culture* (Berkeley, CA, 1993).

21 Sandnes, *Belly and Body*, pp. 149–51, 153, 167.

22 S. E. Hill, *Eating to Excess: The Meaning of Gluttony and the Fat Body in the Ancient World* (Santa Barbara, CA, 2011), pp. 36–8.

23 C. M. Conway, *Behold the Man: Jesus and Greco-Roman Masculinity* (Oxford, 2008), p. 150.

24 W. Braun, *Feasting and Social Rhetoric in Luke 14* (Cambridge, 1995), p. 38.

25 O. Temkin, *Hippocrates in a World of Pagans and Christians* (Baltimore, MD, 1991), p. 131; Hill, *Eating to Excess*, pp. 110–15.

26 Clement of Alexandria, *The Stromata, or Miscellanies*, in *The Ante-Nicene Fathers* [1885], ed. P. Schaff (Grand Rapids, MI, 1956), vol. II, p. 791.

27   Jerome, *Against Jovianus*, in *The Principal Works of Saint Jerome* (New York, 1892), pp. 750–51.

28   C. W. Bynum, *Holy Feast and Holy Fast: The Religious Significance of Food to Medieval Women* (Berkeley, CA, 1988), p. 36.

29   Quoted in H. Musurillo, 'The Problem of Ascetical Fasting in the Greek Patristic Writers', *Traditio*, XII (1956), p. 16; see also G. de Nie, 'Images of Invisible Dynamics: Self and Non-Self in Sixth-century Saints Lives', in *Studia Patristica*, XXXV (2001), pp. 52–64.

30   P. Brown, *The Body and Society: Men, Women, and Sexual Renunciation in Early Christianity* (New York, 1988), p. 316; see also Hill, *Eating to Excess*, pp. 115–20.

31   John Chrysostom, *Ephesians*, in *Nicene and Post-Nicene Fathers: First Series* [1886–89], ed. P. Schaff (Grand Rapids, MI, 1956), vol. XIII, p. 206.

32   Chrysostom, *Timothy*, in *Nicene*, vol. XIII, p. 788.

33   Ibid., p. 787.

34   Chrysostom, *Hebrews*, in *Nicene*, vol. XIIII, p. 941.

35   Chrysostom, *Corinthians*, in *Nicene*, vol. XII, p. 580.

36   J. E. Salisbury, *The Beast Within: Animals in the Middle Ages* (New York, 1994), p. 4.

37   P. Descola, *Par-delà nature et culture* (Paris, 2005), p. 103.

38   Quoted in Salisbury, *Beast Within*, p. 177.

39   T. M. Shaw, *The Burden of the Flesh: Fasting and Sexuality in Early Christianity* (Minneapolis, MN, 1998), pp. 143–4.

40   Chrysostom, *Ephesians*, in *Nicene*, vol. XIII, p. 206.

41   Chrysostom, *Acts of the Apostles*, in *Nicene*, vol. XI, p. 415.

42   In order to be healthy one must 'take away what is superfluous; give what is sufficient, and as much as can be digested'. Chrysostom, *Hebrews*, in *Nicene*, vol. XIIII, pp. 940–41

43   Chrysostom, *First Corinthians*, in *Nicene*, vol. XII, p. 425; Shaw, *Burden of the Flesh*, pp. 143–4; see also B. Leyerle, 'Refuse, Filth and Excrement in the Homilies of John Chrysostom', *Journal of Late Antiquity*, II/2 (Fall 2009), pp. 337–56.

44   Chrysostom, *Second Colossians*, in *Nicene*, vol. XIII, p. 518.

45   D. Ø. Endsjø, *Greek Resurrection Beliefs and the Success of Christianity* (London, 2009).

46   Tertullian quoted in V. E. Grimm, *From Feasting to Fasting, the Evolution of a Sin: Attitudes to Food in Late Antiquity* (New York, 1996), p. 136.

47   C. W. Bynum, *The Resurrection of the Body in Western Christianity, 200–1336* (New York, 1995), pp. 31–2, n. 36.

48   Augustine, 'The Enchiridion', *On the Holy Trinity; Doctrinal Treatises; Moral Treatises*, in *Nicene*, vol. III, p. 577.

49   C. R. Moss, 'Heavenly Healing: Eschatological Cleansing and the Resurrection of the Dead in the Early Church', *Journal of the American Academy of Religion*, LXXIX/4 (2011), pp. 991–1017.

50   Augustine, *The City of God against the Pagans*, trans. R. W. Dyson (Cambridge, 1998), book XXII, ch. 19, p. 1149; ch. 20, pp. 1151–2.

51   P. C. Miller, *The Corporeal Imagination: Signifying the Holy in Late Ancient Christianity* (Philadelphia, PA, 2009), pp. 3–4.

52 P. Cramer, *Baptism and Change in the Early Middle Ages, c. 200–c. 1150* (New York, 1993), pp. 212–13.

53 Bynum, *Holy Feast*, p. 211; S. E. Mullins, 'Myroblytes: Miraculous Oil in Medieval Europe' (PhD dissertation, Georgetown University, 2017).

54 R. Bartlett, *Why Can the Dead Do Such Great Things? Saints and Worshippers from the Martyrs to the Reformation* (Princeton, NJ, 2013), p. 249.

55 Bynum, *Holy Feast*, p. 145.

56 S. E. Hill, '"The Ooze of Gluttony": Attitudes towards Food, Eating, and Excess in the Middle Ages', in *The Seven Deadly Sins: From Communities to Individuals*, ed. R. Newhauser (Leiden, 2007), pp. 57–70.

57 Grimm, *From Feasting*, p. 190.

58 A. Hagen, *Anglo-Saxon Food and Drink* (Hockwold cum Wilton, 2006), p. 417.

59 Quoted in P. J. Patrick, '"Greed, Gluttony and Intemperance"? Testing the Stereotype of the "Obese Medieval Monk"' (doctoral dissertation, Institute of Archaeology, University College London, 2004).

60 J. J. Verlaan et al., 'Diffuse Idiopathic Skeletal Hyperostosis in Ancient Clergymen', *European Spine Journal*, XVI/8 (2007), pp. 1129–35; Patrick, '"Greed, Gluttony and Intemperance"?'

61 J. Le Goff, *La Civilisation de l'occident médiévale* (Paris, 1965), pp. 414–15, 438; D. Alexandre-Bidon, 'Trop gourmand? Le corps obèse dans l'iconographie médiéval', in *Le Corps du gourmand d'Héraclès à Alexandre le Bienheureux*, ed. K. Karila-Cohen and F. Quellier (Rennes, 2012), p. 136.

62 P. Camporesi, *The Incorruptible Flesh: Bodily Mutation and Mortification in Religion and Folklore*, trans. T. Croft-Murray (Cambridge, 1988), p. 78.

63 Quoted in J. Le Goff, *The Medieval Imagination*, trans. A. Goldhammer (Chicago, IL, 1988), p. 84.

64 Camporesi, *Incorruptible*, p. 76.

65 Bynum, *Resurrection*, pp. 134–5.

66 P. L. Reynolds, *Food and the Body: Some Peculiar Questions in High Medieval Theology* (Leiden, 1999).

67 T. Aquinas, *Of God and His Creatures*, trans. J. Ricaby (London, 1905), p. 530n.

68 M. J. Brosamer, 'Medieval Gluttony and Drunkenness: Consuming Sin in Chaucer and Langland' (doctoral dissertation, Department of English, UCLA, 1998), p. 320.

69 *The Annals of Lampert of Hersfeld*, trans. I. S. Robinson (Manchester, 2015), pp. 108, 133–4. Translation modified L. von Hersfeld, *Lamperti monachi Hersfeldensis opera*, ed. O. Holder-Egger (Hanover, 1894), pp. 100, 117.

70 R. Gasse, 'The Practice of Medicine in *Piers Plowman*', *The Chaucer Review*, XXXIX/2 (2004), p. 186.

71 G. Chaucer, *The Canterbury Tales*, ed. R. Boenig and A. Taylor (Peterborough, Canada, 2008), pp. 437–8.

72 Dante Alighieri, *The Divine Comedy*, vol. I: *Inferno*, trans. R. M. Durling (Oxford, 1996), canto VI, 16 (pp. 100–01).

73 M. E. Goodich, *From Birth to Old Age: The Human Life Cycle in Medieval Thought, 1250–1350* (Lanham, MD, 1989), p. 110. As one might expect, fasting was recommended as a cure for lustful thoughts.

74 I. Rosé, 'Le Moine glouton et son corps dans les discours cénobitiques réformateurs (début du ıxe siècle–début du xııe siècle)', in *Corps du gourmand*, ed. Karila-Cohen and Quellier, p. 200.

75 M. Bayless, *Parody in the Middle Ages: The Latin Tradition* (Ann Arbor, MI, 1997), pp. 137, 151.

76 Quoted in S. Vecchio, 'La Faute de trop manger: La gourmandise médiévale entre éthique et diététique', in *Trop gros? L'obésité et ses représentations*, ed. J. Csergo (Paris, 2009), p. 43.

77 Quoted in M.-C. Pouchelle, *The Body and Surgery in the Middle Ages*, trans. R. Morris (New Brunswick, NJ, 1990), p. 172. See also pp. 168–72.

78 Dhuoda, *Handbook for William: A Carolingian Woman's Counsel for Her Son*, trans. C. Neel (Lincoln, NE, 1991), pp. 43–4.

79 Denis the Carthusian, *Liber utilissimus de quatuor hominis novissimis* (Paris, 1548), p. 77; P. Camporesi, *The Fear of Hell: Images of Damnation and Salvation in Early Modern Europe*, trans. L. Byatt (Cambridge, 1990), p. 18. Many thanks to Cara Polsley for her Latin translation. See also T. Oestigaard, 'The Materiality of Hell', *Material Religion*, v/3 (2009), pp. 312–31.

5 Noble Fat? Corpulence in the Middle Ages

1 Vegetius, *Epitome of Military Science*, trans. N. P. Milner (Liverpool, 1993), p. 6; R. M. Grant, *Early Christians and Animals* (London, 1999), pp. 29–30.

2 J. Cadden, *Meanings of Sex Difference in the Middle Ages* (Cambridge, 1993), pp. 39–42.

3 J. Le Goff and N. Truong, *Une histoire du corps au Moyen Age* (Paris, 2003), p. 68.

4 M. Montanari, *Medieval Tastes: Food, Cooking, and the Table*, trans. B. Archer Brombert (New York, 2015), p. 94.

5 Quoted ibid., *Medieval Tastes*, p. 95.

6 H. Pleij, *Dreaming of Cockaigne: Medieval Fantasies of the Perfect Life*, trans. D. Webb (New York, 2001), pp. 152–62.

7 F. Quellier, *Gourmandise: Histoire d'un péché capital* (Paris, 2010), pp. 56–75. On 'body utopias' – that is, 'the basic human utopia of a full stomach and adequate clothing and shelter' – see L. T. Sargent, 'Everyday Life in Utopia: Food', in *Food Utopias: Reimagining Citizenship, Ethics and Community*, ed. P. V. Stock, M. Carolan and C. Rosin (London, 2015), p. 14.

8 H. Klemettilä, *Animals and Hunters in the Middle Ages* (London, 2015), pp. 76–7.

9 J.-L. Flandrin, 'Le Goût et la nécessité: Sur l'usage des graisses dans les cuisines d'Europe occidentale (xive–xviiie siècle)', *Annales: Histoire, sciences sociales*, xxxviii/2 (1983), pp. 369–401.

10 M. Maimonides, 'Two Treatises on the Regimen of Health', trans. A. Bar-Sela, H. E. Hoff and E. Faris, *Transactions of the American Philosophical Society*, (liv/4 1964), p. 19.

11 Flandrin, 'Le Goût', pp. 369–401; V. von Hoffmann, *From Gluttony to Enlightenment: The World of Taste in Early Modern Europe* (Urbana, IL,

2016); P. Rambourg, 'Manger gras: Lard, saindoux, beurre et huile dans les traités de cuisine du Moyen Age au xxe siècle', in *Trop gros? L'obésité et ses représentations*, ed. J. Csergo (Paris, 2009), p. 81.

12 M. Nicoud, *Les Régimes de santé au Moyen Age: Naissance et diffusion d'une écriture médicale (xiiie–xve siècle)* (Rome, 2007), pp. 15–16.

13 Avicenna, *The Canon of Medicine* [book 1], trans. O. C. Gruner (London, 1930), verse 761, p. 395.

14 Ibid., *Canon*, verse 221, p. 168.

15 Avicenna, 'On Cosmetics', *Canon of Medicine* (Rome, 1593), pp. 173–4. Available at: http://ddc.aub.edu.lb [Saab Medical Library, American University of Beirut], accessed August 2018.

16 J. Ziegler, *Medicine and Religion, c. 1300: The Case of Arnau de Vilanova* (Oxford, 1998), p. 165.

17 *The School of Salernum: Regimen sanitatis Salernitanum*, trans. J. Harington (New York, 1920), pp. 134, 138.

18 Quoted in M. Stolberg, '"Abhorreas pinguedinem": Fat and Obesity in Early Modern Medicine (*c.* 1500–1750)', *Studies in History and Philosophy of Biological and Biomedical Sciences*, XLIII (2012), p. 372.

19 M.-C. Pouchelle, *The Body and Surgery in the Middle Ages*, trans. R. Morris (New Brunswick, NJ, 1990), p. 112.

20 'But þe heed in his owen composicioun haþ litil fleissch and fatnes in comparisoun to oþir members; and þat for scharpnesse of witte and help of vndirstonding.' Bartholomaeus Anglicus, *On the Properties of Things: John Trevisa's translation of Bartholomaeus Anglicus, De proprietatibus rerum*, ed. M. C. Seymour (Oxford, 1975), vol. 1, p. 170.

21 J. Ziolkowski, 'Avatars of Ugliness in Medieval Literature', *Modern Language Review*, LVVIX/1 (1984), pp. 1–20.

22 *Certeyne Rewles of Phisnomy* [fifteenth century], in *Secretum secretorum: Nine English Versions*, ed. M. A. Manzalaoui (Oxford, 1977), p. 12.

23 *The Secrete of Secretes* ['Ashmole' version, fifteenth century] in *Three Prose Versions of the Secreta secretorum*, trans. J. Yonge (London, 1898), pp. 108, 110.

24 *The Gouernance of Prynces, or Pryvete of Pryveteis* [1422], in *Secretum secretorum*, pp. 227, 235.

25 Quoted in J. Ziegler, 'The Physiognomist's Kidney in the Fifteenth Century', *Journal of Nephrology*, XVII/4 (2004), p. 601.

26 S. Vecchio, 'La Faute de trop manger: La gourmandise médiévale entre éthique et diététique', in *Trop gros? L'obésité et ses représentations*, ed. J. Csergo (Paris, 2009), p. 44; H. Klemettilä, *Epitomes of Evil: Representations of Executioners in Northern France and the Low Countries in the Late Middle Ages* (Turnhout, 2006), p. 206.

27 Matthew of Vendôme, *Ars versificatoria* [The Art of the Versemaker], trans. R. P. Parr (Milwaukee, WI, 1981), pp. 38–9, 43.

28 R. Barnhouse, *The Book of the Knight of the Tower: Manners for Young Medieval Women* (Basingstoke, 2006), p. 193.

29 W. I. Miller, *The Mystery of Courage* (Cambridge, MA, 2000), p. 187.

30 M. Montanari, 'Peasants, Warriors, Priests', in *Food: A Culinary History from Antiquity to the Present*, ed. J.-L. Flandrin and M. Montanari

(New York, 1999), p. 179; A. Riera-Melis, 'Society, Food, and Feudalism', ibid., p. 260.

31 P. Squatriti, 'Personal Appearance and Physiognomics in Early Medieval Italy', *Journal of Medieval History*, xiv/3 (1988), p. 195.

32 See S. Butler, 'Visconti, Filippo Maria, Duke of Milan [1392–1447]', in *The Late Medieval Age of Crisis and Renewal, 1300–1500: A Biographical Dictionary*, ed. C. J. Drees (Westport, CT, 2001), p. 493; D. Alexandre-Bidon, 'Trop gourmand? Le corps obèse dans l'iconographie médiéval', in *Le Corps du gourmand d'Héraclès à Alexandre le Bienheureux*, ed. K. Karila-Cohen and F. Quellier (Rennes, 2012), p. 138.

33 G. Lubkin, *A Renaissance Court: Milan under Galeazzo Maria Sforza* (Berkeley, CA, 1994), p. 9.

34 R. M. Karras, *From Boys to Men: Formations of Masculinity in Late Medieval Europe* (Philadelphia, PA, 2003), pp. 64–5.

35 Vegetius, *Knyghthode and Bataile* (London, 1935), stanza 22 (pp. 9–10).

36 J. Thomas, *Corps violents, corps soumis: Le policement des mœurs à la fin du Moyen-Age* (Paris, 2003), p. 43.

37 R. Llull, *The Book of the Ordre of Chyualry*, trans. W. Caxton (London, 1926), p. 63.

38 Karras, *From Boys to Men*, pp. 64–5.

39 Quoted in T. Scully, *The Art of Cookery in the Middle Ages* (Woodbridge, 1995), p. 180.

40 Plutarch, *Moralia*, trans. H. N. Fowler (Cambridge, MA, 1960), vol. x, pp. 123–5.

41 C. W. Bynum, *The Resurrection of the Body in Western Christianity, 200–1336* (New York, 1995), p. 219.

42 W. Pfeffer, *Proverbs in Medieval Occitan Literature* (Gainesville, FL, 1997), p. 56.

43 J. Mandeville, *The Travels of Sir John Mandeville* (London, 1915), p. 205.

44 Pleij, *Dreaming*, p. 131; Thomas, *Corps violents*, p. 106.

45 Einhard, *The Life of Charlemagne*, in *Charlemagne's Courtier: The Complete Einhard*, trans. P. E. Dutton (Orchard Park, NY, 1998), pp. 30–31.

46 Montanari, 'Peasants, Warriors, Priests', p. 180.

47 J. L. Nelson, *Courts, Elites, and Gendered Power in the Early Middle Ages* (Aldershot, 2007), pp. 17–19; S. Maclean, *Kingship and Politics in the Late Ninth Century: Charles the Fat and the End of the Carolingian Empire* (Cambridge, 2003).

48 Maclean, *Kingship and* Politics, p. 2; Charles was not called 'the Fat' in Abbo's ninth-century chronicle. Cf. Abbo of Saint-Germain-des-Prés, *Viking Attacks on Paris*, trans. N. Dass (Paris, 2007).

49 S. L. Gilman, *Diets and Dieting: A Cultural Encyclopedia* (New York, 2008), p. 286.

50 T. Reuter, ed., *The New Cambridge Medieval History*, vol. III, *c.* 900–1024 (Cambridge, 1999); J. F. O'Callaghan, *A History of Medieval Spain* (Ithaca, NY, 1983), p. 679; pp. 123–4; R. Collins, *Early Medieval Spain: Unity in Diversity, 400–1000* (Basingstoke, 1995), p. 238.

51 M. Hatzaki, *Beauty and the Male Body in Byzantium* (New York, 2009), p. 36.

52 A. Luchaire, *Les Premiers Capétiens (987–1137)* [1911] (Paris, 1980), p. 176; J. Bradbury, *The Capetians: Kings of France, 987–1328* (New York, 2007), pp. 113, 118; Orderic Vitalis, *Ecclesiastical History*, trans. M. Chibnall (Oxford, 1978), vol. v, p. 212.

53 Suger, *The Deeds of Louis the Fat*, trans. R. Cusimano and J. Moorhead (Washington, DC, 1991), pp. 24, 135.

54 Ibid., pp. 143, 151–5.

55 Henry, Archdeacon of Huntingdon, *Historia anglorum: The History of the English People*, trans. D. Greenway, (Oxford, 1996), pp. 606–7, translation modified. Henry, Archdeacon of Huntingdon, *Historia anglorum* [*c.* 1154], ed. T. Arnold (London, 1879), p. 312.

56 Bradbury, *Capetians*, pp. 130, 147.

57 William of Malmesbury, *Gesta regum anglorum: The History of the English Kings*, vol. 1, trans. R.A.B. Mynors (Oxford, 1998), pp. 732–3.

58 Nicoud, *Les Régimes*, pp. 150–3, 283–4.

59 *School of Salernum*, p. 109.

60 G. Vigarello, *Le Sain et le malsain: Santé et mieux-être depuis le Moyen Age* (Paris, 1993), pp. 61–2.

61 X. Brooke and D. Crombie, *Henry VIII Revealed: Holbein's Portrait and Its Legacy* (London, 2003), p. 19.

62 B. Grosvenor, ed., *Lost Faces: Identity and Discovery in Tudor Royal Portraiture* (London, 2007), p. 54.

63 Brooke and Crombie, *Henry VIII*, p. 22.

64 J. Ridley, *Henry VIII* (London, 1985), pp. 348–9, 409.

65 N. R. Smith, 'Portentous Births and the Monstrous Imagination in Renaissance Culture', in *Marvels, Monsters, and Miracles: Studies in the Medieval and Early Modern Imaginations*, ed. T. S. Jones and D. A. Sprunger (Kalamazoo, MI, 2002), p. 282.

66 P. Boaistuau, *Histoires prodigieuses les plus mémorables* (Paris, 1560), pp. 104–5.

67 S. Davies, 'The Unlucky, the Bad and the Ugly: Categories of Monstrosity from the Renaissance to the Enlightenment', in *The Ashgate Research Companion to Monsters and the Monstrous*, ed. A. S. Mittman and P. J. Dendle (London, 2012), pp. 70–71.

68 Quoted in von Hoffmann, *From Gluttony*, p. 42.

69 G. Vigarello, *The Metamorphoses of Fat: A History of Obesity*, trans. C. J. Delogu (New York, 2013), p. 46.

70 A. Laddis, 'The Legend of Giotto's Wit and the Arena Chapel', in *The Cambridge Companion to Giotto*, ed. A. Derbes and M. Sandona (Cambridge, 2004), pp. 227–8.

71 Pouchelle, *Body and Surgery*, pp. 126–7; Thomas, *Corps violents*, p. 106.

72 R. Mellinkoff, *Outcasts: Signs of Otherness in Northern European Art of the Late Middle Ages* (Berkeley, CA, 1993), vol. 1, pp. 138–40.

73 Pleij, *Dreaming*, p. 376.

74 K. Moxey, *Peasants, Warriors and Wives: Popular Imagery in the Reformation* (Chicago, IL, 1989), pp. 46, 63–4.

75 Quoted in J. E. Hutton, *A Short History of the Moravian Church* (London, 1895), p. 16.

76 Alexandre-Bidon, 'Trop gourmand?', p. 143.

77 Mellinkoff, *Outcasts*, pp. 122, 128.

78 H. A. Oberman, *Luther: Man between God and the Devil*, trans.
    E. Walliser-Schwarzbart (New Haven, CT, 2006), p. 5; see also
    P. Camporesi, *The Incorruptible Flesh: Bodily Mutation and Mortification
    in Religion and Folklore*, trans. T. Croft-Murray (Cambridge, 1988),
    pp. 80–81.

79 S. L. Gilman, *Fat Boys: A Thin Book* (Lincoln, NE, 2004), pp. 54–7.

80 O. Christin, 'La Foi comme chope de bière: Luther, les moines, les
    jeûnes', in *Trop gros?*, ed. Csergo, p. 47.

81 L. Roper, 'Martin Luther's Body: The "Stout Doctor" and his
    Biographers', *American Historical Review*, CXIV/2 (2010), p. 362.

82 A. Cunningham, 'Paracelsus Fat and Thin: Thoughts on Reputations
    and Realities', in *Paracelsus: The Man and His Reputation, His Ideas
    and Their Transformation*, ed. O. P. Grell (Leiden, 1998), pp. 53–77.

83 Paracelsus, *Hermetic and Alchemical Writings*, vol. I: *Hermetic Chemistry*,
    ed. A. E. Waite (London, 1894), p. 261.

84 Paracelsus, *Opus paramirum*, in *Essential Theoretical Writings*, trans.
    A. Weeks (Leiden, 2008), pp. 466–7.

6 The Fat of the Land; or, Why a Good Cock is Never Fat

 1 Joseph Dejardin traces the proverb to a song recorded in *Le Nouveau
    entretien des bonnes compagnies* (1635), though its ideational core is evident
    in Girolamo Mercuriale's gloss on Aristotle: *pinguia corpora sunt veneri
    inepta* (fat bodies are unfit for Venus). Dejardin, *Dictionnaire des spots ou
    proverbes Wallons* (Liège, 1891), p. 214; Mercuriale, *Praelectiones Patauinae
    cognoscendis et curandis humani corporis affectibus* (Venice, 1603), p. 429.

 2 F. Loux and P. Richard, *Sagesses du corps: La santé et la maladie dans les
    proverbes françaises* (Paris, 1978), pp. 17–18, 266. While these proverbs
    were recorded in the nineteenth century, they are consistent with sayings
    uttered centuries earlier.

 3 Were we to transpose these ideas to the Middle Ages, we might find
    that the only proper place for 'a parasite, an ignoble digestive tube who
    grows fat, refuses work and calls into question the natural order of
    society' would be the Land of Cockaigne. F. Quellier, *Gourmandise:
    Histoire d'un péché capital* (Paris, 2010), p. 65.

 4 W. Mieder, *Proverbs: A Handbook* (Westport, CT, 2004), p. 15.

 5 E. Demange, 'Obésité', in *Dictionnaire encyclopédique des sciences
    médicales*, ed. A. Dechambre (Paris, 1864–80), vol. XIV, p. 14.

 6 Isidore of Seville, *The Etymologies*, trans. S. A. Barney et al. (Cambridge,
    2006), p. 224.

 7 Ambroise Paré, *On Monsters and Marvels* [1573], trans. J. L. Pallister
    (Chicago, IL, 1995), p. 55: '*Exemple de fertilité: on la connoist à ceux qui sont
    fort gras, fessus, et ventrus, tant qu'ils creuent en leur peau, force leur est de
    demeurer tousiours couché ou assis, pour ne pouuoir porter la grosse masse de
    leur corps*'. Paré, *Des monstres et prodiges*, in *Œuvres complètes d'Ambroise
    Paré*, ed. J.-F. Malgaigne (Paris, 1840), p. 34.

 8 D. Alexandre-Bidon, 'Trop gourmand? Le corps obèse dans
    l'iconographie médiéval', in *Le Corps du gourmand d'Héraclès à Alexandre*

le Bienheureux, ed. K. Karila-Cohen and F. Quellier (Rennes, 2012), p. 140.

9 P. Camporesi, *Juice of Life: The Symbolic and Magic Significance of Blood*, trans. R. R. Barr (New York, 1995), p. 114. On the etymological link between 'human' and 'humus' (earth), see B. Sax, 'What Is this Quintessence of Dust? The Concept of the "Human" and its Origins', in *Anthropocentrism: Humans, Animals, Environments*, ed. R. Boddice (Leiden, 2011), p. 23.

10 M.-C. Pouchelle, *The Body and Surgery in the Middle Ages*, trans. R. Morris (New Brunswick, NJ, 1990), p. 161; Palladius, *Traité d'agriculture*, trans. R. Martin, (Paris, 1976) vol. I.

11 Paracelsus, *Hermetic and Alchemical Writings*, vol. I: *Hermetic Chemistry*, ed. A. E. Waite (London, 1894), p. 120.

12 G. Tétart, *Le Sang des fleurs: Une anthropologie de l'abeille et du miel* (Paris, 2004), pp. 109–10: 'Oil fattens [the land] because it is unctuous and thick.' J.-P. Camus, *Les Diversitez* (Lyon, 1610), vol. V, p. 482: 'If, as rural *doxa* claims, the earth is lowly, it is not just because it makes back-breaking demands, but because it is inseparable from its vile composition.' D. Laporte, *History of Shit*, trans. N. Benabid and R. el-Khoury (Cambridge, MA, 2000), pp. 38–9.

13 'Swa swa fætt eorþe cenð þæt behydd ys on hyre, ealswa flæs fætt forðgelætt leahter' [*sicut pinguis terra germinat quod absconsum est in ea sic et caro pinguis producit vitium*]. E. W. Rhodes, ed., *Defensor's Liber scintillarum with an Interlinear Anglo-Saxon Version Made Early in the Eleventh Century* (London, 1889), p. 104. The Anglo-Saxon *leahter* used to translate the Latin *vitium* (crime, sin, fault, disease and injury) may also mean 'laughter'. Many thanks to Jan-Frans van Dijkhuizen for bringing this expression to my attention.

14 G. Comet, 'The Development of Farming Implements between the Seine and the Rhine from the Second to the Twelfth Centuries', in *Medieval Farming and Technology: The Impact of Agricultural Change in Northwest Europe*, ed. G. Astill and J. Langdon (Leiden, 1997), p. 26.

15 Paracelsus, *Hermetic and Alchemical Writings*, vol. II: *Hermetic Medicine and Hermetic Philosophy*, ed. A. E. Waite (Chicago, IL, 1910), p. 45.

16 F. Bacon, *Sylva sylvarum, or, A Naturall Historie* (London, 1635), p. 147 (par. 595).

17 H. Schwartz, *Never Satisfied: A Cultural History of Diets, Fantasies and Fat* (New York, 1986).

18 Blith wrote approvingly of waters that conferred upon less fertile land 'Thicknesse, Soyle or Filth, which I call Richnesse'. W. Blith, *The English Improver, or, A New Survey of Husbandry* (London, 1649), p. 27.

19 G. Markham, *Markham's Farewel to Husbandry, or, The Enriching of All Sorts of Barren and Sterile Ground in Our Nation* (London, 1676), pp. 26–7.

20 Laporte, *History of Shit*, p. 15.

21 Artemidorus, *The Interpretation of Dreams: Oneirocritica*, trans. R. J. White (Torrance, CA, 1990), p. 174.

22 Laporte, *History of Shit*, p. 39.

23 J. Burroughs, *Moses His Choice, with His Eye Fixed upon Heaven* (London, 1641), p. 362.

24 J. Bunyan, 'The Barren Fig-tree, or, The Doom and Downfall of the Fruitless Professor', in *The Works of the Eminent Servant of Christ, Mr John Bunyan*, 3rd edn (London, 1767), vol. I, p. 825.

25 H. von Staden, 'Women and Dirt', *Helios*, XIX/1/2 (1992), p. 9; S. S. Morrison, *Excrement in the Middle Ages: Sacred Filth and Chaucer's Fecopoetics* (New York, 2008), p. 7.

26 C. W. Bynum, *The Resurrection of the Body in Western Christianity, 200–1336* (New York, 1995), pp. 31–2, n. 36.

27 The name Gethsemane is actually Aramaic for 'oil press'. 'Second Sunday after Pentecost', in *The Sermons of Saint Anthony of Padua*, trans. P. Spilsbury. http://www.documentacatholicaomnia.eu/03d/1195-1231,_Antonius_Patavinus,_Sermones,_EN.pdf, accessed 4 October 2018.

28 W. Langland, *Piers Plowman III: The C Version*, ed. G. Russell and G. Kane (London, 1997), C.12.224, p. 449.

29 S. Brant, *The Ship of Fools* [1494], trans. A. Barclay (Edinburgh, 1874), vol. I, p. 248.

30 Quoted in K. Bergdolt, *Wellbeing: A Cultural History of Healthy Living*, trans. J. Dewhurst (Cambridge, 2008), p. 178.

31 B. L. Mack, *A Myth of Innocence: Mark and Christian Origins* (Minneapolis, MN, 2006), pp. 159–60.

32 J. W. Hassell, *Middle French Proverbs, Sentences, and Proverbial Phrases* (Toronto, 1982), p. 246.

33 E. Strauss, ed., *Dictionary of European Proverbs* (London, 1994), vol. I, p. 18.

34 W. P. Marvin, *Hunting Law and Ritual in Medieval English Literature* (Cambridge, 2006), p. 78.

35 J. E. Salisbury, *The Beast Within: Animals in the Middle Ages* (New York, 1994), pp. 132, 177.

36 J. Mandeville, *The Travels of Sir John Mandeville* (London, 1915), pp. 120, 334.

37 D. G. Neal, *The Masculine Self in Late Medieval England* (Chicago, IL, 2008), p. 67.

38 Pouchelle, *Body and Surgery*, p. 173.

39 M. Bayless, *Parody in the Middle Ages: The Latin Tradition* (Ann Arbor, MI, 1997), pp. 137, 151.

40 O. Christin, 'La Foi comme chope de bière: Luther, les moines, les jeûnes', in *Trop gros? L'obésité et ses représentations*, ed. J. Csergo (Paris, 2009), p. 53.

41 A. Paré, *De la génération de l'homme*, book 23, ch. 44, in *Œuvres d'Ambroise Paré* (Paris, 1579).

42 L. Joubert, *Erreurs populaires au fait de la médecine et régime de santé* (Bordeaux, 1578), pp. 240–41, 243.

43 L. de Serres, *Discours de la nature, causes, signes, & curation des empeschemens de la conception, & de la stérilité des femmes* (Lyon, 1625), p. 437.

44 F. Loux, *Le Jeune Enfant et son corps dans la médecine traditionnelle* (Paris, 1978), p. 75.

45 Recorded around 1423, quoted in Hassell, *Middle French Proverbs*, p. 129.

46 Aetios of Almida, *The Gynaecology and Obstetrics of the VIth Century AD*, trans. J. V. Ricci (Philadelphia, PA, 1950), p. 60.

47 A. J. Lepp, 'The Rooster's Egg: Maternal Metaphors and Medieval Men' (doctoral dissertation, University of Toronto, 2010), p. 226n.

48 P. Biller, *The Measure of Multitude: Population in Medieval Thought* (Oxford, 2000), p. 253.

49 Thomas Aquinas, *Basic Writings of Saint Thomas Aquinas*, ed. A. C. Pegis (Indianapolis, IN, 1997), vol. I, p. 1096.

50 A. Lindgren, 'The Wandering Womb and the Peripheral Penis: Gender and the Fertile Body in Late Medieval Infertility Treatises' (doctoral dissertation in History, University of California, Davis, 2005), p. 121; J. Cadden, *Meanings of Sex Difference in the Middle Ages* (Cambridge, 1993), pp. 242–3.

51 Hildegard of Bingen, *Holistic Health*, trans. M. Pawlik and P. Madigan (Collegeville, MN, 1994), pp. 67–8.

52 F. Kelly, *A Guide to Early Irish Law* (Dublin, 1988), p. 74.

53 H. R. Lemay, 'William of Saliceto on Human Sexuality', *Viator*, XII/12 (1981), p. 173; Hildegard, *Holistic Health*, p. 96.

54 *Soranus' Gynecology*, trans. O. Temkin (Baltimore, MD, 1991), p. 29.

55 *The Trotula: A Medieval Compendium of Women's Medicine*, trans. M. H. Green (Philadelphia, PA, 2001), pp. 113–15, 121–3; Lindgren, 'Wandering Womb', pp. 31, 194–5.

56 P. Camporesi, *The Incorruptible Flesh: Bodily Mutation and Mortification in Religion and Folklore*, trans. T. Croft-Murray (Cambridge, 1988), p. 78.

57 Lindgren, 'Wandering Womb', p. 127.

58 Pouchelle, *Body and Surgery*, p. 191. 'Although all body was feared as teeming, labile, and friable, female body was especially so. Out of it came fluids and excrescences, and such products were seen more as putrefaction than as growth and new life. To theologians, hagiographers, and medical writers, fertility itself became decay.' Bynum, *Resurrection*, p. 221.

59 J. Evelyn, *A Philosophical Discourse of Earth* (London, 1675), pp. 90–91.

60 J. Maubray, *The Female Physician, Containing all the Diseases Incident to That Sex* (London, 1724), p. 384.

61 S. Switzer, *Ichnograpia Rustica, or, The Nobleman, Gentleman, and Gardener's Recreation* (London, 1718), vol. III, p. 145.

62 G. Cheyne, *An Essay of Health and Long Life*, 10th edn (London, 1745), p. 113.

63 S. Toulalan, '"To[o] Much Eating Stifles the Child": Fat Bodies and Reproduction in Early Modern England', *Historical Research*, LXXXVII/235 (2014), pp. 65–93; see also Toulalan, '"If slendernesse be the cause of unfruitfulnesse; you must nourish and fatten the body": Thin Bodies and Infertility in Early Modern England', in *The Palgrave Handbook of Infertility in History: Approaches, Contexts and Perspectives*, ed. G. Davis and T. Loughran (London, 2017), pp. 171–97.

64 W. Whiter, *Etymologicon universale, or, Universal Etymological Dictionary* (Cambridge, 1822), vol. I, p. 92.

65 Columella, *On Agriculture*, trans. H. Boyd (Cambridge, MA, 1960), vol. I, pp. 110–11.

66 N. W. Gómez, *The Tropics of Empire: Why Columbus Sailed South to the Indies* (Cambridge, MA, 2008), pp. 214–23.

67 J. Goliński, *British Weather and the Climate of the Enlightenment* (Chicago, IL, 2007), p. 171.

68 Quoted in K. M. Phillips, *Before Orientalism: Asian Peoples and Cultures in European Travel Writing, 1245–1510* (Philadelphia, PA, 2014), p. 102.

69 D. Arnold, *Colonizing the Body: State Medicine and Epidemic Disease in Nineteenth-century India* (Berkeley, CA, 1993), pp. 28–9.

70 J. Arbuthnot, *An Essay concerning the Effects of Air on Human Bodies* (London, 1733), p. 155.

71 S.J.K. Pearce, *The Land of the Body: Studies in Philo's Representation of Egypt* (Tübingen, 2007).

72 Aelian, *On the Characteristics of Animals*, trans. A. F. Scholfield (Cambridge, MA, 1959), vol. II, p. 369.

73 M. H. Katz, 'Fattening Up in Fourteenth-century Cairo: Ibn al-Ḥāǧǧ and the Many Meanings of Overeating', *Annales Islamologiques*, XLVIII/1 (2014), pp. 31–54.

74 P. Alpini, *De medicina Aegyptiorum* (Venice, 1591); Alpini, *La Médecine des Egyptiens* [1581–4], trans. R. de Fenoy (Cairo, 1980), pp. 294–5.

75 O. Dapper, *Description de l'Afrique* (Amsterdam, 1686), p. 94.

76 P. d'Avity, *Description générale de l'Afrique* (Paris, 1637), p. 264.

77 P. Gordon, *Geography Anatomiz'd, or, The Geographical Grammar* (London, 1732), p. 303.

78 Observing that soft water contained 'fat and oily Particles', the German geographer Bernhard Varen claimed in 1650 that the Seine was a river blessed with 'fat and soft Waters' that rendered the land fertile as well. B. Varenius, *A Compleat System of General Geography*, trans. Mr Dugdale, 2nd edn (London, 1734), pp. 328, 344.

79 Abbé [Maria Dominicus] de Binos, *Voyage par l'Italie, en Egypte au Mont-Liban et en Palestine, ou Terre Sainte* (Paris, 1787), vol. I, p. 290.

80 Arbuthnot, *Essay*, p. 124.

81 R. Boyle, 'The Divine Original and Incomparable Excellence of the Christian Religion', in *A Defence of Nature and Revealed Religion* (Dublin, 1737), vol. II, p. 377.

82 J.-B. Du Halde, *Description géographique, historique, chronologique, politique et physique de l'Empire de la Chine et de la Tartarie chinoise* (Paris, 1735), vol. II, p. 670.

83 M. Sheller, 'Natural Hedonism: The Invention of Caribbean Islands as Tropical Playgrounds', in *Tourism in the Caribbean: Trends, Development, Prospects*, ed. D. Timothy Duval (London, 2004), p. 24.

84 C. Merchant, *The Death of Nature: Women, Ecology, and the Scientific Revolution* (San Francisco, CA, 1980).

85 Herodotus, *Histories*, trans. A. D. Godley (Cambridge, MA, 1969), vol. IV, p. 301.

86 Hippocrates, *Airs, Waters, Places*, trans. W.H.S. Jones (Cambridge, MA, 1923), p. 133.

87 T. More, *Utopia* [1516], trans. R. M. Adams (New York, 1992), pp. 37, 57; see also T. W. Africa, 'Thomas More and the Spartan Mirage', *Historical Reflections/Réflexions Historiques*, VI/2 (1979), pp. 343–52.

88 Montesquieu, *The Spirit of Laws* [1748], book XVIII, ch. 4, trans. Thomas Nugent (Kitchener, 2001), p. 300.

7 Spartan Mirages: Utopian Bodies and the Challenges of Modernity

1 T. Campanella, *La città del sole/The City of the Sun*, trans. D. J. Donno (Berkeley, CA, 1981), pp. 37, 71, 89; quote on pp. 54–5.

2 K. Bergdolt, *Wellbeing: A Cultural History of Healthy Living*, trans. J. Dewhurst (Cambridge, 2008), p. 179.

3 Ibid., p. 220.

4 R. M. Bell, *How to Do It: Guides to Good Living for Renaissance Italians* (Chicago, IL, 1999), p. 168.

5 L. Valla, *On Pleasure* [*De voluptate*] [1431], trans. A. K. Hieatt and M. Lorch (New York, 1977), p. 130.

6 M. Jendrysik, 'Fundamental Oppositions: Utopia and the Individual', in *The Individual and Utopia: A Multidisciplinary Study of Humanity and Perfection*, ed. C. Jones and C. Ellis (London, 2015), p. 30.

7 Strabo, *Geography*, book IV, IV.6, trans. H. C. Hamilton (London, 1903), vol. I, p. 296.

8 S. Dupleix, *Mémoires des Gaules* (Paris, 1619), p. 53; R. de Bussy-Rabutin, *Histoire amoureuse des Gaules* (Liège, 1680), p. 1. However, Strabo had insisted that the details reported by Ephorus were 'not applicable' to the 'present state' of the Gauls as he encountered them.

9 Bergdolt, *Wellbeing*, p. 177.

10 Cf. E. Levy-Navarro, *The Culture of Obesity in Early and Late Modernity* (Basingstoke, 2008).

11 G. Vigarello, *Histoire de la beauté: Le corps et l'art d'embellir de la Renaissance à nos jours* (Paris, 2004), p. 22.

12 G. Vigarello, *Le Corps redressé: Histoire d'un pouvoir pédagogique* (Paris, 2001), p. 21; Vigarello, *Histoire de la beauté*.

13 S. Connor, *The Matter of Air: Science and the Art of the Ethereal* (London, 2010), p. 328; see also G. Lipovetsky, *De la légèreté: Vers une civilisation du léger* (Paris, 2014); and S. Gilman, *Stand Up Straight! A History of Posture* (London, 2018).

14 V. von Hoffmann, *From Gluttony to Enlightenment: The World of Taste in Early Modern Europe* (Urbana, IL, 2016), pp. 101–36.

15 Ibid., p. 144; see also E. C. Spary, *Eating the Enlightenment: Food and the Sciences in Paris, 1670–1760* (Chicago, IL, 2012), pp. 17–50.

16 R. L. Spang, *The Invention of the Restaurant: Paris and Modern Gastronomic Culture* (Cambridge, MA, 2000), p. 48.

17 Connor, *Matter of Air*, p. 312.

18 Quoted in Spary, *Eating*, p. 204.

19 J. A. Brillat-Savarin, *Physiologie du goût, ou, Méditations de gastronomie transcendante* [1825] (Paris, 1842), p. 9.

20 F. Quellier, 'Du ventre au palais: Le corps du gourmand dans les traites de civilité (XVIe–début XIXe siècle)', in *Le Corps du gourmand d'Héraclès à Alexandre le Bienheureux*, ed. K. Karila-Cohen and F. Quellier (Rennes, 2012), pp. 58–61.

21 G. Vigarello, *The Metamorphoses of Fat: A History of Obesity*, trans. C. J. Delogu (New York, 2013), p. 71.

22 M. Jeanneret, *A Feast of Words: Banquets and Table Talk in the Renaissance*, trans. J. Whiteley and E. Hughes (Chicago, IL, 1991), p. 80; H. M. Nunn, 'Home Bodies: Matters of Weight in Renaissance Women's Medical Manuals', in *The Body in Medical Culture*, ed. E. Klaver (Albany, NY, 2009), pp. 15–36.

23 Quellier, 'Du ventre au palais', p. 59.

24 Vigarello, *Metamorphoses*, p. 61.

25 M. Stolberg, '"Abhorreas pinguedinem": Fat and Obesity in Early Modern Medicine (*c.* 1500–1750)', *Studies in History and Philosophy of Biological and Biomedical Sciences*, XLIII (2012), pp. 370–78.

26 L. Joubert, quoted in J. Gleyse, 'La Renaissance de la "fabrication du corps" par l'exercice physique au XVIe siècle: Discours, pratique, preservation d'un patrimoine, ou transgression d'un interdit?' *Annales canadiennes d'histoire/Canadian Journal of History*, XLI/1 (2011), pp. 1–33.

27 Vigarello, *Histoire de la beauté*, pp. 129–30.

28 L. Boia, *Forever Young: A Cultural History of Longevity*, trans. T. Selous (London, 2004), pp. 70–73.

29 N. Laneyrie-Dagen, *Rubens* (Paris, 2003), p. 120.

30 Quoted in J. M. Muller, 'Rubens's Theory and Practice of the Imitation of Art', *The Art Bulletin*, LXIV/2 (1982), p. 232.

31 P. P. Rubens, *Théorie de la figure humaine*, ed. N. Laneyrie-Dagen (Paris, 2003), p. 71.

32 Ibid., pp. 89–91.

33 Vigarello, *Metamorphoses*, p. 59.

34 P. Parker, 'Virile Style', in *Premodern Sexualities*, ed. L. Fradenburg and C. Freccero (New York, 1996), pp. 202–3.

35 A. Brumley, '"As Horace Fat" in a Thin Land: Ben Jonson's Experience and Strategy', in *Historicizing Fat*, ed. E. Levy-Navarro (Columbus, OH, 2010), p. 118.

36 M. Alexander and E. Bramwell, 'Mapping Metaphors of Wealth and Want: A Digital Approach', in *Proceedings of the Digital Humanities Congress, 2012: Studies in the Digital Humanities*, ed. C. Mills, M. Pidd and E. Ward (Sheffield, 2014). Available at: www.hrionline.ac.uk.

37 Isidore of Seville, *The Etymologies*, trans. S. A. Barney et al. (Cambridge, 2006), p. 218; Vigarello, *Metamorphoses*, pp. 71–3.

38 N. Pellegrin, 'Corps du commun, usages communs du corps', in *Histoire du corps. 1. De la Renaissance aux Lumières*, ed. G. Vigarello (Paris, 2005), p. 488n.

39 Avicenna, *Poème de la médecine*, trans. H. Jahier and A. Noureddine (Paris, 1956), verse 60, p. 15, and 211–12, p. 25.

40 A. Lindgren, 'The Wandering Womb and the Peripheral Penis: Gender and the Fertile Body in Late Medieval Infertility Treatises' (doctoral dissertation in History, University of California, Davis, 2005), p. 31.

41 F. Petrarch, *Remedies for Fortune Fair and Foul. Book II: Remedies for Adversity*, trans. C. H. Rawski (Bloomington, IN, 1991), vol. III, p. 244.

42 T. Elyot, *The Castel of helth* (London, 1534), p. 70.

43 L. Joubert, *Treatise on Laughter* [1579], trans. G. D. de Rocher (Tuscaloosa, AL, 1980), p. 125.

44 Paré, *Œuvres*, book 1, ch. XVIII, p. 33.

45 Quoted in P. Camporesi, *Juice of Life: The Symbolic and Magic Significance of Blood*, trans. R. R. Barr (New York, 1995), p. 41.

46 Joubert, *Treatise*, p. 125.

47 G. Della Porta, *La Physionomie humaine* (Rouen, 1655), p. 530.

48 M. J. van Lieburg, *The Disease of the Learned: A Chapter from the History of Melancholy and Hypochondria*, trans. D. M. Speer (Oss, 1990).

49 M. Bakhtin, *Rabelais and His World*, trans. H. Iswolsky (Bloomington, IN, 1984), pp. 101, 303–67.

50 A. Julian, *De l'art et jugement des songes, et visions nocturnes* (Lyon, 1557), unpaginated.

51 M. de Vulson, *The Court of Curiositie* (London, 1669), pp. 66–7, 191, 195. Similar claims appeared in other dream books, such as F. van Hove, *Oniropolus, or, Dreams Interpreter* (London, 1680), pp. 58, 71.

52 C. Sorel, *Les Récréations galantes* (Paris, 1672), pp. 242, 247–8, 260.

53 A useful snapshot of physiognomic ideas about the virtuous face from 1503 to 1694 is offered in M. Porter, *Windows of the Soul: Physiognomy in European Culture, 1470–1780* (Oxford, 2005), pp. 184–6.

54 P. Dormer, Earl of Chesterfield, *Miscellaneous Works* (Dublin, 1777), vol. II, p. 28. This untitled essay originally appeared in *Common Sense*, 37 (19 February 1737).

55 P. Dormer, Earl of Chesterfield, letters CLVIII (2 August 1748) and CCLXXV (16 March 1752), in *Letters Written by the Earl of Chesterfield to His Son* (Philadelphia, PA, 1876), p. 173, 487–8.

56 Chesterfield, letter CLXI (5 September 1748), ibid., p. 181.

57 Chesterfield, letter XCIX (8 August 1745), ibid., p. 96.

58 B. Platina, *On Right Pleasure and Good Health*, trans. M. E. Milham (Asheville, NC, 1999).

59 C. J. Berry, *The Idea of Luxury: A Conceptual and Historical Investigation* (Cambridge, 1994), pp. 113, 145–6, 164, 170–71.

60 J. E. Crowley, *The Invention of Comfort: Sensibilities and Design in Early Modern Britain and Early America* (Baltimore, MD, 2001), pp. 3–7, 69–73; Hoffmann, *From Gluttony*, p. 163.

61 R. Sassatelli, 'Consuming Ambivalence: Eighteenth-century Public Discourses on Consumption and Mandeville's Legacy', *Journal of Material Culture*, II/3 (1997), pp. 339–60.

62 L. Dacome, 'Useless and Pernicious Matter: Corpulence in Eighteenth-century England', in *Cultures of the Abdomen: Diet, Digestion and Fat in the Modern World*, ed. C. E. Forth and A. Carden-Coyne (New York, 2005), p. 199.

63 J. J. Winckelmann, *Reflections on the Imitation of Greek Works in Painting and Sculpture*, trans. E. Heyer and R. C. Norton (La Salle, IL, 1987), p. 7.

64 Quoted in W. Menninghaus, *Disgust: The Theory and History of a Strong Sensation*, trans. H. Eiland and J. Golb (Albany, NY, 2003), p. 71.

65 N. Elias, *The Civilizing Process* (Oxford, 2000), pp. 102, 138.

66 Menninghaus, *Disgust*, p. 92.

67 Winckelmann, *Reflections*, p. 7.

68 W. Hay, *Deformity: An Essay* (London, 1754), p. 35.

69 D. J. [Louis, chevalier de Jaucourt], 'Obésité', in *Encyclopédie, ou, Dictionnaire raisonné des sciences, des arts et des métiers* (Neufchâtel, 1751), vol. XI, p. 300.

70 [Louis, chevalier de] Jaucourt, 'Sparte ou Lacédémone', in *Encyclopédie, ou, Dictionnaire raisonné des sciences, des arts et des métiers*, ed. D. Diderot and J. le Rond D'Alembert (Lausanne, 1781), vol. XXXI, p. 548.

71 'CORPULENCE', in *Encyclopédie, ou, Dictionnaire raisonné des sciences, des arts et des métiers* (Neufchâtel, 1754), vol. IV, p. 269.

72 J.-J. Rousseau, 'Constitutional Project for Corsica [drafted 1765]', in *Political Writings*, trans. F. Watkins (Madison, WI, 1986), p. 317, translation modified. See also G. Garrard, *Rousseau's Counter-Enlightenment: A Republican Critique of the Philosophes* (Albany, NY, 2003), pp. 66–7.

73 G.-T.-F. Raynal, *Histoire philosophique et politique des établissements des Européens faits les deux Indes* (The Hague, 1774), vol. I, p. 84.

74 A. C. Vila, *Enlightenment and Pathology: Sensibility in the Literature and Medicine of Eighteenth-century France* (Baltimore, MD, 1998), pp. 81, 233.

75 C.-A. Vandermonde, *Essai sur la manière de perfectionner l'espèce humaine* (Paris, 1756), vol. I, pp. 67–8.

76 J.-A. Lelarge de Lignac, *De l'homme et de la femme, considérés physiquement dans l'état du mariage* (Lille, 1774), vol. I, pp. 56–61.

77 Ibid., pp. 56–61.

78 On the persistence of such imagery into the early twentieth century, see Christopher E. Forth, 'Spartan Mirages: Fat, Masculinity, and "Softness"', *Masculinidades y cambio social/Masculinities and Social Change*, I/3 (2012), pp. 240–66.

79 A. Le Camus, *Abdéker, ou, L'Art de conserver la beauté* (Paris, 1754), vol. I, pp. 57–9.

80 A. Le Camus, *Médecine de l'esprit* (Paris, 1753), vol. II, pp. 14–15.

81 Quoted in A. de Baecque, *The Body Politic: Corporeal Metaphor in Revolutionary France, 1770–1800*, trans. C. Mandell (Stanford, CA, 1997), pp. 1, 74, 137–42, 240–41.

8 Grease and Grace: The Disenchantment of Fat?

1 J. Bianchini, 'An Account of the Death of the Countess Cornelia Baudi [*sic*], of Cesena', *Annual Register*, VI (1763), p. 92. See also 'Lettre de M. le Marquis Scipion Maffei au R.P.D. Hippolite Bevilaqua', *Memoires pour l'histoire des Sciences et des beaux Arts* (November 1731), vol. IV, pp. 1922–38.

2 P.-A. Lair, *Essai sur les combustions humaines* (Paris, 1800), pp. 45, 54.

3 W. Wadd, *Cursory Remarks on Corpulence, or, Obesity Considered as a Disease*, 3rd edn (London, 1816), p. 53.

4 C. Merchant, *The Death of Nature: Women, Ecology, and the Scientific Revolution* (San Francisco, CA, 1980); T. Laqueur, *Making Sex: Body and Gender from the Greeks to Freud* (Cambridge, MA, 1990), pp. 154–5; V. von Hoffmann, *From Gluttony to Enlightenment: The World of Taste in Early Modern Europe* (Urbana, IL, 2016), p. 143; A. Rabinbach, *The Human Motor: Energy, Fatigue, and the Origins of Modernity* (Berkeley, CA, 1990), pp. 51–2; G. Vigarello, *The Metamorphoses*

of Fat: A History of Obesity, trans. C. J. Delogu (New York, 2013), pp. 127–8.

5 E. C. Spary, *Eating the Enlightenment: Food and the Sciences in Paris, 1670–1760* (Chicago, IL, 2012), p. 204n.

6 D. I. Levine, 'Managing American Bodies: Diet, Nutrition, and Obesity in America, 1840–1920' (doctoral dissertation in the History of Science, Harvard University, 2008).

7 A.K.K. Hansen, 'Fatness: Concepts and Perceptions in Western European Medicine, *c.* 1700–1900' (doctoral dissertation, University of Copenhagen, 2013), p. 94.

8 M. E. Chevreul, *Recherches chimiques sur les corps gras d'origine animale* (Paris, 1823).

9 G. Vigarello, *Concepts of Cleanliness: Changing Attitudes in France since the Middle Ages*, trans. J. Birrell (Cambridge, 1988), p. 62.

10 A. Vesalius, *On the Fabric of the Human Body*, book 1: *The Bones and Cartilages* [1543], trans. W. F. Richardson (San Francisco, CA, 1998), p. 374.

11 'Les Chirurgiens de la ville y allerent apres & en rapporterent des sacs plein de graisse d'hommes, qu'ils avoient tirez des corps'. H. van Haestens, *La Nouvelle Troye, ou, Memorable Histoire du siege d'Ostende* (Leiden, 1615), p. 147.

12 M. Brocard, *Lumières sur la sorcellerie et le satanisme* (Divonne-les-Bains, 2007), p. 29.

13 K. Stuart, *Defiled Trades and Social Outcasts: Honor and Ritual Pollution in Early Modern Germany* (Cambridge, MA 1999), pp. 157–8; G. Ferrari, 'Public Anatomy Lessons and the Carnival: The Anatomy Theatre of Bologna', *Past and Present*, CXVII (1987), p. 101; D. Cotugno, *A Treatise on the Nervous Sciatica, or, Nervous Hip Gout* (London, 1775), pp. 127–8.

14 P. Camporesi, *The Fear of Hell: Images of Damnation and Salvation in Early Modern Europe*, trans. L. Byatt (Cambridge, 1990), p. 129.

15 J. Hill, *A History of the Materia Medica* (London, 1751), pp. 875–6. This is what Shakespeare had in mind when he has the fat character, Falstaff, describe himself as 'a mountain of mummy'. See R. Sugg, *Mummies, Cannibals and Vampires: The History of Corpse Medicine from the Renaissance to the Victorians* (London, 2011), p. 38.

16 A. Cabanès, *Remèdes d'autrefois: Comment se soignaient nos pères* (Paris, 1905), pp. 51–2.

17 K. Thomas, *Religion and the Decline of Magic* (New York, 1997), pp. 189–90. Thus one Munich physician accused of practising white magic defended himself by showing that he only used 'natural means' that included 'herbs, roots, and human fat'. Stuart, *Defiled Trades*, p. 161.

18 R. K. Jain and D. Fukumura, 'Angiogenesis in Development, Disease, and Regeneration', in *Strategies in Regenerative Medicine*, ed. M. Santin (New York, 2009), p. 204.

19 R. Fludd, *Doctor Fludds Answer vnto M. Foster, or, The Sqve[e]sing of Parson Fosters Sponge* (London, 1631), member III, p. 13.

20 Paracelsus, *Hermetic and Alchemical Writings*, vol. 1: *Hermetic Chemistry*, ed. A. E. Waite (London, 1894), p. 169; J. J. Wecker, *Le Grand Thrésor, ou, Dispensaire et antidotaire tant general que special ou particulier des remedes*

servans à la santé du corps humain (Geneva, 1610), pp. 513–14; Stuart, *Defiled Trades*, p. 160; Sugg, *Mummies*.

21 M. Taussig, *Shamanism, Colonialism, and the Wild Man: A Study in Terror and Healing* (Chicago, IL, 1987), pp. 237–8; M. L. Price, *Consuming Passions: The Uses of Cannibalism in Late Medieval and Early Modern Europe* (London, 2003), p. 110.

22 A. Molinié-Fioravanti, 'Comparaisons transatlantiques', *L'Homme*, XXXII/122–4 (1992), pp. 165–83.

23 *Voyages de Labat*, cited in J.-N. Démeunier, *L'Esprit des usages et des coutumes des différens peuples* (Paris, 1786), vol. II, p. 132.

24 J. Bulwer, *Anthropometamorphosis: Man Transform'd, or, The Artificial Changeling Historically Presented . . .* (London, 1653), p. 356.

25 J.-B. Labat, *Nouveau voyage aux îles de l'Amérique* (The Hague, 1724), vol. II, p. 108.

26 F. T. Elworthy, *Horns of Honour and Other Studies in the By-ways of Archaeology* (London, 1900), p. 187. See also R. Kieckhefer, *Magic in the Middle Ages*, 2nd edn (Cambridge, 2014), p. 98.

27 Camporesi, *Fear of Hell*, p. 129.

28 Kieckhefer, *Magic in the Middle Ages*, pp. 195–6.

29 P. de Lancre, *Tableau de l'inconstance des mauvais anges et démons* (Paris, 1613), p. 106.

30 B. Jonson, 'The Masque of Queens' (1609), in *The Works of Ben Jonson* (London, 1692), p. 348.

31 T. Middleton, *The Witch* [1615] (Whitefish, MT, 2004), p. 12; see also Price, *Consuming Passions*, pp. 61–2.

32 C. F. Otten, ed., *A Lycanthropy Reader: Werewolves in Western Culture* (Syracuse, NY, 1986), p. 27.

33 C. Abry and A. Joisten, 'Trois notes sur les fondements du *complexe de Primarette*: Loups garous, cauchemars, prédations et graisses', *Le Monde alpin et rhodanien*, XXX/1–2 (2002), pp. 135–61.

34 C. Avramescu, *An Intellectual History of Cannibalism*, trans. A. I. Blythe (Princeton, NJ, 2009), p. 255.

35 J. Crétineau-Joly, *Histoire de la Vendée militaire*, 2nd edn (Paris, 1843), vol. II, p. 67. This story may have originated in the early nineteenth century, and is not verified by documentary evidence. A. Gérard, *La Vendée: 1789–1793* (Seyssel, 1992), p. 275.

36 Hill, *History*, p. 876.

37 A.-J.-B. Parent-Duchâtelet, *Hygiène publique, ou, Mémoires sur les questions les plus importantes de l'hygiène* (Paris, 1836), vol. II, pp. 22–4. This volume reprints Parent-Duchâtelet and J.-P. d'Arcet's *De l'influence et de l'assainissement des salles de dissection* (1831).

38 A.L.A. Fée, *Cours d'histoire naturelle pharmaceutique* (Paris, 1828), vol. I, p. 78.

39 Sugg, *Mummies*, pp. 245–55.

40 S. Connor, *The Book of Skin* (Ithaca, NY, 2004), p. 204.

41 M. de Navarre, *L'Heptameron* (Paris, 1560), p. 382.

42 M. Muret, *Traité des festins* (Paris, 1682), pp. 212–14.

43 On the animal imagery pertaining to gluttony, see Hoffmann, *From Gluttony*, pp. 50–55.

44 H. E. Hessus, *The Poetic Works of Helius Eobanus Hessus*, vol. 4: *Between Erasmus and Luther, 1518–1524*, trans. H. Vredeveld (Leiden, 2016), p. 99.

45 R. Cotgrave, *A Dictionarie of the French and English Tongues* (London, 1611), unpaginated.

46 H. Beaumont [Joseph Spence], *Crito, or, A Dialogue on Beauty*, 2nd edn (London, 1752), pp. 28–36, 48–9.

47 F. McNeill, *Poor Women in Shakespeare* (Cambridge, 2007), p. 45.

48 Jonson, 'Bartholomew Fair' (1614), in *Works*, p. 405.

49 K. M. Phillips and B. Reay, *Sex before Sexuality: A Premodern History* (Cambridge, 2011), p. 171.

50 S. Toulalan, '"Unripe" Bodies: Children, Sex and the Body in Early Modern England', in *Bodies, Sex and Desire from the Renaissance to the Present*, ed. S. Toulalan and K. Fisher (Basingstoke, 2011), pp. 131–50.

51 Cotgrave, *Dictionarie*, unpaginated. See also Gordon Williams, *A Dictionary of Sexual Language and Imagery in Shakespearean and Stuart Literature* (London, 1994), p. 972.

52 A. Oudin, *Curiositez françoises, pour supplément aux dictionnaires* (Rouen, 1656), pp. 198–9.

53 D. Erasmus, *On Good Manners for Boys* [*De civilitate morum puerilium*] [1530], in *Collected Works of Erasmus*, ed. J. K. Sowards (Toronto, 1985), vol. XXV, p. 283.

54 M. Stolberg, 'Sweat: Learned Concepts and Popular Perceptions, 1500–1800', in *Blood, Sweat and Tears: The Changing Concepts of Physiology from Antiquity into Early Modern Europe*, ed. M. Horstmanshoff, H. King and C. Zittel (Leiden, 2012), pp. 503–22.

55 Vigarello, *Concepts*, pp. 60, 73.

56 A. Corbin, *The Foul and the Fragrant: Odor and the French Social Imagination* (Cambridge, MA, 1986), p. 158.

57 Hansen, 'Fatness', pp. 85–9.

58 K. O. Kupperman, 'Fear of Hot Climates in the Anglo-American Colonial Experience', *William and Mary Quarterly*, XLI/2 (1984), p. 223.

59 N. Baker, *Plain Ugly: The Unattractive Body in Early Modern Culture* (Manchester, 2010), pp. 120–21.

60 T. Venner, *Via recta ad vitam longam* (London, 1638), p. 267.

61 K. M. Brown, *Foul Bodies: Cleanliness in Early America* (New Haven, CT, 2009), p. 59; L. Dacome, '"Useless and Pernicious Matter": Corpulence in Eighteenth-century Britain', in *Cultures of the Abdomen: Diet, Digestion and Fat in the Modern World*, ed. C. E. Forth and A. Carden-Coyne (New York, 2005), pp. 185–204; M. Stolberg, '"Abhorreas pinguedinem": Fat and Obesity in Early Modern Medicine (*c.* 1500–1750)', *Studies in History and Philosophy of Biological and Biomedical Sciences*, XLIII (2012), pp. 370–78.

62 Joubert, quoted in J. Gleyse, 'La Renaissance de la "fabrication du corps" par l'exercice physique au XVIe siècle: Discours, pratique, preservation d'un patrimoine, ou transgression d'un interdit?' *Annales canadiennes d'histoire/Canadian Journal of History*, XLI/1 (2011), pp. 1–33.

63 F. Bacon, *Sylva sylvarum, or, A Natural History*, in *The Works of Lord Bacon* (London, 1850), vol. I, p. 160.

64 G. Cheyne, *An Essay on Regimen* (London, 1740), p. 145.

65 Ibid., p. 46.

66 Ibid., p. 209. See also A. Guerrini, *Obesity and Depression in the Enlightenment: The Life and Times of George Cheyne* (Norman, OK, 1999).

67 A. Le Camus, *Abdéker, ou, L'Art de conserver la beauté* (Paris, 1754), vol. I, p. 59.

68 Corbin, *Foul and the Fragrant*, p. 62; J.-P. Albert, 'Le Légendaire médiéval des aromates: Longévité et immortalité', in *Le Corps humain: Nature, culture, surnaturel* (Montpellier: Actes du 110e Congrès International des Sociétés Savantes), CX (1985), pp. 37–48.

69 Brown, *Foul Bodies*, p. 33.

70 E. Cockayne, *Hubbub: Filth, Noise and Stench in England, 1600–1770* (New Haven, CT, 2007), p. 63.

71 M. Martin, *Selling Beauty: Cosmetics, Commerce, and French Society, 1750–1830* (Baltimore, MD, 2009), p. 16.

72 Cockayne, *Hubbub*, p. 60; V. Smith, *Clean: A History of Personal Hygiene and Purity* (Oxford, 2007), pp. 192–3. Fat was not the only material whose putrescent qualities could be quasi-alchemically transformed for the purposes of cleansing. In nineteenth-century London, dogshit was collected and sold as a substance called 'pure' for the purposes of cleaning and 'purifying' leather. J. Scanlan, 'In Deadly Time: The Lasting on of Waste in Mayhew's London', *Time and Society*, XVI/2–3 (2007), pp. 189–206.

73 P. Tarin, *Anthropotomie, ou, l'Art de disséquer* (Paris, 1750), vol. I, p. 7.

74 M. Fourcroy, 'GRAS DES CIMETIÈRES', *Encyclopédie méthodique*, vol. IV: *Chimie et métallurgie* (Paris, 1805), p. 480. This article reproduces Fourcroy's memorandum from the 1780s on the state of exhumed bodies.

75 T. Beddoes, *Observations on the Nature and Cure of Calculus, Sea Scurvy, Consumption, Catarrh, and Fever* (London, 1793), pp. 98–9. Francis Bacon had argued earlier that 'You may turn (almost) all Flesh into a Fatty Substance.' Bacon, *Sylva sylvarum, or, A naturall historie* (London, 1635), p. 167 (par. 678).

76 In 1801 the architect Pierre Giraud proposed introducing a process of vitrification that would turn such fatty substances into glass, thus achieving what Philippe Ariès calls 'a new form of the human body, rendered incorruptible and imperishable', that reflected new interest in preserving the bodies of departed loved ones. Ariès, *The Hour of Our Death*, trans. H. Weaver (New York, 1981), p. 514.

77 Corbin, *Foul and the Fragrant*, pp. 20–21.

78 Ibid., p. 21.

79 Vigarello, *Concepts*, p. 107.

80 C. Lucas, *An Essay on Waters* (London, 1756), pp. 211, 216.

81 W. Grant, *Observations on the Nature and Cure of Fevers*, 3rd edn (London, 1779), vol. I, p. 264.

82 D'Aumont, 'Diarrhée', in *Encyclopédie, ou, Dictionnaire raisonné des sciences, des arts et des métiers*, ed. D. Diderot and J. le Rond D'Alembert (Lausanne, 1782), vol. X, p. 912.

83 Corbin, *Foul and the Fragrant*, p. 144.

84 Le Camus, *Abdéker*, p. 57.

85 M. Flemyng, *A Discourse on the Nature, Causes, and Cure of Corpulency* (London, 1760), pp. 8, 20–22; see also Levine, 'Managing American Bodies', pp. 46–57.

86 Wadd, *Cursory Remarks*, p. 186.

87 J. L. and J. Comaroff, *Of Revelation and Revolution: The Dialectics of Modernity on a South African Frontier*, vol. 2 (Chicago, IL, 1997), pp. 189, 225, 336.

88 Alpini, *Médecine*, pp. 294–5. See also W. Tullett, 'Grease and Sweat: Race and Smell in Eighteenth-century English Culture', *Cultural and Social History*, XIII/3 (2016), pp. 1–16.

89 G. Shahani, 'Food, Filth and the Foreign: Disgust in the Seventeenth-century Travelogue', in *Disgust in Early Modern English literature*, ed. N. K. Eschenbaum and B. Correll (Farnham, 2016), p. 107.

90 A. S. Smith, 'Living off the Fat of the Land: Resource Exploitation at Kasteelberg, Southwestern Cape, South Africa', *Nyame akuma*, XXXVI (1991), pp. 20–23; T. Burke, *Lifebuoy Men and Lux Women: Commodification, Consumption, and Cleanliness in Modern Zimbabwe* (Durham, NC, 1996), pp. 23–34.

91 R. Ouellet, 'Sauvages d'Amérique et discours hétérologique', *Études littéraires*, XXII/2 (1989), pp. 115–16.

92 Shahani, 'Food, Filth and the Foreign', p. 115.

93 P. Kolb, *The Present State of the Cape of Good-Hope*, trans. G. Medley (London, 1731), pp. 49–50, 52.

94 G. E. Lessing, 'Laocoön: An Essay on the Limits of Painting and Poetry' [1766], in *Classic and Romantic German Aesthetics*, ed. J. M. Bernstein (Cambridge, 2003), p. 125.

95 Corbin, *Foul and the Fragrant*, p. 85.

96 A. Richerand, *Nouveaux élémens de physiologie* (Paris, 1807), vol. II, pp. 73–5.

97 Quoted in J. Smith and H. Smith, *Rejected Addresses, or, The New Theatrum Poetarum* [1812] (London, 1873), p. 13n.

98 T. Cooke, *A Practical and Familiar View of the Science of Physiognomy* (London, 1819), p. 231.

99 G. Mars and V. Mars, 'Fat in the Victorian Kitchen: A Medium for Cooking, Control, Deviance and Crime', in Harlan, *The Fat of the Land: Proceedings of the Oxford Symposium on Food and Cookery 2002*, ed. H. Walker, (Bristol, 2003), pp. 216-36.

100 A Lady, *The Home Book, or, Young Housekeeper's Assistant* (London, 1829), pp. 18–19.

101 The slang terms for a 'cheat' included *graisseur* and *suiffard* (the latter also denoting an elegantly dressed individual). L. Sainéan, *Le Langage parisien au XIXe siècle* (Paris, 1920), pp. 164, 369, 419, 521.

102 A. McClintock, *Imperial Leather: Race, Gender and Sexuality in the Colonial Contest* (London, 1995), pp. 207–31.

103 'Living Grease – Fat-paunched Devotees at the Shrine of Terpsichore – Adipose Tissue Ambling in a Ball Room', *St Louis Globe-Democrat* (21 January 1877), p. 7.

104 W. A. Alcott, *Vegetable Diet: As Sanctioned by Medical Men and by Experience in All Ages*, 2nd edn (New York, 1859), p. 247.

105 'On the Propensity of Several Nations to Greasy Meats and Drinks',
     The Literary Magazine, and American Register, II/7 (1804), p. 47.
106 C. Nemeroff and P. Rozin, '"You are What You Eat": Applying the
     Demand-free "Impressions" Technique to an Unacknowledged Belief',
     Ethos, XVII/1 (1989), pp. 50–69.

9 Savage Desires: 'Primitive' Fat and 'Civilized' Slenderness

 1 E. Dodwell, *A Classical and Topographical Tour through Greece, during
    the Years 1801, 1805, and 1806* (London, 1819), vol. II, p. 24.
 2 For an example of this claim, see C. Fellows, *A Journal Written during
    an Excursion in Asia Minor* (London, 1839), p. 2.
 3 C. Henricy, *Les Mœurs et costumes des peuples de l'Afrique et de l'Océanie*
    (Paris, 1847), p. 62.
 4 P. Alpini, *De medicina Aegyptiorum*, (Venice, 1591); Alpini, *La Médecine
    des Égyptiens*, [1581–4], trans. R. de Fenoy (Cairo, 1980), p. 294.
 5 See, for example, S. L. Gilman, *Fat Boys: A Thin Book* (Lincoln, NE,
    2004); H. Schwartz, *Never Satisfied: A Cultural History of Diets, Fantasies
    and Fat* (New York, 1986); G. Vigarello, *The Metamorphoses of Fat:
    A History of Obesity*, trans. C. J. Delogu (New York, 2013); A. E. Farrell,
    Fat Shame: Stigma and the Fat Body in American Culture (New York,
    2011); J. L. Huff, 'Corporeal Economies: Work and Waste in
    Nineteenth-century Constructions of Alimentation', in *Cultures of the
    Abdomen: Diet, Digestion and Fat in the Modern World*, ed. C. E. Forth
    and A. Carden-Coyne (New York, 2005), pp. 31–49; Huff, 'A "Horror
    of Corpulence": Interrogating Bantingism and Mid-nineteenth Century
    Fat-Phobia', in *Bodies Out of Bounds*, ed. J. E. Braziel and K. LeBesco
    (Berkeley, CA, 2001), pp. 39–59; J. Coveney, *Food, Morals and Meaning:
    The Pleasure and Anxiety of Eating* (New York, 2000); N. Mackert,
    'Feeding Productive Bodies: Calories, Nutritional Values and Ability
    in Progressive Era U.S.', in *Histories of Productivity: Genealogical
    Perspectives on the Body and Modern Economy*, ed. P.-P. Bänziger and
    M. Suter (London, 2016), pp. 117–35.
 6 J. A. Brillat-Savarin, *Physiologie du goût, ou méditations de gastronomie
    transcendante* [1825] (Paris, 1842), p. 228.
 7 C. Laes, 'Writing the History of Fatness and Thinness in Graeco-Roman
    Antiquity', *Medicina nei secoli: Arte e scienza*, XXVIII/2 (2016), p. 592.
 8 P. Roussel, *Système physique et morale de la femme* (Paris, 1775), pp. 120–21.
 9 *Le Miroir des belles femmes, ou, L'Art de relever par les grâces les charmes de
    la beauté* (Paris, 1800), p. 4.
10 H. Streets, *Martial Races: The Military, Race and Masculinity in British
    Imperial Culture, 1857–1914* (Manchester, 2004), pp. 94–5, 156–85. See also
    M. Sinha, *Colonial Masculinity: The 'Manly Englishman' and the
    'Effeminate Bengali' in the Late Nineteenth Century* (Manchester, 1995).
11 J. Johnson, *The Influence of Tropical Climates on European Constitutions*,
    2nd edn (London, 1818), pp. 391–2.
12 J. Ogilvie, ed., *The Imperial Dictionary, English, Technological and
    Scientific* (Glasgow, 1859), vol. I, p. 1000.
13 G. Bacon, 'Two Indian Days', *The Ludgate*, VIII (1899), p. 437.

14 H. Craik, *Impressions of India* (London, 1908), p. 233.

15 S. L. Blanchard, *Yesterday and To-day in India* (London, 1867), p. 89.

16 E. Hull, quoted in E. M. Collingham, *Imperial Bodies: The Physical Experience of the Raj, c. 1800–1947* (Cambridge, 2001), p. 147.

17 A. Allardyce, *The City of Sunshine: A Novel* (Edinburgh, 1877), vol. I, p. 246.

18 R. Kipling, *From Sea to Sea: Letters of Travel* (New York, 1899), vol. II, pp. 223–7, 249.

19 A. Burnes, 'Lieutenant Burnes on Sinde', *Calcutta Monthly Journal and General Register*, II (1836), p. 166.

20 B. M. Norman, *Rambles by Land and Water, or, Notes of Travel in Cuba and Mexico* (New York, 1845), p. 157.

21 J. L. Kipling, *Beast and Man in India: A Popular Sketch of Indian Animals in Their Relations with the People* (London, 1891), p. 234.

22 Quoted in K. M. Phillips, *Before Orientalism: Asian Peoples and Cultures in European Travel Writing, 1245–1510* (Philadelphia, PA, 2014), p. 185.

23 Quoted in D. Waines, *The Odyssey of Ibn Battuta: Uncommon Tales of a Medieval Adventurer* (London, 2010), p. 174.

24 See J.-B.-L. Durand, *Voyage au Sénégal fait dans les années 1785 et 1786* (Paris, 1807), p. 89.

25 M. Park, *Travels to the Interior Districts of Africa* (London, 1800), p. 181.

26 R. Caillié, *Journal d'un voyage à Temboctou et à Jenné, dans l'Afrique centrale* (Paris, 1830), vol. I, pp. 99–100. For a description of similar developments in Tunisia, see H. Salamon and E. Juhasz, '"Goddesses of Flesh and Metal": Fattening Jewish Brides in Tunisia', *Journal of Middle East Women's Studies*, VII/1 (2011), pp. 1–38.

27 S. L. Gilman, 'Black Bodies, White Bodies: Toward an Iconography of Female Sexuality in Late Nineteenth-century Art, Medicine, and Literature', *Critical Inquiry*, XII (1985), pp. 204–42; and A. Fausto-Sterling, 'Gender, Race, and Nation: The Comparative Anatomy of "Hottentot" Women in Europe, 1815–1817', in *Deviant Bodies: Critical Perspectives on Difference in Science and Popular Culture*, ed. J. Urla and J. Terry (Bloomington, IN, 1995), pp. 19–48.

28 C. C. Crais and P. Scully, *Sarah Baartman and the Hottentot Venus* (Princeton, NJ, 2008), p. 93.

29 W. Wadd, *Cursory Remarks on Corpulence, or, Obesity Considered as a Disease*, 3rd edn (London, 1816), p. 56.

30 W. M. Reddy, *The Navigation of Feeling: A Framework for the History of Emotions* (Cambridge, 2001), p. 223.

31 R. Chambers, *The Book of Days: A Miscellany of Popular Antiquities* (London, 1864), vol. II, p. 621.

32 C. J. Andersson, *Lake Ngami, or, Explorations and Discoveries during Four Years' Wanderings in the Wilds of South Western Africa* (London, 1857), pp. 146–7.

33 A. Burdo, *Niger et Bénué: Voyage dans l'Afrique centrale* (Paris, 1880), pp. 236–7, 274–5.

34 H. Beaumont [Joseph Spence], *Crito; or, A Dialogue on Beauty*, 2nd edn (London, 1752), p. 35.

35 For instance, see Rev. Dr J. L. Krapf, 'East-Africa Mission', *Church Missionary Record*, XVII (1846), p. 6.

36 Quoted in M. M. Smith, *How Race Is Made: Slavery, Segregation, and the Senses* (Chapel Hill, NC, 2006), p. 44.

37 J. Carne, *Lives of Eminent Missionaries* (London, 1833), vol. II, p. 122.

38 T. L. Nichols, *Woman, of All Ages and Nations* (New York, 1849), p. 16.

39 S. Baring-Gould, *The Mystery of Suffering* (London, 1877), p. 50.

40 G. F. Angas, *Savage Life and Scenes in Australia and New Zealand*, 2nd edn (London, 1847), vol. I, p. 73.

41 G. Bennett, *Wanderings in New South Wales, Batavia, Pedir Coast, Singapore, and China* (London, 1834), vol. I, p. 295; G. H. Haydon, *Five Years' Experience in Australia Felix* (London, 1846), p. III.

42 Brillat-Savarin, *Physiologie du goût*, p. 223.

43 Ibid., p. 9.

44 'The Physician. – No. XII. On Corpulence', *New Monthly Magazine*, X (1824), p. 181.

45 H. Giles, *Lectures and Essays* (Boston, MA, 1850), vol. I, p. 2.

46 H. de Balzac, *Théorie de la démarche* (Paris, 1938), p. 632; L. Huart, *Physiologie du flâneur*, part 2 (Paris, 1841), pp. 12–13.

47 'Editors Table: A Talk with Some of Our Correspondents', *The Knickerbocker*, XI/4 (1838), pp. 389–90.

48 P** de Saint-Frajou, *Obésité, ou, Excès d'embonpoint: Moyens propres à la prévenir et à la combattre* (Paris, 1834), p. 9.

49 T. A. James, *Count Cagliostro, or, The Charlatan*, (London, 1838), vol. I, p. 3.

50 Quoted in 'Progress of the Human Species', *Hogg's Weekly Instructor*, L (1849), pp. 33–4.

51 A. Kingsford, *Health, Beauty, and the Toilet: Letters to Ladies from a Lady Doctor* (London, 1886), p. 9.

52 B. Wilson, *The Making of Victorian Values: Decency and Dissent in Britain: 1789–1837* (London, 2007), pp. 25–6.

53 'The corpulence (obesity) and "big bellies" (dyspepsia) of which many of them boast as the indices of health, are the very reverse, being the surest proof of the most afflicting maladies that human flesh is heir to . . . A liberal use of beefsteaks, beer, and exercise may, no doubt, in many cases, successfully counteract for a time the influence of putrid effluvia arising from shops and slaughter-houses; but daily experience proves, in every corner of the capital, that these form no infallible cure.' Unsigned, 'Sanitary Improvement in the Slaughter-house, Larder, and Butcher's Shop', *The Farmer's Magazine*, XLIII/4 (October 1855), p. 333. This phenomenon was observed in France as well. See A. Maccary, *Traité sur la polysarcie* (Paris, 1811), p. 77.

54 C. Lawrence, 'Medical Minds, Surgical Bodies: Corporeality and the Doctors', in *Science Incarnate: Historical Embodiments of Natural Knowledge*, ed. C. Lawrence and S. Shapin (Chicago, IL, 1998), p. 194.

55 J. L. Huff, 'Freaklore: The Dissemination, Fragmentation, and Reinvention of the Legend of Daniel Lambert, King of Fat Men',

in *Victorian Freaks: The Social Context of Freakery in Britain*, ed. M. Tromp (Columbus, OH, 2008), pp. 37–59; M. Kennedy, '"Poor Hoo Loo": Sentiment, Stoicism, and the Grotesque in British Imperial Medicine', in *Victorian Freaks*, pp. 79–113.

56 W. J. Baldwin, 'On the Debasement of National Character by Commerce', *The Tradesman, or, Commercial Magazine*, X/4 (April 1813), p. 294.

57 Collingham, *Imperial Bodies*.

58 J. Duke, *How to Get Thin, or Banting in India*, 2nd edn (Calcutta, 1870), pp. 7–8, 32.

59 A Modern Pythagorean, 'Colonel O'Shaughnessy in India', *Blackwood's Edinburgh Magazine*, XXI (1827), pp. 653–4.

60 An Old Resident, *Real Life in India* (London, 1847), p. 149.

61 T. K. Chambers, *Corpulence, or, Excess of Fat in the Human Body* (London, 1850), p. 140.

62 W. L. MacGregor, *Practical Observations on the Principal Diseases Affecting the Health of the European and Native Soldiers in the North-western Provinces of India* (Calcutta, 1843), p. 200.

63 A. Hervey, *Ten Years in India, or, The Life of a Young Officer* (London, 1850), vol. I, p. 75.

64 Hydaspes, *The Truth about the Indian Army and Its Officers* (London, 1861), p. 42.

65 J. Duke, *Banting in India: With Some Remarks on Diet and Things in General*, 3rd edn (Calcutta, 1885), p. 11.

66 G. Vigarello, *Histoire de la beauté: Le corps et l'art d'embellir de la Renaissance à nos jours* (Paris, 2004); P. N. Stearns, *Fat History: Bodies and Beauty in the Modern West* (New York, 1997), p. 158.

67 Wadd, *Cursory Remarks*, pp. 45, 56.

68 R. Verity, *Changes Produced in the Nervous System by Civilization* (London, 1837), pp. 58–9.

69 É. Celnart, *Manuel des dames, ou, L'Art de l'élégance*, 2nd edn (Paris, 1833), p. 125.

70 [Anonymous] *The Art of Beauty, or, The Best Methods of Improving and Preserving the Shape, Carriage, and Complexion* (London, 1825), p. 78.

71 A. Debay, *Hygiène et perfectionnement de la beauté humaine*, 4th edn (Paris, 1864), pp. 180–81.

72 Brillat-Savarin, *Physiologie du goût*, p. 217.

73 J. J. Brumberg, *The Body Project: An Intimate History of American Girls* (New York, 1997), pp. xx–xxi.

74 A.-M. Bureaud-Riofrey, *Éducation physique des jeunes filles, ou, Hygiène de la femme avant le mariage* (Paris, 1835), p. 128.

75 See 'A Short Chapter on Bustles', *Irish Penny Journal*, I/18 (1840), pp. 140–41; and G. A. Sala, 'Lady Chesterfield's Letters to Her Daughter', *The Welcome Guest*, I/7 (1860), p. 134.

76 E. O'Connor, *Raw Materials: Producing Pathology in Victorian Culture* (Durham, NC, 2000), pp. 153–4; N. Durbach, *Spectacle of Deformity: Freak Shows and Modern British Culture* (Berkeley, CA, 2010).

77 S. de Lorraine, *Les Secrets de la beauté du visage et du corps* (Paris, 1855), pp. 31, 37.

78 Kingsford, *Health, Beauty, and the Toilet*, p. 9.

79 A. H. de Hell, 'Les Arméniennes à Constantinople', *La Revue de l'Orient: Bulletin de la Société Orientale*, VII (1845), p. 138.

80 P. Belouino, *La Femme: Physiologie, histoire, morale* [1845], 2nd edn (Paris, 1853), p. 217.

81 A.-F.-F. Roselly de Lorgues, *La Croix dans les deux mondes, ou, La Clef de la connaissance*, 4th edn (Paris, 1847), pp. 94–5.

82 Henricy, *Mœurs et costumes*, p. 82.

83 W. Banting, *Letter on Corpulence*, 3rd edn (London, 1864), p. 43.

84 E. Monin, *Hygiène de la beauté* (Paris, 1890), pp. 16–20.

85 E. A. Fletcher, *The Woman Beautiful* (New York, 1901), p. 409.

86 Schwartz, *Never Satisfied*, p. 124.

87 K. Vester, 'Regime Change: Gender, Class, and the Invention of Dieting in Post-Bellum America', *Journal of Social History*, XLIV/1 (2010), pp. 39–70.

88 W. I. Miller, *The Anatomy of Disgust*, (Cambridge, MA, 1997) p. 54.

89 B. Dijkstra, *Idols of Perversity: Fantasies of Feminine Evil in Fin-de-Siècle Culture* (Oxford, 1986), pp. 83–96.

90 J. R. Goodall, *Performance and Evolution in the Age of Darwin* (London, 2002), p. 191.

91 A. Macaulay, 'Judging the Bodies in Ballet', *New York Times*, 3 December 2010, www.nytimes.com.

92 A. K. Silver, *Victorian Literature and the Anorexic Body* (Cambridge, 2004), p. 27.

93 A. Parent-Duchâtelet, *La prostitution dans la ville de Paris* (1836; Paris, 1857), vol. I, pp. 186–7. For observations about Algerian prostitutes, see C.-A. Rozet, *Voyage dans la régence d'Alger: ou, Description du pays occupé par l'armée française* (Paris, 1833), vol. II, p. 26; and C. Leynadier and M. Clausel, *Histoire de l'Algérie française* (Paris, 1848), vol. III, p. 148.

94 C. Lombroso and W. Ferrero, *The Female Offender* (New York, 1909), pp. 113–14.

95 H. T. Finck, *Primitive Love and Love-Stories* (New York, 1899). Subsequent references to this text are cited in parentheses.

96 Ibid., p. 284.

97 Ibid., p. 370.

98 Ibid., p. 154.

99 Ibid., p. 418.

100 Ibid., p. 61.

101 Ibid., p. 281.

102 Duke, *Banting in India*, p. 55.

103 R. White, 'The Women of Brassempouy: A Century of Research and Interpretation', *Journal of Archaeological Method and Theory*, XIII/4 (2006), pp. 262–3, 277–8.

104 É. Piette, 'La Station de Brassempouy et les statuettes humaines de la periode glyptique', *L'Anthropologie*, VI (1895), pp. 150–51.

105 M. Beck, 'Female Figurines in the European Upper Paleolithic', in *Reading the Body: Representations and Remains in the Archaeological Record*, ed. A. E. Rautman (Philadelphia, PA, 2000), pp. 202–5.

106 M. A. von Andel, 'Adeps Hominis: A Relic of Prehistoric Therapy', *American Journal of Pharmacy*, XCIV (1922), pp. 665–71; C.J.S. Thompson, 'Some Curiosities of Ancient Materia Medica', *The Western Druggist*,

xv/4 (1893), pp. 144–7; Anonymous, 'From the Editor's Notebook', *The Medical Standard*, xxvii/2 (1904), pp. 89–90.

10 Bodily Utopianism: Modern Dreams of Transcendence

1 A. Huxley, *Brave New World* (London, 2004), p. 177.
2 K. Bergdolt, *Wellbeing: A Cultural History of Healthy Living*, trans. J. Dewhurst (Cambridge, 2008), p. 220.
3 J. Csergo, 'Quand l'obésité des gourmands devient une maladie de civilisation: Le discours médicale, 1850–1930', in *Trop gros? L'obésité et ses représentations*, ed. J. Csergo (Paris, 2009), p. 27.
4 A. E. Farrell, *Fat Shame: Stigma and the Fat Body in American Culture* (New York, 2011), pp. 3–4.
5 H. Addison, *Hollywood and the Rise of Physical Culture* (New York, 2003).
6 G. Vigarello, *The Metamorphoses of Fat: A History of Obesity*, trans. C. J. Delogu (New York, 2013), p. 166.
7 Ibid., p. 148.
8 In America and elsewhere, dieting culture became popular partly because it offered 'a moral counterweight to growing consumer indulgence'. P. N. Stearns, *Fat History: Bodies and Beauty in the Modern West* (New York, 1997), p. 60.
9 J. Guthman, *Weighing In: Obesity, Food Justice, and the Limits of Capitalism* (Berkeley, CA, 2011), p. 183.
10 R. Levitas, *The Concept of Utopia*, 2nd edn (Oxford, 2011), p. 209.
11 R. Levitas, *Utopia as Method: The Imaginary Reconstitution of Society* (Basingstoke, 2013), p. 5.
12 M. A. Vásquez, *More Than Belief: A Materialist Theory of Religion* (New York, 2011), p. 10; see also p. 116.
13 C. McGinn, *The Meaning of Disgust* (Oxford, 2011), p. 181; C. Fischler, 'Pensée magique et utopie dans la science', in *Pensée magique et alimentation aujourd'hui*, ed. C. Fischler (Paris, 1996), pp. 1–17.
14 L. Sfez, *La Santé parfait: Critique d'une nouvelle utopie* (Paris, 1995).
15 N. Le Dévédec, *La Société de l'amélioration: La perfectibilité humaine des Lumières au transhumanisme* (Montreal, 2015); C. Lafontaine, *La Société postmortelle: La mort, l'individu et le lien social à l'ère des technosciences* (Paris, 2008).
16 A. Byers and P. Stapleton, 'Introduction', in *Biopolitics and Utopia: An Interdisciplinary Reader*, ed. P. Stapleton and A. Byers (New York, 2015), p. 5.
17 A. Rabinbach, *The Human Motor: Energy, Fatigue, and the Origins of Modernity* (Berkeley, CA, 1990), p. 44.
18 J. Hoberman, *Mortal Engines: The Science of Performance and the Dehumanization of Sport* (New York, 1992).
19 Here the 'powerful and protean world of work, production, and performance is set against the decrescent order of fatigue, exhaustion, and decline'. Rabinbach, *Human Motor*, p. 63; see also J. L. Huff, 'Corporeal Economies: Work and Waste in Nineteenth-century Constructions of Alimentation', in *Cultures of the Abdomen: Diet,*

Digestion and Fat in the Modern World, ed. C. E. Forth and
A. Carden-Coyne (New York, 2005).

20 Quoted in D. Lupton, *Food, the Body and the Self* (London, 1996), p. 7.

21 R. Sassatelli, *Fitness Culture: Gyms and the Commercialisation
of Discipline and Fun* (London, 2010), p. 145.

22 D. Ø. Endsjø, *Greek Resurrection Beliefs and the Success of Christianity*
(London, 2009), p. 22.

23 T. Inch, *Inch on Fitness* (London, 1923), p. 52.

24 C. Cogdell, *Eugenic Design: Streamlining America in the 1930s*
(Philadelphia, PA, 2004).

25 Z. Bauman, *Liquid Modernity* (Cambridge, 2000), p. 128.

26 S. S. Friedman, 'Periodizing Modernism: Postcolonial Modernities and
the Space/Time Borders of Modernist Studies', *Modernism/Modernity*,
XIII/3 (2006), p. 433.

27 R. Griffin, *Modernism and Fascism: The Sense of a Beginning under
Mussolini and Hitler* (Basingstoke, 2007), p. 39.

28 T. Clark, 'The "New Man's" Body: A Motif in Early Soviet Culture', in
*Art of the Soviets: Painting, Sculpture and Architecture in a One-party State,
1917–1992*, ed. M. C. Bown and B. Taylor (Manchester, 1993), pp. 33–50;
E. Gentile, 'L'"Homme nouveau" du fascisme: Réflexions sur une
expérience de révolution anthropologique', in *L'Homme nouveau dans
l'Europe fasciste (1922–1945): Entre dictature et totalitarisme*, ed. M.-A.
Matard-Bonucci and P. Milza (Paris, 2004), pp. 35–63.

29 L. Nead, *Victorian Babylon: People, Streets and Images in Nineteenth-
century London* (New Haven, CT, 2000), p. 8.

30 J. Lears, *Rebirth of a Nation: The Making of Modern America, 1877–1920*
(New York, 2009), p. 1

31 T. J. Jackson Lears, 'American Advertising and the Reconstruction of
the Body, 1880–1930', in *Fitness in American Culture: Images of Health,
Sport, and the Body, 1830–1940*, ed. K. Grover (Amherst, MA, 1989), p. 63.

32 Griffin, *Modernism*, p. 141.

33 A. Carden-Coyne, *Reconstructing the Body: Classicism, Modernism, and
the First World War* (Oxford, 2009), pp. 4, 25.

34 Friedman, 'Periodizing Modernism', p. 432.

35 H. B. Segal, *Body Ascendant: Modernism and the Physical Imperative*
(Baltimore, MD, 1998), p. 2.

36 Cogdell, *Eugenic Design*.

37 Carden-Coyne, *Reconstructing*, p. 124.

38 Ibid., pp. 35, 249.

39 Ibid., p. 25.

40 Ibid., p. 155.

41 Ibid., p. 256.

42 Addison, *Hollywood*, pp. 10–12.

43 Sylvia of Hollywood, *Streamline Your Figure* (New York, 1939), p. 31.

44 Carden-Coyne, *Reconstructing*, p. 256.

45 A. Levinson, quoted in I. Karthas, *When Ballet Became French: Modern
Ballet and the Cultural Politics of France, 1909–1939* (Montreal, 2015), p. 201.

46 K. J. Parkin, *Food Is Love: Advertising and Gender Roles in Modern
America* (Philadelphia, PA, 2007), p. 174.

47 M. Cowan, *Cult of the Will: Nervousness and German Modernity* (University Park, PA, 2008), p. 113.

48 Quoted in A. Denning, *Skiing into Modernity: A Cultural and Environmental History* (Berkeley, CA, 2015), p. 76.

49 L. Heywood, *Dedication to Hunger: The Anorexic Aesthetic in Modern Culture* (Berkeley, CA, 1996), p. 68.

50 Farrell, *Fat Shame*.

51 H. T. Finck, *Girth Control: For Womanly Beauty, Manly Strength, Health, and a Long Life for Everybody* (New York, 1923), pp. 2–4. See also Farrell, *Fat Shame*, pp. 59–68.

52 F. Fanon, *Les Damnés de la terre* (1961; Paris, 2002), p. 45.

53 G. Hébert, *Muscle et beauté plastique: L'éducation physique féminine* (Paris, 1921), p. 114.

54 F. Heckel, *Maigrir: Pourquoi? comment?* (Paris, 1930), p. 28.

55 P. Sloterdijk, *You Must Change Your Life: On Anthropotechnics*, trans. W. Hoban (Cambridge, 2013), pp. 12, 13.

56 H. Schwartz, *Never Satisfied: A Cultural History of Diets, Fantasies and Fat* (New York, 1986), p. 64.

57 Ibid., p. 81.

58 Cogdell, *Eugenic Design*; see also E. N. Jensen, *Body by Weimar: Athletes, Gender, and German Modernity* (Oxford, 2010), and J. Tumblety, *Remaking the Male Body: Masculinity and the Uses of Physical Culture in Interwar and Vichy France* (Oxford, 2012).

59 Cowan, *Cult of the Will*, p. 4.

60 M. Cowan, 'Imagining the Nation through the Energetic Body: The "Royal Jump"', in *Leibhaftige Moderne: Körper in Kunst und Massenmedien, 1918 bis 1933*, ed. M. Cowan and K. M. Sicks (Bielefeld, 2005), p. 71.

61 L. H. Gulick, *The Efficient Life* (New York, 1907), p. 36.

62 R. S. Copeland, *Over Weight? Guard Your Health: Among Adults the Overweights Have a Greater Prospect of Early Death Than Have the Underweights* (New York, 1922), p. 11.

63 P. H. Nystrom, *Economics of Retailing*, 3rd edn (New York, 1930), vol. II, p. 332.

64 E. B. Lowry, *The Woman of Forty* (Chicago, IL, 1920), p. 44; Copeland, *Over Weight?*, p. 11.

65 H.-J. Stiker, *A History of Disability*, trans. W. Sayers (Ann Arbor, MI, 1997), p. 10. See also A. Herndon, 'Disparate but Disabled: Fat Embodiment and Disability Studies', *NWSA Journal*, XIV/3 (2002), pp. 120–37.

66 Sloterdijk, *You Must Change*, p. 57.

67 N. Mackert, 'Feeding Productive Bodies: Calories, Nutritional Values and Ability in Progressive Era U.S.', in *Histories of Productivity: Genealogical Perspectives on the Body and Modern Economy*, ed. P.-P. Bänziger and M. Suter (London, 2016), pp. 117–135.

68 D. I. Levine, 'Managing American Bodies: Diet, Nutrition, and Obesity in America, 1840–1920' (doctoral dissertation in the History of Science, Harvard University, 2008), pp. 149–50.

69 J. Coveney, *Food, Morals and Meaning: The Pleasure and Anxiety of Eating*, 2nd edn (London, 2006), p. 62. The word 'spiritual' as it is used here 'does

not necessarily equate with "theological" but refers to the means by which individuals are required to construct themselves with a "correct" concern for the "proper" way of behaving in relation to eating': Coveney, *Food, Morals and Meaning*, p. xvi.

70 E. A. Fletcher, *The Woman Beautiful* (New York, 1901), p. 411.

71 W. M. Beardshear, 'Presidential Address: The Three H's in Education', *National Educational Association: Journal of Proceedings and Addresses of the Forty-first Annual Meeting* (Chicago, IL, 1902), pp. 55–65.

72 R. M. Griffith, *Born Again Bodies: Flesh and Spirit in American Christianity* (Berkeley, CA, 2004), p. 4.

73 Griffith, *Born*, p. 16. This is why Sloterdijk sees in early twentieth-century sportive culture the 'de-spiritualization of asceticisms'. Sloterdijk, *You Must Change*, p. 64.

74 T. Inch, *Inch on Fitness* (London, 1923), pp. 26, 29.

75 Griffith, *Born*, pp. 27–39.

76 Ad for Marienbad Reduction Pills, *The Illustrated American*, X/113 (16 April 1892), unpaginated.

77 M. B. Stack, *Building the Body Beautiful: The Bagot Stack Stretch-and-Swing System* (London, 1934), p. 7; see Cowan, *Cult of the Will*, p. 75, and J. J. Matthews, 'They Had Such a Lot of Fun: The Women's League of Health and Beauty between the Wars', *History Workshop Journal*, XXX (1990), pp. 22–54.

78 Gulick, *Efficient*, p. 35.

79 R. L. Alsaker, *Eating for Health and Efficiency* (New York, 1921), p. 223.

80 W. Johnston, *The Fun of Being a Fat Man* (Boston, MA, 1922), pp. 28, 35.

81 C. E. Forth, '"Nobody Loves a Fat Man": Masculinity and Food in Film Noir', *Men and Masculinities*, XVI/4 (2013), pp. 387–406; A. Bilton, *Silent Film Comedy and American Culture* (London, 2013), pp. 111–35.

82 A. Summerville, *Why Be Fat? Rules for Weight-reduction and the Preservation of Youth and Health* (New York, 1916), p. 38.

83 L. Williams, *Obesity* (London, 1926), p. 3.

84 H. Béraud, *Le Martyre de l'obèse* (Paris, 1922), p. 10.

85 S. L. Katzoff, *Timely Truths on Human Health* (Bridgeport, CT, 1921), p. 83.

86 A. H. Douthwaite, 'On the Control of Obesity', *British Medical Journal*, 3824 (1934), p. 699.

87 H. Bruch and G. Touraine, 'Obesity in Childhood: v. The Family Frame of Obese Children', *Psychosomatic Medicine*, II/2 (1940), pp. 203–4.

88 S. Wickware, 'Psychosomatic Medicine: Upset Emotions Can Cause Illness, Obesity, Even Accidents', *Life*, XVIII/8 (19 February 1945), p. 52; see also S. L. Gilman, *Fat Boys: A Thin Book* (Lincoln, NE, 2004).

89 Béraud, *Martyre*, p. 39.

90 W. H. Sheldon, *The Varieties of Human Physique: An Introduction to Constitutional Psychology* (New York, 1940); P. Vertinsky, 'Embodying Normalcy: Anthropometry and the Long Arm of William H. Sheldon's Somatotyping Project', *Journal of Sport History*, XXIX/1 (2002), pp. 95–133.

91 W. H. Sheldon, *The Varieties of Temperament: A Psychology of Constitutional Differences* (New York, 1944), pp. 43–4.

92 W. A. Schonfeld, 'Inadequate Masculine Physique: A Factor in Personality Development of Adolescent Boys', *Psychosomatic Medicine*, XII/I (1950), pp. 49–54.

93 Le Dévédec, *La Société*, p. 114.

94 W. J. Robinson, 'Who May and May Not Marry', *American Journal of Clinical Medicine*, XXIII/9 (1916), pp. 739–45, esp. 743–4.

95 B. G. Jefferis and J. L. Nichols, *Searchlights on Health: The Science of Eugenics* (Naperville, IL, 1919), p. 171.

96 Quoted in Denning, *Skiing*, p. 76.

97 P. H. Roeser, *Vieillesse et longévité* (Paris, 1910), p. 173.

98 See F. P. Weber, *Fatness, Overweight, and Life Assurance* (London, 1901).

99 M. Gullette, *Safe at Last in the Middle Years: The Invention of the Midlife Progress Novel* (Berkeley, CA, 1988).

100 M. L. Stewart, *For Health and Beauty: Physical Culture for Frenchwomen, 1880s–1930s* (Baltimore, MD, 2001), pp. 130–45.

101 C. W. Saleeby, *Health, Strength and Happiness* (London, 1908), pp. 309–10.

102 Gulick, *Efficient*, p. 35.

103 L. Williams, *Middle Age and Old Age* (London, 1925), p. 7.

104 Alsaker, *Eating*, p. 221.

105 Lowry, *Woman of Forty*, p. 40.

106 Copeland, *Over Weight?*, p. 111.

107 A. Hemmerdinger, *La Fin du martyre de l'obèse* (Paris, 1932), p. 31.

108 S. G. Blythe, *Get Rid of That Fat* (New York, 1928), p. 7.

109 L. H. Peters, *Diet and Health: With Key to the Calories* (Chicago, IL, 1918), p. 103.

110 Saleeby, *Health*, pp. 304–5.

111 C. S. Read, *Fads and Feeding* (London, 1908), p. 54.

112 J. C. Whorton, *Inner Hygiene: Constipation and the Pursuit of Health in Modern Society* (Oxford, 2000), p. 126.

113 Levitas, *Concept*, p. 209.

114 I. Zweiniger-Bargielowska, 'The Culture of the Abdomen: Obesity and Reducing in Britain, circa 1900–1939', *Journal of British Studies*, XLIV/2 (2005), pp. 239–273; K. Vester, 'Regime Change: Gender, Class, and the Invention of Dieting in Post-Bellum America', *Journal of Social History*, XLIV/1 (2010), pp. 39–70.

115 Carden-Coyne, *Reconstructing*, p. 179.

116 Ibid., pp. 248–9. Yet for most of the century, women continued to be treated primarily as mothers entrusted with the physical and moral health of the 'race'. I. Zweiniger-Bargielowska, *Managing the Body: Beauty, Health, and Fitness in Britain, 1880–1939* (Oxford, 2010), pp. 124–36.

117 G. Lipovetsky, *De la légèreté: Vers une civilisation du léger* (Paris, 2014), p. 113.

118 J. J. Brumberg, *Fasting Girls: The Emergence of Anorexia Nervosa as a Modern Disease* (Cambridge, MA, 1988); Brumberg, *The Body Project: An Intimate History of American Girls* (New York, 1997).

119 B. M. Mensendieck, 'It's Up to You' (New York, 1931), p. 19.

120 C. Fischler, *L'Homnivore: Le goût, la cuisine et le corps* (Paris, 2001), p. 363; see also G. Vigarello, *Histoire de la beauté: Le corps et l'art d'embellir de la Renaissance à nos jours* (Paris, 2004), pp. 215–7.

121 Hemmerdinger, *La Fin du martyre*, p. 15.

122 'On ne prend pas du ventre, on l'accepte.' Quoted in Vigarello, *Histoire*, p. 218.

123 Sylvia of Hollywood, '*No More Alibis!*', (Chicago, IL, 1935) p. 13.

124 C. Lalo, *La Beauté et l'instinct sexuel* (Paris, 1922), p. 56.

125 Hemmerdinger, *La Fin du martyre*, p. 28.

126 S. de Lorraine, *Les Secrets de la beauté du visage et du corps* (Paris, 1855), pp. 31, 37.

127 G. Pfister, 'The Medical Discourse on Female Physical Culture in Germany in the 19th and Early 20th Centuries', *Journal of Sport History*, XVII/2 (1990), p. 190.

128 M. Hau, *The Cult of Health and Beauty in Germany: A Social History, 1890–1930* (Chicago, IL, 2003), pp. 72–5.

129 Hemmerdinger, *La Fin du martyre*, p. 19.

130 S. de Beauvoir, *The Second Sex* [1949], trans. H. M. Parshley (New York, 1989), p. 158.

131 Beauvoir, *Second Sex*, p. 262; Beauvoir, *Le Deuxième Sexe*, (Paris, 1949), vol. I, p. 394.

132 Beauvoir, *Second Sex*, pp. 534–6, translation modified; Beauvoir, *Le Deuxième Sexe*, vol. II (Paris, 1949), pp. 351–2.

133 L. Binswanger, 'The Case of Ellen West: An Anthropological-Clinical Study', in *Existence: A New Dimension in Psychiatry and Psychology*, ed. R. May, E. Angel and H. Ellenberger (New York, 1958), p. 349.

134 G. Weiss, *Body Images: Embodiment as Intercorporeality* (New York, 1999), pp. 100–01. See also A. Bray, 'The Silence surrounding "Ellen West": Binswanger and Foucault', *Journal of the British Society for Phenomenology*, XXXII/2 (2001), pp. 125–46.

135 Beauvoir's long-time partner, Jean-Paul Sartre, objected to fat on personal as well as philosophical grounds. Avoiding exercise while occasionally going on diets, Sartre loved to eat but feared gaining weight. His reasons for this resonated with the wider culture of his day. Claiming that 'fatness was something I thought of as surrender and contingency', Sartre confessed that 'My sole worry is I'll get fat.' Quoted in H. Rowley, *Tête-à-tête: The Tumultuous Lives and Loves of Simone de Beauvoir and Jean-Paul Sartre* (New York, 2005), pp. 97, 229. It made some sense, then, that fat would cross his mind when trying to convey the 'nausea' he felt towards embodied existence. Through the protagonist of his novel *Nausea*, Sartre expressed an urge 'to drive existence out of me, to rid the passing moments of their fat [*vider les instants de leur graisse*], to twist them, dry them, purify myself, harden myself'. Sartre, *La Nausée* (Paris, 1938), p. 243.

136 N. Changfoot, 'Transcendence in Simone de Beauvoir's *The Second Sex*', *Philosophy and Social Criticism*, XXV/4 (2009), pp. 391–410.

137 Farrell, *Fat Shame*, p. 115.

138 G. Greer, *The Female Eunuch* [1970] (New York, 2003), p. 38.

139 J. Carey, 'Introduction', *The Faber Book of Utopias*, ed. J. Carey (London, 1999), p. xii.

Conclusion: Purity, Lightness and the Weight of History

1 'Woman Wonders: "Will I be Fat in Heaven?"', www.larknews.com, 12 September 2012.

2 C. G. Banks, '"There Is No Fat in Heaven": Religious Asceticism and the Meaning of Anorexia Nervosa', *Ethos*, XXIV/1 (1996), p. 119.

3 Once again, here I employ Coveney's use of the word 'spiritual'. J. Coveney, *Food, Morals and Meaning: The Pleasure and Anxiety of Eating*, 2nd edn (London, 2006), p. xvi.

4 N. Allon, 'Group Dieting Interaction' (doctoral dissertation in Sociology, Brandeis University, 1972).

5 G. Ignatow, 'Culture and Embodied Cognition: Moral Discourses in Internet Support Groups for Overeaters', *Social Forces*, LXXXVIII/2 (2009), pp. 643–9.

6 R. M. Griffith, *Born Again Bodies: Flesh and Spirit in American Christianity* (Berkeley, CA, 2004), pp. 13, 16. See also F. Parasecoli, 'God's Diets: The Fat Body and the Bible as an Eating Guide in Evangelical Christianity', *Fat Studies*, IV/2 (2015), pp. 141–58.

7 A. Chalanset, 'Des merveilleux nuages au rêve de pierre', in *Légèreté: Corps et âme, un rêve d'apesanteur*, ed. A. Chalanset (Paris, 1996), p. 19. Reminding us that 'cosmic' and 'cosmetics' have etymological roots in *Kosmos*, Claude Fischler may not be exaggerating when he identifies the modern body as 'the means and stake of the new religion, of the new link between the self and the universe'. C. Fischler, *L'Homnivore: Le goût, la cuisine et le corps* (Paris, 2001), p. 368.

8 D. Harvey, *A Brief History of Neoliberalism* (Oxford, 2005), p. 2.

9 Z. Bauman, *Liquid Modernity* (Cambridge, 2000), p. 122.

10 J.-P. Corbeau, 'Les Canons dégraissés: De l'esthétique de la légèreté au pathos du squelette', in *Corps de femmes sous influence: Questionner les norms*, ed. A. Hubert (Paris, Les Cahiers de l'Ocha, 10, 2004), p. 51.

11 Harvey, *Brief History*, p. 19.

12 P. Skrabanek, *The Death of Humane Medicine and the Rise of Coercive Healthism* (Bury St Edmunds, 1994).

13 J. Guthman and M. DuPuis, 'Embodying Neoliberalism: Economy, Culture, and the Politics of Fat', *Environment and Planning D: Society and Space*, XXIV (2006), pp. 427–48; C. D. Elliott, 'Big Persons, Small Voices: On Governance, Obesity, and the Narrative of the Failed Citizen', *Journal of Canadian Studies*, XLI/3 (2007), pp. 134–49.

14 Coveney, *Food, Morals and Meaning*, p. 141.

15 A. R. Bitar, *Diet and the Disease of Civilization* (New Brunswick, NJ, 2018).

16 C. Fischler, 'Pensée magique et utopie dans la science: De l'incorporation à la "diète méditerranéenne"', in *Pensée magique et alimentation aujourd'hui*, ed. C. Fischler (Paris, Les Cahiers de l'Ocha, 5, 1996), pp. 111–27.

17 C. Piatti, 'Slow Food Presidia: The Nostalgic and the Utopian', in *Food Utopias: Reimagining Citizenship, Ethics and Community*, ed. P. V. Stock, M. Carolan and C. Rosin (London, 2015), pp. 88–106.

18 A. R. Johnson, 'The Paleo Diet and the American Weight Loss Utopia, 1975–2014', *Utopian Studies*, xxv/2 (2015), p. 103; see also J.-D. Vigne, 'The "Prehistoric Diet": Myths and Scientific Realities', in *Selective Eating: The Rise, Meaning and Sense of 'Personal Dietary Requirements'*, ed. C. Fischler, trans. C. Schoch and W. Snow (Paris, 2013), pp. 93–106.

19 G. Apfeldorfer, 'Maigrir comme acte magique', in *Pensée magique et alimentation aujourd'hui*, ed. C. Fischler (Paris, Les Cahiers de l'Ocha, 5, 1996), p. 79. Fischler calls this the 'principle of incorporation', which is closely related to the idea of magical thinking. Fischler, *L'Homnivore*.

20 C. Durif-Bruckert, *La Nourriture et nous: Corps imaginaire et normes sociales* (Paris, 2007), pp. 60, 79, 81, 154.

21 L. F. Monaghan, *Men and the War on Obesity: A Sociological Study* (London, 2008), p. 101.

22 M. Warin, *Abject Relations: Everyday Worlds of Anorexia* (New Brunswick, NJ, 2009), p. 107. An earlier Australian study reveals very similar impressions. Cf. D. Lupton, *Food, the Body and the Self* (London, 1996), p. 82.

23 K. Chayka, 'The Oppressive Gospel of "Minimalism"', *New York Times*, 26 July 2016, www.nytimes.com/.

24 A. Haynes, *Clean Sweep: The Ultimate Guide to Decluttering, Detoxing, and Destressing Your Home* (New York, 2008).

25 P. Walsh, *Lose the Clutter, Lose the Weight: The Six-week Total-life Slim Down* (Emmaus, PA, 2016). To make this connection, Walsh relies on a study correlating hoarding and 'obesity'. K. R. Timpano et al., 'Consideration of the BDNF Gene in Relation to Two Phenotypes: Hoarding and Obesity', *Journal of Abnormal Psychology*, cxx/3 (2011), pp. 700–707.

26 J. F. Millburn, 'A Minimalist's Thoughts on Diet', www.theminimalists. com/diet/.

27 Bauman, *Liquid Modernity*, p. 128.

28 Apfeldorfer, 'Maigrir comme acte magique', p. 79.

29 Warin, *Abject Relations*, p. 129. See also A. Lavis, 'Engrossing Encounters: Materialities and Metaphors of Fat in the Lived Experiences of Individuals with Anorexia', in *Fat: Culture and Materiality*, ed. C. E. Forth and A. Leitch (London, 2014), pp. 91–108.

30 Warin, *Abject Relations*, p. 106.

31 Ibid., p. 123.

32 L. Boltanski, 'Les Usages sociaux du corps', *Annales: Histoire, sciences sociales*, 1 (1971), pp. 205–33.

33 P. Bourdieu, *Distinction: A Social Critique of the Judgement of Taste*, trans. Richard Nice (Cambridge, MA, 1984), p. 178.

34 Griffith, *Born*, p. 228; S. Strings, 'Obese Black Women as "Social Dead Weight": Reinventing the "Diseased Black Woman"', *Signs*, xli/1 (2015), pp. 107–30; M. Nichter, *Fat Talk: What Girls and Their Parents Say about Dieting* (Cambridge, MA, 2000), pp. 159–80.

35 'To be displaced from the status of full humanity, and, particularly, to be rendered as "animal," is, in the context of a deeply anthropocentric system, to be marginalized in the most fundamental of ways.' K. A. Hardy, 'Cows,

Pigs, Whales: Nonhuman Animals, Antifat Bias, and Exceptionalist Logics', in *The Politics of Size: Perspectives from the Fat Acceptance Movement*, ed. R. Chastain (Santa Barbara, CA, 2015), vol. I, p. 194.

36 'Controversial "Save the Whales" Billboard Swap', www.peta.org, 24 August 2009).

37 G. Critser, 'Let Them Eat Fat: The Heavy Truths about American Obesity', *Harper's Magazine* (March 2000), p. 47.

38 R. Mille, *Gros et heureux de l'être* (Paris, 1978). 'Nous, les obèses, savons que nous sommes mortels.' Available at: http://dicocitations.lemonde.fr.

39 L. Keith, *The Vegetarian Myth: Food, Justice and Sustainability* (Crescent City, CA, 2009), p. 78.

40 M. Pollan, *The Omnivore's Dilemma: A Natural History of Four Meals* (New York, 2006), p. 321.

41 S. Solomon, J. Greenberg and T. Pyszczynski, *The Worm at the Core: On the Role of Death in Life* (New York, 2015).

42 'It is the fear of collapse, the sense of dissolution, which contaminates the Western image of all disease . . . We project this fear into the world in order to localize it, and indeed, to domesticate it.' S. L. Gilman, *Disease and Representation: Images of Illness from Madness to AIDS* (Ithaca, NY, 1988), p. 1.

43 M. Allison, 'Eating toward Immortality: Diet Culture Is Just Another way of Dealing with the Fear of Death', www.theatlantic.com, 7 February 2017.

44 Warin, *Abject Relations*, p. 135.

45 Durif-Bruckert, *La Nourriture*, p. 147.

46 Corbeau, 'Les Canons dégraissés', p. 54.

47 G. Nicolosi, 'Biotechnologies, Alimentary Fears and the Orthorexic Society', *Tailoring Biotechnologies*, II/3 (2006/7), pp. 37–56; C. Rangel, S. Dukeshire and L. MacDonald, 'Diet and Anxiety. An Exploration into the Orthorexic Society', *Appetite*, LVIII (2012), pp. 124–32.

48 C. Adamiec, 'When Healthful Eating becomes an Obsession', in *Selective Eating*, p. 158. See also N. S. Koven and A. W. Abry, 'The Clinical Basis of Orthorexia Nervosa: Emerging Perspectives', *Neuropsychiatric Disease and Treatment*, XI (2015), p. 385.

49 B. Gerisch, 'The Body in Times of Acceleration and Delimitation', *Time and Society*, XVIII/2–3 (2009), p. 375.

50 M. Nussbaum, *Hiding from Humanity: Disgust, Shame, and the Law* (Princeton, NJ, 2004), p. 109.

51 C. Lavin, *Eating Anxiety: The Perils of Food Politics* (Minneapolis, MN, 2013), pp. 80–81.

52 C. McGinn, *The Meaning of Disgust* (Oxford, 2011), p. 181.

53 M. Hauskeller, 'Messy Bodies: From Cosmetic Surgery to Mind Uploading', *Trans-humanities*, VI/2 (2013), p. 69.

54 D. Leder, *The Absent Body* (Chicago, IL, 1990).

55 Margrit Shildrick, *Dangerous Discourses of Disability, Subjectivity and Sexuality* (Basingstoke, 2009), p. 33.

56 S. Ahmed, *The Cultural Politics of Emotion* (London, 2015), pp. 90–91.

57 Without going so far as to reject completely projects for physical improvement, we can certainly explore ways of *reframing* that quest

in less damaging ways. In fact, some people already do so. Despite
the coercive potential of our modern healthism, we know that not all
who pursue fitness regimens are 'cultural dopes' mindlessly seeking to
emulate unrealistic physical ideals. Nor is every weightlifter beholden
to fantasies of omnipotence. By cultivating an appreciation for exercise
as an 'immersive practice', it is possible to engage with our bodies
without buying into a damaging ethic of competitive transcendence.
M. M. Lelwica, *Shameful Bodies: Religion and the Culture of Physical
Improvement* (London, 2017), p. 47; N. Crossley, *Reflexive Embodiment
in Contemporary Society* (Maidenhead, 2006), p. 56; L. Heywood,
'Building Otherwise: Bodybuilding as Immersive Practice', in *Critical
Readings in Bodybuilding*, ed. A. Locks and N. Richardson (New York,
2013), p. 134.

SELECT BIBLIOGRAPHY

Bennett, Jane, *Vibrant Matter: A Political Ecology of Things* (Durham,
  NC, 2010)
Braziel, Jana Evans, and Kathleen LeBesco, eds, *Bodies Out of Bounds: Fatness
  and Transgression* (Berkeley, CA, 2001)
Brown, Peter, *The Body and Society: Men, Women, and Sexual Renunciation
  in Early Christianity* (New York, 1988)
Brumberg, Joan Jacobs, *Fasting Girls: The Emergence of Anorexia Nervosa
  as a Modern Disease* (Cambridge, MA, 1988)
Bynum, Caroline Walker, *The Resurrection of the Body in Western Christianity,
  200–1336* (New York, 1995)
Campos, Paul, *The Obesity Myth: Why America's Obsession with Weight
  Is Hazardous to Your Health* (New York, 2004)
Carden-Coyne, Ana, *Reconstructing the Body: Classicism, Modernism,
  and the First World War* (Oxford, 2009)
Cogdell, Christina, *Eugenic Design: Streamlining America in the 1930s*
  (Philadelphia, PA, 2004)
Collingham, E. M., *Imperial Bodies: The Physical Experience of the Raj,
  c. 1800–1947* (Cambridge, 2001)
Colls, Rachel, 'Materialising Bodily Matter: Intra-action and the
  Embodiment of "Fat"', *Geoforum*, XXXVIII (2007), pp. 353–65
Coveney, John, *Food, Morals and Meaning: The Pleasure and Anxiety of Eating*,
  2nd edn (London, 2006)
Csergo, Julie, ed., *Trop gros? L'obésité et ses représentations* (Paris, 2009)
Durif-Bruckert, Christine, *La Nourriture et nous: Corps imaginaire et normes
  sociales* (Paris, 2007)
Farrell, Amy Erdman, *Fat Shame: Stigma and the Fat Body in American
  Culture* (New York, 2011)
Fischler, Claude, *L'Homnivore: Le goût, la cuisine et le corps* (Paris, 2001)
Forth, Christopher E., and Ana Carden-Coyne, eds, *Cultures of the Abdomen:
  Diet, Digestion and Fat in the Modern World* (New York, 2005)
Gilman, Sander L., *Fat Boys: A Thin Book* (Lincoln, NE, 2004)
—, *Fat: A Cultural History of Obesity* (Cambridge, 2008)
Griffin, Roger, *Modernism and Fascism: The Sense of a Beginning under
  Mussolini and Hitler* (Basingstoke, 2007)

Griffith, R. Marie, *Born Again Bodies: Flesh and Spirit in American Christianity* (Berkeley, CA, 2004)

Grimm, Veronica E., *From Feasting to Fasting, the Evolution of a Sin: Attitudes to Food in Late Antiquity* (New York, 1996)

Hill, Susan E., *Eating to Excess: The Meaning of Gluttony and the Fat Body in the Ancient World* (Santa Barbara, CA, 2011)

Hoffmann, Viktoria von, *From Gluttony to Enlightenment: The World of Taste in Early Modern Europe* (Urbana, IL, 2016)

Jensen, Erik N., *Body by Weimar: Athletes, Gender, and German Modernity* (Oxford, 2010)

Karila-Cohen, Karine, and Florent Quellier, eds, *Le Corps du gourmand d'Héraclès à Alexandre le Bienheureux* (Rennes, 2012)

Kolnai, Aurel, *On Disgust*, ed. B. Smith and C. Korsmeyer (Chicago, IL, 2004)

Levy-Navarro, Elena, *The Culture of Obesity in Early and Late Modernity* (Basingstoke, 2008)

—, ed., *Historicizing Fat in Anglo-American Culture* (Columbus, OH, 2010)

Loux, Françoise, and Philippe Richard, *Sagesses du corps: La santé et la maladie dans les proverbes françaises* (Paris, 1978)

Lupton, Deborah, *Food, the Body and the Self* (London, 1996)

Menninghaus, Winfried, *Disgust: The Theory and History of a Strong Sensation*, trans. H. Eiland and J. Golb (Albany, NY, 2003)

Miller, Daniel, ed., *Materiality* (Durham, NC, 2005)

Miller, William I., *The Anatomy of Disgust* (Cambridge, MA, 1997)

Monaghan, Lee F., *Men and the War on Obesity: A Sociological Study* (London, 2008)

Murray, Samantha, *The 'Fat' Female Body* (Basingstoke, 2008)

Nussbaum, Martha, *Hiding from Humanity: Disgust, Shame, and the Law* (Princeton, NJ, 2004)

Pouchelle, Marie-Christine, *The Body and Surgery in the Middle Ages*, trans. R. Morris (New Brunswick, NJ, 1990)

Rothblum, Esther, and Sondra Solovay, eds, *The Fat Studies Reader* (New York, 2009)

Saguy, Abigail C., *What's Wrong with Fat?* (New York, 2013)

Sandnes, Karl Olav, *Belly and Body in the Pauline Epistles* (Cambridge, 2002)

Schwartz, Hillel, *Never Satisfied: A Cultural History of Diets, Fantasies and Fat* (New York, 1986)

Shildrick, Margrit, *Dangerous Discourses of Disability, Subjectivity and Sexuality* (Basingstoke, 2009)

Stearns, Peter N., *Fat History: Bodies and Beauty in the Modern West* (New York, 1997)

Stolberg, Michael, "Abhorreas pinguedinem": Fat and Obesity in Early Modern Medicine (*c.* 1500–1750)', *Studies in History and Philosophy of Biological and Biomedical Sciences*, XLIII (2012), pp. 370–78

Sugg, Richard, *Mummies, Cannibals and Vampires: The History of Corpse Medicine from the Renaissance to the Victorians* (London, 2011)

Toulalan, Sarah, '"To[o] Much Eating Stifles the Child": Fat Bodies and Reproduction in Early Modern England', *Historical Research*, LXXXVII/235 (2014), pp. 65–93

—, '"If Slendernesse Be the Cause of Unfruitfulnesse; You Must Nourish and Fatten the Body": Thin Bodies and Infertility in Early Modern England', in *The Palgrave Handbook of Infertility in History: Approaches, Contexts and Perspectives*, ed. G. Davis and T. Loughran (London, 2017), pp. 171–97

Tumblety, Joan, *Remaking the Male Body: Masculinity and the Uses of Physical Culture in Interwar and Vichy France* (Oxford, 2012)

Vigarello, Georges, *Histoire de la beauté: Le corps et l'art d'embellir de la Renaissance à nos jours* (Paris, 2004)

—, *The Metamorphoses of Fat: A History of Obesity*, trans. C. J. Delogu (New York, 2013)

Warin, Megan, *Abject Relations: Everyday Worlds of Anorexia* (New Brunswick, NJ, 2009)

Zweiniger-Bargielowska, Ina, *Managing the Body: Beauty, Health, and Fitness in Britain, 1880–1939* (Oxford, 2010)

ACKNOWLEDGEMENTS

This project has been called 'ambitious' so many times that I now consider the term a euphemism for 'rather mad'. Given the scope of the book, though, one can sort of see the point. The mixture of amusement and pity some of my historian colleagues expressed at my last book project, which covered a mere four hundred years, faded to incredulity and genuine concern when they learned about this one. But more has been going on here than simple 'ambition' (or madness). Beginning as a survey of perceptions of fatness in the modern era, this project was guided by my ongoing inquiries into why moral and physical 'softness' enjoys such an ambiguous status in Western culture, particularly in reference to gender and the body. Thus, despite appearances, it is a logical extension of the core themes explored in my previous book, *Masculinity in the Modern West*.

When invited to embark on this project, I had planned to focus on the modern era, devoting at most one chapter to the period from antiquity to the Renaissance. Being less familiar with this era, I assumed it could be addressed fairly easily. At the time, I, like many people, was under the impression that fatness really wasn't much of an issue prior to the modern era. Immersing myself in ancient sources not only revealed the unexpected complexity of what I was dealing with, but made it clear that the classical and biblical worlds were more important than I had imagined for understanding how ideas about fatness and softness have been bound together. As the structure and scope of the book widened to accommodate this realization, I found myself pushed well outside of my scholarly comfort zone, and rather enjoying the experience. But I knew this would not be the book I was asked to write.

The focus of the book was further complicated when I decided to stop ignoring the constant references to 'fat' in agriculture and tried to see what, if anything, these had to do with the body. This opened up a whole new world of possibilities, drawing me towards anthropological models of materiality and the senses that encouraged me to conceptualize fat in terms of tactility as well as visuality, and to approach fat bodies as matters of substance as well as size and shape. My engagement with scholarship on disgust smuggled the insights of psychology and philosophy into the project and also prompted me to consider the role played by animality in historical treatments of fattening. All of this required substantial conceptual alterations to the original plan, and deepened its interdisciplinary perspective.

My editor at Reaktion Books, Vivian Constantinopoulos, gracefully allowed some major deviations from the original prospectus and generously accommodated the numerous extensions and expansions I required to complete it. Many others have contributed to the development of this book. Special thanks go to my Classics colleagues, Anthony Corbeill and John Younger, for guiding me into ancient texts and culture. Thanks also to Barnea Levi Selavan, who from his base in Jerusalem kept me well supplied with suggestions for reading on fat in the ancient world and elsewhere. Early drafts of various chapters were read by Heike Bauer, Anthony Corbeill, Hahna Curtin, Venita Datta, Andrew Denning, Karen Downing, Anna Greenwood, Alison Leitch, Nina Mackert, Willemijn Ruberg, Damon Talbott, Joan Tumblety, John Younger and Ina Zweiniger-Bargielowska. Two especially generous colleagues, John Cerullo and Richard Sugg, were kind enough to read and comment on the entire manuscript.

Many others engaged in conversations and correspondence that yielded much useful information, advice and/or feedback: Elinor Accampo, Michael Baskett, Chris Bishop, Nicole Boivin, Kim Bond, Jeffrey Jerome Cohen, Avery Ray Colter, Ivan Crozier, Vicki Cummings, Michel Delville, Jan Frans van Dijkhuizen, Sergey Dolgopolski, Anne Dotter, Pilar Galiana Abal, Marwa Ghazali, Robbie Gordy, Lesley Hall, Allan Hanson, Michael Hau, Bob Jameson, Daniel King, Helen King, Scott Knowles, Erika Kuijpers, Inger Leemans, Bill Leeming, Alison Leitch, Blake Leyerle, Brittany Lockard, Deborah Lupton, Valerie Mars, LeRoy McDermott, Wolfgang Mieder, Kate Mitchell, John Monroe, Steven Muhlberger, Samantha Murray, Sally Pemberton, James Quinn, Heather Ruiter, Ayu Saraswati, Sonya Satinsky, Charlie Sedlock, Barnea Levi Selavan, Tricia Starks, Christianna Stavroudis, Kristine Steenbergh, Erin Stewart, David Titterington, Sarah Toulalan, Leslie Tuttle, Dale Urie, Lorenzo Veracini, Andrea Weiss, Roger Westcombe, Richard Wilk, Ron Wilson, Verena Winiwarter, James Woelfel, Paul Zimdars-Swartz and Sandra Zimdars-Swartz. As the final chapter and conclusion were the most difficult to write, conversations with Mark Landau, Greta Olson and Willemijn Ruberg were especially productive and encouraging. Friendly disagreements with Nina Mackert were very useful in prompting me to make my ideas more precise.

Portions of this work were presented in a variety of scholarly venues, including the Obesity Seminar Series hosted by the Unit for Biocultural Variation at Oxford University, the Society of Fellows in the Humanities at Columbia University, the Society of European Historians at the University of Arkansas, and the Gender Seminar hosted by the Hall Center for the Humanities at the University of Kansas. Conference papers on aspects of this project were presented at meetings of the American Historical Association, the Western Society for French History, the American Association for the History of Medicine, and the Popular Culture Association. I had the opportunity to try out my conceptual approach in a keynote address delivered at 'Disgust: History, Language, Politics and Aesthetics of a Complex Emotion', a conference hosted by the University of Liège, Belgium. Many thanks to Michel Delville, Andrew Norris and Viktoria von Hoffmann for inviting me to speak. Other ideas were refined during my time as an International Research Fellow at Erfurt University, Germany. I owe a debt of gratitude to Jürgen Martschukat, Nina

Mackert, Nina Wiedemeyer and the rest of the Cultural Techniques Research Group for hosting me. As a subsequent series of talks in Europe promoted further reflection, thanks also go to hosts and audiences at the University of Leiden, University of Utrecht, vu University Amsterdam, Center for the History of Emotions at the Max Planck Institute for Human Development, Albert Ludwig University of Freiburg and the University of Turku.

At the University of Kansas this project was supported by the Keeler Family Intra-University Professorship, the University of Kansas General Research Fund and the now defunct Jack and Shirley Howard Chair of Humanities and Western Civilization. As always, ku's Interlibrary Loan crew was a model of efficiency and resourcefulness. I am also grateful to Maddalena Marinari and Hahna Curtin for their research assistance, and to Anthony Corbeill, Marwa Ghazali, Fatima Mohamed, Cara Polsley, Erin Stewart and Andrea Weiss for translation help. Many thanks to Jon Foulk of otrcat. com, who generously donated some excellent old radio shows featuring fat detectives, and to EphemeraForever.com for providing an image for Chapter Ten. Sylvia Mullins generously shared with me her dissertation on medieval myroblytes, and Anne Katrine Kleberg Hansen kindly sent me a copy of her dissertation on medical perceptions of fatness. LeRoy McDermott was nice enough to share with me his images of and thoughts on Neolithic figurines.

My family has put up with this project for so long that they are surely happy to see the back of it. Many thanks to my wife Pilar and my sons Declan and Logan for listening and contributing over the years. Sarah Trulove's reasonable but, at the time, irritating question about fat and disgust played a significant role in shaping my inquiries. As this book is a long – and long delayed – answer to that question, I dedicate it to her.

PHOTO
ACKNOWLEDGEMENTS

The author and publishers wish to express their thanks to the below sources of illustrative material and/or permission to reproduce it.

Alte Pinakothek, Munich: p. 137; © Estate of Peggy Bacon, courtesy of Kelly Brook: p. 247; from Mary Bagot Stack, *Building the Body Beautiful* (London, 1931): p. 256; Bibliothèque nationale de France, Paris: pp. 180, 181; photos Bridgeman Images: pp. 102, 104 (Alinari), 105 (Alinari), 130 (private collection), 163 (De Agostini Picture Library/S. Vannini); British Museum, London: pp. 54, 65; photos © The Trustees of the British Museum, London: pp. 54, 65, 121; EphemeraForever.com: p. 265; Galleria Nazionale d'Arte Antica, Rome: p. 123; Gemäldegalerie Alte Meister, Dresden: p. 128; courtesy of Historical Collection, Eskind Biomedical Library, Vanderbilt University Medical Center, Nashville, TN: pp. 184, 197; Library of Congress, Washington, DC: p. 216; The Metropolitan Museum of Art, New York (Open Access): p. 129; Musée des Beaux-Arts, Lyon: p. 30; Musée du Louvre, Paris: pp. 72, 73, 132; Museo del Prado, Madrid: p. 66; Museum Mayer van den Bergh, Antwerp: p. 144; private collection: p. 250; © RMN-Grand Palais (Musée d'Archéologie nationale) / Franck Raux: p. 23; Collection of Stanford Research into the Impact of Tobacco Advertising (tobacco.stanford.edu): p. 252; Galerie Tarantino, Paris – photo Luc Pâris: p. 59; Wellcome Library, London: pp. 125, 223.

Carole Raddato has published the image on p. 81 online under conditions imposed by a Creative Commons Attribution Share Alike 2.0 Generic license; Matthias Kabel has published the image on p. 20 online and Bullenwächter has published the image on p. 188 online under conditions imposed by a Creative Commons Attribution Share Alike 3.0 Unported license; Livioandronico2013 has published the image on p. 176 online under conditions imposed by a Creative Commons Attribution Share Alike 4.0 International license. Readers are free to share – to copy, distribute and transmit these works – or to remix – to adapt these works under the following conditions: they must attribute the work(s) in the manner specified by the author or licensor (but not in any way that suggests that they endorse you or your use of the work(s)) and if they alter, transform, or build upon the work(s), they may distribute the resulting work(s) only under the same or similar licenses to those listed above).

INDEX

Page numbers in *italics* refer to illustrations